D1713237

Latinos in a Changing Society

Latinos in a Changing Society

Edited by
Martha Montero-Sieburth and
Edwin Meléndez

Westport, Connecticut
London

Library of Congress Cataloging-in-Publication Data

Latinos in a changing society / edited by Martha Montero-Sieburth and Edwin Meléndez.
      p.   cm.
   Includes bibliographical references and index.
   ISBN-13: 978–0–275–96233–3 (alk paper)—ISBN 978–0–275–96234–0 (pbk: alk paper)
   ISBN-10: 0–275–96233–4 (alk paper)—ISBN 0–275–96234–2 (pbk: alk paper)
   1. Hispanic Americans—Social conditions.   2. Hispanic Americans—Statistics.
   3. Immigrants—United States—Social conditions.   4. Social change—United States.
   5. United States—Social conditions—1980-   6. United States—Ethnic relations.
   I. Montero-Sieburth, Martha.   II. Meléndez, Edwin.
   E184.S75L3688   2007
   305.868'073—dc22   2006035013

British Library Cataloguing in Publication Data is available.

Library of Congress Catalog Card Number: 2006035013
ISBN-13: 978–0–275–96233–3 (cloth)
            978–0–275–96234–0 (pbk)
ISBN-10: 0–275–96233–4 (cloth)
            0–275–96234–2 (pbk)

First published in 2007

Praeger Publishers, 88 Post Road West, Westport, CT 06881
An imprint of Greenwood Publishing Group, Inc.
www.praeger.com

Printed in the United States of America

The paper used in this book complies with the
Permanent Paper Standard issued by the National
Information Standards Organization (Z39.48–1984).

10   9   8   7   6   5   4   3   2   1

Contents

Introduction

Martha Montero-Sieburth and Edwin Meléndez

The 1990s were touted as the decade of Latino empowerment, a period of crossover music, the rise of generation Ñ, the coming of age for second- and third-generation Latinos, and the rise of immigration flows that competed with the earlier massive immigration to the United States at the turn of the century. While the 1990s did not prove to be the decade of Latino advancement envisioned by many, it became the period of Latino insertion into the U.S. landscape allowing for the steady growth and presence of Latinos to be felt. Surpassing the black or African-origin population in 2000, persons of Hispanic or Latino origin are currently the largest minority population group in the United States. As reported by the U.S. Census, by 2005 Latinos constituted 14.4 percent of the total population, and ethnic and racial minority groups as a whole comprised 34.2 percent. These figures represent an increase of 5.4 percentage points in the Hispanic share of the total population in a decade and an 8.7 percent increase for racial and ethnic minorities as a whole. Considering the impact of these demographic changes on the country, it is understandable that the expansion of the Latino population and particularly of undocumented immigrants has become one of the most controversial political issues over the last decade.

The current debates on immigration, immigrants, and the future citizenship of Latinos are among the most contentious of the new century. Immigration and Latinos have become emblematic of radical changes being experienced in the United States. Not only have the demographics demonstrated a rise in the Latino population as compared to the 1990s, but trends in immigration according to Passel and Suro have also shown that during 1992–2004, while there has been a rise, peak, and decline of the numbers of immigrants, its composition has changed dramatically.[1] First, the number of unauthorized immigrants, primarily from Mexico, has continued to grow while the number of legal immigrants has decreased. Second, we have also experienced dramatic changes in the settlement patterns of immigrants throughout every state of the Union.[2] Beyond the traditional southwestern belt (California, Texas, Arizona), the central state of Illinois, and the eastern states of New York and New Jersey, states such as Iowa, Minnesota, Utah, and southern states such as Georgia, Tennessee, and Mississippi are experiencing unprecedented growth in the numbers of Latinos, in the development of Latino businesses, and of ethnic enclaves (U.S. Census Bureau).[3] Finally, the national origin of Latinos, from the initial groups of Mexicans, Puerto Ricans, and Cubans, has also changed to include incoming groups from Central America and the Caribbean.

The heightened presence of Latinos has also induced great advances in our understanding of this population. Manifestations of what is yet to come are evident in the growing numbers of publications found in newsstands, research journals, and academic publications. At the dawn of the new century, a proliferation of books on Latinos cover a broad range of topics including identity formation, politics, social and cultural issues, health, economic, and community development.[4] Research on Latino communities has expanded from the between-group analysis characteristic of the 1990s, to the within-group and comparative analysis of Latinos in different regions and socioeconomic contexts.[5] Studies of Colombians, Central Americans, and in particular Salvadorans are evident in the literature. Notable examples of such comparative studies are those fostered by the National Science Foundation Partnership for International Research and Education, directed by Richard Alba and with co-principal investigators, Margaret Gibson, Jennifer Holdaway, Carola Suárez-Orozco, and Mary Waters with a focus on the children of immigrants in schools; and, the Immigration Project of the Suárez-Orozcos at New York University focusing on global and local issues of immigration.[6]

Indeed various studies in this volume point to longitudinal and critical analysis of the conditions faced by the traditional Latino groups. The studies in this volume look at the topic from various vantage points. For example, Edwin Meléndez examines Puerto Ricans in terms of their circular migration and the labor market conditions they encounter, while Guillermo Grenier, Lisandro Pérez, Sung Chang Chun, and Hugh Gladwin scrutinize the first and second generation ideologies of Cuban Americans in South Florida. In addition, transnational studies of Latinos in the United States and their communities in their countries of origin are also being conducted by various centers and institutes that focus on border issues and transnational influences.[7]

Given the importance of Latino issues in the current social and economic times, the publication of *Latinos in a Changing Society* is both timely and prescient in its contributions to the current discourse of how Latinos are being influenced by U.S. norms and culture and how Latinos are also affecting U.S. society. This volume contributes to our need for comprehensive analysis of how Latin communities compare and contrast with other underserved groups and how changes are taking place within specific Latino groups. The opportunities that Latinos and dominant mainstream interests share are identified in this volume, but so are the discriminatory workplace practices and the many areas in need of change.

More poignantly, the volume attempts to present in the current atmosphere of anger and suspicion toward immigrants, an analytical perspective that is too often absent from politically motivated debates about Latinos and their role in a changing society. Undocumented immigrants are often portrayed as people who come to this country to take advantage of a generous welfare system. This volume critically examines such issues as the disparity in poverty among Latino groups, the lack of access to health services, the Latino commitment to labor participation, the ways that Latino parents engage in schools and in their communities, and the educational dropout rates of Latinos across the country and the underlying causes of those rates. Unlike publications that seek to summarize knowledge about the Latino population in the United States, *Latinos in a Changing Society* provides a broader range of insights into the types of policy analysis, research, and public consciousness needed to advance the educational, social, cultural, and political participation and incorporation of Latinos in the new century. In particular, we address often ignored areas of study such as the Latinos' underserved public services status and the institutional challenges Latino parents face in schools, in the job market, or in the political system.

The chapters of *Latinos in a Changing Society* are divided into two parts. Part I: The Changing Demographics of Latinos, presents an overview chapter followed by four unique cases: Dominicans in the United States, Mexicans in New England, Cubans in South Florida, and Puerto Rican migrants to the United States. Part II: The Changing Social, Educational, and Legal Issues Affecting Latinos, discusses Latino college student adjustment, the involvement of Mexicana/Latina mothers in schools, the policing of the Latino community, Latino access to health and social programs, a case study of the migration, settlement, and incorporation of Latinos in Lawrence, Massachusetts, and a final chapter that examines the relationship of social networks to Latino immigrants in the labor market.

OVERVIEW OF CHAPTERS

"The New Nativism and Latinos in a Changing Society," written by Martha Montero-Sieburth and Edwin Meléndez, presents an overview of the issues covered in greater detail in the book and examines how xenophobia has escalated in California and in the Commonwealth of Massachusetts post-September 11, 2002, with proposition 187, proposition 227, and question 2, which have altogether eradicated bilingual education. The chapter sets the context and the tone for subsequent chapters. In it, Montero-Sieburth and Meléndez weave together current and historical responses to immigrants and show the extent to which some critical barriers to health access and educational opportunities continue to persist into the present.

Chapter two by Ramona Hernández, "Living on the Margins of Society: Dominicans in the United States," is an original contribution to sociological research on the discussion of Dominicans in the United States and poverty. One of the most common statements about Latino poverty is that it is a transitory phenomenon and that it can be eradicated. Linda Chávez, among others, argues that most employment and income statistics are skewed owing to the large number of immigrants among the Latino population.[8] Over time, their statistics can be expected to converge with average economic outcomes. But what if the economic conditions affecting Latinos are historically different from those affecting previous immigrants?

Written with incisive candor, Hernández points out that even when the U.S. economy has had a booming economic situation, Dominicans lived below the poverty level despite the fact that they undertook migration to improve their socioeconomic standing. She further alleges that the economic hardships faced by Dominicans may be greater than the statistical data show because of the way she provides data based on how the computational analysis was done. Addressed in her chapter is the invisibility that has been attributed to Latinos in poverty, but also the undertow of the anti-immigrant sentiment and its indictment of immigrants as being unwanted. She makes a strong claim to consider immigration to the United States as a two-way condition of gains and pains where accommodation cannot necessarily be fostered by living on the margins of society.

Chapter three, "The 'Si Se Puede' Newcomers: Mexicans in New England," by Montero-Sieburth, paints a portrait of Mexicans who have settled in Massachusetts, Maine, Rhode Island, New Hampshire, Connecticut, and Vermont through the reported interviews of leaders within Mexican organizations. Using only viable and functioning Mexican organizations and their identified leaders as proxies, Montero-Sieburth identifies in her findings the general settlement pattern of Mexicans in New England gathered over several years of ethnographic research. The author explains who the Mexicans in New England are, what their emerging leadership appears to be like, and how the collaboration of community-based organizations, religious organizations, student groups, and the General Mexican Consulates of Boston and New York has contributed to their development.

While the study demonstrates the evolution of the organizations and their leaders, the focus is on identifying the current needs of Mexican communities in New England and describing the types of relationships that persist among the Mexican communities, the Consular offices, the government of Mexico, and the United States. This is the first study of its kind to identify the needs of Mexicans in New England through the leaders of Mexican organizations. It provides a portrait of a group that is the minority Latino group in New England and the majority Latino group in the nation.[9]

Guillermo Grenier, Lisandro Pérez, Sung Chang Chun, and Hugh Gladwin's chapter is entitled "There Are Cubans, There Are Cubans, and There Are Cubans: Ideological Diversity among Cuban Americans in Miami." This is an innovative presentation of the rise of moderate political voices and organizations as a challenge to the monolithic image of what they call "exile politics" of the earlier generations of Cubans who left at the height of the Cold

War. Using the FIU Cuba Poll of 2004, Grenier, Pérez, Chun, and Gladwin show the variance in ideologies between first- and second-generation immigrants who appear to be more conciliatory than their parents and those who do not live within the Miami enclave. They argue that the paradoxical nature of the Cuban-American situation presents on the one hand the successes of Cubans, but on the other hand, also presents the frustration of being exiles. In their estimation the "core identity of Cubans in the United States" is that of the exile and not of the immigrant.

Completing Part I is Edwin Meléndez's analysis of whether Puerto Rican migration to and from the United States contributes to increasing the poverty rates among Puerto Ricans in the United States. Using two time periods, the 1980s and 1990s, Meléndez suggests that migration patterns do in fact respond to broader patterns of population changes and evolving labor markets in Puerto Rico and the United States, but that the fluctuation in the annual flow in relation to the population is very modest, implying that there are most likely no significant effects from the composition of migratory flows. Nevertheless, Meléndez does identify some critical changes in the composition and characteristics of Puerto Rican migrants. He points out that not only are recent emigrants older, they have less education and they are attached to the labor force while recent immigrants, who are also older, have significantly more education. He also points out how those who lived in Puerto Rico have higher unemployment rates and weaker labor force attachment than those who return. The occupational distribution of emigrants and immigrants, for both men and women, largely resemble those of the sending country. This chapter is a first approximation to the 1991 to 2000 data by the ramp survey of the Puerto Rican Planning Board, and as such is an indicative study of the demographic and labor market conditions in both countries.

Part II brings our attention to higher education by examining the adjustment needed by a Latino college student in the chapter presented by Regina Jean-Van Hell, and on the role of parents and education, in the chapter by Esperanza de la Vega and Willamette College. While the former is a quantitative study using regression analysis, the latter is qualitative focusing on the meaning given education by Latina mothers. Regina Jean-Van Hell's chapter on "Latino College Students' Adjustment: The Influence of Familism, Acculturation, and Social Supports," is based on a quantitative analysis of the adjustment factors in terms of the influence of familism, or familial ties, acculturation, and social supports that are experienced by Latino College students. Familism in this study was not related to college adjustments even though there was a high number of adjusted (86 out of 90) Latino college students based on assessed pathology and not perception of college adjustment.

Jean-Van Hell's research confirms the studies that show that Latino students who are acculturated to Anglo culture are better adjusted to the academic environment. But her study raises questions about how to view familism for Latinos of different subgroups and how families relate to relationships between different generations, socioeconomic, and educational levels. She concludes by highlighting the need of first generation Latino college students to adjust to the academic environment in order to complete their degree and succeed, but she also emphasizes the need to study familism in order to better understand the cultural challenges that Latino college students face as they enter post-secondary education.

Esperanza de la Vega in chapter seven, "Mexicana/Latina Mothers and Schools: Changing the Way We View Parent Involvement," presents the findings of a qualitative study of the ways in which Latina mothers integrate language and culture into their everyday lives. With detailed quotations from each of the parents of her study, de la Vega demonstrates how aspects of culture such as *respeto* (respect), being *bien educado* (well-educated), sharing *dichos o consejos* (sharing sayings and ways of behaving through sayings), and building up *confianza* (confidence) are part of the building blocks that Latinas use with their children and families. She points to the need for schools to integrate these parents and allow them to participate more vocally and openly in schools.

De la Vega argues that these values and relationship building blocks are a prerequisite for creating positive collaborative environments for parents and schools. Cues from school personnel, such as openness that welcomed parents, included them in school, and asked them to participate, were vital to their engagement in her study. De la Vega refers to this two-way process as a culturally responsive Latino parent involvement approach that differs from the mainstream framework currently employed by schools, which often does not encourage Latino parents' participation and often employs deferential behaviors.[10]

Chapter eight, "Policing the Latino Community: Key Issues and Directions for Future Research," written by Cynthia Perez McCluskey and Francisco A. Villarruel, points out the lack of data on Latino populations in criminal justice research, the absence of consistent methods of race and ethnic classification, and the absence of ethnicity data in national arrest statistics.[11] Throughout the chapter, McCluskey and Villarruel identify the key issues that most affect Latinos and policing, citing the need for (1) data representation of Latinos, (2) literature on sociocultural factors about extended family systems and the use of informal social control networks, (3) understanding respect as a highly valued pattern within Latino communities, (4) the role of religious organizations within the Latino community, and (5) verbal and nonverbal communication patterns among Latinos, which are often misunderstood by the police and therefore viewed with suspicion.

The authors argue that Latino representation in data collection needs to be expanded. Additionally, research that builds upon community experiences with police, community attitudes toward the law, as well as systematic social observation research and research on social and cultural issues needs to be broadened. Moreover, research that examines structural contexts within which police and Latino interactions unfold is critical in untangling organizational, structural, and sociocultural influences on police and Latino relations. Among the factors that need research are styles of policing in the context of community and minority relations, immigration patterns from countries of origin and reasons for arriving in the United States, and neighborhood characteristics that influence attitudes toward the law.

The next set of chapters examine aspects of Latino social, economic, health, and incorporation issues. Chapter nine by Héctor R. Cordero-Guzmán and Victoria Quiróz-Becerra, titled "Cracking the Safety Net: Latina/o Access to Health and Social Programs in the Post-Welfare Era," focuses on social policy and family health issues, which have arisen from the post-welfare era. The authors portray their chapter as a "plan of action" based on three key issues: (1) ensuring access to social programs and health services, (2) monitoring changes in the health status of the Latino population and the specific causes for change, and (3) arguing for and developing preventive approaches as well as broadening the access to the health care system. Of particular importance is the focus they present on the persistent and yet strong relationship that exists between poverty and access to health.

Cordero-Guzmán and Quiróz-Becerra advocate the adoption of preventive health care approaches, with proactive investments in social welfare programs that stimulate the socioeconomic development of Latinos in the United States and throughout the hemisphere. Undoubtedly, this chapter adds an important point of view to the growing body of knowledge about Latino health and to the ongoing debate concerning access.[12] Even with the recent interest in health care reform and a renewed interest in the problems of access to health services, the debate has mostly centered on costs—containment and financing. Such a debate overlooks critical issues, which include the barriers presented by language differences and geographic and institutional barriers. Left out of the discussion is the importance of services that take into account the culture of the patient and also respond by providing access to Latino health professionals. All these affect the ability of Latinos to obtain adequate health care. Health officials and policymakers need to engage Latino health providers and researchers in discussions about improving access and health care delivery services to Latinos.

Cordero-Guzmán and Quiróz-Becerra conclude by signaling that the post-welfare era reforms have not brought about universal health coverage or the elimination of poverty among Latino families. Instead, welfare and immigration reform, they argue, have undermined the development of these goals. They call for a reinvigorated U.S. social policy that will adopt comprehensive measures. Not to do so puts at risk the socioeconomic development of Latinos in the United States.

Chapter ten by Ramón F. Borges-Méndez, "The Latinization of Lawrence: Migration, Settlement, and Incorporation of Latinos in a Small Town of

Massachusetts," traces the origin and development of the Latino community in Lawrence through several migratory streams, through what Borges-Méndez calls "network vines grounded in cities through the Northeastern seaboard (and abroad)" that produces "big barios in small cities" (p. 247). Borges-Méndez describes how Puerto Ricans and Dominicans have moved into manufacturing and low-end service jobs. As a result they find themselves part of some of the highest poverty rates in the region. In some neighborhoods like North Lawrence, Latinos tend to settle and then remain there. While renewal is not forthcoming in such neighborhoods, the rise of organizations has heightened political incorporation of Latinos, but not to the extent that they have been able to overcome institutional racism and political exclusion.

Borges-Méndez concludes with the idea that, as welfare programs have been diminished and in many cases replaced with very limited and subsidiary programs, Latinos in the society with such devolution have not been able to be incorporated. In fact, he points out that these changes have led to limiting the local governments' capacity to serve the changing and demographically different populations and have made it more difficult for Latinos to form the service-oriented organizations that have tended to characterize the organizational infrastructure of Latinos elsewhere in large cities. Social organizations play a significant role in advancing Latinos through several stages of political incorporation. These include participation in nationality based organizations, the development of Latino empowerment, the incorporation of Latinos in transnational politics, and finally a pan-Latino organizational framework. Borges-Méndez alleges that such stage development is taking place for Latinos in Lawrence as they employ diverse strategies to increase their political representation. Dominicans appear to have taken the lead in using their transnational linkages with the Dominican Republic, while Puerto Ricans are experiencing changes in their local political brokerage as their local politics have been subsiding.

Luis M. Falcón's analysis of survey data described in chapter eleven, "Social Networks and Latino Immigrants in the Labor Market: A Review of the Literature and Evidence," indicates that Latinos and Asian immigrants make substantial use of networks as a strategy to facilitate settlement and find employment. But little is known about how and whether such networks may hurt immigrants over time. Falcón points out that while the study of social networks and economic behavior is important in understanding the disparities in immigrant groups, he cautions the need for empirical testing of notions proposed by many who seek to understand how social networks can produce, on the one hand, social mobility and, on the other, inequality. Throughout the chapter, Falcón raises questions about our understanding of social networks and the flow of information in such organizations. He also raises questions about gender differences in the use of such social networks, and compares the evolution of such communities among Latino and Asian group affiliations. He leaves the reader thinking about the tension that can be found as ethnic communities age and a native-born ethnic generation emerges. Such probing questions help us configure the dilemmas of social networks and labor market issues for Latino immigrants.

CONCLUSION

The research in *Latinos in a Changing Society* represents a cross section of efforts across disciplines to provide a better understanding of how the social context affects Latino populations and how they in turn affect society. In many ways, we seem to be experiencing the downside of a cycle of adaptation on the part of new populations after a three-decade wave of heightened and continued immigration. Nativist sentiments are evident in job markets, educational and service institutions, and in political processes.

For many observers, ethnic conflict is part of the assimilation or integration process. In time, they say, we will reach a more promising stage of tolerance and understanding. Latinos' contributions to the economy will be acknowledged, and new elected officials will voice and defend their interests. For others, understanding how Latinos contribute to the landscape of America has not yet worked its way into their consciousness. Perhaps this is partly because of the so-called tendency of blacks and whites to find the other invisible. The heightened fear generated by the current fight against terrorism, the anti-immigrant fear, and the demographic growth and expansion of Latinos, all contribute to this lack of understanding.

Today, there is not a state in the Union that does not have Latinos. Their presence is ever growing, especially in the Midwest, the South, and the Northwest.[13] Without doubt, their legacy will mark economic, social, and political changes in this new century. The Latinization of the United States is already occurring within its borders as Carlos Fuentes so aptly has expressed. Not only has the consumption of salsa overtaken that of catsup, but the artistic influence of crossover Latino music has become evident as Latino tunes gain center stage and in the numbers of Spanish and English speaking entertainers who have found a profitable niche. Latin American influences and the Latino presence are ubiquitous in the United States. Latinos are in fact, making and remaking America.

The future research agenda for Latino scholars is likely to be shaped by the need to develop more appropriate conceptual frameworks. These should be developed from an understanding of the unique past historical period and with an unflinching look at the ways in which today's institutions can respond to the new challenges. The research and ideas presented in *Latinos in a Changing Society* are but a modest contribution toward reaching these ambitious goals.

NOTES

1. Jeffrey S. Passel and Roberto Suro, "Rise, Peak and Decline: Trends in U.S. Immigration 1992–2004," Report of the Pew Hispanic Center, Washington, D.C., September 2005.

2. See the report of Steven Camarota, "Immigrants in the United States—2000. A Snapshot of America's Foreign-Born Population," Center for Immigration Studies, 2001, retrieved April 15, 2006, http://www.cis.org/articles/2001/back1012.html.

3. See Blanca Torres, "As Latino Population Grows, So Do Businesses," *Contra Costa Times*, retrieved March 2006, http://www.contracostatimes.com/mld/cctimes/1415776. htm. Torres cites from the U.S. Census Bureau report on Latino-owned businesses in the United States, that they grew 31 percent from 1997 to 2002, which is three times the national average for all businesses. Latino businesses account for 7 percent of all U.S. businesses. See the actual Census Bureau report, "Hispanic-Owned Firms: 2002, 2002 Economic Census, Survey of Business Owners," U.S. Census Bureau, March 2006.

4. See the two volume encyclopedia edited by Lourdes Díaz Soto, *The Praeger Handbook of Latino Education in the United States*, being published by Greenwood, November 30, 2006. and the Latino-based publications cited by Temple University Press and Harvard University Press as examples.

5. See the extensive set of publications from the Pew Hispanic Center, particularly the report by Roberto Suro, "Counting the 'Other Hispanics:' How Many Colombians, Dominicans, Ecuadorians, Guatemalans and Salvadorans are there in the United States?" Pew Hispanic Center, Washington, D.C., May 2002.

6. See Richard Alba's extensive research of second- and third-generation immigrants in the United States, France, and Great Britain titled "Socio-Economic Attainments of Second Generations in Immigration Societies: An Analysis of Canada, Germany and the U.S.," sponsored by the Russell Sage Foundation, and "The Children of Immigrants in Schools" with Josh de Wind, Margaret Gibson, Jennifer Holdaway, Carola Suárez-Orozco and Mary Waters, funded by the National Science Foundation, as examples of this growing trend, which has become commonplace through research centers in Europe. Also see the work of Marcelo Suárez-Orozco and Carola Suárez-Orozco as co-directors of The Institute for Globalization and Education in Metropolitan Settings, IGEMS, Co-Director, Immigration Studies at NYU.

7. Among the multitude of centers focused on Latino issues are the Tomas Rivera Policy Center, the Pew Hispanic Center, the National Council of La Raza, and a myriad of institutes linked to universities or think tanks dedicated to research of Latinos.

8. See Linda Chávez. (1991). *Out of the Barrio*. New York: Basic Books.

9. The 2000 U.S. Census reports that there are 35.3 million Latinos in the United States, constituting 12.5 percent of the total 281.4 million inhabitants in the United States. Of these, Mexicans constitute 58.5 percent of the Latino population, 9.6 percent are Puerto Rican, 3.5 percent are Cuban, 2.2 percent are Dominican, 4.8 percent are Central American, 3.8 percent are South American, and 17.3 percent are Other Latinos with Spaniards representing 0.3 percent of the total. The total number of Latinos in the New England area is 875,225.

10. See the six-step framework created by Joyce Epstein in Joyce L. Epstein, Lucretia Coates, Karen Clark Salinas, Mavis G. Sanders, Beth S. Simon. (1997). *School, Family, and Community Partnerships*. Thousand Oaks, California. Corwin Press, Inc. Also Joyce L. Esptein. (2001). *School, Family, and Community Partnerships: Preparing Educators and Improving Schools*. Boulder, CO: Westview Press.

11. See the growing literature with examples such as D.L. Carter. (1983). "Hispanic Interaction with the Criminal Justice System in Texas: Experiences, Attitudes, and Perceptions," *Journal of Criminal Justice*, 11, 213–227; D.L. Carter. (1985). "Hispanic Perception of Police Performance: An Empirical Assessment," *Journal of*

Criminal Justice, 13, 487–500; D. L. Carter. (1986). "Hispanic Police Officers' Perception of Discrimination," *Journal of Police Studies*, 79, 204–210. L. Herbst and S. Walker. (2001)."Language Barriers in the Delivery of Police Services: A Study of Police and Hispanic Interactions in a Midwestern City," *Journal of Criminal Justice*, 29, 329–340. Morales, A. (1972). *Ando Sangrando (I Am Bleeding): A Study of Mexican-American Police Conflict.* La Puente: Perspectiva Publications.

12. See, for example, the report from Minority Health Initiatives on Improving Health Coverage and Access for Latinos, Families USA, January 2006, retrieved March 12, 2006 from www.familiesusa.org. Also see the Kaiser Commission on Medicaid and the Uninsured, *Key Facts: Health Insurance Coverage and Access to Care Among Latinos* (Washington, D.C.: Kaiser Family Foundation, June 2000).

13. Steven Camarota and Nora McArdle, "Where Immigrants Live: An Examination of State Residency by Country of Origin in 1990–2000," Center for Immigration Studies, September 2003. Also see the report prepared by Rakesh Kochhar, Roberto Suro, and Sonya Tafoya for a presentation at "Immigration to New Settlement Areas," Pew Research Center, July 26, 2005. Also see "The New Latino South: The Context and Consequences of Rapid Population Growth," Report of the Pew Hispanic Center, July 26, 2005.

PART I

The Changing Demographics of Latinos: Specific Cases

CHAPTER 1

The New Nativism and Latinos in a Changing Society

*Martha Montero-Sieburth
and Edwin Meléndez*

Historians and social scientists view the mid-1960s, the years in which the Cold War was at its height, as an important turning point in American life. The United States was deploying forces all over the world to contain the proliferation of unfriendly regimes while it was also establishing political and economic hegemony over international markets. America had opened full-scale war fronts in Southeast Asia and maintained low-intensity and high-support military operations in Central and South America, which in later years mushroomed into civil wars.

The Civil Rights movement was underway in this period, challenging the unequal status quo that disenfranchised many groups and condemned them into an underclass. At stake were the legal rights, educational opportunities, social and economic benefits, and political incorporation of minorities, who had systematically and historically been denied access and opportunity. President Johnson's War on Poverty funded through a series of programs directed at health, education, and welfare propounded to eradicate the disparities between the haves and the have-nots.[1]

The time was ripe for African Americans to rally to the call, recognizing that separate but equal education did not translate into an equality of economic opportunities nor educational experiences. Armed with the spirit and intent of the laws enacted after the Civil Rights Act of 1964, African Americans assumed the social and political leadership at the national level. Through their struggle, they created spaces for other ethnic groups to emerge in defending their rights. Through the Chicano movement, Latinos would later use the political platforms that had been enacted by African Americans to protest the broken promises of a democratic society.

While the focus for African Americans largely revolved around reducing the historical disparities caused by racial inequality, for Latinos, particularly Mexican Americans, issues of land tenure, unemployment, discrimination, segregated schools, linguistic differences, and lack of visible political representation made *la causa*, the cause, a viable struggle. In response to the demands made by Chicanos, the government enacted liberal reforms in immigration policy to ease family reunification and increase the proportion of Third World immigrants to the United States. Such reforms prevailed until the early 1980s when the impact of the new immigrants, particularly from Latin America began to be felt as their numbers grew.[2]

In 2000, the U.S. Census reported that for the first time in American history persons of Hispanic or Latino origin constituted the largest minority population group, surpassing the black or African origin population. By 2004, Latinos were estimated to account for 41.3 million, or 14.1 percent of the total population, and were projected to become 24.4 percent of the total population by 2050.[3] Assuming current demographic trends continue, around 2050 about half of the nation's population will be white and the other half will be Latino, African American, and other racial groups.[4]

Such rapid growth of Latinos and other ethnic groups has set into motion a growing fear of the social, economic, cultural, and political impact these minority groups may demographically have. No where is the new nativism more clearly stated than in Samuel Huntington's book, *Who Are We? The Challenges to America's National Identity*. In it, Huntington alleges that Latinos are not assimilating as well as other groups of the past, and the immigration of Latinos is fracturing and damaging America's cultural identity.[5] In contrast to the old nativism of the turn of the century, the new nativism is based on a new racial construct where immigration has become synonymous with the growing presence of Latinos and undocumented immigrants from Mexico, an ethnic group regarded as a different race and, perhaps more notably, cementing racial diversity in the country. Notwithstanding Huntington's book and other popular opinions, rapid demographic change and the social convergence of race and ethnicity require a closer look. In this chapter, we provide an overview on the origins and social, political, and economic dynamics influenced by this insidious ideology.

THE GENESIS OF THE NEW NATIVISM

Though immigration and the birth of children of immigrant parents constitute by far the greater source of demographic change in the country, the current immigration wave is still short of historical standards. Figure 1.1 shows the percent foreign born from 1850 to 2000.

Even if the trend is clearly in the upswing, the share of foreign born remains below the record level of 14.8 percent established in 1980. However, when we look at the absolute number of foreign born, the prior record for a decade of 14.2 million foreign born population in the United States established in the 1930s

Figure 1.1
Percent Foreign Born of Total U.S. Population: 1850–2000

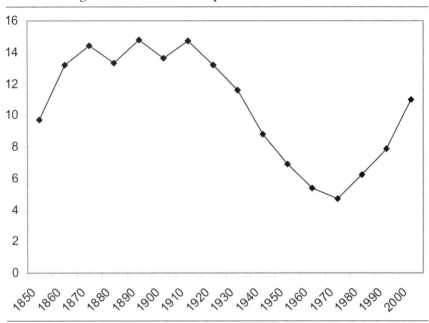

Source: U.S. Bureau of the Census.

has been surpassed in each of the last two decades. As depicted in Table 1.1, the foreign born reached a peak of 31 million in the 1990s.[6]

In addition to the growing share of immigrants, it is important to understand changes in the composition and concentration and how these changes relate to the growing share of ethnic and racial groups in the country. For one, the new wave of immigrants is predominantly people of color and, specifically, foreign born Latinos constitute about half of the flows. Secondly, there are significant differences in the ethnic composition when compared to that of the immigration waves at the beginning of the twentieth century. According to the Immigration and Naturalization Services, in 1993 there were about 3.5 million undocumented immigrants in the United States. However by 2005, over 10.3 million unauthorized migrants in the United States were reported in a Pew Hispanic Center report. Of these, 5.9 million or 57 percent, are from Mexico. About half were in California, but other states also had sizable numbers: New York, 449,000; Texas, 357,000; Florida, 322,000; Illinois, 176,000; and New Jersey, 116,000.[7] Finally the presence of racial minorities is significantly higher today than what it was at the turn of the twentieth century. As depicted in Table 1.1, by 2000 the combined share of racial and ethnic minorities exceeded 38 percent of the population.

Nativism is fueled by a combination of factors, such as the growing share of immigrants of the total population, the unprecedented proportion of people

Table 1.1
Nativity, Race, and Ethnicity of the Population: 1970–2000

| | U.S. Population | | Racial and Ethnic Minorities | | | | | | | |
| | | | Non-Hispanic | | | | Hispanic | | | |
Year	Total	Foreign-Born	Black	AIAN	Asian & PI	Total	Foreign-Born Hispanics	Native Hispanics	Total
2000	282,193,477	31,107,890	34,658,190	2,475,956	10,641,833	42,687,224	14,157,815	28,529,409	107,413,278
1990	248,709,873	19,767,316	29,986,060	1,959,234	7,273,662	22,354,059	7,841,650	14,512,409	73,498,681
1980	226,545,805	14,079,906	26,495,025	1,420,400	3,500,439	14,608,673	4,172,851	10,435,822	55,931,592
1970	203,210,158	9,619,302	22,580,289	763,504	1,356,638	9,589,216	1,802,332	7,786,884	42,106,617
					Percent					
2000	100	11.0	12.3	0.9	3.8	15.1	5.0	10.1	38.1
1990	100	7.9	12.1	0.8	2.9	9.0	3.2	5.8	29.6
1980	100	6.2	11.7	0.6	1.5	6.4	1.8	4.6	24.7
1970	100	4.7	1.1	0.4	0.7	4.7	0.9	3.8	20.7

Source: U.S. Bureau of the Census.

of color when both racial and ethnic minorities are considered, and the large concentration of new immigrants in a few states. It is precisely in California and other states where immigrants are concentrated where the new nativism has found fertile political ground. In California, for example, the new nativist movement won political battles to disallow undocumented immigrants' access to public schools and other public services such as medical care, legal services, training, and higher education. The successful English-only campaigns in Florida, the backlash on bilingual education in New York and Massachusetts as well as other states, and the introduction of English as the official but not exclusive language in 22 states, suggest that there is fertile and growing political ground for the replication of the California experience.

A most important spillover of anti-immigrant sentiment is the impact that the proposed state legislations may have on citizens and legal residents of Latin American descent. Recent historical experiences are instructive in understanding the impact of such legislation on Latinos. With the enactment of the Immigration Reform and Control Act (IRCA) of 1986, Congress passed the first comprehensive overhaul of the nation's immigration system in 66 years. IRCA increased border control, imposed stiffer sanctions on employers who hire undocumented workers, and offered a partial amnesty to undocumented immigrants. A few years after, the U.S. General Accounting Office issued a report, *Immigrant Reform*, the most comprehensive study of discrimination against Latinos ever conducted.[8] The authors used a variety of methods and assembled an impressive amount of data to assess whether the IRCA had adversely affected Latinos' employment opportunities. In a hiring audit conducted in Chicago and San Diego, pairs of low-skilled Anglo-American and Latino job seekers were sent to apply for jobs advertised in local newspapers that only required a high school diploma. Latinos were three times as likely as the closely matched Anglo-Americans to encounter job discrimination.

In a separate study, the General Accounting Office conducted a survey based on a stratified sample of 6,317 employers nationwide to establish the link between discrimination against foreign-looking natives and IRCA. The employer group showed a widespread pattern of discrimination "across a variety of industries in all areas of the nation among employers of various sizes."[9] In fact, employers were turning away Latino and Asian-American job applicants because of their foreign accent or appearance. A year later, a survey sponsored by the National Science Foundation reported that whites continued to hold negative stereotypes of blacks and Latinos, the Equal Employment Opportunity Commission announced that there was an alarming rise of 20 percent in discrimination complaints against employment agencies since 1990, and the Federal Reserve Board reports that there is racial discrimination in the granting of mortgages and that such discrimination is consistent across all income groups. Finally, in 1994, then-President Clinton ordered that federal agencies running programs affecting the environment must not discriminate against poor communities with concentrations of minorities.[10]

There is little doubt that the widespread pattern of discrimination against Latinos was exacerbated by IRCA. During the early 1990s, during times of slow economic growth, immigrants often become scapegoats for growing unemployment and stagnant wages, particularly in regard to other racial minorities. Significant backlash was occurring not only in California, but also in Florida and New York. In these two states, the Haitian and Cuban refugee crises and the secondary migration of Mexicans moving from the West to the East Coast, exacerbated by the aspirations of conservative politicians, unleashed the worst fears of American citizens.

Influenced by these events, the Commission on Immigration Reform recommended, with the endorsement of President Clinton, that the number of legal immigrants allowed to enter the United States each year be reduced by one third. The commission, chaired by the late Democratic congresswoman Barbara Jordan, proposed to reduce the number of visas for workers and refugees and to eliminate preferences for family members, an issue that raises Civil Rights concerns. Congress considered recommendations by a special Task Force on Immigration Reform and produced even tighter controls on the level and composition of immigrants. This lead to the erection of barriers with high tension electrical wires along the Rio Grande as a visible statement echoing the keep out policy of the United States. However, the most punitive effects resulting from the work of the commission are reflected on the restrictions imposed on various educational and social support programs. Educational programs in many urban centers were either reduced or eliminated. For example, bilingual education programs, originally designed to help students learn English using their native language as the medium of instruction, have now been supplanted in many states by Sheltered English Immersion and English as a Second Language programs.[11]

The consequences of restricting education, health, and welfare services to serve only legal U.S. residents or citizens has deterred many immigrants from seeking health services. Proposition 200 in Arizona is a case in point whereby evidence of a person's legal status is required in order to receive medical or welfare benefits. Latino clients tend to shy away from receiving services due to the fear associated with having to share one's legal status and the actual costs for such services. Latinos tend to also not frequent dentists. It is not surprising to hear reports from some Latino dentists about the number of Latino clients who loss their teeth rather than use preventive dental care because of their inability to pay for such care.[12] Of greater concern is the fear of losing future pension reserves from social security, even for those who are legally in the United States. Such fears have provoked an unprecedented number of alien residents to become U.S. citizens in the past 10 years after being in this country for several decades. Waiting lists for becoming a U.S. citizen run into the thousands in some states and extended delay periods of several years are common. By April 1997, setbacks in immigration policies across the country included among others anti-immigration laws denying immigrants welfare benefits, making deportation easier for undocumented immigrants, granting border patrol police more authority to turn anyone away who claimed to seek asylum, and limiting the time period for any undocumented persons in the United States staying for more than six months to not be able to reenter the United States for 3 to 10 years if deported, or after leaving voluntarily.[13]

In sum, the reforms that Chicanos gained in the 1960s in California and the Southwest and those of Puerto Ricans and other Latinos in the Northeast recognizing the presence and contributions of Latinos, have slowly eroded through the implementation of anti-immigrant and anti-bilingual education policies. The backlash spearheaded by new nativism is signaling both the growing fear of the presence of Latinos as well as their inroads into the American landscape. In this new century, the significance of the events of the past 46 years is even more compelling for contemporary America. Clearly with the decline and elimination of affirmative action policies at the institutions of higher learning, the growing trend for setting race-free entrance criteria for examination schools, the prevailing racial divisions between ethnic groups, a growing economy beset by sociocultural and political needs of poor and underserved communities, and the daily reporting of social inequities and injustices through the media, the present situation for Latinos while appearing to be fragile and vulnerable needs closer examination.[14] In the next section we examine the experience of Latinos in California, the birth place of new nativism politics.

THE POLITICS OF NEW NATIVISM: RESTRICTING EDUCATION AND OTHER PUBLIC SERVICES IN CALIFORNIA

Perhaps one of the most significant developments in recent history has been the growing backlash of the new nativism against Latinos expressed in legal, public, and educational policies. No other state has served as a battleground pioneering new nativism grassroots strategies as California has over the last decade. In this section we examine the aftermath of Proposition 187 and Proposition 227 (The Unz Proposal) in California, one of the early case studies of political strategies for the new nativism, and Question 2 in Massachusetts, one of the first states where this strategy was replicated.

In November 1994, California voters overwhelmingly supported Proposition 187: Sixty-two percent of the electorate favored the so-called Save Our State Initiative. As law, it denies undocumented immigrants access to public schools and other public services such as medical care, legal services, training, and higher education. In addition, teachers, doctors, and legal enforcement officials were to inform state and federal authorities of foreigners who were in the country illegally. Over 75 percent of Hispanic voters rejected the law, 75 percent of nonwhite voters favored the law, and African Americans were divided 50/50.[15] Of course, this is not the sole challenge to Latinos in recent years. We have to remember the wave of English-only campaigns in Florida, California, Texas, and many other state legislatures; the battleground in which

bilingual education has existed; and the repeal of bilingual education initiatives introduced in California and approved through Proposition 227, or the
English for Children Initiative known as the Unz Proposal.[16]

Proposition 227, which passed with a high margin of votes, 3.2 million to
2 million in 1998, restricts Latino immigrants' access to education in various
ways: it requires the use of sheltered English immersion in public schools; it
limits students to one program option per district; it does not provide students with access to a core curriculum; it allows mixed age groups; it requires
that teachers have only a good knowledge of English without certification,
bilingual proficiency, or second language training; and, it limits students to
a one-year stay. The availability of foreign language courses and bilingual
two-way immersion programs is also highly restricted. The initiative outlaws
bilingual education for children less than 10 years of age (K–5th grade) and
precludes older students from taking required courses for graduation or college entrance. Clearly, Latino students are unlikely to achieve fluency within
the year, will not be developmentally on grade level, and will be unable meet
the performance standards and testing for English proficiency.[17] Under this
initiative, parents with children who are fluent in English and score at or
above the average for their grade level on English standardized tests may
receive a waiver from the program. However, 19 other parents of the same
grade level must petition for a waiver, thereby restricting Latino parents from
making any educational demands. Parents are foreclosed from choosing an
appropriate program, having their children maintain their native language,
and mobilizing toward effecting change.[18]

Following Proposition 187 and Proposition 227 has been the overwhelming support for Question 2 in Massachusetts—measures that have eroded
opportunities offered by bilingual education. The earlier propositions, as well
as Question 2, have contributed to the demise of bilingual education as we
know it and have provided a rationale for more local control of the best educational practices. Referendum Ballot 2 in the Commonwealth of Massachusetts stipulated that the state law for transitional bilingual education in public
schools would be replaced with a law requiring, only with limited exceptions,
all public school children to be taught in English in all subjects and being
placed in English language classrooms. Ironically, Proposition 2 against bilingual education was overwhelmingly passed by 68 percent in Massachusetts in
2002, even though Massachusetts had been the first state to propose bilingual
education programs in the 1970s. Using slogans promising "English for the
Children," the antibilingual education campaign with widespread media coverage won over voters, including Latinos, in favor of English immersion.[19]

The logical argument of Proposition 187 is simple: undocumented immigrants take jobs and social resources from citizens. Proposition 227 asserts
that English language learners spend too much time in bilingual classes, cost-
ing the state too much. Former California governor Pete Wilson argued in
his reelection campaign that undocumented immigrants cost the state more
than $2 billion a year and thousands of jobs to American workers. Question 2

in Massachusetts emphasized the need for children to learn English and suggested that delays in English language learning would be costly and unproductive. Thus, the law stipulates early exit and entry into all English learning environments within a one-year limit to native language exposure. While on the surface, both California propositions and Question 2 in Massachusetts focused on resources and costs as the critical electoral issues; they are inherently anti-immigrant.

Judging by the electoral support for both Pete Wilson's candidacy and Proposition 187, and the arguments leveled against immigrant costs, both propositions touched deep sentiments among the voters. However, the studies used to support these arguments are controversial and basically flawed, ignoring much of the critical research that supports native language learning and achievement, the time needed to learn a second language, and the importance of developmental learning for the future productivity of immigrants.[20] Most academic research questions both the magnitude of the cost and the assumptions behind the estimates. According to a survey conducted by experts at the Tomás Rivera Policy Institute, the estimated cost of public services is exaggerated because the state taxes immigrants pay are often ignored.[21] In 1992 alone, as reported in an Urban Institute study, undocumented immigrants paid an estimated $732 million to the state of California.[22] As important, most studies find that undocumented immigrants tend not to take advantage of public services because they fear exposure and also because they confront a hostile environment.[23] Indeed, when their contributions to the public coffers from sales and income taxes are considered, immigrants give more to public finances than they receive in public services.[24] Other studies conclude that immigrants are less likely than natives of similar socioeconomic background to receive income transfers.[25] Obviously, fear of apprehension discourages the undocumented population's use of public assistance. Hayes-Bautista indicates that California Latinos, in comparison with African Americans or whites, are least likely to apply for welfare. Moreover, immigration has a stabilizing effect on the Mexican American family.[26] Other studies also suggest that recent Mexican immigrants "tend to rely heavily on friendship and kinship networks for support."[27] De Freitas argues that the tightening of program regulations has made undocumented immigrants ineligible to benefit from most programs.[28]

Proposition 187 and Proposition 227 would be bad policies even if immigrants did not contribute to the economic development of the region directly through higher consumption and taxes and indirectly by supplying needed labor in key industrial sectors. Denying educational opportunities to approximately 300,000 school-age children and the thousands of students enrolled in higher education will have a direct impact on the quality of the labor force, long-term poverty, and increased social conflict.[29] California educators argue that with an average classroom size of more than 30, the loss of a few pupils per classroom will not lead to proposed savings for taxpayers. Except in a few areas of high concentration, school district administrators will be able to cancel classes, lay off teachers, or outright close entire schools. In the long run, the costs in dropout rates, teacher salaries and school closings would be greater. No doubt, the detrimental effects of slashing costs in areas of immigrant concentration will certainly go beyond the possible savings to taxpayers. The social impact of pushing thousands of school-age children out on the streets will first be evident in increased gang violence and petty crimes and secondarily on youngsters' malnutrition and health deterioration.

In 1988, Marcello Medina reported that the cost for dropping out of the educational system for Hispanics results in "$441,000 lost in life-term earnings over those of a typical high school graduate, and $1,082,000 in lost earnings compared to a college graduate."[30] By 2004, those numbers have overall increased to more than 1.2 million students who did not graduate from U.S. schools. The cost in lost wages, taxes, and productivity of dropouts in general, according to the Alliance for Excellent Education, is more than $325 billion, "a number larger than the gross domestic product (GDP) of countries such as Turkey ($301 billion), Austria ($290 billion), and Saudi Arabia ($250 billion), according to 2004 figures from the World Bank."[31] In the long run, we should expect dramatic increases in the persistently poor population and many other social dislocations associated with long-term poverty. Latino poverty is directly linked to such labor-market dynamics as industrial restructuring and discrimination, to the way institutions react to demographic change, and to immigrants' response to the new social environment.[32] To the extent that these conditions persist, unequal employment and social outcomes for Latinos are not a transitory but an enduring phenomenon.

THE IMPACT OF DEMOGRAPHIC CHANGE AND XENOPHOBIA: THE AFTERMATH OF PROPOSITIONS 187 AND 227 IN CALIFORNIA

The implementation of Propositions 187 and 227 has also contributed to engendering widespread discrimination in California. The targeting of Latinos, and in particular, Mexicans, has begun to have an effect in terms of schooling. Mexican immigrants already have lower enrollment figures in public schools than any other group, and they tend to be overwhelmingly tracked into the lower mathematics and science courses.[33] Moreover, anecdotal data suggest that even though Proposition 187 targets the denial of public services to undocumented immigrants, and Proposition 227 limits the time period students can be in bilingual classes and the role that parents might have in making decisions, increased discrimination already exists against all Latinos in private and public sectors. Newspapers reported that shortly after the proposed legislation was embraced by the electorate, three girls were denied pizza in a restaurant, a woman alleged she was denied services at a San Joaquin County office, and a 14-year-old boy said that Asian students told him to go back across the border.[34] No doubt such discriminatory processes and practices will continue to influence other states. These examples of heightened racial and ethnic conflict are likely to extend to the whole nation in coming years.

Yet even with the passing of Proposition 187 and Proposition 227, known as the Unz Proposal, and the widespread acceptance of its premises by those who supported them, there has been resistance to their implementation. Proposition 187 was stalemated in the courts because several challenges were filed by opponents and Latino parents. On November 21, 1995, a U.S. District court overturned key provisions of Proposition 187 on the basis that because immigration was a federal concern, states had no authority to regulate its implementation.[35] By July 1999, former Governor Gray Davis of California agreed not to contest the federal ruling against Proposition 187 because it was being considered as unconstitutional, and as a consequence, Proposition 187 was negotiated out of existence.

Davis was recalled from office in October 2003, and he was succeeded by Republican Arnold A. Schwarzenegger in November 2003, who had voted for Proposition 187. While Schwarzenegger was strongly supported by Latinos during his election, his track record in meeting the needs of Latinos in California during his tenure has been riled with missteps. His approval rating among Latinos who voted for him in 2003 fell from 30 percent to 17 percent by 2005. Not only did Schwarzenegger stumble over border issues, by rejecting legislation benefiting immigrants and opposing the granting of driver's licenses to illegal immigrants, but he also stumbled in relation to health and welfare spending cuts. Thus it is not surprising that Latinos distrust the approval of Proposition 49, the After School Education and Safety Program Act of 2002, which would offer tutoring, homework assistance, and enrichment activities starting in 2004 as an initiative that would curve juvenile crime.[36]

Proposition 227 has also met with resistance as some bilingual teachers in California have ignored its implementation by continuing to teach as they previously had in bilingual programs. In some schools, principals have not put into practice any of the policies and have used the parental waivers to conduct business as usual. A recent five-year study of Proposition 227, conducted by the American Institutes for Research (AIR) and WestEd, found no conclusive evidence favoring one instructional approach for English learners. In fact the study shows that students across all language classifications in all grades have experienced performance gains on state achievement tests, the performance gap between English learners and native English learners has remained constant, and staff has been capable in addressing English learners' academic and linguistic needs as well as focusing school-wide on English language development. In other words, quality of instruction rather than language of instruction contributes to the students' success.[37] Thus, even though both propositions have legally passed, Latinos have resisted and continue to oppose their implementation in schools and at the community level.

In August 1999, the town of El Cenizo, Texas, mostly consisting of foreign-born residents, became the first U.S. city to stipulate that its official business could be conducted in Spanish. Moreover, the townspeople made it known that local authorities could not help border patrols apprehend undocumented immigrants.[38] Those actions have more recently been offset by the establishment of vigilante groups such as the Minutemen along the border in 2004 and by actions taken by police in using trespassing laws in New Hampshire to arrest undocumented immigrants, an allegation that was dismissed in August 2005.[39]

To understand the overwhelming support for Proposition 187 and Proposition 227, it is necessary to assess demographic trends and the relation to electorate composition in California, which is now one of the most diverse majority minority states in the nation. In 1994, California's population was 56.3 percent white, 26.3 percent Latino, 9.4 percent Asian, and 7.4 percent African American. However, according to a statewide exit poll conducted by the *Los Angeles Times*, 81 percent of California's electorate was white, while only 8 percent were Latino, 5 percent were African American, and 4 percent were Asian.[40] Obviously, the wide margin of victory for the proposition reflects the fact that 63 percent of whites, the largest electoral bloc in the state, voted in favor of Proposition 187 and the Unz Proposal. The margin of victory was substantial across gender, age, income, education, and religious lines. It is significant to note that the majority of Democrats (64%) voted against the proposition, but the majority of both Republicans (78%) and independents (62%) voted in favor of it. One can only conclude that Governor Wilson's reelection, with 56 percent of the vote, was heavily influenced by his support of Proposition 187, and Proposition 227 was highly influenced by the private sector interest groups favoring Ron Unz.

The exit poll also revealed a troublesome pattern for the Democratic Party coalition and for race relations in California. As one could have expected, Latinos voted overwhelmingly (77%) against the proposed legislation, but only about half the African Americans and Asians voted against Proposition 187. A similar pattern was also true for Proposition 227. Thus, it appears that ethnic polarization is wider than just whites versus ethnic and racial minorities. Similarly, even in the agricultural Central Valley, where the region's economy is heavily dependent on seasonal immigrant labor, the Proposition 187 passed 69 percent to 39 percent, results that suggest an electoral divide between the farmers and corporations dependent on immigrant labor for their businesses and the popular electorate in the region. Only in the liberal district of the San Francisco Bay area did the electorate reject the initiative. All in all, the results of the election suggest that the white electorate voted as a block against the immigrant population, while the majority of people of color were underage, lacked citizenship, or simply did not vote.

Proposition 187 and the Unz Proposal reignited a deep sentiment that goes well beyond immigrants' rights and California. Similar to the tax revolts of the late 1970s and early 1980s, for example Proposition 13 in California and Proposition 21/2 in Massachusetts, groups have already organized in such disparate states as Florida, New York, and Arizona to pass Proposition 187-type laws.[41] The *Los Angeles Times* article reported that the same group that launched the initiative for Proposition 187 also targeted affirmative action and financial aid to Mexico.[42] This so-called California civil rights initiative proposed to end affirmative action as a policy tool to remedy discrimination, and we have already seen the effects of this on several of the California campuses. While this initiative was the brainchild of two professors from the University of California at Berkeley, the grassroots nativist movement fueled support for the new initiative by linking the immigration issue to affirmative action. They claimed that affirmative action, which was designed to remedy discrimination against African Americans, was incorrectly being used to benefit many other groups. As the Republican Party gained a majority in Congress, affirmative action has become a more pressing policy issue at the national level. The convergence of immigration and affirmative action issues has tremendous political implications: the realignment of national politics is increasingly based on racial politics.

There is a close relationship between the growing nativist and anti-civil rights sentiments, the dissolution of the liberal coalition around the Democratic Party, and the anger of the white electorate toward federal-run government. The primary factor underlying these issues is a stagnant U.S. standard of living. Targeting immigrants, minorities, and single mothers receiving financial assistance is easier than understanding how global competition, corporate restructuring, and new technologies have affected economic growth and income distribution during the past two decades. Former Secretary of Labor Robert Reich described the American working class as an anxious class unable to understand how middle-class wages have stagnated for 20 years and looking for easy solutions to the problem.[43] Indeed, the isolationist sentiment can affect U.S. efforts to penetrate international markets as much as nativism can affect productivity in the domestic market. Despite the ideological debate drawing media and partisan political interest, a more comprehensive view on the incorporation and contributions of Latinos in the United States, the changes that will continue to affect us in the twenty-first century, and how we need to respond to such changes is addressed in the next section.

CHALLENGES FOR THE NEW CENTURY

Americans and Latinos alike will no doubt be affected in this century by several compounding social and public issues. Among these will be the nation's response to: (1) The deconstruction of racial and ethnic categorization in favor of new social and cultural identities; (2) The legalization of the employment status of millions of undocumented immigrant workers and the opening of employment opportunities for Latinos beyond secondary labor markets; (3) The importance of education in the lives of Latino youth from kindergarten to secondary and post-secondary opportunities; (4) The growing concern for health care delivery and services for Latinos; and (5) The integration and political incorporation of new immigrants and their growing need for greater representation and attainment of political strength.

The Deconstruction of Racial and Ethnic Categorization toward the Construction of New Social Identities

We are currently witnessing the deconstruction of racial and ethnic categorization along relational lines, where race and ethnicity are no longer simply viewed as fixed and defined phenotypes, but rather as socially constructed definitions. The most recent census categories already reflect some of the shifts that are occurring in the meaning of ethnicity and race, where being biracial can now be counted in terms of multiple categories. Louis Mirón attributes this shift in definition as being based on the multiplicity of roles that individuals assume in different situations.[44] The current official use of group definition has undergone several changes starting with the use of Hispanic surnames prior to the 1970s, to Hispanic, to Latino, and by biracial and self-identification criteria in the 1990s. Such shifts reflect how terminology and identification of the past, which seemed inflexible, has now begun to yield to the social pressures and demands of changing identities with shifting populations.

The questioning of the notion of race as a biological category belies the stress on the Bell Curve and the rekindling of genetic explanations.[45] New categories, which identify biracial children and the use of Hispanic before or after the use of the term, are currently under consideration by the census bureau. Ethnic groups are moving away from the use of monolithic labels favoring instead more inclusive, pan-ethnic considerations and hybrid concepts. Some critical theorists such as Mirón advance the notion that:

The central point about understanding ethnic identity as social process is that the process is relational. That is, there is not personal ethnic identity apart from a relationship to other ethnic and non-ethnic identities. Identity formation within the social context of ethnicity . . . is inseparable from the broader social relations of power and material and ideological structures.[46]

The term Latino became the nomenclature of the 1990s, and it is likely to generate new social identities in this millennium. Even the notion of borderlands espoused by Gloria Anzaldúa to express the growing diffusion of Latino identity beyond its own situated context, into a cultural and political context has now become commonplace amongst critical writers and pedagogues such as Henry Giroux, Peter McLaren, and many others.[47] We are no doubt in the throes of change, and that change has also been dramatically reflected in the changing composition of the U.S. population over the last 30 years.

As the Latino population grows, it is apparent that the labels used as identifiers will continue to undergo change. Latinos increasingly describe themselves by their ethnicity rather than race. "Racial ethnic labels are used in the United States as code words for behavioral patterns associated with poverty, destitution, and deviant/criminal behavior," says Martha Giménez.[48] In most cases, the word Latino has replaced the word Hispanic. According to

Giménez, "Hispanics are not a minority group in the historical sense of the concept but an extraordinarily heterogeneous population whose members differ in terms of nationality, race, ethnicity, culture, socioeconomic status, and social class."[49] For example, ethnicity, once categorized solely by race, now incorporates class and culture. Latinos are represented through a myriad of self-definitions and characterizations. In fact, a current pan-ethnicity movement blurs the once-strict definitions of Latinos. Felix Padilla as well as José Calderón, both speak of the creation of a pan-ethnic identity based not on a transplanted cultural heritage but on situational and collective action that transcends distinct national and cultural identities.[50] The social categories of race are being subsumed under the category of borders so that ethnicity becomes prominent in its relation to identity and self-esteem. Even when they have limited or no knowledge of their family language and culture, Latinos proudly self-identify in terms of their heritage. Joshua Fishman aptly pointed out in his studies of New York communities that ethnicity may well outlive the loss of language.[51]

Yet as important as ethnicity may be, according to Gimenez, Lopez and Muñoz, Latino heterogeneity, instead of being taken at face value, is overshadowed. What emerges is a race-like character still subject to stereotyping and discrimination. Even though the most successful Latinos appear to be exceptions to the rule, their good fortune is attributed to their having overcome their Hispanicness and assimilating into the mainstream.[52] Understanding such complexities requires ascertaining how Latinos view themselves rather than how they are viewed by others, and more important, how their differences are recognized rather than minimized.

Undocumented Immigrant Workers and Employment Opportunities

The legalization of the employment status of millions of undocumented immigrant workers and the opening of employment opportunities for Latinos beyond secondary labor markets are two of the most contentious yet critical issues for Latinos. The recent demonstrations in favor of a progressive immigration policy reform, one that concedes amnesty for the millions of undocumented workers and facilitates their citizenship, constitute the most significant evidence to date of a Latino pan-ethnic identity. In April 2006 hundreds of thousands of immigrant workers and other supporters organized manifestations across the country that culminated in a "day without immigrants" on May 1, the International Workers Day. Immigrant workers, Latinos in general, and a progressive coalition of supporters organized massive demonstrations in major cities across the country and protested pending legislation that would criminalize undocumented immigrants. The unification of Latino voices and the strength of peaceful street demonstrations resulted in President Bush forwarding to Congress a more favorable legislation. Though the compromise contains stiff border control and employer sanctions provisions, in general the legislation allows for the eventual legalization of close to 10 million workers and a significant increase in visas for guest workers and family reunification.[53]

The question of the economic impact of immigrants has been at the forefront of public policy and popular opinion debates. In general, there are two perspectives on the question of the economic impact of immigration. On the one hand, there are those who regard the impact of undocumented immigrants, and more generally the rapid expansion of unskilled workers, as adverse to the employment opportunities of other minorities and imposing excessive costs on local public systems. For example, in 2002, a report from the Rand Corporation emphasized the need for the United States to revise its immigration laws and to admit those with English language and professional skills, because the costs in education and health care alone of unskilled laborers would erode the economic gains emanating from the current strong economy.[54] A second view on the impact of immigrants on the economy contends that the economy of the 1990s was fueled by the availability of a reserve group of workers willing to satisfy a growing demand for unskilled labor. A case in point is the study conducted by Sum, Uvin, Khatiwada, and Ansel of the Commonwealth of Massachusetts, where immigrant workers have become the principal source of new labor and where between 1980 and 2004, their share in the labor force nearly doubled from 8.8 percent to 17.0 percent. Without their participation, the authors conclude that the labor force would have shrunk.[55] Thus it would appear that depending on the state of the economy, Latino immigrants provide needed labor for jobs that were of little interest to other ethnic groups.

The issue of immigrants taking jobs from native workers has received wide attention. Surveys of the literature point to the conclusion that immigrants are not interchangeable with natives in the workplace and that the newcomers' entry into local labor markets has had a negligible effect, if any, on natives' earnings and employment.[56] In particular, these studies find little or no detrimental effect on other minorities' employment or wages. The major injury seems to be to the earnings of other Latino immigrants, although these effects are relatively small. Even increases in areas of high Latino concentration such as Los Angeles cause limited displacement of native workers and, in fact, there is a large degree of complementarity between native and immigrant workers. A reasonable explanation for such parallelism is that immigrants are employed in certain industries—labor-intensive manufacturing in Los Angeles and New York City, for example. This segmentation of Latino workers precludes competition with natives employed outside these niches. In his analysis of the New York City restaurant industry, Roger Waldinger offers concrete examples of labor-market segmentation impeding competition between blacks and Latinos.[57]

Studies concerning patterns of regional and industrial incorporation of immigrants are also important in this regard. Latino immigrants tend to concentrate within a few standard metropolitan survey areas, where, through networks, they establish employment niches in certain industries. Today, most of the restaurant services of the country are filled with Latinos working from the ranks of busboys to chefs and waiters in large numbers. The irony of Proposition 187 is that, in California, Latinos provide the majority of seasonal agricultural laborers for an industry that certainly profits most from a continuous supply of undocumented immigrants. And who can doubt that American consumers benefit from the low cost of California fruits and groceries?

Whether consumers benefit from cheaper agricultural produces from California or not, few analysts will question the relevance of a steady labor supply to sustain an aging native population. Hernández, Siles, and Rochín describe the new reality in which Latino youth in the United States find themselves as a veritable social revolution.[58] With an aging white population becoming the burden of support, Latino youth will have to contribute to the support of retired people. Working people faced a ratio of 17 retired persons per 3 active workers in 1950, but by the year 2000, this ratio has increased to 2.5 workers per retiree.[59] This development foreshadows demands for educational policies and practices that take into account better jobs and training for Latinos and inclusion of more than one language as part of the educational system. Thus, the issues of educational and economic reform, English as a Second Language, bilingualism, cultural awareness and sensitivity, as well as equity will continue to be central to social policy. Already states such as California and Texas are considered to be minority majority states, and according to Hernández, et al., Latino youth will be entering the labor market at increasing rates but without knowing if they will have a preferred place in better-paying occupations.[60] Given the graying of America and the growth of Latinos, it may be as Hernández, et al. suggest, that Latino youth are as important to the future of the majority population as they are to the future of Latinos themselves.[61] This has serious implications for retirement and pension plan payments. No doubt it will be those in the workforce, particularly underrepresented groups, who will bear the burden of supporting the elderly. To the degree that this workforce can translate their social and cultural capital into skilled, productive, and useful knowledge, there may be serious limitations on the lifestyle that can be expected in the future for all Americans.

THE EDUCATION OF U.S. LATINOS FROM KINDERGARTEN TO HIGHER EDUCATION

The education of U.S. Latinos is a compelling paradoxical issue. While their sheer numbers in elementary and secondary schools have expanded dramatically, their enrollment in post-secondary education is at an all-time high, and their access to graduate programs at the master's and doctoral levels shows steady gains during the 2000s on. Latinos—not necessarily just the poor but those of the middle class as well—have the highest dropout rates of any ethnic group in the United States.[62] In fact, the current status of Latino youths' educational attainment poses a national threat. With the large numbers of Latino high school dropouts, including students from high-income families, a massive uneducated labor force is being created, which will have the costly consequence of widening the education gap between Latinos, blacks, and whites.

Moreover, there are growing concerns as to whether access to preschool programs such as Head Start has long-term benefits lasting through elementary, middle, and high schools for Latinos. Head Start evaluations indicate that middle-class children derive the most benefit from these programs, and that they provide limited coverage for underserved children.[63] Thus the issue to be examined is, how do Latinos become incorporated into the educational system in ways that allow them to compete with their white mainstream counterparts? Are compensatory programs such as Head Start and bilingual and special education classes, vehicles that prepare Latinos in the same ways as their white counterparts? The underlying premise is that given the opportunity, Latino students should not only do well in school, but through the competencies gained, they should successfully meet prescribed academic standards. The leveling of the playing field toward achieving parity is assumed to be inherent in the delivery of educational programs. These assumptions fail to examine the structural and systemic obstacles Latino students face, the day-to-day experiences they share, their constant exposure to discriminatory practices, and their perceived low status, all of which reinforce their sense of failure.

An overall view of the Latino experience in education indicates advancement in post-secondary and higher education. However, further data indicate that at the high school level, there is retrenchment attributable to inadequate learning opportunities and systemic discrimination. Similarly, it is widely assumed that Latinos, like any other students, should simply be treated as any other kids. The problem inherent in this philosophy is that it lacks a special approach to or concern for the students' cultural and linguistic attributes and their migrant or immigrant status, and it disregards the importance of these influences on the lives of Latino students.

This generalized color-blind criterion tends to set Latinos students up for failure. On the one hand, their ethnicity is usually recognized in terms of the relative numbers to be counted as necessary resources, but on the other hand, their unique conditions for learning—as first language speakers from a primary culture not yet assimilated into the secondary language and culture and in some cases, lacking schooling experiences—are not seriously considered. In this dilemma, close examination of the factors that engage or disengage students in and out of school reveals that the solutions require multilevel and multilayered analyses.[64] There are no easy answers to these issues, but clearly the shift that has taken place in explaining the educational experiences of Latinos through models of cultural deprivation and deficit to the more systemic questioning of how schools and health care agencies respond to their specific needs has begun to ground Latinos' experiences within more comprehensive frameworks.

We can no longer ignore the presence of Latinos and their fundamental contributions to the United States. As present and future citizens, they are shaping the discourse that must be developed in each of these areas. The

Suárez-Orozcos have identified some striking differences among immigrant and U.S.-born Latinos. Whereas Mexican-born adolescents are highly motivated to learn to speak English and use the educational system, U.S.-born Latino adolescents appear to be defiant, uninterested in academic pursuits, and unmotivated. They attribute this to the fact that Mexicans see their achievements in terms of the familial obligations and ties to the social group, which still instills much of their core values, while U.S.-born Latinos struggle with identity, peer influences, and allegiances often fragmenting their choices.[65]

Another contributory issue is the role of Latino families. If they are to play more than perfunctory roles in determining school policy, parents must be trained in decision-making processes leading to their development as productive, vocal, and active members of school councils. Empowering Latino parents is fast emerging as a guarantee that effective learning is a top priority. Networks of parents, teachers, students, and administrators are widening as parents mobilize and communities demand better education for their students.[66] The interface between schools, communities, and homes is narrowing and becoming, as the late John Ogbu argued, continuous rather than discontinuous.[67]

The research of Luis Moll and others has also demonstrated that within Latino communities there are funds of knowledge that have not necessarily been identified, tapped, or utilized by schools.[68] What appear to be directives for educating Latinos are no longer prescriptions for success. The focus has shifted from explaining why Latinos can't succeed to providing detailed maps of their roads to success and influence.[69] The conditions under which Latinos learn—school structures, curricula, teacher preparation, role models—are at the center of these analyses.

However, the various social contexts that generations of Latinos have confronted seem to make an important difference. After controlling for social origins, other factors, such as social-psychological attributes, cognitive ability, and timing of immigration, have a significant effect on young Latinos' education. Further research addressing the questions and explanations to guide policymakers in enacting changes still has to be undertaken. Some questions relate to retention and advancement of Latino students at different levels, how tracking affects entry into higher-level courses, whether high school completion is affirmation that the goals of school-to-work programs have been realized, and whether higher education and graduate studies indeed advance the careers of Latinos. Without a doubt, Latino education is inextricably tied to issues of ethnicity, degree and visibility of ethnic group representation among other groups, and distribution of equitable educational services for all students.

HEALTH CARE DELIVERY AND SERVICES FOR LATINOS

The nation's health care delivery system faces complex challenges. For the past decade or so, U.S. health care costs have been rising significantly faster than other sectors of the economy. According to Heather Boushey and Marya Murray Díaz, during the 1990s and into the 2000s, health care costs rose much faster than inflation, and costs for dependent or family coverage shifted from employers to employees thus requiring Medicaid to respond through the State Children's Health Insurance Program (SCHIP), thus placing additional financial stress on the already saturated budget deficit states.[70] In 2002, nearly 113 million Americans under age 65 were without employer-provided health insurance for at least some part of 2002, and a growing number are experiencing a drop in the percentage of those with employer provided health insurance, affecting in particular the coverage of children.[71] Yet among these, children, Latinos, and young adults (ages 18 to 25) are the least likely to have health insurance.[72] In fact, Boushey and Díaz argue:

Latinos are less likely than other racial/ethnic groups to be covered, even once we account for differences in other characteristics, both because they do not receive health insurance from their employers, and they access Medicaid in smaller shares than other racial/ethnic groups.[73]

Access to quality medical care in many urban centers and rural areas has been lacking, and long-term-care coverage is meager. Moreover, health consumers and medical providers alike have been baffled by unreasonable and excessive paperwork and bureaucracy. Owing primarily to these factors, health care reform is a social policy area that received significant attention during former President Clinton's Administration. According to Boushey and Diaz, health insurance premiums rose faster than overall inflation and worker's earnings between 1992 and 2003, except in 1996, 2002, 2003, and 2004, where increases in costs have been double-digit.[74] Even though several states such as Maine and Massachusetts are contemplating legislation for universal health coverage, the lack of health insurance coverage is one of the most critical issues facing the United States today, as the numbers of uninsured Americans rises.

While the recent interest in health care reform seemed to offer a timely opportunity to address Latinos' problems in accessing health services, and the reasons for Latinos' poor health, the debate has centered on cost containment and financing. By and large, the discussions have overlooked such critical issues as language, geographic and institutional barriers, and the paucity of Latino health professionals and culturally competent services, which affect the ability of Latinos to obtain adequate health care services.

Not only are Latinos disproportionately represented among the nation's uninsured and underinsured, but they are also severely underrepresented in health policymaking and medical occupations. The scarcity of Latinos in health research positions results in a shortage of well-documented research on this population.[75] The limitations of national data sets on Latino mortality and morbidity trends were even noted by the Government Accounting Office as early as the 1990s.[76] These factors contribute significantly to a poor understanding of Latino health needs and problems, which hinders the development of adequate programs and services. They also result in limited knowledge of the effect of health policy on Latinos.

It is essential, therefore, that health officials and policymakers engage Latino health providers and researchers in discussions about improving access and health care delivery services to Latinos. It is important to seek mechanisms through which Latino health professionals can participate actively in and influence the identification of priority Latino health issues and develop solutions to the population's health problems. Medical institutions and staff, in attempting to satisfy different clientele in hospital and community settings, focus their teaching on issues of diversity and ethnicity.

The ethnicity of patients and their families plays a significant role in determining the types of health care they can expect to receive and the types of services providers can deliver and support. Just as the ongoing national debate about health care centers on matters of ethnicity, future students will have to concern themselves with receiving an appropriate education, one hewn from the current educational reform movement to introduce more meaningful actions.

Another important finding that influences the relation of education to health can be found in the medical literature. Less educated people are significantly more prone to higher mortality and morbidity rates than those who have a college education. For example, a recent report from the U.S. Department of Health and Human Services found that among people between 25 and 64 years old, the death rate of those with less than a high school education was more than twice that of those who attended college for at least one year.[77]

Clearly, low levels of educational achievement do not bode well for Latinos' health. Therefore, it is apparent that the interdependence of health and education as it affects Latinos requires a deeper analysis of the issues than that supported by traditional research results.

Toward the Social, Economic Integration and Political Participation of the New Immigrants

The integration and political incorporation of the new immigrants and their participation in the United States is a critically important concern in this century. The new immigrant populations are racially and ethnically mixed and, in many cases, have been politically or economically displaced from their country of origin by war or unemployment. Slightly more than 1.5 million legal and illegal immigrants annually arrive in the United States, and over 750,000 births by immigrant women take place.[78] Of these, close to 700,000 enter as permanent residents, 100,000–150,000 enter legally as refugee or asylees seeking protection, and about 300,000 enter as undocumented immigrants.

How are the new immigrants adapting to these circumstances? It is well established in the literature that immigrants develop specific family and community links before coming to the United States. These so-called networks facilitate information and resources that allow not only travel, but also employment opportunities. In the United States, these immigrants develop social networks that emulate the historical linkages that exist between the American foreign and economic policies regarding their countries and their actual presence and concentration throughout the United States.

By and large, the new immigrants, in varying degrees and contingent on their types of networks and support, contribute directly to the economic development of the United States immediately upon arrival. Asian immigrants, particularly Koreans, can count on family and religious networks for financial backing as they establish themselves. Latinos, on the other hand, seek out family support mechanisms and community-based agencies as sources that lead to employment. These immigrants represent skilled workers who provide needed hands in expanding industries and accept jobs that native workers are unwilling to perform: witness the numbers of service workers in the food, restaurant, and cleaning industries and in the care services.

While these parallel institutions may provide entry opportunities into the labor market, they may also limit the opportunities for mobility out of the lowest cluster of occupations. On the one hand, labor unions may not respond to the needs of the workers nor do they promote leadership among laborers, but on the other, once union leaders recognize the growing power of Latino laborers, aggregating them into the leadership of the union seems to bode well for both sides.

Population growth increases the demand for goods and services, stimulating long-term economic growth; and in an increasingly global economy, immigrants provide key links for international trade and commerce. Not only do immigrants stimulate growth in the United States, but through the remittances of money and goods back to their families, they contribute to the economic development of their countries of origin and to the building of infrastructures and the reduction of poverty.[79] According to the Inter-American Development Bank's Multilateral Investment Fund (MIF), close to $45.8 billion was sent in 2004 to Latin America and $17 billion a year alone is sent to Mexico. More importantly, immigrants' contribution to the economy of their home country aids in reducing the need for financial assistance from the United States.

It should be apparent from the earlier discussion that concerns central to Latino political participation are redefining contemporary American politics. Immigration, international trade, and affirmative action are but a few of the issues that directly affect social policy formulation at the state and federal levels. These topics have divided the democratic coalition and are reshaping presidential and local elections. At a first approximation, the relative gains in political representation and access to public policy process have not yielded any discernible gains in education, employment, and economic development. One of the greatest challenges to Latino researchers is to reexamine the conceptualization of political participation and its implicit gender bias.

Mainstream studies of Latino political participation focus on leadership as derived from official positions in elected or appointed office or in formal organizations. Thus, people narrowly define leadership in terms of representation, ignoring other critical aspects of participation and, ultimately, the underlying forces that make viable such participation. Immigrant communities have developed multiple forms of political participation not only in recognizable political structures, but also in established parallel organizations and institutions of ethnic solidarity. For once it is apparent that, in contrast to other periods of relatively high immigration, these new populations comprised of people from Asia and Latin America represent a challenge to preconceived notions of how ethnic groups incorporate into economic, social, and public life. Race is an essential element of social life in the United States—there are no other industrialized countries, for instance, with a population share of racial and ethnic minorities similar to the United States. Undoubtedly these levels of diversity have been characterized in the United States mainly in terms of black and white. Yet the growing diversity of races and cultures challenges existing typologies of social problems and prescribed solutions. Old conceptual formulas lack explanatory power to produce strategies to cope with new realities.

In a milieu, where xenophobic fears prevail and budgetary cuts at the federal and state levels provide less social and public services, the differences between and within ethnic groups for obtaining limited resources escalate, creating unnecessary and conflictive divisions. These perceived conflicts are likely to create defensive stances and posturing about rights and privileges and instead of unifying efforts toward common goals, may result in further distancing Latinos from other ethnic groups. Alternatively, Fraga and Ruiz de Velasco advance a policy-based strategy based on informed public interest. They suggest that Latinos pursue political incorporation that outlines a conceptualization of benefit based not upon gains by a few, but rather benefits many segments of the population. In other words, these authors advocate civil rights within a multicultural state. They suggest that a strategy focused solely on the articulation of rights promotes failure and that if long-term public commitment is to be gained in the human and economic capital of such communities, then it needs to be sought by coalition building.[80] In creating these coalitions, it will be important for Latinos as well as other groups to maintain their social capital, that is, the beliefs, shared values, and familial structures as well as cultures of the groups that serve as bases for the development of their communities.

Another aspect that warrants special consideration is how institutions respond to the challenges posed by rapid population change. The reported research documents the extent to which job-market organizations, such as corporations and unions, institutions of higher education, and health delivery and political systems, are not responding adequately to these challenges. Would the educational system prove to be a social equalizer for Latinos as it was for other ethnic groups before them? Would Latinos' electoral victories and the emergence of a new democratic coalition precede access to public-sector jobs as it did for African Americans? Would a new economic expansion provide favorable conditions for changing employers' views on Latinos' contribution in the workplace? Can the democratic coalition survive the challenge of racial politics and nativist sentiments?

More than rhetorical, these are questions that may help us in assessing whether institutional responses to the new social realities perpetuate a subordinated position for Latinos rather than promoting incorporation and equal participation. Evidently the process of incorporation and full participation in social institutions is going to be substantially different for Latinos than the historic experience of other ethnic groups.

CONCLUSIONS

As the demographic landscape changes and expands, the characterization of the United States as a monolithic culture is also changing, adding new levels of social, economic, and political complexities and greater demands from diverse cultures. Crossovers and borderlands merge and reemerge in music, song, dance, and rituals, and even the all-American sports don new faces drawn from Caribbean and Latin American countries.[81] Similarly the effects of such shifts also mean the need for economic and political representation.

Americans today are experiencing the integration and political incorporation of new immigrants into the fabric of this changing society, which carries with it the demands for different types of knowledge, competencies, and skills than those required of immigrants who came to the United States at the turn of the century. Latinos are also becoming conscious of the need for the creation of new coalitions amongst diverse ethnic groups, in the midst of shifting economic realities and communities. Rather than competing for limited economic and social resources, the need in the future will be toward the creation of national agendas based on common interests and the building of bridges amongst diverse and disparate groups. Subsumed under these issues is the impact that each has directly on employment and income, education, health, and political participation.

Previous immigrant waves coincided with and responded to periods of rapid economic expansion. But the nature of industrial expansion and economic growth today is radically different from that at the turn of the century and the postwar expansions. Though the knowledge-based economy has spurred economic growth, the so-called new economy has also increased inequality in income distribution and provides fewer advancement opportunities for low-skilled, young, and foreign-born workers. Limited economic opportunities, in turn, exacerbate nativist sentiments and racial conflict in job markets where low-wage workers are concentrated and local areas were the impact of immigration on social services is more apparent. To the extent that economic limitations continue to produce a bifurcated pattern of employment opportunities and access to limited social services, the conditions in which new immigrant populations filter into job markets and establish socially-balanced settlements become substantially different when compared with previous historical processes.

Latinos, who were part of the American landscape before Columbus arrived, are actively engaged in developing their communities. Generations of Mexican Americans are native to the Southwest, as conquered peoples of the state of Texas, and Arizona, while Puerto Ricans travel freely between the island and the continent. Even though recent immigrants always speak of returning home, communities in Chicago, Los Angeles, New York, and many other urban and rural areas, attest to the expansion of Latino home bases, of community-based organizations and federations linked to their countries of origin. Their transnationalism is undisputed. Towns throughout the United States have begun to recognize themselves in terms of the ethnic identities of their population. Cities such as Lawrence and Lowell, in Massachusetts have been distinctly shaped by the Dominicans and Puerto Ricans who have made them their homes.

To the extent that they can foster their own visions of change in the American society, Latinos will be the negotiators of the democratic ideals so treasured in the American Constitution. They may well be on their way to becoming the agents of change in fostering America's future. As Padraig O'Malley, the editor of the *New England Journal of Public Policy*, in his 1995 preface to a special issue of the journal devoted to Latinos wrote:

Latinos may well change the American sense of it identity, not just challenge but abnegate some of the core beliefs American has about itself. Change may be incremental, but the sum of the increments always overwhelms the parts. They become in their aggregate the critical mass that presages not change but revolution, the shining pathfinder that illuminates the new course of history.[82]

NOTES

1. See Luis Ricardo Fraga and Jorge Ruíz de Velasco. (1995). "The Declining Significance Rights: Civil Rights in a Multicultural Society," Working Paper, Stanford Center for Chicano Research, for an explanation of this issue as it pertains to African Americans and Latinos in particular. They point out that the Civil Rights Act of 1964 was also followed by the Economic Opportunity Act of 1984 and the Elementary and Secondary Education Act of 1965.

2. See the extensive debate on immigrants that some of these sources characterize: Michael Fix and Jeffrey S. Passel. (1994). *Immigration and Immigrants: Setting the Record Straight.* Washington, D.C.: The Urban Institute; Maureen Goggin and Mark Feeney. (1998). "Open and Shut: The United States Prides Itself on Being a Nation of Immigrants—But for How Much Longer?" *Boston Globe,* 1998; "Undocumented Mexican Immigrants: Dispelling the Myths and Fears." LARASA Report, a Publication of Latinos in Colorado, January 1995; Georges Vernez and Alland Abrahamse (Eds.) (1996). *How Immigrants Fare in U.S. Education.* Santa Monica: Rand Corporation, for

the first systematic effort in explaining the experiences and performance of immigrant children in the United States; and Alan Booth, Ann C. Crouter and Nancy Landale (Eds.) (1997). *Immigration and the Family. Research and Policy on U.S. Immigrants.* New Jersey: Lawrence Erlbaum Associates Publishers.

3. 2004 U.S. Census Bureau Brief and National Population Estimates.

4. 2004 U.S. Census Bureau, and U.S. Interim Projections by Age, Sex, Race, and Hispanic Origin.

5. See Samuel Huntington. (2004). *The Challenges to America's National Identity.* New York: Simon and Schuster.

6. Vernez and Abrahamse (1996) point out in *How Immigrants Fare in U.S. Education,* that "although the current number of immigrants is the highest at any time in the U.S. history, its proportion in the U.S. population is lower than in any decade from the middle of the 19th century until the 1930s, when it ranged from 13.2 to 14.7 percent" (p. 1).

7. Data from the U.S. Bureau of the Census. See also J. S. Passel. (2005). "Unauthorized Migrants: Numbers and Characteristics." Background Briefing Prepared for Task Force on Immigration and America's Future. Washington, D.C.: Pew Hispanic Center. Also note the analysis of trends in immigration depicted by Jeffrey S. Passel and Roberto Suro. (2005). *Rise, Peak, and Decline: Trends in U.S. Immigration 1992–2004.* Washington, D.C.: Pew Hispanic Center.

8. See the extensive reports from the General Accounting Office on Immigration such as "Immigration Enforcement: Weaknesses Hinder Employment Verification and Worksite Enforcement Efforts," GAO-05–813, August 31, 2005; "Homeland Security: Some Progress Made, but Many Challenges Remain on U.S. Visitor and Immigrant Status Indicator Technology Program," GAO-05–202, February 23, 2005; "Immigration Statistics: Information Gaps, Quality Issues Limit Utility of Federal Data to Policymakers," GGD-98–164, July 31, 1998; "Immigration Reform," Washington, D.C.: U.S. Government Printing Office, 1990.

9. Ibid.

10. Jonathan Fox and Michelle C. Boomgaard. *Latinos in the United States.* http://www.bsos.umd.edu/cidcm/mar/ushispan.htm. p. 1–19.

11. "Summary of Provisions and Implications for the Ron K. Unz Initiative: English Language Education for Immigrant Children," San Diego County Office of Education, 1998.

12. Personal communication from Dr. Silvia Ponce, dentist working with Latino communities in Boston, Massachusetts, June 2000.

13. Jonathan Fox and Michelle C. Boomgaard. *Latinos in the United States.* http://www.bsos.umd.edu/cidcm/mar/ushispan.htm. p. 1–19.

14. George Pappas. (1993). "In Understanding Racism toward the Latino Community." Maria Guajardo (ed.). LARASA Report. Latin American Research and Service Agency. October, p. 1–4.

15. Ricardo Sandoval and Susan Feriss. (1995). "The Dilemma of Immigration. How Should Hispanic Policymakers respond to Proposition 187? The Answers Still Aren't Clear." *Hispanic Business,* February, p. 18–21.

16. "Summary of Provisions and Implications for the Ron K. Unz Initiative: English Language Education for Immigrant Children," San Diego County Office of Education, 1998.

17. Ibid.

18. Ibid.

19. Jorge Capetillo-Ponce. (2004–2005). "Challenges to Multiculturalism." *The New England Journal of Public Policy.* Fall/Winter, vol. 20, No. 1, pp. 139–147.

20. See Antonia Darder. (1993). *The Struggle for Educational Justice: Bicultural Studies in Education.* Institute for Education in Transformation. The Claremont Graduate School.

21. Jeffrey Passel S. (1994). *How Much Do Immigrants Really Cost?* Claremont, CA: Tomas Rivera Center. Also see Tom Abate. (2005). "What Immigration Brings California Study Evaluated the Costs, Benefits of a Huge Influx of Foreign Workers," *San Francisco Chronicle*, December 11.

22. Adapted from Erick Schive. (1994). "Proposition 187 is Not Just Cruel, It is Hypocritical," *Business Week*, November 14.

23. Leif Jensen. (Spring 1988). "Patterns of Immigration and Public Assistance Utilization, 1970–1980." *International Migration Review*, 22, No. 1.

24. See the reports from Jeffrey S. Passel. (1994). "Immigrants and Taxes: A Reappraisal of Huddle's 'The Cost of Immigrants,' " Washington, D.C.: The Urban Institute; Jeffrey S. Passel and Rebecca L. Clark. (1994). "How Much Do Immigrants Really Cost? A Reappraisal of Huddle's 'The Cost of Immigrants,' " Washington, D.C, The Urban Institute, including; Julian Simon. (1981). "What Immigrants Take From and Give to the Public Coffers." Final Report to the Select Commission on Immigration and Refugee Policy, Washington, D.C.

25. See Francine Blau. (1984). "The Use of Transfer Payments by Immigrants," *Industrial Labor Relations Review*, 37, No. 2 (January): 222–239; and Marta Tienda and Leif Jensen. (1986). "Immigrants and Social Program Participation," *Social Science Research*, 15, 372–400.

26. David Hayes-Bautista, Werner O. Schink and Jorge Chapa. (1988). *The Burden of Support: Young Latinos in an Aging Society*. Stanford, CA: Stanford University Press.

27. Leif Jensen. (1988). "Patterns of Immigration and Public Assistance Utilization, 1970–1980." *International Migration Review*, 22, No. 1 (Spring).

28. Gregory De Freitas. (1991). *Inequality at Work: Hispanics in the U.S. Labor Force.* New York: Oxford University Press. Also see Martin Carnoy, Hugh Daley, and Raul Hinojosa Ojeda. (1990). *Latinos in a Changing U.S. Economy, Comparative Perspectives on the U.S. Labor Market since 1939.* Inter-University Program for Latino Research. New York: Research Foundation of the City University of New York.

29. See Derrick Z. Jackson. (1994). "For California Educators, Proposition 187 Is a Lesson in Racism," *Boston Globe*, November 16; and Diane Seo. (1994). "Case May Become Legal Test for Proposition 187," *Los Angeles Times*, November 12; "California Adoption of Proposition 227: Learning Delayed, Learning Denied." *NABE NEWS*. National Association for Bilingual Education, Vol. 21, no. 7, June 15, 1998. Also see the "Summary of Provisions and Implications for the Ron K. Unz Initiative: English Language Education for Immigrant Children," San Diego County Office of Education, 1998.

30. Marcello Medina, Jr. (1988). "Hispanic Apartheid in American Public Education," *Educational Administration Quarterly*, 24, no. 3 (August): 336–349.

31. *Alliance for Excellent Education.* Vol. 5, No. 5, March 6, 2006. Retrieved April 1, 2006 from http://www.all43d.org/press/pr_022806.html.

32. See Peter Lobo. "Are the Streets Paved with Gold?" An Examination of the Socioeconomic Outcomes of Asian and Latino Immigrants to the United States. Population Studies Center, University of Michigan, PSC Research Report No. 93–282, for an explanation of the types of differential correlation that exist for Latinos as

compared to Asians between occupational background at the time of entry into the United States and socioeconomic performance.

33. See Carola and Marcelo Suárez-Orozco. (1995). *Transformations. Migration, Family Life and Achievement Motivation among Latino Adolescents.* Stanford University Press.

34. Gordon Dickson. (1994). "Proposition 187 Used to Deny Pizza, Girls Say," *USA Today,* November 21.

35. Jonathan Fox and Michelle C. Boomgaard. *Latinos in the United States.* http://www.bos.umd.edu/cidcm/mar/ushispan.htm. p. 1–19.

36. Suzanne Herel. "After-School Enrichment Plan OKd: Measure to Designate $550 million for activities starting in '04," *San Francisco Gate,* pp. 1–2. Retrieved April 14, 2006 from http://sfgate.com/cgi-bin/article.cgi?file=/c/a2002.

37. Thomas B. Parrish, Maria Pérez, and Amy Merickel. (2006). "Effects of the Implementation of Proposition 227 on the Education of English Learners, K-12. Findings from a Five-Year Evaluation." Submitted to California Department of Education by American Institutes for Research and West Ed, January 24. A previous study conducted by Patricia Gándara. (2000). In the Aftermath of the Storm: English Learners in the Post 227 Era," *Bilingual Research Journal, 24:* 1 and 2, Winter and Spring, showed that two years after the implementation of proposition 227, there was little evidence that the achievement scores of California's English learners had long-term benefits.

38. The *English First* Web site cites a newspaper article from Reuters titled "Texas Town Adopts Spanish as Official Language" (August 16, 1999), as an example of El Cenizo, Texas, where the Mayor reports that because most of the town's residents speak only Spanish, the city council voted to make Spanish, not English the town's official language, thus providing access to the residents. Retrieved August 28, 1999 from http://www.englishfirst.org/elcenezo/elcenezoresuters81699.htm.

39. See "New Hampshire Judge Dismisses Immigrants' Trespass Charges." *Boston Globe.* August 13, 2005.

40. See "A Look at the Electorate," *Los Angeles Times,* November 9, 1994.

41. See Maria Puente. (1994). "States Setting the Stage for Their Own Proposition 187's," *USA Today,* November 18.

42. See Patrick McDonnell. (1995). "For Them, Proposition 187 is Just the Beginning," *Los Angeles Times,* June 28.

43. See John Forrel. (1995). "Meet the New Comeback Kid: Secretary of Labor Robert Reich," *Boston Globe*, April 2, 34.

44. Louis F. Mirón. (1996). *The Social Construction of Urban Schooling: Situating the Crisis.* New York: Hampton Press, Inc.

45. See Richard Hernstein and Charles Murray. (1994). *The Bell Curve: Intelligence and Class Structure in American Life.* New York: Free Press.

46. Louis F. Mirón. (1996). *The Social Construction of Urban Schooling: Situating the Crisis.* New York: Hampton Press, Inc., p. 111.

47. Henry Giroux. (1991). *Post Modernism, Feminism and Cultural Politics: Redrawing Educational Boundaries.* Albany: SUNY; and (1993). Border Crossings: Cultural Workers and the Politics of Education. New York: Routledge Paul, p. 27.

48. Martha Giménez. (1993). "U.S. Ethnic Politics: Implications for Latin Americans," *Latin American Perspectives, 19,* No. 4 (Fall): 7–17.

49. Ibid. p. 10.

50. Felix Padilla. (1985). *Latino Ethnic Consciousness: The Case of Mexican Americans and Puerto Ricans in Chicago.* Notre Dame: University of Notre Dame Press. Also see

José Calderón. (1992). "Hispanic and Latina: The Viability of Categories for Panethnic Unity, in The Politics of Ethnic Construction, Hispanic, Chicano, Latina?" *Latin American Perspectives, 19*, No. 4, pp. 37–44.

51. Joshua Fishman. (1980). *Bilingual Education in the United States under Ethnic Community Auspices, Alatis*, (ed.). Georgetown University Round Table on Languages and Linguistics. Current Issues in Bilingual Education. Washington, D.C.: Georgetown University Press, 8–13.

52. Martha Giménez, Fred A. Lopez and Carlos Muñoz, Jr. (1992). "The Politics of Ethnic Construction: Hispanic, Chicano, Latino?" *Latin American Perspectives, 19*, No. 4, Fall, pp. 1–106.

53. See the Close Up Foundation information Web site, www.closeup.org. Retrieved May 30, 2006.

54. Steven Haider, Robert F. Schoeni, Yuhua Bao, Caroline Danielson. (2001). *Immigrants, Welfare Reform and the Economy in the 1990s*. Santa Monica, CA: Rand Corporation.

55. Andrew M. Sum, Johan Uvin, Ishwar Khatiwada, Dana Ansel with Paulo Tobar, Frimpomaa Ampaw, Sheila Palma, Greg Leiderson. (2005). *The Changing Face of Massachusetts*. Boston: MA. The Massachusetts Institute for a New Commonwealth and Center for Labor Market Studies. June 2005.

56. George Borjas. (2005). "The Economic Integration of Immigrants in the United States: Lessons for Policy." *Poverty International Migration and Asylum*. Edited by George Borjas and Jeff Crisp. Palgrave Macmillan, pp. 241–250. George Borjas. (2001). *Heaven's Door: Immigration Policy and the American Economy*. Princeton University Press, 2001. Also see earlier work of George Borjas. (1990). *Friends or Strangers: The Impact of Immigrants on the U.S. Economy*. New York: Basic Books; Michael J. Greenwood and John M. McDowell. (1988). *The Labor Market Consequences of U.S. Immigration: A Survey*. Washington, D.C. Immigration Policy Group, U.S. Department of Labor; Julian Simon. (1989). *The Economic Consequences of Immigration* New York: Basil Blackwell; and Robert D. Reischauer. (1989). "Immigration and the Underclass," *The Annuals 501* (January): 120–131.

57. See the extensive research on this subject by Roger Waldinger, with Michael Licther. (2003). *How the Other Half Works: Immigration and the Social Organization of Labor*. University of California Press; and also his earlier work Roger Waldinger. (1987). "Changing Ladders and Musical Chairs: Ethnicity and Opportunity in Postindustrial New York," *Politics and Society 15*, 369–401.

58. Rudy Hernandez, Marcelo Siles, and Refugio Rochin Jr. (2000). "Latino Youth: Converting Challenges to Opportunities," In *Making Invisible Latino Adolescents Visible: A Critical Approach Building Upon Latino Diversity*, ed. Martha Montero-Sieburth and Francisco A. Villarruel. New York: Garland Press, pp. 1–28.

59. Ibid. p. 1.

60. Ibid., p. 7.

61. Ibid., p. 8.

62. Wendy Schwartz. (1997). *Immigrants and Their Educational Attainment: Some Facts and Findings*. ERIC Clearinghouse on Urban Education. According to Maria Puente and Sandra Sanchez, while the Latino population is projected to increase by 61 percent in the next 15 years, its dropout rate is expected to be twice as high as that of blacks and more than three times that of whites. See Pedro Pedraza and Melissa Rivera (Eds.) (2005). *Latino Education: An Agenda for Community Action Research. A Volume of the National Latino/a Education Research and Policy Project*. New York: Erlbaum

Press; Robert Slavin and Margarita Calderón (eds.) (2001). *Effective Programs for Latino Students.* Hillsdale, NJ: Erlbaum; and Ralph Rivera and Sonia Nieto. (1993). *The Education of Latino Students in Massachusetts: Issues, Research and Policy Implications.* Boston: Mauricio Gaston Institute for Latina Community Development and Public Policy, University of Massachusetts Boston, for an extensive analysis of some of these issues, particularly tracking discriminatory practices and dropout rates and measures for success of Latinos.

63. See Vernez and Abrahamse (1996) point out in *How Immigrants Fare in U.S. Education.* Santa Monica: Rand Corporation.

64. See Martha Montero-Sieburth. (1993). "The Effects of Schooling Processes and Practices on Potential 'At Risk' Latino High School Students." In Ralph Rivera and Sonia Nieto (eds.) *The Education of Latino Students in Massachusetts: Issues, Research and Policy Implications.* Mauricio Gaston Institute for Latino Community Development and Public Policy and the University of Massachusetts Press, pp. 217–242.

65. Carola Suárez Orozco and Marcelo Orozco-Suárez. (1995). *Transformations. Migration, Family Life, and Achievement Motivation Among Latino Adolescents.* Stanford University Press.

66. For example, in the greater Boston metropolitan areas, several organizations including the Latino Parents Association, Parents' Place, teaches parents how to become advocates by offering training in education and in self motivation and encouraging parents to become involved in the schooling of their children.

67. John Ogbu. (1982). "Cultural Continuities and Schooling," *Anthropology and Education Quarterly, 13,* No. 4: 290–307.

68. Luis Moll. (1992). "Bilingual Classroom Studies and Community Analysis: Some Recent Trends," *Educational Researcher, 21,* No. 2 (March): 20–24.

69. For explanations of success for Latinos, see the Introduction titled "Latino Youth and America," by Francisco A. Villarruel and Martha Montero-Sieburth in *Making Invisible Latino Adolescents Visible. A Critical Approach to Latino Diversity.* New York: Falmer Press, 2000, pp. xiii–xxxii; "An Overview of the Educational Models Used to Explain the Academic Achievement of Latino Students: Implications for Research and Policies into the New Millennium," by Martha Montero-Sieburth and Michael Christian Batt, In Robert E. Slavin and Margarita Calderon (eds.) *Effective Programs for Latino Students.* New Jersey: Erlbaum Associates Publishers, 2001, pp. 331–368; and Henry (Enrique) Trueba (2004). *The New Americans: Immigrants Transnationals at Work.* New York: Rowman and Littlefield.

70. See Heather Boushey and Mayra Murray Diaz. *Health Insurance Data Briefs # 1: Improving Access to Health Insurance. Center for Economic and Policy Research.* Retrieved on April 15, 2004 from http://www.cepr.net/publications/health_insurance_1_2004_04.html.

71. Ibid.

72. Ibid.

73. Ibid. p. 5.

74. Ibid. Also see Kaiser Family Foundation. *Employer Health Benefits. 2003 Summary of Findings,* p. 2, http://www.kff.org/insurance/loader.cfm?url=commonspot/security/getfile.cfm&PageI=20688.

75. See the extent this issue has been discussed from the key findings from the Kaiser Women's Health Survey. "Women and Health Care: A National Profile." Report prepared by Alina Salgnicoff, Usha R. Ranji and Roberta Wyn. Kaiser Family Foundation, July 2005 to H. Amaro, "Health Data on Hispanic Women: Methodological

Limitations." *Proceedings of the 1993 Public Health Conference on Records and Statistics.* National Center for Health Statistics, 1993; H. Amaro. (1993). "Testimony on the Disadvantaged Minority Health Improvement Act," U.S. Senate Committee on Labor and Human Resources, Washington, D.C., June 30; J. Delgado and L. Estrada. (1993). "Improving Data Collection Strategies," *Public Health Reports, 108*, 540–545; National Council of La Raza. (1993). "Improving Hispanic Health Status." *Agenda Supplement 11*, no. 2 (Winter); National Health Policy Summit. (1992). "Summary of Discussions and Recommendations in Assessing Hispanic Health Needs." April; and Surgeon General's National Hispanic/Latino Health Initiative. (1993). "One Voice, One Vision: Recommendations to the Surgeon General to Improve Hispanic/Latino Health," U.S. Department of Health and Human Services, June.

76. General Accounting Office. (1992). *Hispanic Access to Health Care: Significant Gaps Exist.* Washington, D.C.: U.S. Government Printing Office.

77. *Health and the United States*, U.S. Department of Health and Human Services, 1994.

78. See *Current Numbers from the Center for Immigration Studies.* Retrieved April 12, 2006 from http://www.cis.org/topics/currentnumbers.html.

79. See the "Tomas Rivera Policy brief on Binational Impact of Latino Remittances," by Rodolfo de la Garza, Manuel Orozco, and Miguel Baraona. Tomas Rivera Policy Institute, March 1997, pp. 1–8. Also see Lori Wiechman. (1997). "Hispanics Budding Power Growing at Phenomenal Rate, Study Says Hispanic Buying Power to hit $348 Billion," *The Arizona Republic Business.* June 19. The buying power of Hispanic consumers is growing at three times the rate of inflation and is gaining on black purchasing power according to a University of Georgia study. This increase is up 65 percent since 1990. Hispanic buying power is also concentrated in California ($112 billion), Texas ($56 billion), and New York ($33 billion). It should be noted in Frederick Rose's report, "Measures Against Immigrants Repeat U.S. History," *The Wall Street Journal*, April 26, 1995, that economic analysts such as George Borjas point out that it takes four generations or 100 years for immigrant families to reach educational and economic parity with natives, thus with the influx of recent immigrants requiring greater skills than those of 100 years ago, means that unless they have access to such education and support, they may be at a greater disadvantage than their immigrant ancestors.

80. Luis Ricardo Fraga and Jorge Ruiz de Velasco. (1995). "The Declining Significance of Rights: Civil Rights in a Multicultural Society." Working Paper Series, No. 50, Stanford Center for Chicano Research, Stanford University, January 30.

81. See "Latin U.S.A.: How Young Hispanics Are Changing America," *Newsweek*, July 2, 1999, for a review of the cross-over music and characteristics of generation the young Latinos who are bicultural in America.

82. From the *Special Issue of Latinos in a Changing Society, Part I*, Summer 1995. University of Massachusetts Press.

CHAPTER 2

Living on the Margins of Society: Dominicans in the United States

Ramona Hernández

LIVING ON THE MARGINS OF SOCIETY: DOMINICANS IN THE UNITED STATES

In 2000, over 3 in 10 Dominican households in New York City, where 60 percent of the Dominican people living in the United States reside, lived below the poverty line. When compared to other racial/ethnic groups, Dominicans had the highest poverty rate in the city, including higher than Hispanics (see Table 2.1). But poverty among Dominicans is hardly a new phenomenon. High pockets of poverty have existed among this group since very early in their migration process. In fact, as reflected in Table 2.1, in 2000, poverty among Dominicans declined slightly by almost 5 percent as compared to previous decades. In 1980, 36 percent of Dominican households lived below the poverty level. In 1990, poverty rate had slightly increased among this group to 36.6 percent.

Moreover, large segments of the Dominican people in the United States have continued to be poor and live below the level of poverty even at moments when the United States has experienced booming economic conditions, which are reflected in a strong dollar in the market, higher levels of exportations, high real estate value, higher levels of productivity, and low unemployment levels. This is also to say that a large segment of the Dominican people live in poverty after migrating to the United States, despite the fact that the migration journey was undertaken precisely to improve their socioeconomic standing. It is important to add here that the segments of the Dominican population that could be facing economic hardship may be much larger than the current percentages provided in this discussion.

Table 2.1
Poverty in New York City 1980, 1990, 2000

Population Group	Poverty Rate (%)		
	1980	1990	2000
Dominican New Yorkers, overall	36.0	36.6	32
New York City Average	18.0	17.2	19.1
Non-Hispanic White Population	8.7	8.2	9.7
Non-Hispanic Black Population	28.3	22.9	23.6
Non-Hispanic Asian Population	—	—	18.2
Hispanic/Latino Population	35.0	31.4	29.7

Sources: 5% Public Use Micro Data Sample, 1980, 1990 and 2000 U.S. Census of Population. Department of Commerce.

The data included here refers only to those homes that were found to live below the poverty level according to U.S. censuses. There are other segments of the poor populations that, if computed into the analysis, could enlarge significantly the size of poor Dominican households. One of these segments is represented by those households that live precisely at the level of poverty, not quite above this imaginary line. In 2003 the Census Bureau set the poverty line at $18,810 for a family of four. According to the definition, only those families whose incomes *were below* the poverty mark lived in poverty. Scholars tend to measure in percentages the distance between the poverty line and the income of a given family to provide a more accurate picture of the size of the families who live in poverty. A family whose income is 125 percent above the poverty level is considered economically solvent. Conversely, a family whose income is 125 percent below the poverty level is 75 percent much poorer than a family whose income falls 50 percent below the poverty line. Needless to say that both families face much more economic hardship than a family whose income falls slightly below the poverty line or matches it. Similarly important is the fact that the Census Bureau does not take into account geographic location when computing the poverty income. Yet, researchers have argued that the cost of living varies from city to city and that the income reflecting the poverty line should be adjusted accordingly to reflect a more accurate picture of the reality faced by the poor.

Looking carefully at the data presented in Table 2.1, two related questions come to mind: (1) why are Dominicans so poor? and (2) why has poverty persisted among U.S. Dominicans?

POVERTY IN THE UNITED STATES: A TABOO

On August 27, 2004, the Center on Budget and Policy Priority issued a press release pointing at the state of affairs for the poor in the United States.

The press release indicates, "the number and percentage of Americans living below the poverty line increased for the third consecutive year in 2003, and the number and percentage of people without health insurance also climbed for the third straight year" (1). Indeed, in 2003 the number of poor Americans increased to 35.5 million, and the number of those who did not have medical health coverage increased to 45 million. In 2003, the Census Bureau defined poor families as those with cash incomes of less than $18,810 a year for a family of four. Among the poor, children, particularly those in families headed by single women, and those living in *extreme poverty* suffered the most economic hardship.[1] Indeed, the number of poor children climbed to 12.9 million, and the number of those living in extreme poverty rose to almost half of all poor, or 15.3 million. The census Bureau defines extreme poverty as those families with cash incomes below half of the poverty line. In 2003, the average poor family had incomes of $8,853 per year, or $738 per month (see Table 2.2).

Poverty has increased in the United States during a period of time when the economy is recovering from its downfall.[2] The growth of prosperity and poverty simultaneously reflects an interesting fact: the U.S. economy behaves in ways that are familiar to economists in third world or developing countries. In the case of the Dominican Republic, for instance, poor people have resorted to leaving home in larger numbers at times when the economy has performed the best, including moments when the Dominican economy has outperformed all Caribbean countries and most countries in Latin America.[3] But what interests us more here is the fact that the press release concerning the deplorable conditions of the poor and their escalating number among the American people did not cause any state of alarm or a state of despair and preoccupation among policymakers or the current head of this nation. The alarming news about the poor in this country resulted in a press release composed by the Center on Budget and Policy Priorities and a couple of other comments expressed casually by people in the media. That is to say that the poor are not perceived as worthy of news nor are they part of the American public discourses.

Table 2.2
Changes in Poverty and Health Insurance (in Millions)

Year	2000	2001	2002	2003
Poverty *(aggregated)*				
All People	31.6	32.9	34.6	35.9
Hispanics	7.8	8	8.5	9
Health Insurance				
All People	39.8	44.1	43.6	45

Source: Center for Budget and Policy Priority, 2004.

The year 2004 was a year of presidential elections, and both main political parties held their national conventions to nominate and accept their respective presidential and vice-presidential candidates. The two selected candidates were John Kerry for the Democratic Party and George W. Bush for the Republican Party. Neither John Kerry's nor George W. Bush's acceptance speeches discussed the issue of poverty in the United States. Their speeches, as those of many past presidential candidates, focused on creating jobs, the issue of taxes, enhancing the incomes and the lives of those identified as the middle class, and now, on the war against terrorism. The faces of millions of poor people, who walk on the streets of many neighborhoods in the United States, remained invisible in the speeches of all four candidates who ran for the two highest political posts in this country. Two of the four made it in November 2nd; and surely, the two men proceeded to implement the plan for the American people they had previously described and in which no specific action or concerns were conveyed about the escalating number of poor people in this country.

POVERTY AMONG IMMIGRANTS

As argued previously, discussions about poverty as a social ill in the United States seldom take place in public spheres. Yet, the issue of poverty in the United States has caught the attention of academics who have dedicated many pages to discussing it whether in scholarly forums or in written forms. As a result, there is a considerable amount of literature examining poverty among U.S. natives and how their lives are impacted by it.[4] This is not the case for Hispanic immigrants. While a good amount of studies focus on Hispanic immigrants in the United States, research on poverty among this group is insufficient. There are a number of motives behind this lack of scholarly research:

1. The perception that immigrants, in general, are people who, for the most part, are better off in the receiving society as compared to their home countries.
2. The belief that Hispanic immigrants are protected by a strong sense of family that alleviates destitution and staggering poverty. Along the same line it is also believed that immigrants in general count on a network system that helps them to accommodate themselves in the receiving society by connecting them with the labor market, housing, social services, and so forth.
3. The view that immigrants tend to settle in declining neighborhoods and that their energy, vitality, and ambitious impetus revitalize an area turning it into a vibrant, dynamic, and effervescent community.
4. The idea that immigrants are "birds of passage," or temporary visitors whose main goal is to secure enough resources to return to their home countries as quickly as possible.
5. The perception that many immigrant groups are transnational, or people who find ways to live in two societies using resources, opportunities and knowledge from both to accommodate themselves.[5]

Most migration literature dealing with the socioeconomic status of Hispanics in the United States is permeated by one of these views. Furthermore, when poverty is discussed among Hispanics, the tendency is to focus on Puerto Ricans and Mexicans, the two largest subgroups among Hispanics/Latinos.[6] Besides the absolute size and the weight that these two groups may affect in the overall Hispanic/Latino population, these groups are also characterized for having been living in the United States for longer periods of time than most Hispanic migrants. They have, therefore, created a good number of voices, whether scholars or activists, of their own who may look at issues that others may not find attractive, credible, or even worthy of studying or discussing.[7]

Of course, each of these views somehow contribute to making poverty among Hispanic immigrants invisible, or at least, not readily perceptible to many. Poverty among Hispanic immigrants is also hidden by the fact that they come to live in a society that has traditionally rejected the poor, has segregated them in neighborhoods, and, which is perhaps more destructive, has developed a system of beliefs that tends to blame the poor for their own material necessity and want. Such actions and beliefs inevitably exonerate the organisms of power from assuming responsibility for the causes behind poverty in the United States.

But the truth of the matter is that whether Hispanic immigrants possess a strong sense of family, count on an ethnic community populated by people of their own kind, or think of themselves as temporary dwellers, or people who are just passing through, this does not prevent them from falling into poverty. The same line of argument can be advanced in terms of this society's attitude in blaming the victims and making the poor accountable for their own poverty: Poverty among Latinos is not going to go away by finding them accountable for their actions. Unless specific social policies are developed to address it, the fate of many Latino subgroups will likely remain the same. Similarly, thinking of migrants as transnational people may lead one to think that migrants live in two worlds; yet, this does not necessarily mean that migrants have resolved their economic life in either society, whether the sending or the receiving society.

EXPLAINING POVERTY

A number of theories have been postulated to explain the origins and the persistence of poverty in the United States. Roughly, three theoretical views lead the discussion:

1. Issues dealing with human capital
2. Perceptions dealing with cultural—or lack of—traits and values
3. Matters dealing with structural socioeconomic causes

The human capital explanation proposes that the origins of poverty are connected to people's lack of education, training, skills, experience, network, and so forth. A variant of the human capital theory is the mismatch perception, or the understanding that a number of workers do not possess the skills, education, or training demanded in a given labor market. Workers who do not possess the necessary training or education required by the labor market become vulnerable, face prolonged levels of unemployment, and hold menial, low-paying, and undesirable jobs. Prolonged unemployment periods and the inability to find a job push segments of the working populations into becoming *marginalized* or *discouraged* workers, or workers who are not counted among the unemployed by the Bureau of Labor Statistics.[8]

James Jennings, a political scientist, has voiced his criticism concerning the human capital theory and has argued that such a theory "focuses on the weaknesses of the individual. There is a presumption that the economic system is effective for everyone who is properly skilled and educated; thus, poverty could be reduced significantly if only impoverished groups could obtain the skills necessary for the available jobs" (Jennings, 1999, 17). On the same vein, others have raised concerns about an aprioristic approach in the valorization of education and its view as a panacea for all ills for all members of society regardless of race and social class (Griffith, Frase, and Ralph, 1989).

The cultural explanation for poverty has been linked to Max Weber in his classic text *The Protestant Ethic and the Spirit of Capitalism*, which discusses the causes of economic success among a given religious group. According to the classic text, Protestants who followed Calvin's dictums managed to succeed over Christians. The triumphant Protestants were characterized for having a work ethic and a way of life that emphasized continuous hard work and continuous savings through the practice of a prudent lifestyle: Protestantism. The puritan point of view proposed a system of belief and a set of practices—a culture—that became the standard of a given group in Europe and that was transported to the nascent United States by the colonists who came to steal land and conquer people.

Variants of Weber's approach are found in the school of thought that proposes that the poor lack proper norms of behavior and values, that they are immoral, and that they are inherently or genetically unequipped. Oscar Lewis's classic analysis of poverty among Puerto Ricans in New York City reflects such a view. In *La Vida: A Puerto Rican Family in the Culture of Poverty*, Lewis argues that "People with a culture of poverty are aware of middle class values, talk about them and even claim some of their own, but on the whole they do not live by them. Thus it is important to distinguish between what they say and what they do" (1966, xlvi). On his part, Charles Murray (1984) takes another angle and proposes the eradication of welfare policies that benefit the poor. In his view, social welfare for the poor creates dependency among the poor, nurtures a way of life, and eliminates the development of incentives that the poor should use to pull themselves up from poverty.

Perhaps the most ardent critic of the cultural approach to poverty is Karl Marx and Friedrich Engels, whose work presents a socioeconomic structural approach to understanding poverty. In Marx and Engel's view the nature of social and cultural formations are intrinsically influenced by the economic base of society—by its mode of production and by the relationships that exist between those who own the means of production and those who do not. The system of ideas or beliefs that informs each institution in a given society is then connected to the economic foundation or its mode of production in that society. This is to say that poverty arises not because poor people lack a given culture, but because they live in a society whose economic system produces precisely a state of inequality among its members and creates a system of ideas and beliefs that justify and help to maintain the established status quo or state of affairs *(Communist Manifesto)*.

Ryan (1976) is a modern critic to the cultural approach and builds his argument from a structural perspective. He argues that there are social forces that are beyond poor people's control and that push them into poverty.

EXPLAINING POVERTY AMONG DOMINICANS: THE TRADITIONAL VIEWS

The traditional answer to the question of why Dominicans are poor in New York City focuses on four variables: Dominicans have low-human capital, they have low household income, they face high unemployment levels, and a significant portion of their homes are headed by a single woman. There is evidence to support the traditional notion on poverty. Tables 2.3, 2.4, 2.5,

Table 2.3
Per-Capita Household Income of Dominicans in New York City 1980, 1990, 2000

Mean Annual Household Per-Capita Income ($)	1980	1990	2000
Dominican New Yorkers, Overall	5,920	6,336	10,032
New York City Average	12,765	16,412	24,010
Non-Hispanic White Population	16,336	23,276	37,391
Non-Hispanic Black Population	8,600	10,894	15,367
Non-Hispanic Asian Population	—	—	19,533
Hispanic/Latino Population	7,085	8,515	12,500

Sources: 5% Public Use Micro Data Sample, 1980, 1990 and 2000 U.S. Census of Population. Department of Commerce. The data for 1980 income are in 1990 dollars and have been adjusted by the change in the U.S. Consumer Price Index between 1980 and 1990 as published by the U.S. Bureau of Labor Statistics. *2000 Census, 5% PUMS.*

and 2.6 provide data on household per capita income, unemployment rates, female-headed homes, and educational attainment among Dominicans for 1980, 1990, and 2000. As reflected on these tables, in each decade studied, Dominicans had the lowest income, their unemployment levels were among the highest if not the highest, they have significant female headed homes, and they have the lowest educational attainment as compared to other racial/ethnic groups in the city, including Hispanics.

In 1980, the annual per capita household income of Dominicans was $5,920. By 1990, the per capita annual household income of the group had increased to $8,659, and by 2000 it had increased to $10,032. What is interesting to note is that while one cannot negate that the annual per capita income for Dominicans has significantly increased from 1980 to 2000, one also needs to take into account that as compared to other groups, in the three decades compared here, Dominicans have had consecutively, the lowest per capita income among all groups. Their lower income is precisely what explains the high percentage change in income among Dominicans from 1990 to 2000.

Data on unemployment reveal similar distressing findings. Table 2.4 shows that in 1980, 14.3 percent of Dominican males and 9.5 percent of Dominican females were unemployed. In 1990, 15.7 percent of males and 18.4 percent of females were then unemployed. In 2000, 8.9 percent of Dominican males and 13.1 percent of Dominican females were unemployed. Note that in 1990 both Dominican men and women had the highest unemployment rate among all groups, and that while in 2000 the unemployment rate of Dominican

Table 2.4
Unemployment Rates in New York City 1980, 1990, 2000

| | Unemployment Rate (%) | | | | | |
| | Male | | | Female | | |
Population Group	1980	1990	2000	1980	1990	2000
Dominican	14.3	15.7	8.9	9.5	18.4	13.1
New York City, Overall	7	8.7	5.5	6.6	8.1	6.5
Non-Hispanic White Population	5	5.5	3.2	6.6	4.9	3.4
Non-Hispanic Black Population	13.1	14.3	9.4	9.9	10.9	8.6
Hispanic/Latino Population	14	12.4	7.5	12.21	13.6	10.9

Sources: 5% Public Use Micro Data Sample, 1980, 1990 and 2000 U.S. Census of Population. Department of Commerce.

males was only second to non-Hispanic blacks, Dominican women were less fortunate and continued to have the highest unemployment level among all women compared.

In the United States, the term *broken home* is commonly used to refer to households with children that are headed by a single woman. The derogative phrase eludes to the significant value this society places on male figures or fathers in the home. But in spite of society's moral judgment, female-headed homes are quite prevalent among Dominican families. In 1980, a single woman headed over 3 in 10 Dominican homes. In 1990, the proportion increased to 4 in 10, and in 2000, the number decreased again to 3 in 10 homes. While in 1990, Dominicans had the highest percentage of families headed by a single woman in the city, in 1980 and 2000 Dominicans were second to non-Hispanic blacks who exhibited 35.6 percent and 40 percent respectively of single female-headed homes.

In looking at educational attainment one finds that yet again, Dominicans show disadvantages as compared to other groups residing in the city. In 1980, 72.0 percent of the Dominican population 25 years of age or older did not have a high school diploma. By 1990, the percentage of non-high school graduates had significantly declined to 52.3 percent, and by 2000, to 49 percent. On the other hand, the percentage of those with "College or More" increased from 3.8 percent in 1980 to 8.0 percent in 1990 and to 10.6 percent in 2000. Despite the positive gains, note in both cases that Dominicans represent the two extremes of the educational pyramid: a disproportionate representation among those who have not completed a high school education and a very low representation among those who possess higher education.

Table 2.5
Female-Headed Families in New York City

	Female-Headed Families (%)		
Population Group	**1980**	**1990**	**2000**
Dominican Population	34	40.7	38.2
New York City Average	19.2	21.7	22.1
Non-Hispanic White Population	9.4	9.2	9.1
Non-Hispanic Black Population	35.6	38.8	40.0
Non-Hispanic Asian Population	—	—	8.1
Hispanic/Latino Population	31.5	34.3	32.0

Sources: 5% Public Use Micro Data Sample, 1980, 1990 and 2000 U.S. Census of Population. Department of Commerce.

Dominicans' low educational attainment matters in a society that increasingly privileges the attainment of formal schooling and training and validates knowledge that has been certified through educational degrees. The trend is not new. In the 1980s, more Dominicans arrived in the United States, particularly to New York City, than in any previous decades, including the 1990s. In 1988, at the time when Dominicans were rapidly arriving, an editorial published in the *Washington Post* described the new state of affairs in the labor market and noted "The educational-linked difficulty facing the large number of workers in this country, who, not that long ago, could qualify for a wide range of entry level, decently paying jobs without sophisticated technical skills or in many cases a high school diploma. As we constantly hear, those jobs are mostly gone, replaced by more technically demanding and autonomous jobs that need employees with higher-order skills" (October 29, 1988).

In the 1990s we came to terms with the reality that the United States has evolved into an advanced service-oriented economy that has a tendency to increasingly depend on technology. Thus, traditional blue-collar work,

Table 2.6
Educational Attainment of the Dominican Population 1980, 1990, 2000
Persons 25 Years of Age or Older

Population Group	Year	Percentage of the Population Completing			
		Less than High School	High School	Some College	College or More
Dominican	1980	72	16.5	7.7	3.8
Population	1990	52.3	20.4	19.3	8
	2000	49	20.5	19.9	10.6
New York City	1980	35.8	30.9	13.5	19.8
Overall	1990	20.8	24.8	24.5	29.9
	2000	19.4	21.0	37.7	21.9
Non-Hispanic	1990	11.7	23.2	23.5	41.6
White	2000	14.5	30	28.5	27
Non-Hispanic	1990	24.9	29.9	29.6	15.6
Black	2000	27.4	29.7	28.4	14.5
Non-Hispanic	2000	18.9	16.3	21.4	43.4
Asian Hispanic/Latino	1990	40.4	25.6	23.1	10.9
Population	2000	47.5	22.1	19.9	10.5

Sources: 5% Public Use Micro Data Sample, U.S. Department of Commerce, 1980, 1990 and 2000 U.S. Census of Population.

particularly jobs associated with the manufacturing and industrial sectors, are rapidly disappearing from the scenario. Joel L. Nelson eloquently has argued that post-industrial societies count on an escalating base of knowledge associated with the acquirement of formal schooling. "My reference to and definition of knowledge here is quite specific: an organized and objective interpretation of information. This knowledge base develops in tandem with raising levels of education and expanding literacy of a more professional and specialized white-collar workforce" (1995, 4).

EXPLAINING POVERTY AMONG DOMINICANS IN THE UNITED STATES: AN UNORTHODOX APPROACH

Every factor discussed previously, without a doubt, impacts on the socioeconomic status of the Dominican people, or any other group for that matter. But while each of these factors may be the result of temporary situations or transitory stages for some population groups, in the case of the Dominican people, poverty has obstinately persisted from decade to decade regardless of how long Dominicans have lived in the city. Of course, needless to say such a high level of persistent poverty among Dominicans unquestionably challenges traditional views concerning the multiple benefits associated with migrating from a poor society to a rich one. Furthermore, persistent poverty among Dominicans also questions the belief that the longer one lives in a receiving society the more chances one has to achieve socioeconomic progress. In other words, while unemployment may be high among those Dominicans who have recently arrived, it should be low among those who have been living here for some time. Table 2.7 shows data on unemployment correlated with time of arrival. The data reflects a significant high unemployment level (14%) among those Dominicans who had arrived before 1980. What is even more disconcerting is that compared to those who had arrived during the 1995–2000 period, unemployment rates among these long-time Dominican residents were still 2 percent higher than the more recent immigrant arrivals. Why is that?

Persistent above average unemployment rate among Dominican workers suggests that unemployment among the group is not seasonal or frictional but *structural*. That is to say that the loss of jobs among the group is caused by a contraction produced on the demand side of the labor market.

The shifting of the economy from manufacturing to service and the increasing loss of blue-collar, unskilled jobs had a devastating effect on Dominican immigrants who are mostly unskilled, blue-collar workers. During 1980, for instance, among all the Caribbean nations the Dominican Republic had the highest proportion of unskilled, blue-collar workers admitted to New York City. From 1982 to 1989, 36.6 percent of Dominicans were specifically classified as operators, fabricators, and laborers. The corresponding proportion for the entire Caribbean, excluding the Dominican Republic, was 21.4 percent. Although during the 1990s a larger share of Dominican immigrants

Table 2.7
Unemployment Rates Dominicans in the Labor Force

Greatest Challenge			Unemployment is lower because more professional people migrated these years.
1	**2**	**3**	**4**
Arrived Before	Arrived Between	Arrived Between	Arrived Between
1980	1980 & 1990	1990 & 1994	1995 & 2000
14%	19.2%	10.2%	12.1%

Source: For 1980 and 1990, 5% *Public Use Micro Data Sample, US Census of Population.* Department of Commerce. For columns 3 and 4, *Current Population Survey.*

came from the professional and technical ranks as compared to previous years, the proportion of those who were blue-collar and unskilled workers continued to dominate the movement. Throughout the decade of the 1990s, 14.8 percent of all those who declared to have an occupation in the Dominican Republic were classified under the category "Professional, Specialty, and Technical."

Table 2.8 presents data on the decline of manufacturing and the share of the population employed in that sector. As reflected on the table, almost one in two Dominicans was employed in the manufacturing sector in 1980. Yet, by 2000, the representation of Dominicans in the manufacturing sector had precipitously declined to 12.4 percent or to four times less than what they had in 1980 (48.6%). But unemployment among Dominicans came about because the displaced workers could not find jobs in the other growing job sectors of the economy, either because they did not have the educational or training qualifications required for those jobs or because there were not enough jobs that Dominicans qualified for.

The inability of the U.S. economy to produce enough blue-collar, low-skilled jobs at a pace capable of matching the needs of the labor force is an issue that seldom appears in the writings among scholars of migration studies. A superficial look at the U.S. economy may lead one to miss the disparity between supply and demand in certain sectors of the labor market, particularly before the facts that immigrant, job-seekers keep coming and that the U.S. continues to create jobs in every sector of the economy. But of course, the question is not whether people come or do not come, or whether a number of

Table 2.8
The Decline of Manufacturing in New York City Persons in the Labor Force

Share of Labor Force	1980	1990	2000
Proportion of New York City Labor Force	18%	12.1%	6.6%
Proportion of Dominican Labor Force	48.6%	25.7%	12.4%

Source: 5% Public Use Micro Data Sample, U.S. Department of Commerce, 1980, 1990, and 2000 U.S. Census of Population. Department of Commerce.

jobs are created regularly. The question lies, rather, among other things, on whether job seekers get jobs and on the number of those who do not, and on an empirical analysis of the elasticity of the labor markets where immigrants tend to be hired. Such analysis needs to take into account the needs of the immigrant population and other labor groups who may compete with immigrants for the same jobs.

There are some valuable studies in the contraction of employment opportunities available to minority workers in this country. In his *When Work Disappears: The World of the New Urban Poor*, sociologist William Julius Wilson examines poverty among blacks. "The demand in the labor market has shifted toward higher educated workers in various industries and occupations. The changing occupational and industrial mix is associated with increases in the rates of joblessness (unemployment and "dropping out" of, or nonparticipation in, the labor force) and decreases in the relative wages of disadvantaged urban workers . . . joblessness and declining wages are also related to the recent growth in ghetto poverty. The most dramatic increases in ghetto poverty occurred between 1970 and 1980, and they were mostly confined to the large industrial metropolises of the Northeast and Midwest, regions that experienced massive industrial restructuring and loss of blue-collar jobs during that decade" (1996, 33–34). From her part, sociologist Clara Rodriguez has cited the narrowing of the manufacturing sector among the major factors causing a high incidence of poverty and unemployment in the Puerto Rican community during the 1950s and 1970s in New York City. The manufacturing sector had been the group's major source of employment since the time of its arrival (Rodriguez, 1979, 208).

Some have argued that the restructuring of the economy created other job markets that were in need of specifically immigrant labor. In her *Mobility of Labor and Capital* (1988), sociologist Saskia Sassen speaks about the shifting of the economy and the development of a simultaneous process that created an abundance of blue-collar and low-paying jobs. She alleges, on the one hand, that the restructuring led to the formation of global cities where an advanced service sector generated a variety of low-paying jobs that require little training and skills, such as night and weekend hotel managers, dog-walkers, and gourmet shop workers. It also led, she argues, to the development of a transformed industrial production that she calls a "downgraded manufacturing sector" (23) of sweatshops and low-paying, dead-end jobs.

Without a doubt jobs have been created in the United States through the shifting of the economy from a mostly industrial based to a more service sector oriented economy. However, the displaced blue-collar, unskilled jobs have not been replaced in a manner that satisfies the needs of the growing labor force that is seeking these jobs. Furthermore, the creation of blue-collar, unskilled jobs is unlikely to return to the level it previously had in the 1950s and the 1960s. The U.S. economy increasingly depends on school-related knowledge and technical training, and those workers who do not enhance their skills and acquire the appropriate knowledge required in today's labor markets are likely to become superfluous and jobless.

RESTRICTING THE ENTRANCE OF UNWANTED PEOPLE

In 1980 we witnessed a shift in the U.S. government's thinking about surplus population. The "benign neglect" approach ceased to exist as the dominant response to the entrance of unneeded immigrants. Legislative efforts began to be introduced that proposed a firm attitude toward unwanted job seekers coming in. As the decade progressed, various immigration laws were approved. It became increasingly clear that the State no longer wished to maintain a passive or even merely discursive attitude before the immigrant flows. With the Immigration Reform and Control Act (IRCA) of 1986, which specifically targeted and penalized employers who hired foreign-born workers who did not have proper work authorization, the State initiated a new modality for regulating and controlling the entrance of migrants. Firm, aggressive, and often punitive measures now became part of immigration legislation.

Benign indifference gave way to an aggressive offensive policy against immigrants coming from the Third World, particularly from Latin America and Asia. Legislation was supported by a mass of federal funds. Sophisticated devices such as infrared eyeglasses, contrived for use to inspect the border with Mexico, which had become an international bridge facilitating the influx of people from Latin America, the Caribbean, and Asia, increased. At the border, the Immigration and Naturalization Service (INS) employed electrified fences, tall cement walls, ferocious and well-trained dogs, aircrafts, watercrafts, special police troops, and other paraphernalia to contain the flow of undocumented immigrants. While until then the new policies had only targeted undocumented migrants, in the mid-1990s, the focus expanded to include documented ones as a pervasive anti-immigration climate took hold of the land.

Indeed, in the past 20 years we have witnessed an increase in the amount of resources allocated to control undocumented immigration. In general, the budget to control unregulated immigration has more than tripled from 1980 to 2004. The budget allocated for border enforcement alone multiplied itself by seven from 1980 to 1995. The attacks of September 11th, 2001 made matters worse and provided additional justification to the U.S. government to allocate even more resources to control unauthorized entrants.

Documented immigration did not escape from condemnation and people raised their voices against immigrants. Increasingly, policymakers became concerned about the need for an urgent action concerning the nation's surplus unskilled foreign workers. Propositions of curtailing immigration flourished among government representatives from the states of Florida, California, Texas, and Louisiana. In June 1992, Senator Robert C. Byrd shared this incident with his peers in the Senate: "I pick up the telephone and call the local garage. I can't understand the person on the other side of the line. I am not sure he can understand me. They're all over the place, and they can't speak English. Do we want more of this?" (Sontag, 1992, E5).

The answer to Senator Byrd's question came in the form of two new laws enacted in 2004: the Anti-Terrorist Act and the Welfare Reform Act. Both legislative acts have been perceived as anti-immigrant.[9] In the process, the anti-immigration climate at the governmental level has succeeded in winning over representative voices from civil society. A national survey on the issue of immigration conducted by Gallup in 1994 revealed that 65 percent of the American people wanted legal immigration curtailed. Two recent studies produced by the Center for Immigration Studies conclude that immigration to the United States needs to be curtailed, because its number has reached unprecedented records and because it nurtures the entrance of terrorists and people who profess different ideological beliefs from ours (Center for Immigration Studies, 2005).

Well-respected scholars, experts in immigration studies, writing from different academic fields have also taken a position on the issue of increasing immigration. George J. Borjas, the author of *Friends or Strangers?* (1990), stated that post 1965 immigrants joined the welfare system at a much faster pace and greater number than old immigrants and that their presence constituted a net loss in revenues to some states (Sontag, 1992, E5). Roger Waldinger, on the other hand, declared that indeed immigrants do take jobs away from African Americans and adds "the immigrant influx makes it unlikely that African Americans would reap-dividends even in a period of full employment" (Waldinger, 1996, Op-Ed).

Along the same line, on June 2nd, 2005, the Census Bureau reported on its Web site that immigrants were taking jobs usually held by youths in the United States: "Last year [2004] 36 percent of those ages 16 to 19 held some sort of job, be it a newspaper delivery route or a full-time position in lieu of high school or college. That is down from 45 percent in 2000 and is the lowest level since 1945."[10] The alarming news pointed out that employers rejected the young because they did not have what employers were looking for: skills, appearance, and attitudes. On the other hand, immigrants were older, were willing to take menial jobs, and were preferred by some employers.

The pervasive anti-immigration wave has reached a peak. Voices adversarial to the influx of Third World immigrants are being heard loud and clear in every corner of this country. Washington no longer desires to send an unclear message regarding immigration: unequipped immigrant job seekers are no longer welcome. Employers have not mounted any opposition. Unwanted job seekers, their children included, must be ready to deal with an inimical ambience.

Recently, the Pew Hispanic Center released a study on the issue of immigration to the United States during the past decade. Contrary to what many thought, the number of immigrants has not continually increased. In fact, it has declined. The study found that "From the early 1990s though the middle of the decade, slightly more than 1.1 migrants came to the United States every year on average. In the peak year of 1999 and 2000, the annual inflow was about 35 percent higher, toping 1.5 million. By 2002 and 2003, the number coming to the country was back around the 1.1 million mark. This basic pattern of increase, peak and decline is evident for the foreign-born from every region of the world and for both legal and unauthorized migrants" (Passel and Suro, 2005, i).

Clearly, the anti-immigrant sentiment is reflected in concrete actions: stricter immigration legislations, increased preventive measures at the border, and faster removals for immigrants who have violated the laws. The United States has made up its mind: immigrants, job-seekers, should stay put at home and resist the temptation to head to the United States. It happens, however, that in this case, neither the sending societies nor immigrants themselves may care about the concerns the United States has about immigration.

EXPORTING UNWANTED HANDS: AN EVIL GAME

Increasingly, capitalist societies have opted for, if not directly facilitated, the emigration of its people, rather than contend with an expanding surplus of laborers. The idea behind stimulating them to leave to other countries is that, presumably, they would have access to a better life. In other texts, I have argued that emigration from the Dominican Republic responded to a government initiative taken during Joaquín Balaguer's first presidency in 1966. The initiative was never promulgated or made into law; it was simply a de facto policy that encouraged people to leave home by facilitating their exodus. During Balaguer's first presidency, consular laws were "liberated," and all Dominicans who applied for passports received them. While the granting of passports can be taken innocently as a step toward the creation of a democratic society, a rapid review of Balaguer's successive governments will certainly leave no one with such a thought. The repressive and abusive governments of Balaguer granted Dominicans passports so they could think it was all right for them to leave and to try and find a better future somewhere else.[11] Needless to say that such a decision exonerated the Dominican government from satisfying the needs of those who day by day packed their belongings and left. Migration then represents more than the willingness or unwillingness of the receiving society to participate in the process. Migration is also the end-result of "behind the door" social policy on the part of sending societies' governments and the need to leave on the part of the migrants.

A TACIT RESOLUTION AGAINST UNWANTED IMMIGRANTS: DECLINING IMMIGRATION, INCREASING DEPORTATION

In a similar manner, through denying entrance by adopting laws that restrict immigration, and by enacting laws that produce increasing deportations, the United States has resolved itself to push out and keep out poor, unwanted Dominicans. Regarding deportation, for instance, in 1996, Congress enacted two laws—the Antiterrorism and Effective Death Penalty Act (AEDPA) and the Illegal Immigration Reform and Immigrant Responsibility Act (IIRIRA), which drastically increased the number of actions and behaviors considered criminal and unlawful for legal or authorized permanent residents. The 1996 laws facilitate and accelerate the process of deportations and make it the mandatory punishment for many more law-violators than ever before. Julissa Reynoso, a lawyer who is currently preparing an extensive study on deportations and human rights' violations states "Changes in criminal justice policies, Immigration and Naturalization Services enforcement policies, and the new mandatory detention system render the new laws far more unforgiving in practice than is apparent from their texts."[12] The new laws eliminated the process whereby an apprehended documented immigrant could demonstrate their ties to this country, their lack of knowledge of their native land, and their possibility for rehabilitation.

The passing of the USA Patriot Act on October 2001, just six weeks after the attack of September 11th, expanded the possibilities of deportation of immigrant people, whether U.S. naturalized or not. The new law deals specifically with people who have been caught on the act of terrorism or who have been accused of plotting to commit terrorist acts against this nation. But the new law also provides room for deporting those people who have been accused of having even some remote affiliation with organizations and people believed to be terrorists or supportive of terrorism. It is precisely this particular provision of the USA Patriot Act that makes many immigrant people and immigrant advocates nervous. The flexibility of the USA Patriot Act to persecute and process people in such a liberal manner provides opponents of immigrants with a mortal weapon that would probably produce numerous casualties and in the process, would liberate this society from unwanted people or surplus population.

A brief look at the number of those admitted into the United States recently from the Dominican Republic will cause one to believe that things have begun to change and that the aggression against certain classes of immigrants has lessened (see Figure 2.1).

Indeed, it appears that the pattern reflecting a downfall in immigration since 1995 began to reverse itself in 2002 when the United States admitted more Dominicans than it has previously admitted since 1996. In 2000, for instance,

Figure 2.1
Dominicans Admitted to the United States, 1965–2004

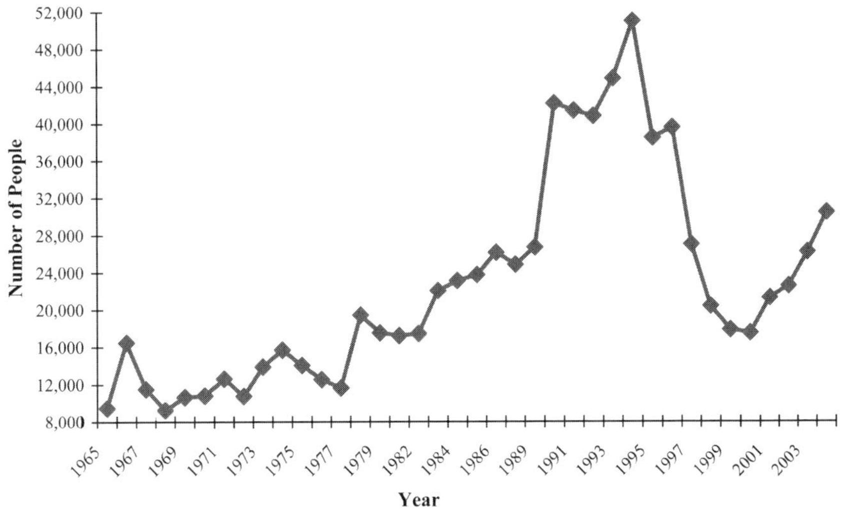

Information on Dominicans admitted to the United States is unavailable for the years 1981 and 1988. Therefore these years have been omitted.

the United States admitted 17,536 Dominicans. In 2001, the number of Dominicans admitted climbed to 21,213, and in 2004, to 30,492 (Office of Immigration Statistics, Department of Homeland Security). Yet, such a conclusion is far from the truth. These numbers reflect *total* number of admitted, and the number of admitted immigrants is made up by two categories: adjustments and new arrivals. "New arrivals" may obtain their permanent visas while waiting in the Dominican Republic; "adjustments," on the other hand, may obtain their permanent residence status while living in the United States. As indicated in Figure 2.2, the number and percentage of "new arrivals" has actually declined since 1996 while the number of adjustments has oscillated with ups and downs since 1996 but increased steadily during the last three years (2000, 2001, and 2002)[13] affecting the overall number of Dominicans who have been admitted with permanent status into the United States. Some may argue that the decline in the number admitted is due to heavy backlog on immigration paperwork now that severe scrutiny permeates the entire immigration process after the attacks of September 11th. In the case of the Dominican people, however, it is clear that the decline began much prior to the attacks and the increasing piling up of immigration paperwork waiting to be processed. I do agree with advocates of immigrant groups who fear that the attacks may in fact provide the United States a solid argument to reject certain immigrant groups.

Looking from 1994 to 2004, the number of Dominican immigrants admitted to the United States shows the following: (1) in 2004 the United States admitted only 40.5 percent of the number of Dominicans admitted in 1994;

Figure 2.2
Immigrants from the Dominican Republic Admitted for Legal Permanent Residence by Class of Admission, 1996–2002

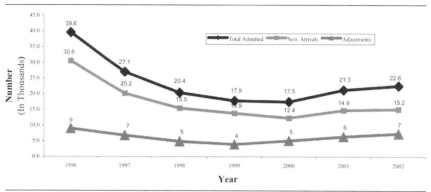

Figure 2.3
Deported to the Dominican Republic 1965–2003

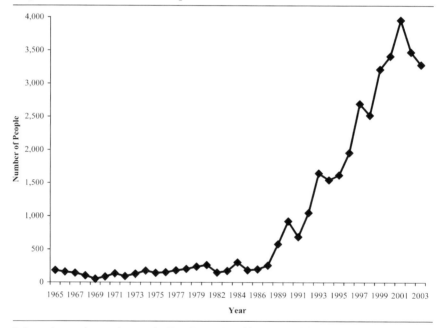

Information on deportations to the Dominican Republic is unavailable for the years 1981 and 1988. These years have been omitted.

(2) *every year,* going backward from 2004 to 1994, shows that the number of Dominicans admitted is well-below that of 1994, or the year when the largest number of Dominicans had been admitted dating as far back as 1966. Data on Dominicans deported t o the Dominican Republic, however, differ from data reflecting admissions to the United States.

On comparing data related to the same decade concerning Dominicans admitted versus Dominicans deported, one finds that the number of those deported to the Dominican Republic has doubled, increasing from 1,640 in 1993, to 3,349 in 2003, and to 3,506 in 2004 (see Figure 2.3).[14] An interesting point to make is that Dominicans deported to the Dominican Republic accounts for almost half of all those deported to the entire Caribbean region.

CONCLUSION

For many of us it is quite obvious that the United States has closed its doors on some immigrants. The doors are closed for those who have no jobs at home, are uneducated, and are unskilled. News reported in the Census Bureau home Web page detailed the following: from 2000 and 2004 the number of immigrants with high school diplomas and college degrees 25 years of age or older increased from 30.7 percent to 33.2 percent and from 32.5 percent to 34.3 percent respectively. In 2001, 2002, and 2003, the United States granted 195,000 visas each year to trained, college-educated workers who were sponsored by employers. In each year, the number of visas granted went up three times the number of visas usually granted on an annual basis for employment purposes. At the same time, older and disabled immigrants are having a harder time trying to secure U.S. citizenship: "The advocates say applications for citizenship are being delayed by procedural changes that include the ending of an outreach program, more backgrounds checks, and increasing rejection of medical certificates that allow some applicants to avoid interviews in English and the citizenship exam. The delay, they say, has put disabled and elderly refugee applicants at risk of losing some government benefits, because to be eligible, they must meet a deadline to become citizens."[15]

The United States is no longer the land of opportunity for those who do not possess the skills and educational background required by today's labor market. Many, in Congress and outside Congress, hold this view. The anti-immigrant sentiment is spreading fast and new laws are proposed to keep unwanted immigrants out or to make their lives more difficult if they are already here. In several states, including New York, immigrants are being told that they may not be able to get a driver's license if they are not properly documented. Advocates for immigrants feel that such a law will prevent immigrants from working and will seriously affect their likelihood of making a living for themselves and their families. Are immigrants hearing the voices that are opposed to their coming? Will they finally listen?

In spite of not being wanted, many of those unwelcome immigrants have already made up their minds. It is unlikely that, if conditions remain unchanged at home, they will simply stay put there. Many of these immigrants left home pressed by economic need, and they had no choice but to listen to their own instinct of survival rather than to stipulated legislation that go against them. With regards to unwanted immigrants that are already here, I suspect that they too will simply close their ears to hostile reasoning. Many have formed families and may not think to go back to where they came from. Nor will their children who were born here and who may only recognize this space as home.

Besides the will of the people, there are many of us who firmly believe that immigration to the United States is not a one-sided coin decided only by the U.S. government. It has never been. Societies that share socioeconomic systems also share the gains and the pains associated with such systems. Hence, on the other side of the coin one finds the direct doing of the sending society's government. As long as we hold down to the current state of affairs, immigration will not cease in the near future, and somehow this country will have to find ways to accommodate, whether willingly or not, those who are coming through the front or back door.

NOTES

1. There is not an official definition for "extreme poverty." In various reports the U.S. Census Bureau and the Children's Defense Fund define "severe poor" and "extreme poverty" as a family whose income falls 50 percent below the federal poverty line.

2. According to most economic indicators, the U.S. economy has been performing well since 2001.

3. See chapter 1 of *The Mobility of Workers under Advanced Capitalism: Dominican Migration to the United States* (2002) for a lengthy discussion on economy growth and emigration in the Dominican Republic.

4. Among important texts dealing with poverty in the United States are: *Progress and Poverty: An Inquiry into the Cause of Industrial Depressions and of Increase of Want with Increase of Wealth; A New Introduction to Poverty: The Role of Race, Power and Politics; No Escape: The Minimum Wage and Poverty;* and *Separate Societies: Poverty and Inequality in US Cities.*

5. The enumerated reasons can be read in the following texts: *Out of el Barrio; New People in Old Neighborhoods: The Role of New Immigrants in Rejuvenating New York's Neighborhoods; Between Two Islands; Birds of Passage;* and *In the Barrios: Latinos and the Underclass Debate.*

6. In this discussion, I will use the terms Hispanic and Latino simultaneously to refer to the same population, or people of Hispanic origins residing in the United States. I am mindful of the ongoing debate surrounding the two terms.

7. The Tomás Rivera Policy Institute and the National Council of La Raza are well known for conducting studies dealing with poverty among Chicanos and Mexican immigrants. In the 1970s and 1980s, Centro de Estudios Puertorriqueños at Hunter College, CUNY, produced important and pioneering research focusing on Puerto Rican poverty.

8. A marginalized worker is one that is slightly attached to the labor force. He/she is a worker *who has looked for work* within the year and wants to work but has not looked for work in the past four weeks prior to completing the census questionnaire. A discouraged worker on the other hand, has not looked for work the four weeks prior to completing the census questionnaire, because he/she believes *that there is no job available.* Neither group is counted among the unemployed.

9. In July 17, 1996, *The New York Times* reported that many immigrants who were living legally in the country had been placed in detention by the INS office and were facing deportation. Under the new Anti-Terrorism bill, any documented immigrant who has been convicted of a felony, including a misdemeanor, perhaps an arrest for smoking marihuana at a young age, is subject to detention and deportation. Similarly, the new Welfare reform imposed many restrictions on aid to legal immigrants who are not naturalized U.S. citizens.

10. This quote was taken from the article "Immigrants taking jobs usually held by US youths" from 06/02/2005, a weekly news brief of US Immigration News found on the website www. workpermit.com (http://www.workpermit.com/news/2005_06_02/us/immigrants_american_youths.htm).

11. Mexico presents a similar case. Besides the *Bracero Program*, which ended in 1965, and which clearly provided superfluous workers to the United States, various governments have attempted, unsuccessfully, to convince the United States to either provide legal documentation to undocumented Mexicans residing in the United States, to allow for a larger number of workers to cross over the border to the United States to work, though they would remain living in Mexico, and to treat humanly and with respect Mexican citizens who are caught trying to cross the border.

12. Unpublished manuscript. "Deportation and Human Rights Violations: The Case of the Dominican People." Julissa Reynoso, 2004.

13. The Department of Homeland Security, Office of Immigration Statistics, has not yet released data on "adjustments" and "new arrivals" for 2003 and 2004. At the time of this writing, October 20, 2005, only *some data* concerning Dominicans admitted to the United States in 2003 and 2004 had been released.

14. The data reported for 2003 and 2004 may change. While only 3,349 Dominicans have been actually deported (or removed, current new term) in 2003 at the time Homeland Security published its *Statistical Annual Report*, during the same 2003 a higher number of Dominicans (or 4,073) had been identified in the same annual report as "deportable aliens," or as aliens *in* and *admitted* to the United States who are subject to any grounds of removal (deportation) stipulated in the Immigration and Nationality Act.

15. The information given is based on two articles entitled "Elderly disabled may have trouble getting US citizenship" from 09/26/2005 and "US immigrants are now more highly educated" from 02/22/2005. Both articles can be found on the website www.workpermit.com under the heading US Immigration News (http://www.workpermit.com/news/2005_09_26/us/elderly_disabled.htm) and (http://www.workpermit.com/news/2005_02_22/ushigher_education_levels_for_us_immigration).

REFERENCES

Borjas, George J. 1990. *Friends or Strangers: The Impact of Immigrants on the U.S. Economy*. New York: Basic Books.

Center for Immigration Studies. August, 2005. "Immigration and Terrorism: Moving Beyond the 9/11. Staff Report on Terrorist Travel," by Janice L. Kephart and "Keeping Extremists Out: The History of Ideological Exclusion, and the Need for Its Revival," by James R. Edwards, Jr.

Center on Budget and Policy Priorities. 2004. "Census Data Show Poverty Increased, Income Stagnated, and the Number of Uninsured Rose to a Record Level in 2003."

George, Henry. 1879. *Progress and Poverty: An Inquiry into the Cause of Industrial Depressions and of Increase of Want with Increase of Wealth.* New York: Robert Schalkenbach Foundation.

Goldsmith, William W. and Edward J. Blakely. 1992. *Separate Societies: Poverty and Inequality in US Cities.* Philadelphia: Temple University Press.

Grasmuck, Sherri and Patricia R. Pessar. 1991. *Between Two Islands: Dominican International Migration.* Berkeley: University of California Press.

Griffith, Jeanne E., Mary J. Frase, and John H. Ralph. 1989. *American Education: The Challenge of Change.* Washington D.C.: Population on Reference Bureau.

Hernandez, Ramona. 2002. *The Mobility of Workers under Advanced Capitalism.* New York: Columbia University Press.

Jennings, James. 1999. "Persistent Poverty in the United States: Review of Theories and Explanations." In *A New Introduction to Poverty: The Role of Race, Power, and Politics,* eds. Louis Kushnick and James Jennings. New York: New York University Press.

Kushnick, Louis and James Jennings. 1999. *A New Introduction to Poverty: The Role of Race, Power, and Politics.* New York: New York University Press.

Lewis, Oscar. 1966. *La Vida: A Puerto Rican Family in the Culture of Poverty.* New York: Random House.

Marx, Karl and Friedrich Engels. 1991. *Communist Manifesto.* New York: WW Norton Publishing Co.

Moore, Joan W. and Raquel Pinderhughes. *In the Barrios: Latinos and the Underclass Debate.* New York: Russell Sage Foundation.

Murray, Charles. 1984. *Losing Ground: American Social Policy, 1950–1980.* New York: Basic Books.

Nelson, Joel L. 1995. *Post Industrial Capitalism: Exploring Economic Inequality in America.* Thousand Oaks: Sage Publications.

Passel, Jeffrey and Roberto Suro. 2005. "Rise, Peak, and Decline: Trends in US Immigration 1992–2004." Washington: The Pew Hispanic Center.

Piore, Michael J. 1979. *Birds of Passage: Migrant Labor and Industrial Societies.* Massachusetts: Cambridge University Press.

Rodriguez, Clara E. 1979. *Labor Migration under Capitalism: The Puerto Rican Experience.* New York: Monthly Press.

Ryan, William. 1976. *Blaming the Victim.* New York: Vintage Books.

Sassen, Saskia. 1988. *The Mobility of Labor and Capital: A Study in International Investment and Labor Flow.* Cambridge: Cambridge University Press.

Schapiro, Isaac. 1987. *No Escape: The Minimum Wage and Poverty.* Washington, D.C.: Center on Budget and Policy Priorities.

Sontag, Deborah. 1992. "Calls to Restrict Immigration Come from Many Quarters." *The New York Times* (December 13): E5.

U.S. Department of Commerce. *1980 U.S. Census of Population, 5% Public Use Micro Data Sample.* Bureau of the Census.

U.S. Department of Commerce. *1990 U.S. Census of Population, 5% Public Use Micro Data Sample.* Bureau of the Census.

U.S. Department of Commerce. *2000 U.S. Census of Population, 5% Public Use Micro Data Sample.* Bureau of the Census.

Waldinger, Roger. 1996. "The Jobs Immigrants Take" [editorial]. *The New York Times* (March 11).

Weber, Max. 1958. *The Protestant Ethic and the Spirit of Capitalism.* New York: Scribners.

Wilson, William Julius. 1996. *When Work Disappears: The World of the New Urban Poor.* New York: Vintage Books.

Winnick, Louis. 1990. *New People in Old Neighborhoods: The Role of New Immigrants in Rejuvenating New York's Communities.* New York: Russell Sage Foundation.

CHAPTER 3

The "Sí Se Puede" Newcomers: Mexicans in New England

Martha Montero-Sieburth

INTRODUCTION

Although Mexicans[1] constitute the largest group of Latinos in the United States, accounting for almost 60 percent of the total Latino population (Census 2000),[2] they are the newest and smallest group[3] among the Latino populations of New England (Crowley, 2001). Mexicans account for 60,173 of the total numbers of Puerto Ricans,[4] Dominicans, Colombians, Central and South Americans within New England (875,225). Connecticut has 23,484 Mexicans, Massachusetts has 22,288,[5] Rhode Island has 5,881, New Hampshire has 4,590, Maine has 2,756,[6] and Vermont has 1,174.

Notwithstanding their small numbers, Mexicans in New England depict part of the national trend of Mexican concentration in immigration, the changing composition of Mexican immigrants, changes in the receiving and sending states, and the settlement and duration patterns of Mexicans in the United States. According to Stephen Camarota's report (2001) of the Center for Immigration Studies' using 2000 census data,[7] Mexico and Spanish-speaking Latin America dominate U.S. immigration. Of the 35.7 million foreign-born in the United States, based on estimates of the March 2004 Current Population Survey (CPS) and Census 2000 American Community Survey, 21.7 million or 61 percent are legal permanent residents, 1.2 million or 3 percent are temporary legal residents, 2.5 million or 7 percent are refugee arrivals post-1980, and 10.3 million or 29 percent are undocumented migrants. Of these foreign-born, 5.9 million or 57 percent are from Mexico, 2.5 million or 25 percent are from Latin American, 1 million or 9 percent are from Asia, 0.6 million or 6 percent are from Europe and Canada, and 0.4 million or 4 percent are from Africa, according to the Pew Hispanic Center. Of the undocumented, the larger numbers are 4.5 million or 43 percent men, ages 18–39; 3 million or 29 percent women, ages 18–39; 1.7 million or 17 percent children under 18; and 1.1 million or 11 percent ages 40 and over (Passel, 2005).[8]

Latin Americans are estimated to be the larger numbers of unauthorized migrant population, but of these Mexicans constitute the largest immigrant group in the United States (Grieco, 2003). Furthermore, the National Population Council of Mexico in 2002, reported that in addition to the 10 million Mexican nationals in the United States, there were also 8 million Mexicans born in the United States of Mexican parentage for the first generation, and close to another 8 million of Mexican origin for the second generation, represented by Chicanos, Mexican Americans, or Mexicanos (López Vega, 2003). Moreover, the National Population Council of Mexico points out that only 1 in 5, or 21 percent of immigrants of Mexican origin has U.S. citizenship, 7 out of 10 Mexicans in the United States live in a house, 53 percent of these immigrants do not have health coverage, and close to 53 percent of the Mexicans earn less than $20,000 a year (CONAPO, 2004).[9]

The composition of Mexican emigrants has also changed during the past 10 years in that they are younger, between the ages of 12 and 34, with an average educational level of 6.2 years of schooling, still dominated by males (95 of each 100),[10] are from urban rather than rural areas, and in some case, indigenous villages. Unlike their predecessors, Mexicans are now remaining in the United States, and many have made inroads toward becoming naturalized. Such changes and human exodus has affected not only the economic stability of Mexico, but also the sustainability of Mexico, which according to the Mexican central bank received $16.6 billion between 2000 and 2004, and this could easily rise to $20 billion in 2005. Such remittances are believed to affect close to 1 million families according to the National Population Council of Mexico (http://www.conapo.gob.mx/prensa).

The traditional sending states of Jalisco, Zacatecas, Guanajuato, and Michoacán, with well over 100 years of migration, were joined during the 1920s by Durango, and Nayarit,[11] and since the 1980s by the states of Aguascalientes, Colima, Morelos, San Luis Potosí,[12] Puebla, Hidalgo, Oaxaca, Guerrero. During the 1990s to the present, Tamaulipas, Chiapas, Veracruz, Chihuahua, Sinaloa, Durango, the state of Mexico and the Federal District have also become sending states (Balboa, 2004; http://www.inegi.gob.mx/est/contenidos).[13] The settlement pattern of Mexicans in the Southwest and Midwest, concentrating in California, New Mexico, Arizona, Texas, and Illinois, has been offset by the exponential growth of Mexicans in Georgia, Tennessee, Louisiana, North Carolina, Minnesota, and Wisconsin (Passel, 2005). Just in Georgia, the Mexican population grew from 20,000 in 1990 to 191,000 in 2000 (Grieco, 2003). As Leopoldo Romero, owner of the Casa Romero restaurant in Boston, Massachusetts states "There are Mexicans all over. I actually see less Mexicans in Guadalajara, Jalisco than in Boston" (personal interview, April 2004).

Between 1990 and 2000, New England has dramatically been affected by these changes. Miren Uriarte and Charles Jones' (2002, 21) report that the white population of New England experienced a decline in outflow not only as a proportion of the total population, but in actual numbers: "There were 37,676 fewer white persons in Rhode Island today than there were in 1990 . . . fueled by losses of 4.2 percent of the white population of each Connecticut and Rhode Island and 1.6 percent of that of Massachusetts."[14] At the same time, there was an increase in the diversity of populations. The numbers of Latinos in Rhode Island alone quadrupled during the past decade, a fact that has made the Latinos in the Ocean state outstrip those in the New England region at a rate of 98.5 percent compared to 54 percent for New England and 57.9 percent for the United States (Uriarte and Jones, 2002).

New Hampshire is reported to have grown in 2000, from 11.4 percent to 1,235,786, in its general population, the largest increase of all East Coast states north of Delaware and centered around Concord, Manchester, and Nashua (Bayles, 2001). Yoel Camayd-Freixas, Gerald Karush, and Nelly Letjer (2006) point out that there were 20,489 or 1.7 percent Latinos at the start of this decade, and New Hampshire had a 95 percent non-Latino white population. Yet by 2000, the number of Latinos, mostly immigrants accounted for 9 percent growth, and in the last decade they grew by 82 percent. They estimate that the Latino population quadrupled, arriving from neighboring Massachusetts and elsewhere, yet they believe that such a trend appears to be in favor of native-born Latinos.[15] Vermont also showed unexpected gains during 1990–2000 in their Latino population.

Today, Massachusetts has the largest concentration of Latinos, and Connecticut and Rhode Island, the denser presence of Latinos. Massachusetts and Connecticut are the most chosen states by Mexicans,[16] only trailed by Rhode Island and Southern New Hampshire. Carlos Rico, the former Consul General of Mexico in Boston, asserts that "Only in New Hampshire are Mexicans a significant component of both the Mexican origin population in New England (12.51%) and of that state's Hispanic community (22.4%)" (2001, 2). In fact, Camayd-Freixas, Karush, and Letjer (2006, 9) note that "41% are from South American and 28% are from Central America. Most Central Americans are from Mexico (65%). This suggests new in-flow links between New Hampshire and the Western US and Mexico."[17] Maine and Vermont, the states with the least numbers of Mexicans, are relative exceptions, because Mexicans account for a larger proportion of their Latino population: 29.4 percent and 21.3 percent, respectively (Rico, 2001). Some cities in Connecticut, Massachusetts, Rhode Island, and New Hampshire during 1990 to 2000 also experienced over 50 percent growth in the Mexican population, while cities in Vermont and Maine[18] had sparse numbers of Mexicans.[19]

With the growth of Mexican nationals in New England, their history, settlement patterns, adaptation, and current needs have become more evident. Mexican authorities and community members (personal communication, September 2004), report that Mexicans in New England are from more diverse states of Mexico, have varied educational experiences ranging from little or no schooling to post-doctoral studies, and have a wide range of socioeconomic backgrounds. They range from privileged students at academic institutions, to professionals, entrepreneurs, businessmen, contractors, house cleaners, day laborers, and prisoners.[20] Among some of the Mexicans in New England there has been a Nobel Prize winner,[21] several prosperous restaurant owners,[22] a number of established professionals,[23] large numbers of students,[24] businessmen, entrepreneurs, mechanics, housecleaners, musicians, artists, fruit and vegetable pickers, and an array of service and factory-oriented workers in the restaurant, landscape, and construction industries.

PURPOSE

Given the uniqueness of the "si se puede" newcomers in New England, the purpose of this exploratory study is fourfold: (1) to present the "pulse" of what is happening to the Mexicans in New England as a preliminary study for future research to be undertaken with the Mexican communities of New England; (2) to identify, and describe the Mexican[25] experience as it has historically evolved in New England over several decades and to identify the current needs of this community; (3) to describe how diverse Mexican communities are being organized through the leadership of directors, presidents, and community members of the Mexican communities in New England; and (4) to identify the conception of leadership currently employed by the Mexican community at large, the types of leaders in charge of Mexican organizations, and the issues that are salient in these communities.

METHODOLOGY

To gain access to the Mexican experience in New England, the design of the research[26] was primarily qualitative with a focus on the in-depth interviews of the perspectives of Mexican leaders of established Mexican organizations as a major data source complemented with (1) *documentation data* from the census, reports and studies from diverse research centers and institutes;[27] (2) *community data and historical records* gathered through interviews with community members, meetings, telephone conversations with the Mexican Consulate personnel in New York and Boston and Latino community members in the New England states; (3) *local lore data* collected by the researcher over a 25-year period;[28] and (4) *contextual descriptions* from the Internet and media information, including newspapers and newsletters.

The interviews served as a proxy approximation to the data of the communities these leaders served. These Mexican leaders[29] were identified by list through the Mexican Consulates in Boston and New York. While leaders of Mexican organizations in Massachusetts, Rhode Island, Maine, and New Hampshire were interviewed each for three hours, Mexican leaders consisting of individuals who headed an organization or had participated as Mexicans in umbrella Latino organizations in Vermont and Connecticut were accessed through telephone interviews of one hour duration.

Understandably the data gathered in this study would not be comprehensive nor representative of the Mexican community at large, because this would require a massive longitudinal research undertaking in New England. However, insights about the concerns identified by these leaders of their communities, the types of organizing and leadership that they are forming or have formed, and the needs they hear from their constituents could be captured as part of a first cut analysis.

The corpus of data was analyzed using cross comparison methods and triangulation of data sources, eliciting concept formation and thematic integration of the transcribed interview notes. All of the documentation and historical data underwent content analysis, and the results were refined through the cross indexing of interview data. The findings focus on the profiles of Mexican leaders, their educational status, and leadership concepts and the types of organizations managed, including the needs, activities, membership, and socioeconomic standing of members. In addition, the types of relationships that the Consulates of Mexico have with the Mexican organizations and communities was identified as well as the role that these leaders of Mexican organizations and communities expect from the Mexican and U.S. governments.

Because the data gathered was extensive and the findings presented require closer examination, several publications on aspects of the Mexicans in New England have been prepared, which range from the historical settlement of Mexicans throughout New England, to the organizations developed, the types of leadership they have defined, and the political consciousness being formed. This chapter reports on the Mexican Diaspora in New England through a historical overview and presents the synthesis of the Mexican leaders' interviews identifying the reported needs of the Mexican communities. Not addressed herein are the range of leadership issues and the role of the Mexican organizations in terms of their contributions to leadership development and transnational politics, which are discussed elsewhere.

HISTORICAL ACCOUNT AND SETTLEMENT PATTERNS OF MEXICANS IN NEW ENGLAND

The establishment of Mexicans, like many other Latino groups in New England, is created by strong economic pushes and pulls, family interests, and emergent and developing social networks.[30] It is a history of nationals, migrants, and immigrants appearing at different time periods, seeking jobs or education, and attempting to create a niche in New England. These communities appear to grow in spurts, "gota por gota," or "drop by drop."

The Classification of Mexicans

There are a number of classifications of Mexicans in the United States. *Mexican nationals* refers to those who are in the United States of Mexican nationality with U.S. visas. These include students at diverse universities, many who have scholarships from the Mexican government and are transient in nature and visitors such as tourists who are in the United States for limited periods to visit families or general visa holders. While students plan to return to Mexico, some obtain work permits as professionals in the public and private sector once they graduate, or receive H-1B visa program authorizations, or solicit their alien registration card once after completing the required five-year stay. *Mexican nationals with U.S. permanent residence* are those who have lived in the United States for more than the five-year limit. They have rights to study and work, but not to vote. Permanent residents may remain in that status for quite some time, and it is known that many Mexicans continue to have such a status, even through they are eligible to obtain U.S. citizenship. *Mexican dual nationals* consist of many who gave up their Mexican citizenship to become American citizens. However with the change in the laws of Mexico in 1993, granting such U.S. citizens the right to regain their Mexican citizenship, many have opted to do so. While the Mexican government closed out such an option after March 2003, it has reopened it again without limitation of time because of the high demand for requests for Mexican citizenship in the consular offices. For these dual nationals, travel with a U.S. and or Mexican passport provides them with greater flexibility, yet for some U.S. politicians, this practice is being viewed as unfavorable and even "un-American." *Undocumented Mexicans* are those who are unauthorized to work in the United States, but often have access to purchasing, under the table, a social security card. These Mexicans become a large part of the labor force, pay taxes, and make up much of the informal infrastructure in childcare, elder care, house and office cleaning services, restaurants, and residential care facilities, where their legal status and even English speaking ability is often not questioned. *Indigenous Migratory Mexicans* represent 30 percent of the 70 percent or 346 municipalities where Indian languages are spoken and have high northward migration to seek agricultural jobs and better life conditions, according to a recent study by CONAPO (The National Council of Population). *Migratory Mexicans* are brought to work in the food industries and are managed by diverse employees, or are seasonal cranberry, potato, broccoli, onion, or other produce workers who return to the southern United States or Mexico based on bilateral agreements between the United States and Mexico. Migratory Mexicans use H2-B visas.[31] *Mexican Americans* are U.S. citizens, with Mexican cultural roots through ancestry to Mexico or Spain, as in the case of New Mexico. They may have limited, some use, or no use of Spanish, yet adhere to Mexican cultural repertoires, identify with Mexicans, and seek their association in order to retain such connections. *Mexicans married to U.S. citizens* retain strong connections to Mexico, but at the same time, share in American culture and expose their families to bicultural, cultural and social activities. These U.S. husbands and wives, regarded as "friends" of Mexico, are integrated into the mosaic of Mexicans in New England.

Prior to the 1980s, the influx of Mexicans in New England was generally of three types: (1) students who were endowed with grants and fellowships provided by the Mexican government or industries and banks could afford to study in New England; (2) professionals—who established businesses, mostly in the service and food industry, medical professions, and social service areas; and (3) migratory workers who flowed in and out of New England.

Mexican intellectuals attended prestigious universities based on the types of personal and family support they had to study abroad and based on the expectation that upon completion of their degree they would return to Mexico follow their careers.[32] Because few except the wealthy could afford to study abroad on their own, the Mexican government in the early 1980s began to expand the funding of fellowships through the National Council of Science and Technology (CONACYT). Today, grants from CONACYT are highly valued, and Mexican students are expected to return to Mexico once they have completed their studies for at least a two-year period. However, many Mexican professionals under the H-I B visa in a specific field or the extended visa program, often stay behind, becoming part of Mexico's brain drain.[33]

Boston, along with many New England cities (Providence, New Haven, Hartford, and Bridgeport, among others) with their numerous colleges and universities are attractive magnets for Mexican students. Not only can these institutions offer fields of study not readily available in Mexico, but they are able to prepare leaders with innovative and advanced thinking into the new century. Boston University, Harvard University, Babcock College in Massachusetts, Brown University in Rhode Island, University of Vermont, and University of Maine, among many other institutions, attract many Mexican students in business, English, management, international relations, urban planning, and other areas. . The formal endorsement and admission of Mexican students to such international and English-speaking programs, provides not only prominence to these institutions, but also generates income, which constitutes a large part of their endowments. Mexicans within these institutions have created their own student organizations and have made outreach programs for the Mexicans in the communities in which these institutions are found. Some of the organizations that exist in Boston are HUMA (Harvard University Mexican Association), with chapters in Mexico City, and fellowship opportunities; the Berklee School of Music Mexican Association; the MIT Mexican Association; Boston University's Mexican Association; Brown University Mexican Association; and fledging associations at Endicott College and Wellesley College. Mexico's public sector has also profited from sending bankers and policymakers to study for short-term or more extended periods, which they capitalize on upon their return.[34] Thus, academia has been and continues to be an enormous draw for Mexicans into New England.

There are also the professional Mexicans who have settled, established their careers, and developed businesses in the New England area. Among these are doctors, dentists, architects, professors, businessmen, and entrepreneurs in the private and public sector. Because many of the Mexicans in the New England area, especially in professional roles, tend to be from Mexico City (*chilangos,* or Mexico City dwellers),[35]differences between regions and cities, from the capital and the provinces of Mexico can subtlety be distinguished. The regionalism as well as localism of Mexico is evident in the strong transnational ties that Mexicans maintain with their towns and cities of origin (Rumbaut, 1995). Whole towns have become transplanted from Mexico into New England cities and towns. For example, Mexican residents in New Haven, Connecticut are primarily from Tlaxcala and Puebla (personal communication of community organizer, October 2004). Mexican residents of Nashua-Manchester, New Hampshire are from Sombrerete, Zacatecas; East Boston[36] harbors people from El Refugio, Jalisco,[37] and Central Falls-Pawtucket is home to people from Alfajayucan, Hidalgo (Rico, 2001).

Finally there are the working-class Mexicans, in the cleaning services of hospitals, offices, and homes; in elder and child care in many of the urban cities; and in the food and restaurant industry (personal communication, October 2004). In addition, there are migrant workers, who harvest the sea cucumber, broccoli, and blueberries and work in the timber industry in Maine, the diary farms in Vermont, construction companies of New Hampshire, and bog cranberries in Rhode Island and Connecticut.[38] In Maine, the migrant workers have sought to find leaders such as Benjamim Guiliani, who through his office directed at enforcing the rights of workers, advocates for their protection. In Boston, UNICCO, a cleaning service organization, has organized its workers. Thus many of the service-oriented organizations hire many Mexicans, who average two or three different jobs each week, working for as many as 80 to 100 hours for entry-level wages.

Immigration Patterns

Driven by economic needs and the existence of established social networks, Mexicans tend to emigrate[39] to New England through four routes: (1) *primary migration*, for those studying in New England or working short term in specific New England states; (2) *secondary migration*, for those arriving after having worked in California, Arizona, New Mexico, and Illinois, and seeking new fortunes; (3) *circulatory migration*, for those returning to New England after having been in Mexico; or (4) *expired visas*, by which a number of Mexicans, who for fear of not being allowed back into the United States because their visas have run out, procure social security cards that allow them to work incognito, while they hope to obtain amnesty and await changes in the federal legislation.

According to Enrico Marcelli (2002), close to 60 percent of undocumented immigrants cross the border legally, but when their visas expire, they become illegal, as visa overstayers. They are characterized as permanent residents, and those who for a variety of reasons, are nonpermanent. Those who gain legal permanence do so through family sponsorship and not through employment. Among the nonpermanent residents are visa overstayers, who remain in the United States knowing that they cannot return to Mexico, because they cannot re-enter the United States for 10 years. Once settled, many seek permanent residence with the help of immigrant lawyers. Others are migratory workers who rotate between Mexico and the United States and return to New England to work. Thus permanent and nonpermanent residents, some rotating between jobs, and others staying on and becoming residents, characterize the residence fluidity and mobility of Mexicans in New England.

Of these Mexicans, Marcelli (2002) points out that about 70–80 percent tend to work in lower skill occupations with the remaining 20–30 percent in professional, administrative, and higher skill jobs. Thus there are (1) the well-established Mexican professionals who make up part of the brain drain of some of the technology companies and settle in the region; (2) the entrepreneurs who have established businesses, including restaurants, specialty food shops, and construction companies; (3) the Mexican graduate students who attend a variety of public and private schools and universities, which include music schools, graduate and post-graduate programs, and technical schools;[40] (4) the seasonal migrant worker who rotates between jobs under temporary visas and bilateral contractual arrangements and who is willing to weather the New England winters; and (5) the undocumented worker or *mojados*, who is not represented by the census numbers, but finds their way into the New England area to relatives or *paisanos* (hometown or country person), and are nonetheless visible among the numbers of professional and student populations.

Compared to Puerto Ricans and Dominicans, who constitute the largest of the Latino groups, followed by Colombians and Central Americans in New England, Mexicans are relatively new. Mexicans were reported in Rhode Island during the 1920s, based on a 1938 *Providence Journal Bulletin*, documented by Martha Martinez.[41] They were starting to grow in Massachusetts, during the 1940s–1960s, according to Leopoldo Romero, who was one of the first Mexicans in Boston.[42] In New Hampshire, Margarita Fernández-Letkowski, current president of the Asociación Mexicana de New Hampshire or the Granite State Mexican Organization in New Hampshire, states that Mexicans became a clustered group around Nashua and Manchester in the manufacturing and industrial sector during the latter part of the 1970s and into the 1980s. Today they are a sizable Mexican community.[43]

In Maine, the need for agricultural laborers gave rise to Mexican migrant workers, in different areas: Presque Isle, recruited to harvest broccoli and sea cucumber; Portland area, for agricultural work; and Paris, Maine, for chicken farm work (personal communication, Boston Consular Personnel, November 2004). Many participate in Maine Migrant Workers' Advocacy Group to consolidate their rights and are guided by Benjamin Guiliani who is the director of this organization. In those cases where Mexicans cannot find an advocate, they form part of the Latino umbrella organizations in different towns. Thus Mexicans tend to seek other Mexicans, particularly when in need, but they also seek each other out for advice, support, and social gatherings.

In Vermont, Mexicans and Mexican Americans who attend the University of Vermont, as well as interested individuals, decided to create an umbrella organization, Latinos Unidos, which has undergone several changes during the past 15 years. The organization has provided a meeting ground for the rising numbers of Mexicans and has been pivotal in identifying support mechanisms such as immigration lawyers and business contacts for Mexicans seeking help. Many working-class Mexicans who live in Vermont are employed in the dairy industry. In Connecticut, Mexicans began to appear during the 1940s and 1960s, attracted by family ties and work in the factories and mills at the height of these industries. Today, Fairfield County, including Bridgeport and Stratford, has mushrooming numbers of Mexican newcomers attracted by social- and service-oriented work and who are in need of social and public services (personal communication, October 2004).[44]

Emigration to Rhode Island concurs with the need for laborers. Complete villages have literally moved into the state since the 1980s. Following in the footsteps of the first Mexican organization (Organización Mexicana de Nueva Inglaterra [OMNI], the Mexican Organization of New England) founded in Boston in 1992 by a group of interested Mexican professionals, La Asociación Social, Cultural y Deportiva Mexicana de Rhode Island, the Social, Cultural and Mexican Sports, Association of Providence, Rhode Island followed in its stead and began to provide informational support and services to Mexican newcomers. Much of the needs of Mexicans had been detected through the churches to which they belong, and in this respect, the organizing for help and for the celebration of religious festivities no doubt has contributed to seasoning Mexicans in their leadership.

The Organización Libre Mexicana de Rhode Island, or the Free Mexican Organization of Rhode Island, established in Pawtucket, is a community-focused organization that organizes special civic, cultural, and social events and conducts money collections for Mexicans in need. Arising as a separate entity to the Providence-based organization, the Organización Libre Mexicana focused on concrete issues, such as celebrating Mother's Day, a St. Valentine's youth pageant, raising funds to help their communities back home through remittances that help build schools and repair buildings, and helping members in personal crisis matters.

During 1985 to 1990, the presence of Mexicans became accentuated, when according to Marcelli (2002), nearly half of the Mexican population arrived in Massachusetts. Since then, the number of emergent Mexican civic, social, and sports organizations provide a sense of the growing and stable presence of Mexicans in Connecticut, New Hampshire, and Rhode Island, and to a lesser degree, Vermont and Maine. As a consequence, Fronteras Unidas, or United Frontiers, has arisen as one of the latest organizations catering to community interests and personal needs of Mexicans and other Latinos in East Boston. The organization was set up in 2003 to help immigrants meet and know each other and to also help them access needed resources and information.

While there are few records of the arrival of Mexicans in New England, what is known tends to be either a newspaper item documented by someone or tends to be anecdotal, and has been passed to later generations. However among the earlier accounts collected by this author of Mexicans who arrived in New England during the 1960s is the story of a known restaurant entrepreneur,

Leopoldo Romero, who established one of the first and best known Mexican restaurants in Boston, Massachusetts. This highly educated Mexican with advanced degrees and with great knowledge of Mexican cuisine, decided to introduce the flavors of authentic Mexican food paralleling the French cuisine that Julia Child had created in Boston. The end result has been an enterprising 40-plus-year-old business, going strong, and influencing the Boston scene with Mexican flavors.

According to Mr. Romero, during the 1960s, the only Latinos were Puerto Ricans and Cubans, who were followed by the Colombians, Chileans, Brazilians, and Mexicans. Their presence began to be felt during the middle 1980s and in the 1990s through the types of organizations that flourished. The Mexicans arriving in New England were students and professors who frequented his restaurant and workers in the industries.

The shifts in the 1964 immigration laws made family reunification possible until the 1989s, and propelled immigration to continue to grow throughout New England. By then, the small but growing Mexican community had expanded, and wholesale groups, such as Goya, created markets in communities interested in Mexican products. Also, construction companies that hired Mexicans, along with other Latinos, had gained a foothold in the industry, and the demand for maintenance work opened jobs for many Latinos, which included many Mexicans.

Mexicans in Rhode Island, according to Martha Martínez (2002), reappeared after the 1980s and 1990s mostly in agricultural work in West Warwick and Coventry. By the mid-1990s, after the North American Free Trade Agreement (NAFTA), Mexicans began to arrive for diverse work opportunities but primarily the jewelry industry. They met hardships, including language barriers, but were able to progress and develop their own businesses in the upper Federal Hill and Olneyville sections of Providence. Today, a mix of agricultural, business, and service-oriented jobs attracts Mexicans to Rhode Island. Its proximity to Boston, the Mexican Consulate, and the Mexican organizations there fuels their continued growth.

Settlement Patterns in New England

While Boston is one of the main entering ports, cities such as Providence, and even as far as New York City, are extensions of a corridor that leads Mexicans to Chelsea, Fitchburg, Framingham, Woburn, and East Boston in Massachusetts; Pawtucket, Central Falls, and the former Italian sections of Providence, Rhode Island; Nashua-Manchester, New Hampshire; Portland and Lewiston, Maine; and Bridgeport, Hartford, New Haven, and outlying areas of Connecticut. Spillovers of Mexicans from New York, Connecticut, and New Jersey have worked their way into not only the urban centers, but rural areas as well.[45] Communities that were once Italian, such as East Boston, Massachusetts, or of mixed ethnicities such as Chelsea, Massachusetts with its Jewish, Franco-American, Italian, and Anglo populations, are now being settled by Mexicans arriving directly from Mexico or via Los Angeles, Chicago, or New York City. Yet unlike the Barrio of New York City, which has a rich Puerto Rican concentration and now Mexican Poblanos (Creuheras, 2001; Moreno Gonzales, 2003),[46] Mexicans are dispersed throughout New England with their major concentration being in major cities or towns and spurious existence in rural areas.

Socioeconomic Push and Pull

Mexicans arriving in the New England area seek not only the opportunities to study, or become professionals, but also to fill the niches of available jobs. For many Mexicans, the need to find people willing to work opens doors for employment, particularly in the restaurant businesses, construction, and social services. Because many Mexicans are willing to *echarle ganas* (give it their all), they readily become employed in a market where hard-working, loyal, and committed laborers are highly valued.[47]

The establishment of Mexican restaurants throughout New England served to promote employment and a base for many Mexicans engendering the production of tortillas. As restaurants opened, owners sought to find the ingredients for Mexican food, such as tortillas, beans, chocolate, and other food products, which in turn created the networks for the procurement of Mexican food products and the wholesale of these products. Their availability also created a demand for the newly acquired taste of tortillas, "harina de maíz, chiles, quesos" corn flour, chili peppers, and cheese, so much so that conventional food suppliers have now introduced Mexican food products alongside their traditional fare and now are part of the take-out food industry.[48]

As the restaurant businesses grew, family members through word of mouth joined the ranks of waiters, dishwashers, and cooks, and families settled in New England. Not only did the employers' help families emigrate, but the employees learned the restaurant trade, and several have started their own Mexican restaurants. Augmenting such restaurants has been the development of tortilla factories. Mr. Romero says, "When a tortilla factory is established, it is because the demand is there." Hence the establishment of Maria and Ricardo's Tortilla Factory in the late 1980s, first in Jamaica Plain and later in 2000 in Quincy, and Cinco de Mayo Tortilla Factory in Chelsea during the 1990s reflects this upward trend. Currently, there are well over 50 Mexican restaurants in the Commonwealth of Massachusetts, and the contiguous states also report having at least 15 to 20 Mexican restaurants in urban areas and fewer in rural areas (personal communication, October 2004). Such numbers attest to the inroads made by these early Mexican businessmen in the current markets. Along with the growth of Mexican restaurants has been the growth of the Mariachis musical businesses, initiated first by Jose Gutierrez, who owns the Mariachi Mexamerica in Boston, followed with the Mariachi Chapala of Jose Luis Sicairos, the Mariachi Son de América of Veronica Robles and Willy Lopez, to other groups such as Cuerdas de Oro owned by Javier and Lucy Iraheta, and Mariachi Real de Jalisco of Carlos Alfredo. These troubadours play at all of the social and civic and cultural events of the diverse Mexican communities and represent an essential part of Mexican culture.[49]

Other businesses followed suit to the start up of restaurants. Jobs were generated and opportunities for work in construction, housecleaning, landscaping, child care and elder care[50] afforded entry into the job markets for Mexicans. Needing inexpensive laborers, the construction companies kept up with the demands by rotating their workforce, giving rise to greater job opportunities, networks, and partnerships for Mexicans, between and across ethnic lines.[51] The demand for construction laborers willing to take the jobs on the spot, created tiers of apprentices working with licensed electricians and plumbers, who learned the trade, pooled their monies together, began to send remittances back home, and set into motion the constant ebb and flow of disposable workers (de la Garza, Orozco, Baraona, 1997, 1998; Orozco, 2003).

The building boom in New England during the 1980s, the expansion of the technology highway, and health care mergers of hospitals and health care centers through the 1990s also created the need for management and cleaning services—care that many Mexicans began to fill and that provided significant entry and advancement opportunities. For these Mexicans, not speaking English did not detract from their work. Thus, Boston's Big Dig during the 1990s to the present, the shift in agricultural production to nontraditional products such as broccoli in Maine, and the service sector employment opportunities created jobs that Mexicans needed. Not only did Mexicans from the West and Midwest begin to arrive in New England, but also from nontraditional states such as Chiapas and the Mixteca, which includes Puebla,[52] Oaxaca, and Guerrero. During 1990–1999, 30 percent of the new immigrants into the United States at the national level arrived from Mexico. Over the same time period Mexicans began to trickle at the rate of 1 percent to states such as Massachusetts (Corchado and Solis, 1999).[53]

Finally the service areas in house cleaning, office building cleaning, and child and elder care expanded considerably. Through informal infrastructures and word of mouth, many Mexicans, and especially those who did not speak English, could readily gain employment. Once such jobs were secured, these were maintained, because Mexicans filled a niche. When the employer depended on the worker who filled the function of the organization or company, networks of support between the entrepreneur and worker were created that eventually lead to the support for their families, many of whom stayed in Mexico, to join the worker under family reunification.[54]

Through the cycle of job demand, procurement, and fulfillment, the circular nature of the *remesas* or remittances, which are particularly notable in the case of Mexicans, was created. The remittances[55] of monies, calculated to be about $10 billion a year, allowed many Mexican newcomers the opportunity to bring their families from Mexico to New England, helped their remaining family in Mexico to subsist, and helped their communities to thrive and be rebuilt (Bendixen and Associates, 2003). Over one million families in Mexico receive remittances from the United States (Lazos, July 2004).

Remittances are perhaps the most significant factor affecting Mexican immigrants today, garnering them a foothold in the United States and in Mexico's economic development. Even the immigrants earning less than $20,000 a year, are able to send between $200 and $250 on average to their families in Mexico (Otero, 2004). During 2003, the central bank of Mexico pointed out that the money sent home by Mexican migrants topped foreign investment and tourism at $6.3 billion (Lazos, July 2004; Stevenson, 2003).

The General Mexican Consulates in Boston and New York have also contributed over the past two decades in identifying the needs of the Mexican community, developing support mechanisms, such as the *consulados móviles* (mobile consulates offering services for registration and legal documents to the Mexican communities), and doing community outreach. Prior to the 1990s, Mexicans in the New England area were represented through honorary consuls who had administrative roles. As the numbers grew, a formalization of roles has taken place with greater emphasis being placed on Mexican communities and the protection of Mexican citizens in the United States.

During the past 20 years, this author has witnessed a shift in the policies of the 10 Consul Generals of Mexico in Boston from the traditional top-down system of administration toward strengthening their relationship with the Mexican community. With the support of the former Consul General of Mexico, Mauricio Chávez Medina, the Mexican Organization of New England was founded in 1992 by a group of professionals, community members, and interested parties. "Instead of the Mexican community being at the doorstep of the Consulate, the Consulate came to the community," says Ricardo Olivares (personal communication, November 2004). Through such initiatives, the Consulate in Boston has presented library books to the University of Massachusetts—Boston, sponsored a series of cultural events and visits by prominent Mexicans, and supported the development of closer relationships between the student organizations and the community-based groups. Most importantly, collaboration between student, community, and consular personnel has made possible the organizing of the 15th of September, Mexico's Independence Day, as a community and student-run celebration. This participative trend changes depending on who is in charge of the Consul of Mexico.

Former Consul General Carlos Rico continued initiatives started by the former General Consul of Mexico in Boston, Hector Vasconcelos. Among these was the 1998 suit filed by the Mexican government and a group of Mexican workers against DeCoster Egg Farm on the basis of discrimination, racism, and rights violation in its treatment of 14 immigrant male and female workers from 1988–1997 (Cubra, 2002). This was the first time that the Mexican government filed a suit in a foreign land to protect its own citizens. A $3.2 million settlement was reached in 2002. Another was the Federation of Mexican Organizations (FOMNI), which was initiated by Consul General Vasconcelos in 1998 and reinstated in 2001 by Consul Carlos Rico as an umbrella organization for student and community-based organizations. The organization's first president was Elizabeth Canali, who served until Julio César Aragón was elected as president in 2001. He served until 2004, when Ana Portillo was elected. Currently, Aragón continues to be the president of his own organization in Rhode Island, and Ana Portillo, who was the former president of the Mexican Organization of New England is the president of the Federation of Mexican Organizations in New England.

FOMNI's goals are (1) to promote an objective image of the Mexican community and Mexico in New England; (2) to engage Mexicans in the civic life of the area, strengthening the organizations and their leadership; (3) to support Mexican groups in their problem-solving; (4) to advocate and uphold the shared interests of the Mexican community with authorities in each of the states; (5) to maintain a constructive and mutually supportive relationship with Latino populations in the area; and (6) to support the protection of Mexicans in the area.

The current General Consul of Mexico in Boston, Porfirio Thierry Muñoz Ledo, has directed much of his attention to the needs of the Mexican community and has made inroads in harnessing resources that help address their needs. The former General Consul of Mexico in New York, Arturo Sarukhán Casamitjan, was known for working toward greater outreach of the Mexican community in New York, Connecticut, and New Jersey. The Mexican Consulate along with Mexican community organizations played an important role during the September 11th tragedy in which over 500 Mexicans lost their lives.

At the same time, the Mexican government has also responded through the creation of the Office of Representation for Mexicans and Mexican Americans in the Exterior, which was followed by the Programs for the Mexican Communities in the Exterior in 1990. Under President Vicente Fox, the National Council for Mexican Communities in the Exterior, the Institute for Mexicans Abroad (IME), and the Consultative Council of the IME were established to inform and protect the interests of Mexicans living abroad. The IME uses the Internet to post information and updated reports on a daily and weekly basis under the LAZOS bulletins, and it also sends the weekly statement from President Fox. In addition, each consulate has a designated community liaison working directly with the Mexican communities. The ex-President of the Federation for Mexican Organizations in New England, Julio César Aragón, until 2006, was a member of the Consultative Council of the IME. That role has now been assumed by Marta Nelson as first counselor with the support of Benjamin Guiliani as a second counselor. Their roles are to take the "pulse" of what the Mexicans in New England need and report these directly to the Mexican government and other interested entities. Thus, the current role of the Consulates is that of narrowing the distance between the Mexican government and its people through greater community initiatives.

FINDINGS FROM INTERVIEWS WITH MEXICAN LEADERS

Based on the lists provided by the Mexican Consulates in Boston and New York, the principal investigator and community researcher identified Mexican leaders to be interviewed in person or by telephone. The lists included directors or presidents of Mexican organizations, shop or restaurant owners, and church activity organizers. The decision was made to interview only those leaders who either directed or managed a Mexican organization and not those who shared information or worked within religious groups. Student organization leaders, while quite active and supportive of the Mexican communities in New England, were not included because they tend to have transient leadership, are directed toward their academic programs, and are not within the purview of the community organizations.

From the total pool of 25 leaders, 6 males and 6 females were identified for the New England states as being directors, presidents, or co-presidents of Mexican community-based organizations through the Consular personnel of the New York and Boston Mexican Consulates and through community organization members knowledgeable about Mexicans and the Mexican organizations. The three-hour interviews took place at their homes or workplace for leaders in Massachusetts, New Hampshire, Rhode Island, and Maine and a one-hour telephone interview was conducted with leaders or informants in Connecticut and Vermont. Not included are Xuchipilli and Las Perlitas, which are dance groups for adults and for children, respectively.

Out of the total nine active and inactive organizations that currently represent Mexicans in New England, six (all active) are represented in this study. These six are primarily found in Massachusetts, Maine, Rhode Island, and New Hampshire, and their focus ranges from migrant work to cultural and social, sports, and community interests. Two that focused on sports and social and cultural affairs have become inactive and are in Connecticut and Vermont. One new Mexican organization was being developed in Connecticut at the time of the study, but whether it has been formalized or not is not known.

From the interviews, the areas identified were (1) the Leadership Identification of Mexicans by the Consulates and Community Members; (2) the Demographic Data of the Leaders; (3) The Needs of the Mexican Communities as Reported by Leaders; (4) the Nature of the Organizations, and Relationships to the Consulate, Government of Mexico and the United States; and (5) the Leadership Roles and Decision-Making Processes. However, only the first four are presented in this chapter, because the discussion of leadership and the role of community organizations as has already been noted will be treated elsewhere. The findings are represented in terms of salient issues or themes. The notion of leader, which is particularly significant, serves as the introduction to this section.

The Concept of Leadership

Under the notion of *leader*, both the Consulate of Boston and New York include directors and presidents of Mexican organizations, community members who own shops or restaurateurs who share information. When such a notion was applied within the Mexican communities visited, other meanings arose, as several community members tend to identify leaders through word of mouth. In such contexts, the term *leader* is applied to a person who can mobilize others, shares important information, and directs groups. Some of the Mexican leaders stated they could not apply the concept directly to themselves because they did not think of themselves as leaders, believing that role was either nobler or beyond the work they did. Instead, they felt that this was a label conferred on them by the community. Interestingly, this was more commonly stated by the leaders from working-class backgrounds or by some of the women in the pool. Yet the middle-class leaders, particularly those who are in their early 30s, did not hesitate to consider themselves as such. One could surmise that coming from an educated background, having been privileged in schooling, and accessing certain cultural capital, assuming the stewardship of some of the community organizations appeared to grant such entitlement.

One definition of a leader referred to "a person that has integrity and has a philosophic base and good principals. Others are to decide whether I am such a leader, but I am constant, have heart, and the ability to move in circles where I am not invited, sometimes not being liked by some, but accepted by others. We are in a society that offers great opportunities and risks." Another said: "I do not define myself as a leader, but as a person who wants to resolve problems and who enjoys the challenges that are presented. To me it is getting things done, that gives me satisfaction." In comparing similarities and differences between Mexican leaders and American leaders, several notions were expressed by both the male and female leaders. American leaders were viewed as having power and the use of their own language, of integrating politics with the economy, and of studying and shaping their leadership, whereas Mexican leaders controlled others, were grassroots in their orientation, and wanted to be genuine but at times also corrupt. Mexican leadership was being developed on social and cultural foundations, not on business networks and power. Who is a leader within the Mexican community? And What are the attributes of such leaders? How does his/her leadership operate? Clearly, these continue to be critical questions in need of further exploration.

Accessing the available databases made it clear that there is a need for having updated and accurate information. The author and community researcher found that much of the data from the Consular offices had changed. People had moved, organizational leaders had left, new leaders were emerging, and the information was lacking. Hence one immediate implication drawn from this research is the need for updated, valid databases that can be found within the Consular offices, but also within the organizations themselves.

Demographic Profiles of Mexican Leaders

The background of the six male and six female leaders indicated they came from Veracruz, Chihuahua, Michoacán, Tlaxcala, Guanajuato, Sonora, Hidalgo, and the Federal District. Six had lived in Mexico City prior to coming to the United States, and the other six had lived elsewhere in the United States (California, Texas, Illinois) before coming to New England.

Most had been in the New England area for 7 to 25 years, with the earliest having arrived in 1974 and the most recent in 1997. One of the Mexican leaders was born in the United States. He left for Mexico as a child, but later returned to spend the rest of his life in New England, later claiming his Mexican citizenship when this was made possible after 1993. Of the 12 leaders, 8 live in the city and 4 in the suburbs. Seven own their own houses or apartments, with 2 owning a second home, and 5 are renters. The range in ages is between 30 to 55 years of age, with the majority arriving in the area during their 20s, a few in their 30s and 40s, and one when he was 11. The majority arrived with families, and only four arrived as single men or women. Of the 12, 9 are married, 2 are divorced, and 1 is single. Eight have young and older grown-up children (from 1 to 4) and four have no children.

Their educational levels are quite varied, from a primary school completer, to four who had partially completed except for one who had completed secondary school, two with a bachelors' degree from Mexican institutions, four with Masters' degrees, and one with a medical degree. They had studied education, social sciences, science, agricultural studies, computer systems, urban planning, civil engineering, and dentistry in Mexico, and four continued to advance their studies and careers in the United States.

All reported ranges of bilingual experiences, from limited English-speaking abilities to full proficiency, yet all use Spanish as a means of communication at home, among family and community members. All of the women considered their language abilities in speaking, reading, writing, and comprehension to be high, with the strongest area being the writing of Spanish. One of the females speaks five languages and is fluent in all. All of the males reported having unequal use of English-speaking abilities, with reading and writing overall being the most difficult, while speaking and comprehension of English was not a problem. All reported that being bilingual and bicultural were essential qualities in being able to advance themselves and the lives of their children, and they also emphasized that having basic if not more advanced knowledge of computer skills, was a necessity. Of the 12, 9 reported using the computer to make their own announcements, bulletin boards, and displays for the civic and cultural events of their organizations. Three described themselves as being advanced in computer literacy, being able to use complex software programs. While all have access to a computer, most use the Internet, and one male uses the computer from 10 P.M to 2:00 A.M. daily to send emails and report information to colleagues.

They are employed as childcare providers, salespersons, managers, urban planners, business administrators, translators, special education teachers, dentists, and jewelry polishers. One volunteers in a state office and another spoke of "being well connected to politicians in a city." Of the 12, 4 own businesses, and the rest are either employed by nonprofit organizations, or work in companies, schools, or corporations. The majority (8 out of 12) use the skills from their work in the organizations they manage. Among the skills they use are "knowing how to deal with people, being able to communicate, sharing transcultural experiences, having organizational vision, and being bilingual." Of the 12, 2 report being of working-class backgrounds while the rest identify as middle class.

When asked if their work opportunities would be the same, better, or worse in Mexico, 4 of the 12 reiterated that their work opportunities would be the same as in Mexico, and 6 stated their work situation was better in the United States: "things are backward in Mexico," "everything takes longer," "you need to know the right person to have the right job," "available opportunities due to your knowledge, things would be the same in Mexico, but economic opportunities, not so." One woman stipulated that "she studied in the U.S., got married here and this is where her life is."

In answering the question about how their work in the United States contributes or not to their role as leaders within the Mexican community, two abstained. Others mentioned, for example, "that her job made her aware of access to political arena in United States and the opening of many doors that can be used to support the Mexican community." "All that I know, I could teach in any school at any level, yet I keep my job separate from my role as a President, yet at times I use the knowledge of the workplace as a transition for contacts that need to be made." Another stated that "the opportunities are either there or not there," or that "through the work, the help to meeting the needs of families could be concentrated," and another mentioned that her area was so specialized, that it was not found in Mexico. Yet another mentioned that her job contributed to her "having a clear vision of reaching objectives and the outcomes of certain tasks." From the profiles, it is clear that the identified Mexican leaders show broad ranges in experiences, education, and backgrounds and have specific individual and community agendas.

Mexican Organizations, Activities, and Membership

Although six active community organizations were identified, each is distinctively different, depending on the mission and vision of the organization and the socioeconomic needs of the Mexican community being served. Each organization ranges in focus from social, cultural, and civic affairs, to more community and specific needs. Among the six organizations, one is more of a social club and mixer, providing networking of mostly middle-class Mexicans; another is locally oriented, attempting to seek work opportunities, the drivers' license, and the use of the identification card or consular card, *matricula;* another responds to the local needs within the host community of Mexicans and to needs in Mexico, such as the building of a new school; another focuses on sports, social and cultural activities, and sharing of information; another responds to critical issues relating to migrant needs, and the most recent is involved in generating funds through social and cultural activities for specific needs such as helping families in need (death of a family member, or illness of a person). Of the 12 leaders of organizations, 7 express political awareness of the role of their communities in New England. Five expressed political inclinations, depending on the length of time in the United States and New England. Of these, one is particularly concerned about advancing other people's thinking in this area, and has become a spokesperson through his continuous emailing of communiqués. Another is aware of the need for political activity, which he learned in Mexico during his politically active times as a student leader, and another uses the social events to target issues, such as showing the movie "A Day without Mexicans," or calling attention to the celebration of César Chávez. Yet none of the organizations manifest any overt political agendas, except for the sentiments and ideas that are expressed by their leaders.

All but two are seasoned organizations, having been in existence for over 10 to 12 years. Only two have more recent beginnings; one is a fledging new organization created several years ago, and the other has been inactive but has become reactivated as of late. All of the organizations are nonprofit—a status acquired with the help of a lawyer. They are registered in each of the states and keep up with maintaining an active status even though their reports on their activities are made known through word of mouth, fliers to their membership, or by email.

While the goals of the organizations are clear in the minds of the 12 leaders, their responsibilities are many in attempting to carry through on the objectives of their organizations. These vary from meeting the needs of Mexicans, making them feel close to Mexico, and learning about services that are available to them, to diffusing Mexican culture and making such culture known, to having economic control and cooperation among members, to protecting Mexicans by educating, and orienting them, and to offering informational workshops. All expressed working anywhere from 20 to 120 hours per month on organizational activities. They all vocalized having massive attendance at celebrations, parties, and raffles, with as many as 300 to 500 people present. Their active membership, however, is reported to be as low as 5 to 15 members per organization, and in the case of the two newly activated organizations, closer to 20 to 25. While they all pointed out that they had monthly meetings, most were called in response to setting up an event or celebration. Of the six, only one requires members to pay dues, the others do not impose any fees because they believe their members cannot afford to pay, so they rely heavily on community c fund raising.

As to the responsibilities of the members and board of directors in carrying out the programs, most pointed out that they could count on the members, at times passively and at other times energetically, depending on the role that the leader assumed. In discussing the knowledge about the organization's statutes, mission, and vision that the members shared, most concurred that their members knew about the statutes in principle, but few had ever seen these in writing, they had not been translated to Spanish, and they had not been disseminated except upon request.

The actual directors, presidents, or vice-presidents make most of the decisions and then attempt to delegate tasks. Once the activity has been planned, then the membership organizes around the selling of tickets or volunteering of time, but for the most part, the role of directing is left to the upper echelons of such organizations. Meetings are often held on a project needed basis and are internally supported by the directors or presidents of the organizations. As one leader remarked, "We are really phantom organizations which exist, but the work is left to a few." Several others pointed out that it was better to make the decisions at the top and carry them through than rely on getting other people who did not have the time to carry through the activities. Hence, several of these organizations seem to respond to crisis without having the time to plan and be pro-active, and as volunteers within those organizations, the leaders assume the burden of responsibility.

The membership of each organization is also quite varied, from Puebla, Guerrero, Chihuahua, Oaxaca, Veracruz, Zacatecas, Jalisco, Sinaloa, to the Federal District. Three of the five organizations' members are mostly from rural areas, one has more urban members, and the other is split between rural and urban areas. The majority of the members of at least four of the organizations have young families, have completed primary and some secondary school, and have incomes between $1,200–$2,500 per month in construction, carpentry, social services, cleaning jobs, and factory work, earning low incomes, yet making enough to live, although with debts. Only one of the organizations stated that their members, mostly professionals with a few being painters, carpenters, or singers, were able to have a satisfactory income, and their members earned well over $2,500 per month.

Thus, it appears that fledging and more seasoned organizations are created out of the needs of the Mexican community in a specific time and space to meet some immediate or more remote needs. The renovation of the organization's vision and mission appears not to be a planned activity, but rather an unfolding of situations, needs, or crisis. Only two of the organizations have had outside organizational managers help them with their objectives and goal setting. The others are by and large home grown and community-based. The need for developing leadership that starts with learning to organize boards and action plans seems to be a definite need.

The Needs of the Mexican Communities in New England Reported through Leaders

Among the needs expressed for the Mexican community *reported through their leaders* are the following. It should be noted that these needs express the reflections that leaders made of the majority and not necessarily the needs of Mexicans in more comfortable situations. Hence, it should be clear that the needs expressed are driven by socioeconomic concerns. Among these in order of importance are:

1. *Acquiring the identification card and driver's license*, which in some cases can be obtained with the use of the *matrícula* or identification card,[56] are two central issues discussed by most of the leaders, particularly because the Mexican consular office has been providing the identification card since 1871 (O'Neill, 2003; Donohue, 2003). Several pointed out that many Mexicans were driving without licenses simply to get to their

jobs. They were concerned that they were putting their lives in danger. The identification card was deemed as critical for banking purposes, obtaining a drivers' license, and simply daily use. Many expressed the lack of support from Police departments, some of which accept the use of the identification card, but others do not.

2. *Legalization of undocumented status was salient* for many as expressed by the leaders. Waiting to see if changes in the federal laws will grant them permanency in the United States was one of the critical concerns for many of the working-class Mexicans and those who have overstayed their visas.

3. *Affordable and accessible housing* for rental and for eventual purchase. Many felt that the rents were so excessive that they had to live with relatives in order to make the monthly payments. Access to buying their own homes was often a determent, because some of the leaders interviewed did not realize that they could purchase a home without being permanent residents. Several expressed awe at the ability of Asian groups in purchasing homes within their own neighborhoods. Of the leaders who owned homes or apartments, several had learned how to access the Latino community-based banking loans, and at least three owned property, which was rental income. Thus, it is clear that information on loans, home purchases, and renting versus owning are all new to many of these Mexicans.

4. *Available work* for them to move up the ranks. Several of the leaders expressed how volatile the job market was and that the need for more permanent jobs was critical for them to be able to live modestly with their families. On the job training and advancement were also mentioned as critical supports.

5. *Educational services* for their children and for adults wishing to learn English and to advance the studies they left behind in Mexico. Some of the adults expressed that they would like to have the time to complete their studies, which they had to leave behind in Mexico, and that access to schools after work was essential for them. The need for better schooling and treatment of their children was also a focus of discussion, particularly because all of the leaders expressed that their members want their children to learn English, but not at the cost of the Spanish. For many of the adults, learning English becomes an arduous process, yet English is needed for the better jobs, so programs that help them learn are much desired. Finally, the issue of helping their youth advance in higher education was mentioned as significantly important, particularly because many of the youth who are undocumented drop out in high school or do not see any opportunities ahead for furthering their education. They expressed the need for grants and funding for such students that would help keep them in school and participate in society. They mentioned that even those students who were legal could not afford to pay for higher education, so a pipeline for educational advancement is greatly needed.

6. *Health insurance for the Mexican communities* was stated as significant. Several of the leaders pointed out the request of many Mexicans to be able to use the social security services of Mexico in the United States for basic medical care. Others felt that they could not afford health insurance over food, so taking care of one's health becomes an unaffordable luxury.

7. *Group cohesion among Mexican leaders and communities.* Several pointed out the need for coalition building rather than the "divide and conquer syndrome," which they felt prevailed in their communities. Several pointed out how difficult it was to organize Mexicans with such diverse backgrounds and experiences and with excessive work and family demands. The leaders expressed that they felt that nationality

in excess did not allow for formation of groups and that the regional emphasis experienced from Mexico often set them apart and created barriers by inciting, as one said, "turf differences." Many expressed the importance of building solidarity among Mexicans of all backgrounds and classes. They clearly saw differences between the Mexican university groups and their communities, and they expressed the need for greater coalition building to reduce such differences. As several pointed out, being viewed as an underclass by non-Mexicans was hard enough, and attempting to provide a positive image of Mexicans was made even harder by the negative portrayal in the media. Thus what they needed was the backing of other Mexicans in order to show that they are a united front. Clearly this sentiment was strongly expressed by many of the leaders, who also saw the advantages of having the solidarity of other Latino groups.

8. *Dealing with discrimination* was also a focus of discussion. For some of the Mexican community leaders, the way that Mexicans are treated by the police is particularly demeaning. The issue of how they are depicted and portrayed was brought up, and it is necessary to create a different image of the Mexican. In addition, they also felt that discrimination among Mexicans needed to change. Social and class differences need not come into play if Mexicans see themselves as a core group.

These in essence represent the concerns of Mexicans in New England as they ponder their futures. Having an education, access to work, banks, drivers' licenses, and economic resources are all fundamental rights that they are attempting to gain. One of the leaders summed it up as "We need communication among and between us, information, and presence."

The Role of Mexican Organizations with Mexican Consulates, Mexican Government, and the United States Government

The relationships that the organizations maintain with the Consulates in New York and Boston reflected several perspectives. On the one hand, there is an informational relationship with the Consulates whereby missives on the mobile consulates are sent to the leaders of these organizations and communication about events is forthcoming. On the other hand, the information is at times devoid of instructions on use and requires that the community pay for duplication materials to be disseminated, creating costs for the organizations. Of the leaders from the six organizations, two identified a relatively stable relationship with the Consulate in Boston. Another two leaders pointed out that there was some degree of distance between the organization and the Consulate in Boston even though the Consulate recognized their efforts. Two suggested that the Consulate was out of reach to them in most of the activities, and the support they received was null, limited, or late. In addition, a community member for Connecticut reported the need to receive feedback from the Consulate in New York. Among the needs these organizations echoed was a need for greater communication and relationship building between the Mexican communities and the authorities of Mexico. While the needs of the Mexican community have grown and are many, the majority of the leaders expressed their concerns for how the Mexican government was responding to such needs and their representation in the United States. Those speaking about the Consulate in New York understood the financial and physical limitations that Consulates have with growing demands. However, receiving economic and educational resources were issues raised by the majority of the leaders for helping their own communities grow their own leadership. The use of the mobile consulates was considered by most to be a useful tool for getting the Mexican community to register with the Consulates and for getting information. However, they felt such information needed to be two-way and equitable to all of the Mexican groups. Several echoed how some organizations received greater support in conducting the mobile consulates than others. In addition, the need for greater relationship building between the Consulate and the Mexican communities was expressed. Three of the Mexican organizations' leaders felt they knew the Consular personnel due to participating in the mobile consulates. Otherwise they would not have such relationships.

Several stated they needed more personal updates of how decisions in Mexico would affect their lives in the United States. One leader said: "Getting the ear of people in the Consulates and being heard are two needs." Another said: "Mexico was too far away and that the need for becoming aware of what was happening had to occur on their doorstep."

Regarding the role that the Mexican government has with the organizations, the leaders asked not only for recognition, knowing "that we exist, and "want to vote," and "be counted," but also for economic and educational resources for services and projects, education using Spanish, educational preparation, data-bases, and political training. One leader commented that "the Mexican government thought Mexicans in New England did not exist, but if they actually took a real census, they would be dramatically surprised." Several also noted that the U.S. government needed to be aware that the Mexican government's role was to protect Mexicans abroad and that "being treated with dignity" was an important criterion. They noted that the United States could provide grants and funding of projects, be aware of the contributions of Mexicans, and establish better bilateral agreements.

In short, these reported statements and the analysis conducted high-lights several issues for consideration of the Mexican communities and their organizations.

1. Mexican communities and organizations could benefit from leadership training, the understanding of how organizations function and how they can grow through concerted efforts between the community-based organizations, leadership pro-grams at institutions of higher learning, and initiatives with the Mexican consular offices. There are nascent leaders in need of training who could eventually create their own prototypes of leadership based on strategies brought from Mexico and tied to democratic tendencies in the United States.

2. The development of gendered leadership, particularly of the women who have taken on the role of presidents or directors and who are breaking ground in attempting to create more dialogical processes for other women in the Mexican community.

3. The understanding of cultural issues as not being isolated from the social and economic concerns. The focus on culture, while positive in terms of identity formation and cultural heritage, also needs to be tied to the advancement of Mexicans within the economic realm. Only then will a basis for developing insights into political strategies become part and parcel of such a process.

CONCLUSION

Clearly, throughout this chapter the use of the monolithic term *Mexicans* hides much of the variations that exist, the idiosyncrasies of each subgroup, and the sense of survival, stability, and advancements that Mexican are experiencing in the United States and in New England. It is the homogeneity and at the same time the heterogeneity of Mexicans that helps us understand their dual cultural and future citizenship existence; "Ni somos de aquí, ni de allá" (We are not only from here, nor from there).

The difference between the Mexican who emigrated post-Mexican Revolution is that today's Mexicans are here to stay. Talk of the "reconquista," the retaking of the lands lost to Mexico after the 1848 Treaty of Guadalupe Hidalgo following the U.S.–Mexico War, abound, and the notion that a border exists is more fictive than a reality in their minds. Mexicans today make up part of the global trends, where the regional markets accelerated by the North American Free Trade Agreement caused a massive restructuring of the rural farmers who could not compete with the agribusinesses in the United States. As Suárez-Orozco points out throughout his research, increasing inequality in Mexico has lead to an uncontainable wave of Mexican immigrants entering the United States.[57] This, in addition to the need for workers, has absorbed many Mexicans into the U.S. economic infrastructure, including women and children whose emigration has increased fivefold since 1986, according to Alfredo Corchado and Dianne Solis (1999).

Among the critical concerns raised by the Mexican population in New England is the legitimacy of their role within the growing Latino populations and their need for integration into a social, educational, and economic infrastructure that respects and acknowledges their contributions. The fact that Mexicans are contributing to the workforce is positive, but that they do so in the lower rungs, without opportunities for educational advancement and economic stability, are challenges that need to be overcome. There is no doubt that the relationship of Mexico through economic, cultural, and social ties to the United States makes the role of Mexicans in New England a pivotal one. The Mexican diaspora will be one of the most important factors in the development of bilateral relation with the United States in future decades (Fernandez de Castro, 2004). Yet in order for Mexicans to have political ascendancy, economic fulfillment, educational access, and entry into the middle management and professional arenas, they will need to consolidate their leadership development, build coalitions and alliances, and develop strong social, cultural, economic, and political platforms with other Latinos. The findings show an emerging sense of leadership for these Mexicans in

New England, with some of the directors of these organizations being pivotal social actors. However, learning how to organize the wide range of interests of these Mexicans in New England, support their needs, and extend their power is clearly a united effort on the part of the community organizations, student groups, and Mexican Consulates. Mexicans can "echarle ganas," give it their all, but they will require training in leadership and mentoring and continued experimentation with their emerging leadership in expanding their community building as the "sí se puede" newcomers in New England.

Mexican Organizations in New England

New England States

The Federation of Mexican Organization of New England (FOMNI)

Maine

The Maine Migrant Workers' Advocacy Group, Inc.

Massachusetts

Organización Mexicana de Nueva Inglaterra (OMNI), Mexican Organization of New England

Asociación de Mexicanos en Berklee

Harvard University Mexican Association (HUMA)

MIT Mexican Student Association (Clubmex MIT)

Asociación Mexicana de Endicott College

Fronteras Unidas

Xuchipilli, Ballet Folklórico

New Hampshire

Granite State Mexican Association of New Hampshire

Rhode Island

Asociación Guadalupana de Rhode Island

Asociación Libre Mexicana de Rhode Island

Asociación Social, Cultural y Deportiva Mexicana de Rhode Island

Estudiantes Mexicanos de Brown University

Las Perlitas de Mexico

Liga Mexicana de Futbol Soccer de Rhode Island

ACKNOWLEDGMENTS

The phrase "sí se puede" (yes, we can or yes, it can happen) was coined by the farm workers in California during the 1960s who protested alongside César Chávez. The phrase has come to symbolize the collective effort of the Latino community in the United States. It is used as a signature by ex-President of the Federation of Mexican Organizations in New England, Julio César Aragón, who resides in Rhode Island and is a former representative of the Mexicans in New England as a counselor within the Institute for Mexicans Abroad.

This chapter is dedicated to the memory of Alicia Cuevas de Montero, the author's mother, who was certainly the oldest Mexican in Massachusetts at the time of her death at age 98 and probably one of the oldest for the rest of New England in 2003. Her legacy as a Mexican woman who experienced the Mexican Revolution of 1910–1917, World War I and II, emigrated to the United States as an adult, lived in the United States for close to 35 years, and shared numerous tales and lessons in the lives of many, has generated a sense of community for future generations.

The undertaking of interviews with Mexicans leaders was made possible through funds from the Mauricio Gaston Institute of the University of Massachusetts—Boston during Spring–Fall 2004. The generosity of former director Dr. Andres Torres' is much appreciated in making this possible.

NOTES

1. The support of the General Consulate of Mexico in Boston and the General Consulate of Mexico in New York made it possible to initiate the contacts with the "leaders" of Mexican organizations. Informational meetings were held with several of the consular personnel throughout Spring, Fall of 2004 until Fall 2005. Their support is highly valued and appreciated.

2. The 2000 U.S. Census reports that there are 35.3 million Latinos in the United States, constituting 12.5 percent of the total 281.4 million inhabitants in the United States. Of these Mexicans constitute 58.5 percent of the Latino population, 9.6 percent are Puerto Rican, 3.5 percent are Cuban, 2.2 percent are Dominican, 4.8 percent are Central American, 3.8 percent are South American, and 17.3 percent are Other Latinos with Spaniards representing 0.3 percent of the total. The total number of Latinos in the New England area is 875,225. However, if numbers for undocumented Latinos are counted, that inclusive figure may be as high as 1,000,000 for all of New England.

3. They are as Suárez-Orozco points out both the oldest and the newest Americans, settling in the Southwest, several hundred years and now the newest, because the majority of the Mexican Americans are either immigrant or first generation.

4. Puerto Ricans are not immigrants, but U.S. citizens; hence Dominicans are by far the largest of the Caribbean and Latin American immigrant Latino groups and account for 25.1 percent or 22,349 of the total of 88,878 during 1990–1998 (Marcelli).

5. Some of the figures for Mexicans in Massachusetts towns are as follows: Boston, 4,126 or 4.4 percent of the total Latino population of 85,089 in 2000; Framingham, 345 of 7,265; Lawrence, 316 of 43,019; Waltham, 609 from 5,031; Salem, 131 of 4,541; Chelsea, 660 of 16,984; Haverhill, 340 of 5,174; and Lynn, 853 of 16,383.

6. Maine is considered to be one of the whitest states in the United States, yet migrant workers from Mexico and Central America who have been seasonal agricultural workers are settling permanently and are requiring services that might be consolidated through a Maine Latino Center (Jenna Russell, "As numbers rise, Latinos in New England seek louder Voice," *Boston Globe*, January 12, 2003).

7. See the report by Steven A. Camarota. "Immigration from Mexico. Assessing the Impact on the United States," Washington, D.C.: Center for Immigration Studies, July 2001. Also see the report by Steven Camarota and Nora McArdle titled "Where Immigrants Live: An Examination of State Residency by Country of Origin in 1990–2000." Center for Immigration Studies, September 2003. The authors signal the growing concerns about the declining diversity and changing distribution of immigrant by country across the United States, but more importantly their ability to integrate and to assimilate.

8. Passel, Jeffrey S. *Rise, Peak and Decline: Trends in U.S. Immigration 1992–2004.* Washington, D.C.: Pew Hispanic Center, September 2005.

9. The National Council on Population (CONAPO) in its study of migration between Mexico and the United States, reports that in 40 years, 17 million Mexicans have left the country, and this has diminished the current population of Mexico, which would have been 120 million instead of the 100 million of today. Moreover, close to 10 million Mexican nationals now live in the United States, with 8.2 million being the children of Mexican parents and 7.8 million second generation descendents of Mexicans (www.milenio.com).

10. Note that according to Mieczyslaw Karczmar, in "Rise in Anti-Immigration Sentiments in the United States," *Frankfurt Voice, Demography Special, Deutsche Bank Research*, July 30, 2002, 80 percent of the U.S. farm workers are Mexican.

11. During the twentieth century, these states after being devastated by the Cristera War (1926 to 1929) experience a massive Mexican migration to the United States according to Juan Balboa, "En 4 años, drástico cambio del mapa migratorio mexicano a los Estados Unidos," *La Jornada*, October, 10, 2004.

12. According to the Consejo Estatal de Población in Mexico, 386,000 people from the state of San Luis Potosi, or 4 percent of Mexico's total population live in the United States and are settling in North Carolina, Florida, and Tennessee.

13. See Juan Balboa, "En 4 años, drástico cambio del mapa migratorio mexicano a Estados Unidos." *La Jornada, México, D. F.*, 10 de octubre de 2004.

14. The data for Rhode Island taken from Miren Uriarte et al., report, and the historical account of Marta Martinez is complemented by, data gathered from Julio Aragon, ex-President of the Federation of Mexican Organizations in New England who also heads up the Mexican Association for Social, Sports and Cultural Programs in Rhode Island.

15. See Camayd-Freixas, Yoel and Gerald Karush, and Nelly Letjer. "Latinos in New Hampshire: Enclaves, Diasporas, and an Emerging Middle Class." In Andres Torres (ed.). *Latinos in New England.* Philadelphia: Temple University Press, 2006, pp. 1–17.

16. According to Marcelli (2002, 2), "among all immigrants, 58 percent settled in Massachusetts and 27 percent settled in Connecticut between 1990 and 1998. Among Latin Americans and Caribbean immigrants, 54 percent settled in Massachusetts and 33 percent in Connecticut."

17. Camayd-Freixas, Yoel and Gerald Karush, and Nelly Letjer. "Latinos in New Hampshire: Enclaves, Diasporas, and an Emerging Middle Class." In Andres Torres (ed.). *Latinos in New England* Philadelphia: Temple University Press, 2006, pp. 1–17.

18. Between 1990 and 2000, the following cities experienced growth in the Mexican populations. In Connecticut, Bridgeport, Mexicans grew from 402 or 1.1 percent to 2,687 or 6.0 percent; Danbury, 443 or 9.2 percent to 1,294 or 11.0 percent; Hartford from 498 or 1.1 percent to 993 to 2.0 percent; New Britain from 107 or 0.9 percent to 625 or 3.3 percent; New Haven with 781 or 4.8 percent to 3,483 or 13.2 percent;

Norwalk from 182 or 2.6 percent to 1,897 or 14.6 percent; Stamford from 912 or 9.3 percent to 1414 or 7.2 percent; Waterbury from 236 or 1.7 percent to 588 or 2.5 percent; W. Haven from 76 or 4.4 percent to 451 or 9.5 percent; Willimantic from 257 or 11.2 percent to 902 or 18.9 percent. In Massachusetts, Boston went from 2,640 or 4.4 percent to 4,126 or 4.8 percent; Chelsea from 120 or 1.4 percent to 660 or 3.9 percent; Framingham from 208 or 4.3 percent to 345 or 4.7 percent; Haverhill from 74 or 2.9 percent to 340 o4 6.6 percent; Lawrence from 84 or .03 percent to 316 or 0.7 percent; Lowell from 143 or 1.4 percent to 282 or 1.9 percent; Lynn from 167 or 2.3 percent to 853 or 5.2 percent; Methuen from 19 or 1.0 percent to 70 or 1.7 percent; New Bedford from 184 or 3.3 percent to 322 or 3.4 percent; Revere from 171 or 10.4 percent to 473 or 10.6 percent; Salem with 47 or 2.0 percent to 131 or 2.9 percent; Somerville with 148 or 3.1 percent to 464 or 6.8 percent. In Rhode Island, Central Falls went from 91 or 1.8 percent to 677 or 7.5 percent; Pawtucket had 254 or 5.1 percent and later 581 or 5.7 percent; Providence had 738 or 3.1 and now has over 2,237 or 4.3 percent; Woonsocket had 79 or 6.9 percent and now has over 168 or 4.2 percent. New Hampshire experienced the growth of Mexicans in Manchester with 391 or 18.3 to 1,220 or 24 percent today, and Nashua with 554 or 23.2 percent to 1306 or 24.2 percent.

19. It should be noted that even the 2000 census data does not represent the current numbers of Mexicans throughout New England. From the interviews gathered for this study, and visits to Mexican communities, it is clear from all of the information gathered, that the numbers of Mexicans are much greater than has been reported based on the interviewee data.

20. In 1999, according to Carlos Rico, former Consul of Mexico in "View from New England: A Preliminary Portrait," Revista, DRCLAS, 2001, the Federal Bureau of Prisons established a Medical Center in Devens, Massachusetts, which concentrates chronically ill prisoners, many of whom are Mexicans being sent by different states and detained Mexican nationals.

21. Former Cambridge resident, now residing in California, Dr. Mario Molina ex-professor of MIT, is a scientist dedicated to ozone layer analysis.

22. Among these are Leopoldo Romero of Casa Romero, German Aguilar and Rafael Osornio of Café el Sol Azteca, Pepe Gutierrez of Tacos el Charro, Juan Martinez of Mi Rancho Grande, Julieta King, former owner of Villa Mexico and Julie's Faire in Woburn, to name just a few.

23. Among these are several psychologists, psychiatrists, entrepreneurs, professors, and doctors including Dr. Enrique Caballero, a leading diabetician at the Harvard Medical School.

24. The range in students varies from those enrolled in community colleges to those who use the cooperative system in Boston-based universities to colleges throughout New England, in specialized fields and at public and Ivy league universities such as Harvard, Brown, Dartmouth, and Yale. Many are active within Mexican-run student organizations.

25. The use of the term "Mexican" herein includes not only Mexican nationals with different legal statuses, but also those who as descendents of Mexicans in their second and third generations identify as Mexicans.

26. The research was conducted by the author as principal investigator, Alicia Morales, a community researcher, and Bessie King, an undergraduate student at Northeastern University who provided contact help. As Mexicans, invested in understanding the issues of the Mexican community, the team continues to be on-going and is still uncovering nascent Mexican "leaders" in New England during 2005–2006.

27. Census data, information, and reports gathered from research institutes such as the Mauricio Gaston Institute for Latino Public Policy and Community Development at the University of Massachusetts-Boston, the David Rockefeller Center for Latin American Studies, the Center for Immigration Studies, and the Institute for Mexicans in the Exterior became additional sources for data. The Institute for Mexicans in the Exterior through Lazos provides for a synthesis of news in the United States and in Mexico, which affects all Mexicans on a daily basis. This is part of the initiative by President Fox under the Institute for Mexicans Abroad, which includes Mexicans living abroad.

28. As an ethnographer of Mexican society and culture, the author gathered data on Mexican communities, particularly those in Massachusetts and to a lesser extent, Rhode Island between 1976 and 2003. She also actively participated in Mexican consular activities of an organizational nature, presented at cultural and social events, served as president of the Mexican Organization of New England for over seven years, supervised graduate student research on the Mexican community, mentored Mexicans into professional roles, and generated greater confluence between the university student groups and members of the Mexican community around civic celebrations. Such a role allowed her to understand the Mexican community in general, but also as an insider and outsider to Mexican culture, to approximate their reality in New England.

29. The use of the term *leader* is widely used within the Mexican community and is often attributed to people who have gained prominence within the communities of Mexicans, have businesses or establishments where Mexicans gather and share information, or are key informants on the communities. While the directors of the Mexican organizations may not associate their work with the use of such a term, they nevertheless adjudicate it to those who they see are able to mobilize and connect people.

30. Records on the Latinos in Boston indicate that among the first groups were Cubans who came to Boston around 1948. Olga Dummont, who left Cuba, is considered to be one of the *madrinas* (godmothers) who helped people get on their feet. Since discrimination was prevalent during the 1950s, Latino social and civic activities were celebrated mostly in private homes. Community centers such as the Casa de Caridad and ABCD became critical in fostering Latino presence (Uriarte, 1996).

31. From the fieldwork visits, a notable trend that is emerging is that of Chinese restaurant owners soliciting Mexican workers at the border and bringing them to work for a duration of 2–3 months and later returning them to the border.

32. It should be noted that Mexican scholarships to study abroad were not supported by the Mexican government until the 1970s through CONACYT, thus students who could study did so through the support of their families.

33. Lindsay Lowell of the Pew Hispanic Center estimates that 12 percent of Mexico's population with higher education is in the United States. Yet Agustin Escobar of CIESAS Occidente, a research institute, points out that although 12 percent of the total labor force from Mexico is in the United States, 30 percent of Mexicans with Ph.Ds are also in the United States (Emigration, Outward Bound, Sept. 26, 2002, Economist). www.economist.com/world/.

34. Many of the Banks of Mexico support their professionals by offering them short-term courses in places like the Harvard Business School and upon their return have them work in international banking practices.

35. Chilango is a term used to identify residents of Mexico city. However, depending on the way that it is stated, it can have implications for identifying chilangos as

distinctively different from the people of the provinces and may have negative infer-
ences about power relationships and social backgrounds.

36. A description of the Mexicans in East Boston was written as part of a two-part
series on the impact of Hispanic Immigration in the Boston area by Tatiana M. With
and was titled "From Mexico to Massachusetts: Northeast Migration Linked to Jobs,
Proposition 187 and Family," *Boston Sunday Globe*, April 14, 1996.

37. Well over 500 immigrants from El Refugio have been arriving in East Boston
for the past 30 years, and at least 1,000 people or two-thirds of the population have left
according to a report by Cindy Rodriguez of *The Globe*. The exodus to Eastie began in
July 1972 when a Mexican American sailor, Ernesto de la Rosa, came for his bride, Ana
Maria and in bringing her to East Boston, created interest for the family to follow.

38. These were services once linked with Franco-Americans, Cape Verdean, Por-
tuguese, and Italian workers.

39. Mexico, as a top-sending country to the United States according to Steven
Camarota and Nora McArdle, increased its share of 16 percent in the 1980s to 22 percent
by the 1990s and to 30 percent by 2000 ("See Where Immigrants Live: An Examination of State Residency of the Foreign Born by Country of Origin in 1990 and 2000,"
Center for Immigration Studies, September 2003).

40. Among some of the celebrated Mexicans who now hold professorships is Mili
Bermejo who teaches at the Berklee School of Music; and Mario Molina, Nobel Prize
winner, who used to teach at MIT and is now in California.

41. See Martha Martinez, *The Latinos of Rhode Island*, Rhode Island Foundation,
2002.

42. Interview conducted with Leopoldo Romero, owner of Casa Romero in Boston,
March 2004.

43. Margarita Fernández-Letowski has been the president of the Granite State
Mexican Association of New Hampshire for over six years after the two previous
directors requested that she assume the leadership of the organization.

44. The organizing of Mexicans that is taking place in several parts of Connecticut
has to do with the community's response to the way that the police have dealt with
racial profiling, detentions, and the use of licenses. Helping immigrants understand
their rights appears to be a growing concern in Connecticut, as reflected through one
of the telephone interviews with several Latino and non-Latino community leaders
(Field notes, October 2004).

45. It is well known that the Barrio, once viewed as Puerto Rican, has now become
inundated with Mexicans from Puebla, so much so that names such as Pueblolandia for
the area are now in common use.

46. Poblanos is the term for people from the state of Puebla, which until recently
was not a feeder state to U.S. immigration, but in the last 10 years has experienced
the exodus of whole towns and villages to places like New York city. According to a
recent study by Francisco Rivera-Batiz at Columbia University, Mexicans are the fastest growing group in New York City and even the city's 186,872 reported Mexicans by
the 2000 Census is most likely an undercount. They are the third largest group after
Puerto Ricans and Dominicans, come from poor, rural communities, have a median
age of 24.3 years old compared to 34.4 for the city overall, and have a mean household
income of $10,231 with an average of 9 years of schooling, working in the service area,
food retail industries where close to 42 percent of Mexican male workers are employed
(John Moreno Gonzales, *Newsday*, September 17, 2003) (see http://www. nynewsday.
com/news).

47. While newly arrived Mexicans are eager to work, the belief is that they tend to drive down wages. Studies show that their contributions are not actually seen until the third generation, when there seems to be sufficient economic payback both in terms of income generated and in terms of contributions to the social system (Miller, 2003).

48. The popularization of Mexican food has grown so extensively that America Take Out corporation has jumped on the bandwagon (www.americatakeout.com).

49. Most of the Mariachi bands are represented not only by Mexicans and Anglos, but musicians from Latin America and the Caribbean, and they are highly solicited by the number of performances given by any of the groups.

50. The field notes from the research appear to describe this type of staging for Mexicans who enter the job market and meet the demands.

51. It is interesting that among the 70 Mexican restaurants identified in the Boston greater metropolitan area, many of the owners are not Mexican, but represent other nationalities, including Salvadorans, Colombians, and Dominicans as owners or partners. Of these restaurants, approximately 15 are actually owned by Mexicans.

52. One of the owners of a local Mexican restaurant in the greater metropolitan area of Boston boasts about having mole made by hand in Puebla, flown into New York city in concentrated blocks, and then brought to Boston via truck in order to serve the legitimate Mole Poblano.

53. See the reports on *The Changing Face of Massachusetts*, prepared by Andrew M. Sum et al., for the Massachusetts Institute for a New Commonwealth. Center for Labor, Market Studies, Sponsored by Verizon, Citizens Bank, Polaroid, Bank of America and Nellie Mae Education Foundation, June 2005, and the *Changing Workforce: Immigrants and the New Economy* in Massachusetts prepared by Andrew M. Sum and W. Neal Fogg et al., for Citizens Bank, the Massachusetts Institute for a New Commonwealth, November 1999.

54. One of the Mexican restaurant owners reports that he has helped his workers obtain their residency status and has helped reunify six families, which amounts to about 30 family members (Fieldnotes, Restaurant owner, Boston, 2001).

55. See the recent report on "Sending Money Home: Remittances to Latin America and the Caribbean," sponsored by the Inter-American Development Bank, Washington, D.C., May 2004.

56. The use of the matricula (consular identification card) has become one of the most controversial issues in the United States. The fact that it has been recognized at certain levels, for example, the Department of the Treasury in the United States, but can be decided upon at the local Police Department levels in cities and towns has created stopgaps for many Mexicans seeking employment and driving licenses.

57. See the research by Henry (Enrique) Trueba, *The New Americans: Immigrants Transnationals at Work*. New York: Rowman and Littlefield Publishers, 2004; and the Suárez-Orozcos, *Transformations. Migration, Family Life and Achievement Motivation among Latino Adolescents*. Stanford, CA: Stanford University Press, 1995; Marcelo Suárez Orozco and Mariela M. Páez, *Latinos: Remaking America*. Los Angeles: University of California Press and David Rockefeller Center for Latin American Studies, Cambridge, MA, 2002; Carola Suarez-Orozco and Marcelo Suarez-Orozco, *Children of Immigration*. Cambridge, MA: Harvard University Press, 2001; Marcelo Suarez-Orozco, *Mexican Immigration and the Latinization of the United States*. Revista. Cambridge, MA: Harvard University. David Rockefeller Center for Latin American Studies, Fall, 2001, pp. 40–41.

REFERENCES

Bayles, Frank. "N. H. Outpaces New England Neighbors." *USA Today*, March 24, 2001 (http:www.cgi.usatoday.com/).

Balboa, Juan. "En 4 años, drástico cambio del mapa migratorio mexicano a Estados Unidos." *La Jornada, México, D. F.*, 10 de octubre de 2004.

Bendixen and Associates. *Remittance Senders and Receivers: Tracking the Transnational Channels.* Washington, D.C., November 24, 2003. Pew Hispanic Center, MIF, FOMIN.

Camarota, Steven A. *Immigration from Mexico. Assessing the Impact on the United States*, Washington, D.C.: Center for Immigration Studies, July 2001.

Camarota, Stephen and Nora McArdle. *Where Immigrants Live: An Examination of State Residency of the Foreign Born by Country of Origin in 1990 and 2000.* Center for Immigration Studies, September 2003.

Camayd-Freixas, Yoel and Gerald Karush, and Nelly Letjer. "Latinos in New Hampshire: Enclaves, Diasporas, and an Emerging Middle Class." In Andres Torres (ed.). *Latinos in New England* Philadelphia: Temple University Press, 2006, pp. 1–17.

Corchado, Alfredo and Dianne Solis. "Mexicans Reshaping America." *The Dallas Morning News*, September 19, 1999. www.dallasnews.com.

Creuheras, Santiago. "The Poblano Diaspora. The View from New York." Revista, Cambridge, MA: Harvard University, David Rockefeller Center for Latin American Studies, Fall 2001, pp. 42–43.

Crowley, Cathleen F. "As Latino Population Surges, So Does Its Power, Influence." *Eagle Tribune*. July 1, 2001. www.eagletribune.com.

Cubra, José Luis. "Mexican Workers Reach Settlement in Landmark Discrimination Suit." *The News, Mexico City*, July 5, 2002. Published by La Prensa in San Diego, California.

de la Garza, Rodolfo, Miguel Baraona, Manuel Orozco, Harry P. Pachon, and Adrian D. Pantoja. *Family Ties and Ethnic Lobbies: Latino Relations with Latin America. Policy Brief, June 1998. Los Angeles*, CA: Tomas Rivera Policy Institute, 1998.

de la Garza, Rodolfo, Manuel Orozco, and Miguel Baraona. *Binational Impact of Latino Remittances. Policy Brief, March 1997.Los Angeles, CA:* Tomas Rivera Policy Institute, 1997.

Donohue, Brian. "Mexico's ID Cards Ignite a Controversy." *The Star-Ledger.* May 15, 2003. www.nj.com.

Fernández de Castro, Rafael. "La Diáspora Mexicana: Retos y Oportunidades." *Reforma*, 26 de octubre de 2004.

Grieco, Elizabeth. "The Foreign Born from Mexico in the United States." Migration Information Source. Migration Policy Institute, October 1, 2003.

Harvard Business School. "What Would Migration Mean for Business." Special to *CNET New.com*, May 25, 2003. (http://new.com.com).

Krissman, Fred. " 'Them and Us'? Assessing Responsibility for Undocumented Migration from Mexico." Working Paper No. 46, Center for Comparative Immigration Studies, University of California, San Diego, La Jolla, California, December 2001.

LAZOS. Bulletin of the Institute for Mexicans Abroad of the Mexican Government, July 2004.

Lopez Vega, Rafael. "Consejo Nacional de Poblacion." *Mexico, D. F.*, 26 de junio de 2003.

Martinez, Marta. "The Latinos of Rhode Island." In Uriarte, Miren with Maria Estela Carrión, Charles Jones, Natalie Carithers, Juan Carlos Gorlier, and Juan Francisco García, (eds). *Rhode Island Latinos: A Scan of Issues Affecting the Latino Population of Rhode Island.* Boston: Mauricio Gaston Institute for Latino Community Development and Public Policy, University of Massachusetts-Boston, Prepared for the Rhode Island Foundation, 2002, pp. 46–51.

Marcelli, Enrico. "Legal Immigration to New England during the 1900s." *Latinos in Massachusetts: Immigration.* The Mauricio Gaston Institute, University of Massachusetts-Boston. April 2002.

Miller, Steve. "New Immigration Drive Down Wages Study Says." *The Washington Times*, 2003. (http://www.washtimes.com/national/).

Moreno Gonzalez, John. "Mexican Population Up. Study: They Are the Fastest Growing Group in the City." *New York, Newsday*, September 17, 2003.

O'Neill. Kevin. "Consular ID Cards: Mexico and Beyond." *Migration Information Source.* April 1, 2003. www.migrationinformation.org.

Otero, Lisandro. "Política y Remesas." *El Sol de México en Línea*, 2004.

Orozco, Manuel. "Remittances, the Rural Sector, and Policy Options in Latin America. The Inter-American Dialogue." *Migration Information Source.* June 1, 2003.

Passel, Jeffrey S. "Rise, Peak and Decline: Trends in U.S. Immigration 1992–2004." Pew Hispanic Center, Washington, D.C., September 2005.

Passel, Jeffrey S. "New Estimates of the Undocumented Population in the United States," *Migration Information Source*, May 22, 2002.

Rico, Carlos F. *View from New England: A Preliminary Portrait.* Revista, Cambridge, MA: Harvard University, David Rockefeller Center for Latin American Studies, Fall 2001, pp. 42–43.

Rumbaut, Ruben G. "Immigrants from Latin American the Caribbean: A Socioeconomic Profile." Julian Samora Research Institute, Statistical Brief No. 6, Michigan State University, 1995.

Stevenson, Mark. "Mexico Central Bank: Money Sent Home by Migrants Tops Foreign Investment, Tourism." *Star-Telegram*, August 29, 2003.

Suárez-Orozco, Carola and Marcelo. *Transformations. Migration, Family Life, and Achievement Motivation among Latino Adolescents.* Stanford, CA: Stanford University Press, 1995.

Suárez-Orozco, Carola and Marcelo M. Suarez-Orozco. *Children of Immigration.* Cambridge, MA: Harvard University Press, 2001.

Suárez-Orozco, Marcelo M. *Mexican Immigration and the Latinization of the United States.* Revista, Cambridge, MA: Harvard University, David Rockefeller Center for Latin American Studies, Fall 2001, pp. 40–41.

Suárez-Orozco, Marcelo M. and Mariela M. Paez. *Latinos: Remaking America.* Los Angeles, CA: University of California Press, and David Rockefeller Center for Latin American Studies, Cambridge, MA, 2002.

Sum, Andrew M. and W. Neal Fogg, with Sheila Palma, Neeta Fogg, Julia Kroshko, Paul Suozzo, Mykhaylo Trubśkyy, Christopher Harrington. *The Changing Workforce: Immigrants and the New Economy in Massachusetts.* Center for Labor Market Studies, Northeastern University, the Massachusetts Institute for a New Commonwealth, Citizens Bank, Inc., 1999.

Sum, Andrew M., Johan Uvin, Ishwar Khatiwanda, and Dana Ansel, with Paulo Tobar, Frimpomaa Ampaw, Sheila Palma, and Greg Leiserson. *The Changing Face of Massachusetts*. Boston, MA: Massachusetts Institute for a New Commonwealth. Center for Labor, Market Studies, Sponsored by Verizon, Citizens Bank, Polaroid, Bank of America and Nellie Mae Education Foundation, 2005.

Trueba, Henry (Enrique). *The New Americans: Immigrants Transnationals at Work*. New York: Rowman and Littlefield Publishers, 2004.

Uriarte, Miren and Charles Jones. "Growth of Latino Population." In Uriarte, Miren with Maria Estela Carrion, Charles Jones, Natalie Carithers, Juan Carlos Gorlier, and Juan Francisco Garcia. *Rhode Island Latinos: A Scan of Issues Affecting the Latino Population of Rhode Island*. Boston: Mauricio Gaston Institute for Latino Community Development and Public Policy, University of Massachusetts-Boston, Prepared for the Rhode Island Foundation, 2002, pp. 23–26.

Uriarte, Miren with Maria Estela Carrión, Charles Jones, Natalie Carithers, Juan Carlos Gorlier, and Juan Francisco Garcia. *Rhode Island Latinos: A Scan of Issues Affecting the Latino Population of Rhode Island*. Boston: Mauricio Gaston Institute for Latino Community Development and Public Policy, University of Massachusetts-Boston, Prepared for the Rhode Island Foundation, 2002.

CHAPTER 4

There Are Cubans, There Are Cubans, and There Are Cubans: Ideological Diversity among Cuban Americans in Miami

Guillermo J. Grenier, Lisandro Pérez, Sung Chang Chun, and Hugh Gladwin

On December 15, 1823, during a heavy blizzard, the ship *Draper C. Thorndike* sailed into New York's harbor from Gibraltar. It carried salt, almonds, and a handful of passengers. Among them was a Cuban priest named Félix Varela, a prominent figure in the nascent movement to free Cuba from Spanish control. The story goes that shortly after disembarking, Varela slipped and fell on an icy Manhattan street. As he was being helped up by friends and former students who greeted him at the dock, one of them jokingly told the priest that there was a legend in New York that predicted that all foreigners who fell on the snow when they arrived were destined to spend the rest of their lives in the city. The priest must have thought the prediction amusing and very far-fetched. After all, he was only 35 years old and found himself in New York almost by accident. The *Thorndike* happened to be the first ship out of Gibraltar after Varela had to literally flee Spain when his pleas for greater Cuban autonomy were violently rejected by the Spanish monarch. Varela probably regarded New York only as a way station until he could return to his native island.

But the legend became reality. Varela would spend the next 30 years of his life in lower Manhattan, establishing parishes and ministering to his flock of poor immigrants, most of them Irish. He never returned to Cuba.

Félix Varela, as a prominent Cuban separatist, could be regarded as the first person with a Cuban (not Spanish) identity who lived in the United States. As such, the arrival of the *Thorndike* on that day in 1823 represents the beginning of the story of Cubans in exile in the United States. It is a fitting start to that story, because Varela's experience established many of the themes of the Cuban presence in this country, themes that would be echoed by virtually every wave of Cubans that has come to the United States since that winter day in 1823: exile identity and the undying hope of return. The Cubans, much like the hero of one of my favorite movies, *Groundhog Day*, seem to keep reliving the same historical experience, in hopes of one day getting it right.

As with Varela's arrival, all major waves of Cuban immigrants throughout the nineteenth and twentieth centuries have been triggered by political conditions in the island. It is an immigration that cannot be understood without reference to its political and policy contexts. Cubans have arrived in the United States as did Varela: "reluctant migrants," defining themselves as exiles who await the opportunity to return and recover the island from the political order that compelled them to leave. Historically many did return, but most shared Varela's fate, spending the rest of their days without ever seeing their island again. This was true of José Martí and his generation, living in Tampa, Key West, and New York while fighting for Cuban independence, and of the numerous exile migrations that occurred prior to the Cuban Revolution in 1959, as well as to the early waves of the post-1959 exiles, many of whom, like my father, will pass their remaining days in the United States. A legacy of frustrated exile has punctuated the Cuban presence in the United States from the very beginning.

Because exile serves as such a powerful unifying experience for a people, the tendency has been to categorize all Cubans living in exile as sharing the same political identity and political culture. Because the exile agenda is one of return (as opposed to the immigrant agenda of resettlement), it is often assumed that all exiles, in this case all Cubans living in exile, share the same views about how this return can be achieved. During the wars of independence, the nationalist discourse emanating from the exile communities was one of unity, proclaiming all Cubans' desire for independence and return. The sometimes colorful (as in yellow) press coverage of the community also painted the Cubans as monolithic in their desire for independence (and the United States stoically ambivalent to the idea of empire building). After the alleged "independence," and during the years of direct domination by the United States, the small exile communities that took turns settling on U.S. soil similarly proclaimed that they spoke for the Cuban people when they expressed the desire to impose regime change on the government du jour on the island.

Reality, of course, was not so neat. During the Wars of Independence, the exile communities were sharply divided as to the course of action best suited to the situation. There were Nationalist/Independentista tendencies, as well those simply wishing reforms but a continuation of Spanish colonial relations, and even those who openly lobbied for the Annexation of Cuba to the United States. Similarly, during the twentieth century, Cubans in exile have lobbied for U.S. intervention against their "enemies" and even for statehood with the same zeal as they often railed against the neocolonial policies of the United States. All this as a way of pointing out that within the long history of exile communities in the United States, there have always been Cubans, and Cubans, and Cubans.

And so it is for the current crop of exiles. The current community of Cuban "exiles," as is the custom to categorize all Cubans arriving in the United States since the triumph of the 1959 Revolution, have attracted more than their share of attention from both the press and the scholarly community because of this assumed monolithic element. While the social-science and popular literature on this community represents a respectable bibliography, the attention has not been evenly distributed across all dimensions of community dynamics and development. By far, most of the literature concentrates on the economic development of the enclave and its impact on the *Latinization* of the region. Explorations of many of the political dimensions of the community have largely escaped detailed analysis.

This is ironic, for political forces are at the core of the very origins of the contemporary Cuban American presence in the United States. Furthermore, the press and the public have consistently focused much more on that third characteristic, in direct contrast to the situation in the scholarly literature. Whatever image most Americans have of Cuban Americans is probably constituted, more than anything else, by political features such as staunch anti-Castroism, militancy, terrorism, political conservatism, and a predominant affiliation with the Republican Party. The anti-Castro characteristic of the community might well be considered to be its master status, establishing the limits and potentials for all group activity.

Yet, is this monolithic political profile of an entire community accurate? There are various attributes of the community that, upon reflection, caution us against making that assessment. First, when we speak of the Cuban American community, we are speaking of a group that has had almost a continuous flow into the south Florida region since 1959. This flow can be categorized into distinct waves, with different pull and push factors. Waves that have found different receptions and acceptance in the region and that have had different modes of departure from the island. There is no reason to assume that members of all waves would harbor identical opinions. Moreover, a growing number of the members of the Cuban American community in south Florida were not born in Cuba. If we refer to the Cubans immigrating to Miami as being composed of waves, the increasing numbers of U.S.-born Cubans are the rising tide of the Cuban community.

Despite this identifiable diversity, the political characteristics of the community are considered to be uniform and dominated by an "exile ideology" established by the first wave of post-revolution migrants. The assumption is that the exile experience shaped the collective identity of those fleeing Castro's revolution, no matter when or how they came, and continues to shape the political identity of Cuban Americans, particularly when dealing with Cuba and U.S.–Cuba policy.

This chapter explores the issue of diversity within the Cuban American population of Miami-Dade County by analyzing the attitudes of different cohorts of Cuban migrants on selected policies. We utilize data from the 2000 Cuba Poll, a telephone survey of 1,175 Cuban Americans in Miami-Dade County conducted by two of the authors in the spring of 2000.[1] While the poll is broad and measures behavioral and attitudinal responses dealing with issues beyond our current concerns, it allows us to focus on a few variables that directly address some of the key elements of the "exile ideology" and its acceptance by the various waves of Cuban migrants. Following Pérez's description of the characteristics of the "exile ideology" (1992), we are particularly concerned with variables that measure (1) the primacy of Cuba for Cuban Americans, (2) a commitment to an uncompromising struggle against the Cuban government, and (3) a similar commitment to the Republican Party. We will measure these dependent variables using the waves and generational characteristics of the respondents as the dependent variables in order to present an exploratory profile of the diversity of the Cuban American community within the heart of the exile community.

CUBAN AMERICANS' DEMOGRAPHIC AND SOCIOECONOMIC PROFILE

Cubans make up the third largest Latino group in the United States, behind Mexicans and Puerto Ricans. As Figure 4.1 shows, the Cuban population increased from 1.05 million to 1.24 million over the last decade. The 19 percent increase in population is below the average Latino population increase of 60 percent during the previous decade. The share of the total Latino population occupied by Cubans decreased from 4.8 percent to 3.5 percent between 1990 and 2000. Cuban Americans are most heavily populated in Miami (Grenier and Stepick, 1992; Pérez, 1992). Approximately 60 percent of the Cuban population resides in Miami-Dade County and Broward County in Florida, and in Hudson County in New Jersey.

Despite their hyper concentration in Miami-Dade County and their alleged obsession with the fate of Cuba, Cuban Americans have become incorporated into the so-called mainstream society quite well. Few immigrant groups have been incorporated so quickly while simultaneously forging a uniquely

Figure 4.1

2000 Cuban Population Concentration by County (1.24 Million)

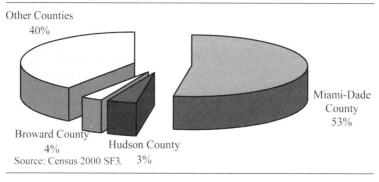

Other Counties
40%

Broward County
4%

Hudson County
3%

Miami-Dade County
53%

Source: Census 2000 SF3.

Table 4.1
Cuban American Profile: 2000

Ethnicity	Foreign Born	College Degree or Higher	Below Poverty	Median Household Income
Cuban	68.5%	21.2%	14.6%	$42,642
Hispanic or Latino	40.2%	10.4%	22.6%	$34,397
Non-Hispanic White	3.5%	27.0%	8.1%	$54,698
Total Population	11.1%	24.4%	12.4%	$50,046

bicultural identity (García, 1996; Pérez, 1992). As Table 4.1 indicates, Cuban immigrants manifest higher levels of income and education than the aggregate of other Latino groups while exhibiting lower poverty levels (Pérez, 1992). Even though they are a community of predominantly first generation foreign-born immigrants (68.5%), their percentage of college graduates and percentage below the poverty line almost equals those of the total population in the United States. The Cubans' experience provides a fascinating case study in American immigration and ethnic history, not only because of the federal government's response to their arrival, or the role they have played in U.S. foreign policy, but because of their adjustment to life in the United States.

WAVE COHORTS AMONG CUBAN IMMIGRANTS

Before the 1959 Cuban Revolution, the United States maintained pervasive economic and political control over Cuba's governance (Poyo, 1989). Many of those who immigrated to the United States before the Revolution were laborers attracted to New York by the factories and service industries of the region (Pérez, 1992). The migration flows initiated after the revolutionary transition of 1959 had a decidedly political, rather than economic, character. Yet, the migration to the United States after 1959 is composed of distinct waves. Each wave has a particular historical motivation for leaving the island and is received in a different socioeconomic and political context than the other waves. Some waves are intense and receive considerable national attention, as were Mariel and the 1994 "balsero crisis," while others are barely ripples. As Figure 4.2[2] reveals, the Cubans who arrived after 1959 came during six distinct periods (Grenier and Perez, 2003).

The first wave of approximately 250,000 Cubans arrived from 1959 to 1964. As with most revolutions, the first people to be affected, and thus the first to leave Cuba, were those in the middle and upper classes (Eckstein and Barberia, 2002; García, 1996; Grenier and Stepick, 1992; Pérez, 1990). The

Figure 4.2
Cuban Migration by Wave of Arrival

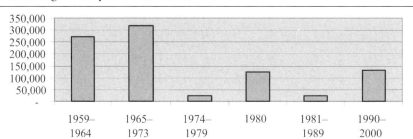

second wave of about 300,000 Cubans arrived during the "freedom flights" from 1965 to 1973. Table 4.2 shows that more technical workers arrived in the 1965 to 1973 cohort group than with the earlier group. The first two cohorts laid the foundation for the creation of a viable Cuban economic enclave in southern Florida. The economic enclave founded by middle-class Cubans in these two cohorts accommodated all subsequent arrivals from Cuba and served as a magnet for immigrants from all over Latin America (García, 1996).

The third cohort consists of those who came to the United States between the periods of 1974–1979, when the migration between the United States and Cuba was diminished. The third wave is also highly educated and includes more professionals than post-1980 cohorts.

The seven-year period of reduced migration came abruptly to an end during the Mariel Crisis of 1980. After Peru refused to turn over Cubans who had killed a guard in the process of crashing through the gates of the Peruvian Embassy, the Cuban government withdrew the remaining guards and thousands of Cubans rushed into the Embassy seeking asylum. Subsequently, Cuban officials opened the port of Mariel to allow all Cubans who wanted to leave the island to do so in an orderly fashion. While the exodus proceeded rather chaotically, 124,776 Cubans did leave from the port of Mariel, and most of them ultimately settled in the South Florida region (Grenier and Stepick, 1992; Nackerud, Springer, Larrison, and Isaac, 1999; Pedraza, 1996; Pérez, 1990; Poyo, 1989). Unlike the earlier cohorts, these 1980 Cubans lived most of their adult lives in Cuba's new revolutionary society. This has prompted some analysts to conclude that this migration included more individuals "pushed" by economic necessity rather than by political motives (Eckstein, 2002). Although felons comprised less than three percent of the Mariel Cubans, this cohort received a hostile reception in the United States (García, 1996; Pedraza, 1985; Portes and Stepick, 1996). Yet, in spite of the odds against them, they demonstrated patterns of adaptation similar to those of the Cubans who had arrived earlier (García, 1996).

Table 4.2
Socio-Economic Profile by Wave Cohorts among Cuban Americans

Wave of Arrival	Mean age	1.5 Gener-ation*	College graduates and more	House-hold income below 20,000	House-hold income 50,000 and more	Profess-ionals	Skilled manual workers
Before 1959	67	29%	31%	30%	33%	31%	3%
1959–1964	60	34%	38%	28%	44%	39%	7%
1965–1973	62	20%	21%	36%	22%	26%	10%
1974–1979	55	21%	39%	8%	17%	30%	6%
1980	54	8%	21%	43%	23%	22%	14%
1981–1989	52	12%	27%	44%	17%	25%	22%
1990–2000	41	2%	29%	49%	1%	25%	20%
U.S. Born	32	NA	51%	1%	65%	59%	8%

*1.5 Generation refer to those who came to the United States aged 1–14.

Throughout the years of 1981–1989, the migration between the United States and Cuba was severely diminished. The few Cuban Americans who came to the United States during this period of time constitute the fifth wave cohort.

The sixth cohort consists of those who came to the United States throughout the years of 1990–2000. After the fall of the Soviet Bloc in 1989, Cuba's importance to U.S. interests was reduced. However, in 1994, a large influx of migrants from Cuba facilitated the historic policy change that officially ended the preferential open door for Cuban immigrants (Nackerud, et al., 1999) and introduced the current "wet-foot/dry-foot" policy (immigrants found at sea are returned to the island while those who make it to land are granted asylum) as well as established the minimum number of visas to be granted to Cubans on the island at 20,000 (Nackerud, et al., 1999). The sixth cohort is different from previous Cuban immigrants in that they left their homeland with tacit approval from the Castro government (García, 1996). Black and mixed-race Cubans are more represented in this cohort as are many who considered themselves revolutionaries for many years until the opportunity to emigrate presented itself. Consequently, the cultural diversity within the Cuban community is now more extensive than ever (García, 1996).

COHORT DIFFERENCES IN ANTI-CASTRO HARD-LINE POLITICAL IDEOLOGY AMONG CUBAN IMMIGRANTS

Table 4.3 presents the variables from the Cuba Poll that we are analyzing in this chapter along with the frequency percentages from the entire sample.

Table 4.3
Percentage Comparison for Measures for Exile Ideology

Measures for Exile Ideology	Cuban: Miami-Dade County
Position of candidate toward Cuba very or somewhat important	77%
Strongly oppose to selling medicine to Cuba	27%
Strongly oppose to selling food to Cuba	35%
Strongly oppose national dialogue among Cuban exiles, dissidents, and representatives of the Cuban government	37%
Strongly approve U.S. ban on business with Cuba	37%
Should not allowed unrestricted travel to Cuba	47%
Against ending embargo	63%

Source: 2000 Cuban Poll.

Except for the first variable measuring the salience of Cuba in considering a political candidate for office, what can be interpreted as the hard line position is presented as a percentage of the entire sample. Only on the issue of the embargo does the hard line opinion dominate. In all other variables, which constitute the policy elements of the embargo, the percentage of Cuban Americans who "strongly oppose" a more conciliatory position constitute the minority of the population.

But how do these sentiments distribute themselves across the different migration cohorts, and what do they say about the Cuban American adherence to an exile ideology? The remaining portion of this section categorizes the appropriate variables into the three elements of the exile ideology that we are exploring: (1) the primacy of Cuba for Cuban Americans, (2) a commitment to the Republican Party, and (3) a commitment to an uncompromising struggle against the Cuban government.

The Primacy of the Homeland

In the exile ideology, the affairs of the homeland represent the community's foremost priority. The public discourse is largely preoccupied with the political status of the homeland. A key element of any exile consciousness is the fact that the members of the community were forced out of their country; emigration was not a choice, as with so many other immigrants, but a survival strategy allowing them to live and fight another day. Emigration is part of an enduring conflict. During the past 40 years there has been a protracted continuation of the intense conflict that occurred since about 1960 and 1962, when the Cuban regime was entrenching itself against the serious attempts by the U.S. government and various sectors of Cuban society to overthrow it. For many

Cubans who lost that conflict and went into exile, the struggle has not ended, and they have tried, with amazing success, to keep the conflict alive.

The desire to recover the homeland shapes the behavior of the exiles in the host country. It is the focus of political discourse and the source of mobilization in the Cuban American community. The U.S. policy toward Cuba and the internal situation in the island continue to predominate. In contrast, a certain apathy characterizes the attitude toward more domestic issues, such as the adoption of English as the official language of Florida.

The importance of Cuba for the Cuban American community is often ridiculed, because Cuba is often seen as central to issues that seem far removed from foreign policy matters, at least to the general public. For example, Miami-Dade County was the only county in the country with an ordinance preventing county funds from being used in any business activity involving Cuban nationals. In most situations, this prohibition was redundant given the federal trade sanctions currently in place, but the ordinance had a direct impact on local cultural organizations working within the legal limits of the federal trade sanctions. Organizations promoting cultural exchanges, musical or in the plastic arts, faced the prospect of having their county funds suspended or at least publicly scrutinized if Cuban artists were involved in local activities. Although the ordinance was judged unconstitutional in 2000, support for it did not go away. When asked in the FIU Cuba Poll 2000 if they supported the principles of the revoked ordinance, 49 percent of Cuban Americans in Miami-Dade said that they did, as compared to 25 percent of non-Cubans.

This obsession with Cuba spills over into the political process in another way. Many Cuban Americans use the Cuba issue as a litmus test for evaluating candidates for local office. "If you want to run for dog catcher," said a Cuban American patron at a sidewalk coffee stand, "you'd better take a hard line position toward Cuba or you'll never get elected." While it may not be that extreme, it is true that Miami politics dances to a Cuban beat. As Table 4.3 demonstrates, Cuban Americans still consider a candidate's position toward Cuba to be of primary importance: 77 percent said that a candidate's position on Cuba was important in determining their vote. Figure 4.3 shows that approximately 61 percent considered a candidate's position on Cuba as *very* important when casting their vote. The 1965–1973 cohorts exhibit the highest percentage among wave cohorts.

Support for the Republican Party

The primacy of the homeland explains the overwhelming preference for the Republican Party, a trait that sets Cubans apart from other Latino groups. Unlike most other Latinos, a majority of Cubans have traditionally voted Republican— due largely to the GOP's perceived strong stance against Fidel Castro (Barreto, de la Garza, Lee, Ryu, and Pachon, 2002; Pérez, 1992). Indeed, their initial attraction to the Republican Party was motivated by their desire to influence policy toward the island, particularly during the presidency of Ronald Reagan (de la Garza and Desipio, 1994). Their high voter registration and voting rates are signaled as examples of Cuban Americans' unique political culture (Highton and Burris, 2002; Hugo, 2003). Their party preference stands in contrast with other Latino voters who have been traditionally Democrat. Cuban American voters in Miami have helped turn Florida into a bastion of Republicanism. In Florida, they often play a crucial role in determining election outcomes.

Registered Republicans far outnumbered registered Democrats among Cubans in Miami in the year 2000, to the tune of approximately 67 percent Republicans and 17 percent Democrats. In the mind of a typical Cuban American, loyalty to the Republican Party demonstrates the importance of international issues in the political agenda of Cubans. If a substantial number in the Cuban community disagreed with elements of the exile ideology, or if there was a greater balance in that agenda, with importance given to purely domestic issues, the Democratic Party would have made greater inroads.

In fact, if Cuban Americans were to view themselves as immigrants in this country, rather than as political exiles, and made judgments about political parties based upon their needs and aspirations as immigrants in the United States, they would be Democrats in overwhelming numbers. This would be true not only because of the general social agenda of the Democrats but also because of the specific experience of Cuban migration. The measures that have greatly facilitated Cuban immigration and the adjustment of Cuban Americans in the United States have all been enacted by Democratic administrations: the Cuban Refugee Emergency Program and its resettlement efforts, the assistance given to the Cuban elderly and the dependent, the establishment of the Airlift or Freedom Flights, and permission for the Mariel boatlift to take place, among others. The fact that Cubans are overwhelmingly Republican is therefore a testimony to the importance of homeland issues and the perception that Republicans are more in tune with the anti-Castro agenda.

As Figure 4.3 shows, 69 percent of Cuban immigrants registered as Republicans, but there exist significant differences among wave cohorts. Cohorts from 1959–1964 and 1974–1979 are most likely to support the Republican Party, whereas the pre-revolutionary cohorts and 1990–2000 cohorts are least likely to support the Republican Party. The commitment to the Republican Party by the earlier cohorts can have a significant impact on elections. Their turnout in presidential elections can be as high as 90 percent, while only between 50 and 60 percent of recent younger cohorts vote (Roman, 1996).

Uncompromising Attitude against Cuban Government

The embargo constitutes the most important uncompromising attitude against the Cuban government. The U.S. government has maintained an embargo policy since 1959, despite mounting pressure in Congress to loosen it. In the view of hard liners, the embargo has been the most important instrument for driving Cuba toward reform. But others suggest that the embargo

Figure 4.3
Importance of Candidates Position on Cuba and Support for the Republican Party by Wave Cohorts

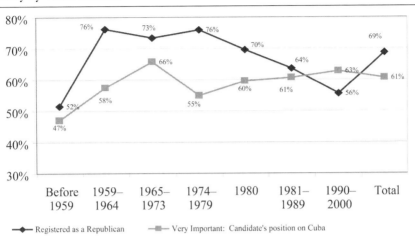

contributes to keeping the country poor, thus hurting the people Cuban Americans are trying to help. This moderate perspective also encourages the initiation of a national dialogue among Cuban Americans and the Cuban government as well as the selling of medicine and food to the island. Some hard-liner Cubans oppose the sale of medicine and food to Cuba, as well as starting a national dialogue, primarily because such assistance and recognition would serve only to sustain the Castro regime.

Table 4.4 suggests that not all Cuban Americans are in agreement about how to deal with the island. Of all respondents, 64.4 percent favor continuing the U.S. embargo of Cuba, emphasizing that there exists strong anti-Castro attitude among Cuban Americans. However, there are significant differences among the cohorts in the support for some of the restrictions imposed by the embargo. For example, 76.7 percent of 1965–1973 cohorts favor continuing the U.S. embargo policy, compared to 40.7 percent of 1990–2000 cohorts. Yet, only 35.6 percent of all respondents oppose the selling of medicine, and 46.4 percent oppose the selling of food to Cuba. In addition, the community is split right down the middle on the issue of initiating a national dialogue between Cuban exiles and the Cuban government.

Again cohort differences are very significant in all three policy measures against Cuba. As expected, those arriving in the earlier waves hold the most intransigent views while the most recent arrivals reveal a more conciliatory perspective. The 1980 and 1981–1989 cohorts fall in-between. It is evident that the time of arrival to the United States is an important variable in understanding the disagreements about how to deal with Cuba among Cuban Americans.

Table 4.4
Uncompromising Attitude Against Cuba by Wave Cohorts

Wave of Arrival	Favor Continuing the U.S. Embargo of Cuba	Oppose Selling Medicine to Cuba	Oppose Selling Food to Cuba	Oppose National Dialogue Among Cuban Exiles and the Cuban Government	N
Before 1959	62.5%	34.3%	44.2%	42.0%	35
1959–1964	71.3%	41.9%	55.7%	57.1%	172
1965–1973	76.7%	47.0%	62.5%	61.0%	211
1974–1979	62.1%	41.9%	51.7%	62.5%	31
1980	67.1%	36.5%	43.3%	53.0%	85
1981–1989	63.3%	37.3%	44.1%	45.4%	59
1990–2000	40.7%	14.9%	22.9%	33.3%	127
U.S.-Born	57.1%	24.8%	31.1%	32.0%	109
Total	64.4%	35.6%	46.4%	49.5%	829

Source: 2000 Cuban Polls.

Prohibiting U.S. travel for pleasure to Cuba is another one of the restrictions imposed by the embargo. In 2003, the Republican-led House and Senate voted to end the travel ban, but later dropped the measure after Bush threatened a veto (*USA Today*, February 10, 2004). Figure 4.4 shows that half of the respondents oppose unrestricted travel to Cuba and, as expected, there are differences among the wave cohorts: 62 percent, 59 percent, and 56 percent of each of the first three wave cohorts oppose unrestricted travel to Cuba while 46 percent of 1980 cohorts, 43 percent of the 1981–1989 cohorts, and only 23 percent of the 1990–2000 cohorts oppose this policy. Like other hardline measures, far fewer of the more recent émigrés opposed unregulated visitation rights. This difference exemplifies significant cohort effect.

Over the last decade, Cuban American travel to Cuba reached its highest level. Travel increased from approximately 7,000 to over 140,000, with an estimated minimum of 100,000 immigrants visiting annually between 1996 and 1999 (Eckstein and Barberia, 2002). The U.S.–Cuba Trade and Economic Council estimates 156,000 U.S. travelers made authorized trips to Cuba in 2003 while as many as 25,000 Americans traveled illegally to Cuba via a third country (*USA Today*, February 10, 2004). However, Figure 4.4 reveals that the actual percentage of those who have traveled to meet their family is still relatively low, with the highest proportion of visitors (54%) coming from the pre-revolutionary cohort. More of the other pre-1980 waves arrivals have visited Cuba than later immigrants. This lower rate of return is influenced by the Cuban government's extremely restrictive entry policy for those leaving the country in 1980 and 1994. These restrictions applied to the 1980 cohort until the end of the 80s and for

Figure 4.4
Travel to Cuba by Wave Cohorts

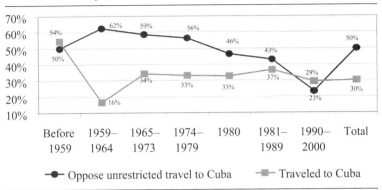

those leaving in the raft exodus of 1994 until 1999 (Eckstein and Barberia, 2002). Interestingly enough, only 16 percent of the 1959–1964 hard-line cohort members made visits to Cuba since they left their homeland, while over 30 percent of each of the other cohorts traveled to Cuba.

GENERATIONAL DIFFERENCES IN ANTI-CASTRO HARD-LINE POLITICAL IDEOLOGY AMONG CUBAN IMMIGRANTS

In addition to time of departure from the island, age of arrival and nativity are important generational variables influencing political culture in the Cuban community. A growing number of the members of the Cuban American community were not born in Cuba. According to the 2000 census SF4, the U.S.-born Cuban Americans make up 31.5 percent of the Cuban population in the United States. They can be expected to have a distinct political ideology from their first generation parents. In addition, it is important to distinguish the "1.5 generation" from the U.S.-born and the first generation. Previous research has failed to distinguish the situation of immigrants who came to the United States as children (the "1.5 generation") versus those who came as adults (the first generation). Rumbaut (1994) found that their pre- and post-immigration experiences and adjustment to U.S. culture differed from both their first generation parents and U.S.-born individuals. 2000 Cuban polls enable us to investigate how Cuban American political ideology is affected by the age at which they came to the United States.

Primacy of Homeland and Support for the Republican Party

As Figure 4.5 shows, U.S-born Cubans are less likely to evaluate a candidate's policy on Cuban issues as very important and are less likely to support

Figure 4.5
Importance of Candidate's Position on Cuba and Support for the Republican Party by Generation

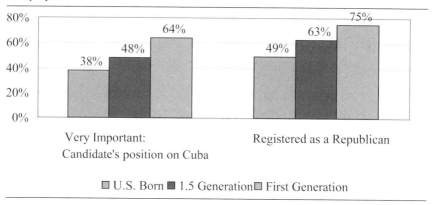

Very Important: Registered as a Republican
Candidate's position on Cuba

☐ U.S. Born ■ 1.5 Generation☐ First Generation

the Republican Party than the first generation and the 1.5 generation. In addition, 1.5 generation Cubans are less likely to evaluate a candidate's policy on Cuban issues as very important and are less likely to support the Republican Party than the first generation. Figure 4.6 demonstrates that the margin is significantly large. While further analysis is necessary to flesh out the reasons for the generational differences, the poll does show that U.S.-born Cuban Americans are more likely to get their news about Cuba from English-language newspapers, as opposed to Spanish-language radio or print media. As a result they are much less exposed to many of the opinions and public discourses that shape the political behavior of older Cubans.

Uncompromising Attitude against Cuban Government

Figure 4.6 presents the generational variation of anti-Castro uncompromising attitude among Cuban Americans. As expected, the first generation Cuban Americans are more likely to favor continuing the embargo, to oppose the selling of medicine and food to Cuba, and to oppose the establishment of a national dialogue than 1.5 generation and U.S.-born Cuban Americans. The 1.5 generation exhibits stronger measures of an uncompromising attitude than U.S.-born counterparts.

Figure 4.7 reveals the generational differences in opposing unrestricted travel to Cuba. First generation Cuban immigrants are more likely to oppose unrestricted travel to Cuba than 1.5 generation and U.S.-born Cuban Americans. In addition, 1.5 generation is more likely to oppose unrestricted travel than U.S.-born counterparts. Figure 4.7 also shows that more first generation Cubans, who are more likely to oppose unrestricted travel to Cuba, actually have visited

Figure 4.6
Generational Differences in Uncompromising Attitude against Cuba

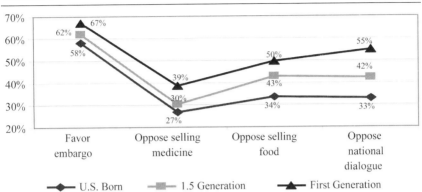

Figure 4.7
Travel to Cuba by Generation

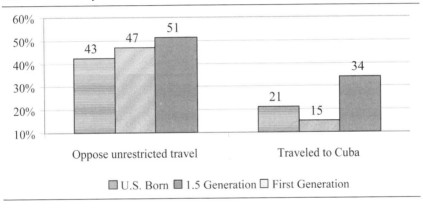

Cuba, compared to the U.S.-born and 1.5 generation. However, interestingly enough, the U.S.-born Cuban Americans were more likely to travel to Cuba than the 1.5 generation counterparts.

DISCUSSION AND CONCLUSION

Departures from the traditional exile ideology began to manifest themselves at the end of the Cold War. With the fall of the Berlin Wall, Cuban exiles who had long struggled to overthrow an entrenched socialist regime now had in Eastern Europe an operational model of how such a thing might be accomplished. Rather than an overnight "rupture" scenario traditionally envisioned by the exiles, the new model involved an evolution that might be led by elements from within the system, a process that could be helped by openness rather than hostility and isolation. Consequently, some Cuban Americans, including some traditional hard liners, began to espouse a strategy of promoting a relaxation of tensions with Havana and engaging elements within Cuba. The rise of this new orientation led in the 1990s to the establishment of several organizations that, in different ways, conceptualized anti-Castro activism in more moderate terms, espousing an elimination of hostility and emphasizing constructive relations with the Cuban government. These new organizations have been committed to a peaceful transition to democracy that would not be based on confrontation and hostility.

These developments served to broaden the ideological spectrum of Cuban exile politics, creating new voices that argued against a continuation of the current U.S. policy. Although these new elements have thus far failed to gain predominance within the community, they have served to challenge what had been a monolithic image of exile politics, providing support for initiatives that challenge the traditional course of U.S.-Cuba relations.

In addition to the rise of moderate political voices and organizations, perhaps an even greater challenge to the continuation of a policy of isolation toward Cuba has developed within the exile community. Cuban Americans whose only motivation is to visit and help family and friends on the island represent a major point of contact between the two countries. Remittances and family visits provide Cuba with more foreign exchange than its tourism industry and fuel the development of a more moderate voice within the Miami community.

The 1994 and 1995 migration accords between the United States and Cuba raised the ceiling for Cuban migration to the United States. Since then, some 20,000 Cubans have come to the United States each year in an authorized fashion, in addition to the smaller number who arrive through unauthorized means. This new influx, added to those who came during and after Mariel, serves to increase the number of Cubans in the United States with an interest in sending remittances and returning to visit relatives. Unlike the earlier migration wave that departed at the height of the Cold War and have sought to keep the anti-Castro struggle alive, newer arrivals are likely to place priority on communicating with their families still in Cuba. The earlier exiles are much less likely to have maintained family ties in the island.

The FIU Cuba Poll has consistently shown that the most recent arrivals to the United States tend to have the most moderate views on how to deal with the island. For example, a majority (54%) of those arriving after 1984 favor lifting the embargo. Among those arriving in the 1960s and 1970s, less than a third favor lifting it.

In addition to the new arrivals, two other important sectors of the Cuban population of the United States tend to add diversity to the political culture: the new generations and those living outside of Miami. The FIU poll shows that members of the second generation born in the United States are much more conciliatory in their views toward island politics than their parents. The same is true of Cubans who do not live within the insularity of the Miami enclave and are therefore less likely to have maintained an exile ideology.

According to the 1995 poll, Cubans living in New Jersey are more likely to favor a dialogue with the Castro regime than those living in Miami. Similarly, New Jersey Cubans are less likely to be influenced by a candidate's position on Cuba as they cast their vote in local and national elections. As the process of concentration in South Florida continues, the arrival in Miami of Cubans who have lived elsewhere in the United States adds yet another source of pluralism to the political landscape.

Yet, despite the obvious attitudinal diversity of the Cuban American population regarding Cuba policy, or perhaps because of this diversity, the persistence of certain hard-line attitudes still require examination. The continued support for the embargo, for example, seems to be impervious to pragmatic policy considerations. It seems that support for the embargo underscores yet another trait of the political culture of Cubans in the United States: the importance of emotion over pragmatism. While admitting that the embargo may be ineffective, and, further, even recognizing that lifting it may well bring about significant changes in Cuba, a majority in the Cuban community continue to oppose any such softening of U.S. policy because of its symbolism. If the United States abandons its hard-line stance against Cuba, the argument goes, Fidel Castro will have won the 40-year struggle. It is therefore a struggle that is based not so much on pragmatism as it is on emotion.

Energizing the emotionalism of the community is the highly personalized nature of the anti-Castro struggle. The enduring presence in Cuba of the historical leader of its socialist revolution is a key factor in maintaining distance and hostility between Cuban exiles and the government in Cuba. For most Cubans in the United States, the culprit responsible for their exile is not a political movement, not a revolution, not a government, but a person. Fidel Castro represents a continuation of a long-standing Cuban tradition in which authority has a primarily personal, not institutional, base.

The least favorable side of emotionalism and irrationality is a traditional intolerance to views that do not conform to the predominant exile ideology of an uncompromising hostility toward the Castro regime. Those inside or outside the community who voice views that are soft or conciliatory with respect to Castro, or who take a less-than-militant stance in opposition to Cuba's regime, are usually subjected to criticism and scorn, their position belittled, and their motives questioned. Liberals, the "liberal press," most Democrats, pacifists, leftists, academics, intellectuals, dialoguers, and socialists are favorite targets. Any dissent within the community is especially difficult, because great pressure can be brought to bear on the individual or group. Moreover, intolerance of opposing views has frequently been a source of friction between Cubans and other groups and institutions in Miami. The exiles' inflexible anti-Castroism has frequently been criticized—and even ridiculed—by non-Cubans in Miami, especially when it manifests itself as attempts to censor cultural events in Miami by artists or intellectuals from Cuba (Grenier and Perez, 2003).

Ultimately, the Cuban American story in the United States is a paradoxical one. On the one hand, Cuban Americans are held up as examples of the immigrant success story. As immigrants, the Cuban American story is one of achievement and victories. It is the story of an immigrant group that has made unprecedented gains in empowering themselves in the new country. The well-documented economic success, as well as equally impressive achievements through the ballot box, has resulted in the creation of a solid ethnic enclave in a region that is often considered to be the harbinger of the multiethnic American future.

Yet, the Cuban American identity is not an immigrant one, but one of exiles. As exiles, Cuban Americans often behave in ways that the rest of the country finds unreasonable and even irrational. The exile story is one of the relentless and enduring pursuit of the exile goal of recovering the homeland by triumphing over the regime, or more accurately, the person, who is responsible for their exile. It is a story of frustration, misunderstandings, and resentment.

The contrast of the two stories is ironic. The core of the identity of Cubans in the United States is as exiles, not immigrants. If the goal of exiles is to recover the homeland, and the job of immigrants is to successfully adjust economically and empower themselves in the new country, then we can reach the conclusion first formulated by our colleague Max Castro: Cubans in the United States have been a failure at what they say they are, and a success at what they say they are not.

NOTES

1. 2000 Cuban Poll was conducted by Guillermo Grenier and Hugh Gladwin at Florida International University with a sample of 1,175 Miami-Dade County residents of Cuban descent, which was generated from a telephone survey using standard random-digit-dialing procedures that ensured that each residential phone had an equal chance of being chosen for the sample (http://www.fiu.edu/orgs/ipor/cuba2000).

2. The numbers of Cuban migrants during each wave were recalculated from Table 1 in Nackerud, et al. The number of Cuban immigrants from 1998 to 2000 was counted as 20,000 per year, assuming that the immigration pact between the United States and Cuba in 1994, which agreed to allow 20,000 Cubans per year to emigrate to the U.S. legally, continued to be in effect.

REFERENCES

Barreto, Matt, R. O. de la Garza, J. Lee, J. Ryu, and H. P. Pachon. 2002. "A Glimpse Into Latino Policy and Voting Preferences." Los Angeles: The Tomas Rivera Policy Institute. University of Southern California.

Cue, Lourdes. 2001. "Election 2000 the Latino Factor." *Hispanic* 14: 1.

de la Garza, Rodolfo, and Luis Desipio. 1994. "Overview: The Link between Individuals and Electoral Institutions in Five Latino Neighborhoods." In *Barrio Ballots: Latino Politics in the 1990 Elections.* Edited by Rodolfo de la Garza, Martha Menchaca, and Luis Desipio. Boulder: West View Press.

Eckstein, Susan, and Lorena Barberia. 2002. "Grounding Immigrant Generations in History: Cuban Americans and Their Transnational Ties." *International Migration Review* 36: 799–837.

García, María Cristina. 1996. *Havana USA: Cuban Exiles and Cuban-Americans in South Florida, 1959–1994.* Berkeley: University of California Press.

Grenier, Guillermo J., and Sung Chun. 2003. "Measuring Cuban Exile Ideology: Key Findings from 2000 Cuban Polls." Presentation. Department of Sociology, University of New Mexico, April.

Grenier, Guillermo J., and Lisandro Perez. 2003. *The Legacy of Exile: Cubans in the United States.* Boston: Allyn and Bacon.

Grenier, Guillermo J., and Alex Stepick III. 1992. "Introduction." In *Miami Now!: Immigration, Ethnicity, and Social Change.* Edited by Guillermo J. Grenier and Alex Stepick III, Gainesville: University Press of Florida.

Highton, Benjamin, and Arthur L. Burris. 2002. "New Perspectives on Latino Voter Turnout in the United States." *American Political Research:* 30: 3, 285–306.

Hugo, Mark. 2003. "Electoral Engagement among Latinos." *Latino Research@ND* 11:2. South Bend, Indiana: Institute for Latino Studies. University of Notre Dame.

Nackerud, Larry, A. Springer, C. Larrison, and A. Issac. 1999. "The End of Cuban Contradiction in U.S. Refugee Policy." *International Migration Review* 33: 176–192.

Pedraza-Bailey, Sylvia. 1985. *Political and Economic Migrants in America: Cubans and Mexicans.* Austin: University of Texas Press.

Pedraza-Bailey, Sylvia. 1996. "Cuba's Refugees: Manifold Migration." In *Origins and Destinies: Immigration, Race, Ethnicity in America.* Edited by Sylvia. Perdraza and Ruben Rumbaut. Albany, NY: Wadsworth.

Pérez, Lisandro. 1992. "Cuban Miami." In *Miami Now!: Immigration, Ethnicity, and Social Change.* Edited by Guillermo J. Grenier and Alex Stepick III. Gainesville: University Press of Florida.

Pérez, Louis A. 1990. *Cuba and The United States.* Georgia: University of Georgia Press.

Pérez-López, Jorge F. 1995. *Cuba's Second Economy: From Behind the Scenes to Center Stage.* New Brunswick, NJ: Transaction Publishers.

Portes, Alejandro, and Alex Stepick. 1996. *City on the Edge: The Transformation of Miami.* Berkley: University of California Press.

Poyo, Gerald. E. 1989. *With All and for the Good of All: The Emergence of Popular Nationalism in the Cuban Communities of the United States, 1848–1898.* Durham, NC: Duke University Press.

Roman, Ivan. 1996. "The Cuban Vote." *Hispanic* 9:8.

Rumbaut, Ruben G. 1994. "The Crucible Within: Ethnic Identity, Self-Esteem, and Segmented Assimilation among Children of Immigrants." *International Migration Review* 28: 748–794.

CHAPTER 5

Changes in the Characteristics of Puerto Rican Migrants to the United States

Edwin Meléndez

INTRODUCTION

The question of whether migration from Puerto Rico to the United States has contributed to increased socioeconomic disadvantage among Puerto Ricans in the United States continues to attract public and academic attention. The composition of immigrants can affect social outcomes directly through its effects on the average education, skills, language proficiency, and labor force participation of the population. These effects could be magnified and contribute to persistent poverty if migrants concentrate in areas where other low-income Puerto Ricans and other Latinos or disadvantaged populations already reside. Also, socioeconomic disadvantaged among Puerto Rican communities in the United States could rise if those who return to Puerto Rico tend to be better educated, more skilled, or have greater labor force participation than those who stay in the United States. If such tendencies were to persist for a prolonged period of time, the composition of migratory flows could be a contributing factor to higher poverty rates for Puerto Ricans in the United States.

The study of the composition of Puerto Rican migration is important for various reasons. To begin with, migration from Puerto Rico to the United States, and return migration, constitutes a special case of a clearly Latino population from a low income country migrating to a higher income country with no legal barriers to their movement, and with very low transportation costs between the two destinations (fairly comparable to the costs of interstate moving). Second, Puerto Rican migration precedes that of other Latin American countries, perhaps with the notable exception of Mexico, and offers a valuable case study for understanding the dynamics of labor market incorporation and assimilation among immigrants, particularly those of Hispanic heritage. Finally, there is a wealth of studies and data documenting the origins, evolution, and current conditions of Puerto Rican migratory flows when compared to other migrants from Latin America and the Caribbean. A deep understanding of a case study such as Puerto Rican migration is above all important when the flows and characteristics of migrants—particularly those flows with a large number of undocumented migrants—might not be captured by formal surveys and other sources of data. In sum, Puerto Rican migration to the United States serves as a well-documented case study (or "natural experiment") that informs the question of "what would happen over time in terms of the volume and composition of migrants if the legal and transportation barriers affecting immigration from other Latin American countries to the United States were completely eliminated (i.e., with citizenship status and substantially reduced transportation and relocation costs)?"

Migration continues to be an important and influential experience in everyday life for the Puerto Rican community in the United States and those in Puerto Rico. While Puerto Ricans in the United States represented about one-third of the total Puerto Rican population residing in both countries in 1970, by the year 2000 the Census of Population estimated that close to half (47%) of the total 7.2 million Puerto Ricans (by birth or parentage) resided in the United States. Projections are that the Puerto Rican origin population in the United States will surpass in numbers those residing on the island by the end of decade. More than any other factor, continued migration from the island to the continent is responsible for the aforementioned population trends, trends that clearly continued over the last decade.

According to the Puerto Rico Planning Board (PRPB) data, 466,948 Puerto Ricans 16 years of age or over left the island between 1991 and 2000, and 134,587 returned during the same period (Table 5.1).

Average annual out-migration from Puerto Rico to the United States increased by 8,450 in the 1990s in comparison to the 1982 to 1988 period,

Table 5.1
Net Migration (16 Years and Over)

Period	Emigrants	Immigrants	Net Migration	Annual Average
1982–1988	–285,787	134,587	–151,200	–21,600
1991–2000	–466,948	166,447	–300,501	–30,050
Change				–8,450

Source: Author's estimates based on unpublished data from the Programa de Planificación Económica y Social, Subprograma de Estadísticas, Encuesta Sobre Información del Viajero, Puerto Rico Planning Board.

from 21,600 to 30,050. In general, fluctuations in net migration from Puerto Rico to the United States continue to be largely determined by the business cycle and relative economic conditions in the two regions. One simple measure of the relative strength of one economy in relation to the other is the differential in the unemployment rate. As depicted in Figure 5.1, trends in net migration are clearly influenced by trends in unemployment differentials.

However, there are other factors influencing the higher average on net migration between the two periods, not all of them conforming to conventional explanations. For instance, the average unemployment rate for the 1990s as a whole of 14 percent was substantially lower than the 20 percent for the 1982–88 period. In fact, among those leaving Puerto Rico (emigrants hereafter) the average unemployment rate was lower during the 1990s than it was in the 1980s. Similarly, general population growth might not be a good explanation for the observed increase in net outflows of migrants to the United States. Throughout the postwar period, the rate of growth of the Puerto Rican population, whether only those in Puerto Rico or in conjunction to those in the United States are considered, has steadily declined, yet net migration increased in the 1990s when compared to the 1980s. Though other social and cultural factors might be at play, the demographic composition and the labor market standing of migrants may offer some clues as to some of the factors influencing the increase in net outflows of migrants from the island.

In terms of the patterns observed in the changes of the characteristics of migrants, the data and analysis that follows show that recent emigrants tend to

Figure 5.1
Net Migration and the Unemployment Differential between Puerto Rico and the United States

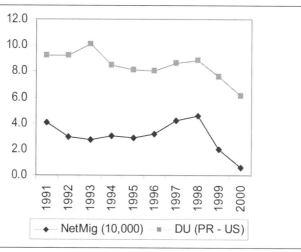

Source: Author's estimates based on unpublished data from the Programa de Planificación Económica y Social, Subprograma de Estadísticas, Encuesta Sobre Información del Viajero, Puerto Rico Planning Board and from Departamento del Trabajo y Recursos Humanos de Puerto Rico, Negociado de Estadísticas del Trabajo, Encuesta de Vivienda.

be older, have less education, and greater employment. These characteristics are associated with longer and more permanent stays in the receiving regions. Older workers with more experience and attachment to the labor force make fewer mistakes (i.e., shorter stays and more frequent trips) in their decision to migrate than younger workers with greater occupational mobility and less attachment to the labor force. Among those leaving the island, return migrants to Puerto Rico are also older in comparison to similar cohorts in previous decades, and they are also more educated. These characteristics are also consistent with a slower rate of return migration from the United States to Puerto Rico. However, age and education affect the rate of return migration but not necessarily the composition of the flows. Regarding the occupational composition, a general indicator of skills among migrants, I found that trends among migrants in the 1990s are similar to the general tendencies and characteristics evident during the 1980s. Changes in the occupational structure of immigrants are very modest with the exception of women in the services occupations and men and women in managerial and professional occupations.[1]

What are the implications of these changes in the characteristics of Puerto Rican migrants for the observed socioeconomic conditions of Puerto Ricans in the United States? Or more specifically, is the composition of migrants a potentially significant factor that can explain the higher poverty among Puerto Ricans in the United States? To begin with, migrants continue to represent a small fraction of the Puerto Rican labor force in both regions. During the last two decades, migratory flows do not have the magnitude that they did during the midst of the great migratory wave of the 1950s. A second argument to consider based on the findings of previous research as well as this study's findings is that the characteristics of the migrant population generally resemble those of the labor force as a whole, and that this pattern has continued in the 1990s. Certainly there are exceptions to these general patterns, as I will explain in more detail in the analysis that follows, but these exceptions are far from sufficient to explain major socioeconomic conditions, such as the poverty rate, among the general Puerto Rican population in the United States. If anything, they appear to represent minor disturbances induced by labor market conditions in both regions.

In the next section of the paper, I present a brief review of the literature on Puerto Rican migration and changes in the characteristics of migrants. Changes from one period to the next seem to be related to specific policies targeting migration and to long-term business-cycle dynamics, both of which will be briefly reviewed. After a short discussion on data and method, I present the main findings of the study and some general conclusions on the implications of these findings.

EVOLVING VIEWS ON THE COMPOSITION OF PUERTO RICAN MIGRANTS

The composition of Puerto Rican migrants has changed dramatically during the post-World War II years. These changes correspond to a large extent to broader political and economic dynamics, which in turn are reflected in four general historical periods of Puerto Rican migration (Falcón, 1990; History Task Force, 1979; Melendez, 1993). The first period corresponds to the great migration wave to the United States of the late 1940s through the early 1960s; the second period is characterized by the appearance of a significant return migration to Puerto Rico from the early 1960s to mid 1970s; the third period corresponds to the economic crisis and economic stagnation that lasted from the mid 1970s to the late 1980s; and, the final and most recent period of the 1990s is characterized by the unprecedented economic expansion of both countries. This last period is the focus of our analysis in this paper.

During the early postwar period, from the late 1940s to the early 1960s, industrialization increased greatly and agriculture declined rapidly. These economic changes prompted a movement of population from rural to urban areas and from the island to the continent. Numerous studies of out-migration during the early postwar period—using different types of data sources including special surveys and decennial censuses—found that there was a significant degree of positive selectivity.[2] These findings held true whether selectivity was measured by educational attainment, labor force attachment, or occupational composition (Friedlander, 1965; Hernandez-Alvarez, 1967; Maldonado, 1979; Mills, Senior and Goldsen, 1947; Reynolds and Gregory, 1965; Senior and Watkins, 1975, Sandis, 1970). Emigrants to the United States were disproportionately young, had higher educational levels, and were more skilled than the general population. No industrial grouping was overrepresented, although agriculture constituted the largest grouping. White-collar and other skilled occupations were overrepresented among emigrants, while less skilled occupations were under-represented. Although Puerto Ricans had a lower socioeconomic profile than the native general population in New York and other receiving areas, those leaving Puerto Rico in the early postwar period represented a more educated and skilled segment of the population.

The 1960s and early 1970s were years of transition for the Puerto Rican economy and migration patterns. In Puerto Rico, industrial production shifted from labor-intensive to more capital-intensive manufacturing, and service industries and government became the largest economic sector. Due to lower unemployment and higher wages in the postwar era, emigration slowed down during this period and return migration became very significant. This was, in short, a period of important new forces that impacted migratory patterns and in the logic of migration itself. During this period of transition, characteristics of migrants to and from the United States began to resemble the general characteristics of the population in Puerto Rico. Patterns in age, education, unemployment, and other characteristics of emigrants challenged the conventional wisdom that migrants constituted a selected, more educated and skilled portion of the island population—a conclusion that has been documented in numerous prior studies (Cintron-Vales,

1974; Cordero, 1989; Ortiz, 1986; Puerto Rico Planning Board, 1974; Tor-ruellas and Vazquez-Calzada, 1982; Vazquez-Calzada and Morales-Del Valle 1980; Zell, 1973).

Furthermore, based on a reinterpretation of the historical evidence, Frank Bonilla and his colleagues raised the hypothesis that Puerto Ricans functioned as an industrial labor reserve of the U.S. labor markets (Bonilla, 1983; Bonilla and Campos, 1986; History Task Force, 1979). In their view, Puerto Rico has been absorbed, or fully integrated, into the class structure of the United States. For the most part, Puerto Ricans were employed as low-wage workers in labor-intensive manufacturing and service industries. For all practical purposes, the island functions as a region of the United States. Because of the economic forces at play, industrial production in Puerto Rico and the Puerto Rico class structure in general became an extension, perhaps an appendix, of the U.S. economy. An important corollary of the industrial reserves thesis is that a portion of the population will move back and forth continuously to satisfy labor demand in *both* areas—a counter-argument to the neoclassical economic analysis that predicts mostly one-way flows from the low-wage region to the high-wage region. The circular migration thesis has occupied much attention among scholars researching Puerto Rican migration since Bonilla and his colleagues first introduced the concept (see for example Basu, 2002; Duany, 2002; Hernandez-Alvarez, 1967; Hernandez-Cruz, 1985; Kuenzy, 1998; Rodriguez, 1989).

The late 1970s and early 1980s was a period of general stagnation and economic crises for both the United States and the Puerto Rican economies (Meléndez, 1985, 1990). For the first time during the postwar era, return migration outpaced emigration for several consecutive years. Emigration continued to be sluggish during the 1970s, and it is not until the early 1980s that significant outflows are observed again (Falcón, 1990). During this period of economic crises, the island's economy turned decisively toward a post-industrial configuration were the service sector provided most of the employment and represented the fastest rates of growth. Because of these changes in the structure of employment, some researchers suggested that migration disproportionately affected those with higher education and skills, the occupational elite (Alameda and Ruiz-Oliveras, 1985; Gutierrez, 1983; Gutierrez and Mayerson-David, 1983). But other, more rigorous studies of the question found no evidence of a brain drain from Puerto Rico, although they found some evidence of an overrepresentation among technical occupations (Ortiz, 1986; Rivera-Batiz, 1987). Moreover, other researchers found evidence of negative selectivity (or a bias toward a lower socioeconomic status) among those returning to the island (Cordero, 1989; Enchautegui, 1989, 1990, 1991). Regardless of how the findings from these contending studies are weighted, the fact remains that there were fundamental changes in the composition of migratory flows in the postwar era compared to the patterns observed in previous decades.

In a monograph titled "Los que se van, los que regresan" ("Those who leave, those who return") published by the Center for Puerto Rican Studies (Meléndez, 1993), I examined 1982 to 1988 data from the ramp survey conducted annually by the Puerto Rican Planning Board. I concluded that there was no evidence to support the contention that migration flows constituted a selected portion of the Puerto Rican population during the periods under investigation. Those who left the island during the 1980s were active participants in the labor force, although their ranks represented much higher rates of unemployment at the time of departure than the general civilian population. Their occupational distribution was fairly similar to that of the general labor force population as a whole, except for an overrepresentation of male technicians. A similar pattern was evident among those returning from the United States to Puerto Rico during the 1980s. They were not predominantly less skilled than the sending population. In short, Puerto Rican migrants to and from the United States in the 1980s resembled the characteristics of the general population in the sending region.

The question of occupational selectivity has been formally studied and tested in a number of studies (Ortiz, 1986; Rivera-Batiz, 1987, 1989). Following these studies, I developed a model in which to use the PRPB data to test the hypothesis that Puerto Rican migrants to the United States have a lower occupational standing when compared to the general population in the sending region (Meléndez, 1994). In contrast to these previous studies, I was able to control for job offers, labor force status at the time of departure, wage differentials by occupations, and the occupational distribution in the receiving area. After controlling for these critical factors identified in the literature, the study found that the occupational composition among emigrants generally corresponded to the distribution of occupations in the home country's labor force. Exceptions to this general pattern were farm workers, laborers, and craft and kindred workers who were overrepresented in the flows. The two most important factors inducing overrepresentation in these occupations were whether the emigrants had received job offers prior to their departure and whether they had been employed at the time of departure. In other words, of the 16 general occupational categories used in the study, favorable employment conditions in the United States greatly influenced the observed selectivity of emigrants in three categories. No positive or negative occupational selectivity was found among immigrants. These findings confirmed those of previous studies that lacked some of the control variables available with the ramp survey.

The main implications of this body of research regarding the persistent disadvantage of Puerto Ricans in the United States when compared to the native U.S. population, is that there are likely to be factors other than migrants' skills and other labor market characteristics that cause socioeconomic inequality and disparities in assimilation. Put simply, the low earnings and high jobless rates that are reflected in above-average poverty rates among Puerto Ricans cannot be primarily attributed to the selective exodus of unskilled workers or the selective return of those with above-average skills. The objective of this study, as explained before, is to ascertain whether there have been significant changes in the characteristics of Puerto Rican migrants to the United States in the 1990s that may indicate that changes in the characteristics of migrants might have become an important factor affecting Puerto Rican poverty in the United States, more so than it has been in the past.

METHOD AND DATA

The data for this study is from the Survey of Travelers (or Encuesta Sobre Información del Viajero in Spanish) conducted by the PRPB. The main objective of the survey is to collect information about the volume and characteristics of travelers from Puerto Rico to the United States. The so called ramp survey is based on a sample drawn from all the commercial flights leaving or entering Puerto Rico from the Luis Muñoz Marín International Airport in San Juan, and more recently from the Rafael Hernández airport in Aguadilla. The period under investigation extends from 1982 to the 1988 and from 1991 to 2000. The data for the 1982 to 1988 period was previously published in an earlier study on the same topic (Meléndez, 1993). The Puerto Rico Planning Board assembled the 1991 to 2000 data and prepared the tabulations specifically for this study.

To date the ramp survey is the most reliable data (and perhaps the only source) in regard to the social and economic characteristics of the migrating population *at the time of departure from or arrival to the island.*[3] The decennial Census of Population, the main alternative source of data for the study of Puerto Rican migration, is generally acknowledged as the most reliable source of information about the social and economic characteristics of the population. However, the Census is not designed to address migrant populations and does not collect data on migrants other than when the person came to live in Puerto Rico.[4] Though imperfect, this approach allows researchers to describe the characteristics of the migrant population surveyed during the decennial census, at one point in time. In addition to an intrinsic bias to undercount migrants, the census is unable to provide specific information about the social characteristics of migrants at the time when migration occurred. The ramp survey, based on a random sample of travelers, provides data on migrants at the time or departure from or arrival to the island, and collects detailed information on labor market and demographic characteristics.

According to the operational definition used by the PRPB, an immigrant is a person 16 years or older who intends to stay in Puerto Rico for three months or longer. Those who are coming to the island to visit family or are returning after a business, leisure, or study trip are excluded from the sample. Conversely, an emigrant is a person who leaves the island intending to remain in the United States for more than three months, and whose purpose for traveling is not to visit family, to study, or for health reasons.[5] A final consideration regarding this sample is that the survey identifies and interviews persons 16 years and older. Most studies on Puerto Rican migration use data on departures and arrivals of passengers to estimate net movement of passengers as a proxy for net migratory flows. These figures are compiled by the Puerto Rico Port Authority and include gross data not adjusted for the purpose of the trip, the length of the stay, the age of the population, or destination and origin of the traveler. Of all the sources of possible differences between the figures reported in this study and the figures reported by the Port Authority, the exclusion of minors and foreigners is perhaps the most significant source of differences in reported figures. Taken as a whole, the PRPB's Survey of Travelers remains the best source of information about Puerto Rico migrants' characteristics. And because it is collected continuously, the survey allows for intertemporal comparisons of such characteristics on a consistent basis.

The basic approach of the study is to compare migratory flows, from Puerto Rico to the United States and from the United States to Puerto Rico, using average data for two decades: from 1982 to 1988 (the ramp survey is only available for these dates during that decade) and from 1991 to 2000. This comparison is intended to identify significant changes in the composition of migrants from the 1980s to the 1990s along some critical dimensions of labor market characteristics of the migrants. The tables assembled (Table 5.2, Table 5.3, Table 5.4, and Table 5.5) examine the 16 years old and over population along critical demographic and labor market characteristics: age and sex; immigrants by occupations and sex; and, labor force status by sex. Finally, I also examine years of school completed by sex for the population 25 years of age or older. In this context, age serves as a proxy for labor market experience, education and occupations are proxies for skills, and obviously labor force status indicates the proportion of workers that were employed prior to migration. The next sections examine the characteristics and composition of Puerto Rican emigrants and immigrants to and from the United States.

Table 5.2
Emigrants by Age and Sex (16 Years and Over)

	1982 to 1988		1991 to 2000		Change	
	Men	Women	Men	Women	Men	Women
Total	177,723	108,068	284,916	250,923		
16–24	45.3%	40.9%	30.8%	29.6%	−14.5%	−11.3%
25–34	29.7%	35.0%	30.3%	28.7%	0.6%	−6.3%
35–44	14.0%	13.9%	17.9%	17.8%	3.9%	3.9%
45–54	6.8%	5.0%	10.1%	10.6%	3.3%	5.6%
55–64	2.7%	3.5%	6.1%	7.3%	3.4%	3.8%
65+	1.3%	1.5%	4.7%	5.9%	3.4%	4.4%

Source: Author's estimates based on unpublished data from the Programa de Planificación Económica y Social, Subprograma de Estadísticas, Encuesta Sobre Información del Viajero, Puerto Rico Planning Board.

Table 5.3
Emigrants by Years of School Completed and Sex
(Persons 25 Years and Over)

	1982 to 1988		1991 to 2000		Change	
	Men	Women	Men	Women	Men	Women
Total	97,170	63,908	217,739	192,976		
6 or less	20.0%	15.1%	19.0%	18.5%	−1.0%	3.4%
7 to 11	39.2%	28.9%	33.5%	30.4%	−5.7%	1.5%
12	22.0%	28.1%	27.9%	27.6%	5.9%	−0.5%
13 to 15	9.7%	14.4%	9.4%	11.1%	−0.3%	−3.3%
16 or more	9.0%	12.4%	9.5%	11.8%	0.5%	−0.6%

Source: Author's estimates based on unpublished data from the Programa de Planificación Económica y Social, Subprograma de Estadísticas, Encuesta Sobre Información del Viajero, Puerto Rico Planning Board.

Table 5.4
Emigrants by Labor Force Status and Sex (16 Years and Over)

	1982 to 1988		1991 to 2000		Change	
Labor Force Status	Men	Women	Men	Women	Men	Women
Percent in Labor Force	81.4%	37.4%	82.0%	34.3%	0.6%	−3.1%
Percent Unemployed	41.0%	34.9%	23.4%	16.3%	−17.6%	−18.6%
Employment to Civilian Population	48.0%	24.3%	62.4%	28.4%	14.4%	4.1%

Source: Author's estimates based on unpublished data from the Programa de Planificación Económica y Social, Subprograma de Estadísticas, Encuesta Sobre Información del Viajero, Puerto Rico Planning Board.

EMIGRATION TO THE UNITED STATES

The most salient demographic characteristics of emigrants of both periods are that they tend to be young and disproportionately male. Of the 284,916 men and 250,923 women who left the island between 1991 and 2000, 61 percent of men and 60 percent of women were younger than 34 years of age (Table 5.2).

However, two major changes are apparent when comparing the 1991 to 2000 cohorts to the data from the previous decade. While men represented 62 percent of total emigration during the 1980s, the proportion of men declined to 53 percent during the 1990s. Equally important is the tendency of emigrants to be older in the 1990s compared to similar cohorts in the 1980s. While the proportion represented by the youngest cohort (16 to 24 years of age) declined by 14.5 percent for men and 11.3 percent for women between

Table 5.5
Emigrants by Occupations and Sex (16 Tears and Over)

Occupation	1982 to 1988		1991 to 2000		Change	
	Men	Women	Men	Women	Men	Women
Professionals	4.4%	15.9%	5.6%	15.0%	1.2%	−0.9%
Technical	4.3%	2.9%	5.7%	6.0%	1.4%	3.1%
Managers	1.6%	1.5%	7.4%	8.7%	5.8%	7.2%
Clerical	2.7%	19.6%	3.3%	26.6%	0.6%	7.0%
Sales	4.1%	3.7%	3.9%	6.0%	−0.2%	2.3%
Crafts	20.2%	2.1%	16.3%	1.6%	−3.9%	−0.5%
Operatives	13.6%	17.5%	11.1%	11.3%	−2.5%	−6.2%
Services	9.3%	13.3%	13.0%	18.8%	3.7%	5.5%
Laborers	8.7%	0.6%	13.9%	0.9%	5.2%	0.3%
Domestics	0.6%	4.9%	0.3%	1.4%	−0.3%	−3.5%
Farmers & Workers	17.4%	1.0%	13.6%	0.8%	−3.8%	−0.2%
Others	13.3%	17.5%	5.9%	3.1%	−7.4%	−14.4%

Source: Author's estimates based on unpublished data from the Programa de Planificación Económica y Social, Subprograma de Estadísticas, Encuesta Sobre Información del Viajero, Puerto Rico Planning Board.

the 1980s and 1990s, all the cohorts 35 years of age or older gained between 3.3 and 5.6 percentage points for both sexes. In short, for the first time during the postwar era, women represent close to half of the emigrants, and the age distribution of those who leave is less skewed toward the youngest.

To assess changes in the educational attainment of emigrants, Table 5.3 presents the years of school completed for emigrants 25 years and over for the 1982 to 1988 and the 1991 to 2000 periods.

The most significant finding is that the distributions of emigrants by educational attainment changed relatively little between the two periods. Men tended to be less educated in the 1980s for those with less than 12 years of schooling, while high school graduates had the greatest gains (of 5.9 percentage points) in the 1990s. In comparison to similar cohorts in the 1980s, women were slightly less educated across all high school and above cohorts. Overall, these patterns suggest a fairly similar distribution of educational attainment among emigrants, though men showed a slight increase in educational levels for the least educated, and women showed a slight increase in representation among the least educated.

Men and women who left the island as emigrants to the United States have very different profiles regarding labor force status. In comparison to the previous decade profile, men continued to have a high participation in the labor force

(82% in the 1991 to 2000 period), but they show a much lower unemployment rate and, therefore, a much higher employment-to-population ratio.

Unemployment for men declined from 41 to 23.4 percent, a 17.6 percentage point decline between the two periods, while the employment-to-population ratio increased by 14.4 percent, to 62.4 percent. Women showed similar tendencies, but the overall representation among those participating in the labor force declined by 3.1 percentage points, from 37.4 percent in the 1980s, to 34.3 percent in the 1990s. Consequently, the significant reduction of 18.6 percent in unemployment among emigrant women resulted in only a slight increase of 4.1 percentage points in the ratio of employment to civilian population, to 28.4 percent. As previously argued, the similarities in the general pattern of unemployment between men and women could be attributed to the relative strength of the two economies. However, the differences in labor force participation and employment to population ratios suggest that there are significant compositional differences between the two flows. In fact, women identified "housewife" as the reason for migration (i.e., indicating that the primary reason for traveling was to accompany their husband) in over 50 percent of the cases.[6]

The changes in occupational distribution data provide some clues as to other underlying labor market dynamics affecting emigrants' labor force participation. Table 5.5 depicts emigrants by occupations and sex.

Between the 1982 to 1988 and 1991 to 2000 periods, the largest gains in occupational representation for women were in managerial and clerical, with 7.2 and 7.0 percentage points change, respectively. These gains in occupational representation were followed by gains in services (5.5), sales (2.3), and technical (3.1), but there were significant losses in representation of operatives (−6.2) and domestics (−3.5). For men, the largest gains are observed among managers (5.8), laborers (5.2), and services (3.7), while the largest losses are observed among craft occupations (−3.9) and operatives (−2.5). The examination of the data suggests that the economic pull seems to be from a strong services economy in the United States relative to a more sluggish service sector in the island.

To recapitulate the key findings regarding the changes in the socioeconomic characteristics of Puerto Rican emigrants to the United States during the 1990s, emigrants are older and somewhat less educated, but they experience lower unemployment rates in the United States than emigrant cohorts in the 1980s. In addition to these general trends, men depicted a similar attachment to the labor force as in the previous decade, but women's labor force participation remained characteristically low during the 1990s. The proportion of managers among emigrants increased for both men and women but other than that, the changes in the occupational distribution of migrants' outflows were relatively small.

IMMIGRATION FROM THE UNITED STATES

The majority of Puerto Ricans returning to Puerto Rico during the 1990s are young. Sixty-two percent of men and 55 percent of women are 34 years of age or younger (Table 5.6).

Table 5.6
Immigrants by Age and Sex (16 Years and Over)

	1982 to 1988		1991 to 2000		Change	
	Men	Women	Men	Women	Men	Women
Total	85,982	48,605	97,249	68,916		
16–24	33.6%	31.3%	32.3%	29.5%	−1.3%	−1.8%
25–34	30.3%	34.2%	29.4%	25.5%	−0.9%	−8.7%
35–44	16.8%	17.1%	15.5%	17.6%	−1.3%	0.5%
45–54	9.0%	9.2%	9.5%	13.2%	0.5%	4.0%
55–64	6.2%	6.6%	6.8%	9.0%	0.6%	2.4%
65+	4.1%	1.5%	6.5%	5.3%	2.4%	3.8%

Source: Author's estimates based on unpublished data from the Programa de Planificación Económica y Social, Subprograma de Estadísticas, Encuesta Sobre Información del Viajero, Puerto Rico Planning Board.

However, the most salient characteristic of the 1991 to 2000 age cohorts is that immigrants are to some extent older when compared to the previous decade cohorts. The 16 to 24 years of age cohorts in the 1991 to 2000 period shows a 1.3 percentage point decline among men and a 1.8 percentage points decline among women when compared to the 1982 to 1988 cohorts. In the most recent period, women returning to Puerto Rico tended to be older than men. In particular, female immigrants in the 25 to 34 years of age category declined by 8.7 percentage points. The increase in the older cohorts was equally pronounced, increasing 10.7 percentage points overall for women 35 years of age and older. Among men, only the 65 years of age and older cohort increased a modest 2.4 percentage points.

Table 5.7 depicts significant gains in the educational attainment of immigrants over 25 years of age. The proportion of immigrants returning to Puerto Rico with less than high school completion declined significantly during the 1990s when compared to the 1980s. Men showed the most improvement in educational attainment among the least educated, with a decline of 18.1 percent in the high school drop out category, while women followed closely behind with a decline of 16.3 percent. The largest gain for men was in the post-college educational category, which increased by 15.1 percentage points, from 11.1 to 26.2 percent.

Overall, male immigrants gained 18.6 percentage points in the high school and above cohorts. Women gains were equally significant, with an increase of 17.7 percentage points overall in the high school and above cohorts. Thus, in relation to the outflows from the island, return migrants have been more educated while those leaving have been less educated. In part, these trends are reflective of the increasing levels of education of the Puerto Rican population

Table 5.7
Immigrants by Years of School Completed and Sex
(Persons 25 Years and Over)

	1982 to 1988		1991 to 2000		Change	
	Men	Women	Men	Women	Men	Women
Total	57,057	33,391	11,349	9,980		
11 or less	53.0%	43.8%	34.9%	27.5%	–18.1%	–16.3%
12	24.5%	29.5%	26.8%	29.0%	2.3%	–0.5%
13 to 15	10.9%	15.8%	12.1%	22.1%	1.2%	6.3%
16 or more	11.1%	10.0%	26.2%	21.4%	15.1%	11.4%

Source: Author's estimates based on unpublished data from the Programa de Planificación Económica y Social, Subprograma de Estadísticas, Encuesta Sobre Información del Viajero, Puerto Rico Planning Board.

in the United States, both in comparison to Puerto Ricans in the island in recent years and in comparison to previous decades. However, the staggering return of the most educated in the 1990s has heightened validity to the old argument about migration to the United States serving as a "training ground" for Puerto Ricans (Friedlander, 1965).

The observed pattern of labor force status for return migrants upon arrival is very similar to those leaving the island during the 1990s. In general, unemployment and labor force participation rates stay about the same for both men and women, but men employment to population ratio experienced a sharp decline. In reference to Table 5.8, the most notable change when considering the patterns observed for emigrants is that the employment to population ratio for men declined 8.4 percentage points, to 70.4 percent.

This drop in employment status among immigrants coincides with an increase in the "retirement" category. Otherwise, the unemployment rate for women also declined moderately by 1.3 percentage points, while the employment ratio stayed about the same (0.2). For men, differences in labor force participation (−2.8%) and unemployment (0.6%) represent relatively modest changes from last decade to more recent years. If any inference is possible from this data, it is that immigrants have maintained a high labor force attachment in the 1990s as they did in the 1980s. Although this may be true, the magnitudes of the changes are modest and may contribute relatively little to the overall changes in the characteristics of the population in the sending and receiving regions.

The differences in occupational employment for returning men and women migrants are apparent in Table 5.9.

For men, the largest changes in occupational flows between the 1982 to 1988 period and the 1991 to 1995 period were for managers (4.7 percentage points) and professionals (3.5), while the most significant declines were in crafts (−3.5 percentage points). For emigrant women, the largest gains in occupational

Table 5.8
Immigrants by Labor Force Status (16 Years and Over)

Labor Force Status	1982 to 1988		1991 to 2000		Change	
	Men	Women	Men	Women	Men	Women
% in Labor Force	84.9%	46.2%	82.1%	46.5%	−2.8%	0.3%
% Unemployed	7.2%	9.4%	7.8%	8.1%	0.6%	−1.3%
Employment to Civilian Population	78.8%	41.9%	70.4%	42.1%	−8.4%	0.2%

Source: Author's estimates based on unpublished data from the Programa de Planificación Económica y Social, Subprograma de Estadísticas, Encuesta Sobre Información del Viajero, Puerto Rico Planning Board.

Table 5.9
Immigrants by Occupations and Sex (16 Years and Over)

Occupation	1982 to 1988		1991 to 2000		Change	
	Men	Women	Men	Women	Men	Women
Professionals	5.2%	11.4%	8.7%	15.6%	3.5%	4.2%
Technical	5.3%	5.4%	6.4%	6.9%	1.1%	1.5%
Managers	2.7%	2.5%	7.4%	8.0%	4.7%	5.5%
Clerical	3.6%	19.5%	4.1%	21.1%	0.5%	1.6%
Sales	4.2%	2.8%	4.0%	3.0%	−0.2%	0.2%
Crafts	15.9%	1.8%	12.4%	1.3%	−3.5%	−0.5%
Operatives	19.2%	24.0%	20.4%	18.0%	1.2%	−6.0%
Services	10.7%	11.4%	10.1%	19.2%	−0.6%	7.8%
Laborers	5.5%	0.4%	6.7%	0.7%	1.2%	0.3%
Domestics	0.9%	5.8%	0.2%	3.4%	−0.7%	−2.4%
Farmers & Workers	14.7%	0.9%	15.6%	0.4%	0.9%	−0.5%
Others	1.2%	14.0%	4.0%	2.5%	2.8%	−11.5%

Source: Author's estimates based on unpublished data from the Programa de Planificación Económica y Social, Subprograma de Estadísticas, Encuesta Sobre Información del Viajero, Puerto Rico Planning Board.

representation were in the services (7.8 percentage points), managers (5.5), and professional (4.2) categories, while the most significant declines are observed in operatives (−2.5). Taken as a whole, gains in management and professional occupations for both men and women seem to reflect the growing proportion in these occupations among the population as a whole, otherwise the analysis shows modest changes in the occupational structure of returning migrants. As was the case with emigrants, the occupational distribution of immigrants largely resemble the level and changes of the occupational distribution of the Puerto Rican population in the island and the United States.[7]

The key findings of this section can be summarized as follows. Return migration to Puerto Rico during the 1990s resembles, to a large extent, the patterns observed during the previous decade. More recent immigrants are relatively older and have higher educational attainment than those in previous decades. These tendencies are likely the result of a shift among the general Puerto Rican population in the United States toward older cohorts and improvements in educational attainment. In regards to labor force status, immigrants in the 1990s have a similar profile when compared to similar cohorts of those returning to Puerto Rico in the 1980s. Changes in the occupational structure of immigrants are very modest with the exception of women in the services occupations, and men and women in managerial and professional occupations. In the next section, I draw some general implications from the analysis of the data.

CONCLUSIONS

Does Puerto Rican migration to and from the United States contribute to increasing poverty rates among Puerto Ricans in the United States? The data presented in this chapter cannot categorically disallow the theory that migratory flows may contribute to increased poverty and inequality among Puerto Ricans in the United States. This chapter represents only a very general analysis of the characteristics of the migrant population in two periods of time, during the 1980s and 1990s. A more detailed analysis of the available data will certainly provide more evidence on this question. Nevertheless, the data and analysis presented suggest that migration patterns respond to broader patterns of population changes and evolving labor markets both in Puerto Rico and the United States. And even in the few instances when these changes may operate to increase Puerto Rican poverty and socioeconomic inequality, the magnitude of the annual flows in relation to the population as a whole are very modest. Thus, the answer to the broader question of the impact of migration on Puerto Rican poverty and socioeconomic inequality seems to be that there are in all probability no significant effects from the composition of migratory flows.

Notwithstanding this general statement about the impact of migration on the socioeconomic characteristics of Puerto Ricans, there are some notable changes in the composition and characteristics of the migrants. Recent emigrants tend to be older, with less education, and with greater attachment to the labor force. Recent immigrants are also older, but they are significantly more educated. However, those who leave the island have higher unemployment rates and weaker labor force attachment when compared to those who return to the island. The occupational distribution of emigrants and immigrants seem to be fairly equal for both men and women. The largest occupational changes seem to be concentrated in the same occupations in both directions, some of which have higher wages and some have lower wages. If there is any impact at all, considering that the migration flows to the United States are much larger than return migration to Puerto Rico, occupational changes in managers and professionals might contribute to improve the average income of the population in the receiving region. These tendencies are in part related to a decline in the demand for low-skill workers in the areas where Puerto Ricans are concentrated in the United States and in Puerto Rico.

To recapitulate the argument of this chapter, the exceptions observed in the analysis of educational and labor force characteristics of migrants are not sufficient to explain broader socioeconomic dynamics of the Puerto Rican population in the United States. On the contrary, the composition and characteristics of migratory flows from Puerto Rico to the United States and return migration from the United States to Puerto Rico seem to be reflective of demographic and labor market conditions in both countries. The available data suggest that there is no discernable pattern of weaker workers in terms of labor market characteristics among those who leave, or of the best workers among those who return. This chapter is only a first approximation to the 1991 to 2000 data provided by the ramp survey of the Puerto Rican Planning Board. Some topics, such as the greater educational attainment among those returning to the island, deserve further scrutiny in future research.

NOTES

The author would like to thank Maggie Perez and Miriam Garcia from the Programa de Planificación Económica y Social, Subprograma de Estadísticas, Encuesta Sobre Información del Viajero, of the Puerto Rico Planning for producing the tabulations for the 1991 to 2000 period. Their assistance was invaluable for completing the study.

1. Meléndez (1994) previously demonstrated that these tendencies by occupational categories could be explained by labor market conditions in the sending and receiving regions.

2. Immigrants' selectivity is a topic that has received extensive attention in the literature, including the selectivity of Puerto Rican migrants to and from the United States, as we will discuss in this section of the chapter. For the purpose of this study, I define the positive selectivity of migrants as a process that results in migrants constituting a self-selected group of workers from the available pool in the sending region who are better prepared for labor market success in the receiving region when compared to those that stay in the sending region. In general, the literature suggests that migrants are positively selected, as measured by wage or income gains over time (Jasso, Rosenzweig, and Smith 2002), occupational or skills differentials (Chiswick, 1999; Lobo and Salvo, 1998), or educational attainment (Feliciano, 2005). However, the degree of such positive selectivity, or the possibility of negative selectivity among migrants, is related to the income distributions of the sending and receiving countries (Borjas, 1987, 1995), the transferability of immigrants' skills to the new labor market, and the cost of both migration and return migration (Chiswick, 1999), among other factors. Furthermore, the earnings gains over time after arrival might be different for

immigrants depending on their ethnic and national characteristics (Livingston, 2002; Lewis-Epstein, Semyonov, Kogan and Wanner, 2003). Recent studies have also found that ethnicity and race among various Latino groups affect the rate of spatial dispersion or assimilation (South, Crowder, and Chavez, 2005a, 2005b).

3. The PRPB uses two questionnaires to collect data, one for departures and one for arrivals. These questionnaires have changed several times throughout the years. The categories of the data presented in this study have been reorganized to facilitate the interpretation of the information and to make it consistent throughout all the years included in the study. The questionnaire used by the PRPB from 1983 to 1984 to 1986 to 1987 was used as a base questionnaire, because this questionnaire was used for the longer period of time. The data for the whole second period under examination (1991 to 2000) was compiled using a new questionnaire adopted in 1991.

4. Some researchers also in the past used a question about residency five years prior to the census to determine migrant status. See Godoy (2003) for an elaboration of this point.

5. In this study, I have selected Puerto Ricans by birth or parentage who are migrants and whose destination or origin is the United States. Migrants to and from other countries, as well as foreign-born persons, have been excluded from the population under study. In order to make the figures reported here as consistent as possible, missing values were treated in the most rigorous way. Cases with missing values for one of the variables included in the study were excluded from the population. For this reason, the figures reported in the tables represent a different population from those reported in previous reports by the PRPB.

6. Data is not shown on the table but available from the author upon requests.

7. See Meléndez 1993 and 1994 for a more detailed analysis of past tendencies in the occupational structure of migrants when compared to the working population as a whole.

REFERENCES

Alameda, Jose I. and Wilfredo Ruiz-Oliveras (1985). "La fuga del capital humano en la economia de Puerto Rico: reto para la actual decada." *Revista de Ciencias Sociales*, 24 (1–2).

Basu, Kisalaya (2002). "Sequential and Circular Migration of Labor: Theory, Decision Rules and Evidence." SUNY Albany, PhD Dissertation.

Bonilla, Frank (1983). "Manos que Sobran: Work, Migration, and the Puerto Rican in the 1980's." In National Puerto Rican Coalition, *Recent Trends in Puerto Rican Migration.* Washington, D.C.: National Puerto Rican Coalition.

Bonilla, Frank and Ricardo Campos (1986). "Evolving Patterns of Puerto Rican Migration." *Industry and Idleness.* New York: Centro de Estudios Puertorriquenos.

Borjas, George (1987). "Self-Selection and the Earning of Immigrants." *American Economic Review*, 77 (4): 13–26.

Borjas, George (1995). Assimilation and Changes in Cohort Quality Revisited: What Happened to Immigrant Earnings in the 1980s? *Journal of Labor Economics*, 13 (2): 201–45.

Chiswick, Barry R. (1999). "Immigration Policy and Immigrant Quality: Are Immigrants Favorably Self-Selected?" *The American Economic Review*, 89 (2): 181–185.

Cintron, Celia and Pedro Vales (1974). *Social Dynamics of Return Migration to Puerto Rico.* Rio Piedras: Centro de Investigaciones Sociales, Universidad de Puerto Rico.

Cordero-Guzman, Hector R. (1989). "The Socio-Demographic Characteristics of Return Migrants to Puerto Rico and Their participation in the Labor Market: 1965–1980." Unpublished M.A. Thesis, The University of Chicago.

Duany, Jorge (2002). "Mobile Livelihoods: The Sociocultural Practices of Circular Migrants between PR and the US." *International Migration Review*, 36 (2), Summer.

Ellis, Mark (1996). "The Circular Migration of Puerto Rican Women: Towards a Gendered Explanation." Bloomington: Indiana University Population Institute for Research and Training, Working Paper No. 98–5.

Enchautegui, Maria E. (1989). "Experience Accumulated Abroad and the Assimilation Patterns of Puerto Rican Return Migrants." Mimeo. Population Studies Center, University of Michigan.

Enchautegui, Maria E. (1990) "The Value of U.S. Labor Market Experience in the Home Country: The Case of Puerto Rican Return Migrants." Mimeo. Population Studies Center, University of Michigan.

Enchautegui, Maria E. (1991) "Subsequent Moves and the Dynamics of the Migration Decision: The Case of Return Migration to Puerto Rico." Mimeo. Population Studies Center, University of Michigan.

Falcón, Luis M. (1990). *Migration and Development: The Case of Puerto Rico.* Washington, D.C.: Commission for the Study of International Migration and Cooperative Economic Development.

Feliciano, Cynthia (2005). "Educational Selectivity in U.S. Immigration: How Do Immigrants Compare to Those Left Behind?" *Demography*, 42 (1): 131–152.

Friedlander, Stanley L. (1965). *Labor Migration and Economic Growth: A Case Study of Puerto Rico.* Cambridge: MIT Press.

Godoy, Ricardo (2003). "Puerto Rican Migration: An Assessment of Quantitative Studies." *Centro Journal*, 15 (2): 207–231.

Gutierrez, E. (1983). "The Transfer Economy of Puerto Rico: Toward an Urban Ghetto?" In J. Heine, Editor, *Time for a Decision: The United States and Puerto Rico.* London: North-South Publishing Co.

Gutierrez, E. and Lucia Mayerson-David. (1983). "Migration and Strategic Considerations for Policy: Social Stratification and the Education Sector." In National Puerto Rican Coalition (Editors), *Recent Trends in Puerto Rican Migration.* Washington, D.C.: National Puerto Rican Coalition.

Hernandez-Alvarez, Jose (1967). *Return Migration to Puerto Rico.* Berkley: Institute for International Studies.

Hernandez-Cruz, Juan E. (1985). "Migración de retorno o circulación de obreros borícuas?" *Revista de Ciencias Sociales*, 27: 81–110.

History Task Force (1979). *Labor Migration under Capitalism: The Puerto Rican Experience.* New York: Monthly Review Press.

Jasso, Guillermina, Mark Rosenzweig, and James P. Smith (2002). "The Earnings of US Immigrants: World Skill Prices, Skill Transferability, and Selectivity." Mimeo. New Immigrant Survey, Princeton University.

Kuenzi, Jeffrey John (1998). "Self-Selection and Migrants' Destination Choice: A Study of Puerto Ricans in the United States and Puerto Rico." University of Massachusetts, Ph.D. Dissertation.

Lewin-Epstein, Noah, Moshe Semyonov, Irena Kogan, Richard A Wanner (2003). "Institutional Structure and Immigrant Integration: A Comparative Study of Immigrants' Labor Market Attainment in Canada and Israel." *The International Migration Review*, 37 (2): 389–420.

Livingston, Gretchen and Joan R. Kahn (2002). "An American Dream Unfulfilled: The Limited Mobility of Mexican Americans." *Social Science Quarterly*, 83 (4): 1003–1012.

Lobo, Arun Peter and Joseph J Salvo (1998). "Changing U.S. Immigration Law and the Occupational Selectivity of Asian Immigrants." *The International Migration Review*, 32 (3): 737–760.

Maldonado, Edwin (1979). "Contract Labor and The Origins of Puerto Rican Communities in the U.S." *International Migration Review*, 13 (1): 103–121.

Meléndez, Edwin (1985). "Accumulation and Crisis in the Postwar Puerto Rican Economy." Unpublished Ph.D. Dissertation, University of Massachusetts.

Meléndez, Edwin (1990). "Accumulation and Crisis in the Open Economy: The Postwar Social Structure of Accumulation in Puerto Rico," *Review of Radical Political Economies*, 22 (2–3): 231–251.

Meléndez, Edwin (1993). *Los Que Se Van, Los Que Regresan New York:* Center for Puerto Rican Studies.

Meléndez, Edwin (1994). "Puerto Rican Migration and Occupational Selectivity, 1982–88." *International Migration Review*, 28 (1): 49–67.

Mills, C. Wright, Clarence Senior, and Rose Goldsen (1947). *Puerto Rican Journey*. New York: Columbia University Press.

Ortiz, Vilma (1986). "Changes in the Characteristics of Puerto Rican Migrants from 1955 to 1980." *International Migration Review*, 20 (3): 612–628.

Puerto Rico Planning Board (1974). *La Migracion Puertorriquena: Sus Tendencias, Caracteristicas, e Implicaciones en la Politica Publica*. San Juan: Puerto Rico Planning Board.

Reynolds, Lloyd G. and Peter Gregory (1965). *Wages, Productivity, and Industrialization in Puerto Rico*. Illinois: Richard D. Irwin.

Rivera-Batiz, Francisco L. (1987). "Is There a Brain Drain of Puerto Ricans to the United States?" *Puerto Rico Business Review*, 12 (June–July): 6–7.

Rivera-Batiz, Francisco L. (1989). "The Characteristics of Recent Puerto Rican Migrants." *Migration World*, 17 (2): 6–13.

Rodriguez, Clara (1989). "Puerto Ricans and the Circular Migration Thesis." *Journal of Hispanic Policy*, 3: 5–9.

Sandis, Eva (1970). "Characteristics of Puerto Rican Migrants to and from the United States." *International Migration Review*, 4 (11): 22–43.

Senior, Clarence and Donald O. Watkins (1975). "Toward a Balance Sheet of Puerto Rican Migration." In Francesco Cordasco (Editor), *Status of Puerto Rico*. New York: Arno Press.

South, Scott J., Kyle Crowder, and Erick Chavez (2005a). "Geographic Mobility and Spatial Assimilation among U.S. Latino Immigrants." *The International Migration Review*, 39 (3): 577–608.

South, Scott J., Kyle Crowder, and Erick Chavez (2005b). "Migration and Spatial Assimilation among U.S. Latinos: Classical Versus Segmented Trajectories." *Demography*, 42 (3): 497–523.

Torruellas, Luz M. and Jose L. Vazquez-Calzada (1982). *Los puertorriquenos que regresaron: analisis de su participacion laboral*. Rio Piedras: Centro de Investigaciones Sociales, Universidad de Puerto Rico.

Vazquez-Calzada, Jose-L. and Zoraida Morales Del Valle (1980). "Probacion de ascendencia puertorriquena nacida en el exterior." *Revista de Ciencias Sociales*, 22 (1–2): 3–27.

Zell, Steven (1973). *Comparative Study of the Labor Market Characteristics of Return Migrants and Non-Migrants in Puerto Rico*. San Juan: Puerto Rico Planning Board.

PART II

The Changing Social, Educational, and Legal Issues Affecting Latinos

Latino College Students' Adjustment: The Influence of Familism, Acculturation, and Social Supports

Regina Jean-Van Hell

This study investigates the cultural value of familism, one of the more significant characteristic of Latinos, and how this value relates to the adjustment to college of Latino undergraduate students in Northeastern universities. The intent is to understand how familism, perception of social support, and level of acculturation affect a student's adjustment and advancement in higher education. The study is also timely and important in light of the increasing numbers of Latino youth attending postsecondary education and the possible passage of the bipartisan Development, Relief, and Education for Alien Minors Act, S. 1545, known as the "Dream Act," which would allow immigrant students who have grown up in the United States to apply for legal status and pursue studies in higher education paying in state tuition fees.

The number of Latinos attending post-secondary education in the twenty-first century has increased dramatically. Statistics from *The Chronicle Almanac* indicate that from the Fall 1991 to Fall 2001 the population of Latinos attending post-secondary education increased by 99.46 percent. From that population (1,560,600) 92 percent attended undergraduate institutions, 6.40 percent attended graduate education, and 0.9 percent pursued professional degrees.[1] About half of the Latinos attending post-secondary education in 2001 were enrolled in two-year public institutions. Thus, Latinos are more likely to attend community colleges than four-year colleges and less selective institutions. This disparity in college outcomes reflects differences in high school preparation as well as their low socioeconomic status. This has been compounded by the fact that federal financial assistance available to Latino college students is in the form of loans, rather than as grants, and the additional cost increases in public college tuitions.[2] These students are also more likely to live at home, attend college part-time, and work full time jobs to support themselves and their families.[3] Statistics show that Latinos are less likely to complete an undergraduate degree even when Latinos have reached their third year of college, as was found by the Inter-University Program for Latino Research, which is a national consortium of 18 Latino-focused research centers.[4] Other data has indicated that "Latinos receive 6 percent of all bachelor's degrees."[5]

Census data (U.S. Census Bureau, 2004) for Latinos over 25 years old indicate the following percentages of educational attainment: (1) 43 percent do not have a high school diploma, (2) 27.4 percent graduated from high school, (3) 13 percent had some college but no degree, (4) 5.2 percent completed an associate's degree, (5) 8.3 percent have a bachelor's degree, and (6) 3.1 percent have advanced degrees. This census data indicate that about 11 percent of the current Latino population has an education with a bachelor's degree and above. As a result, it is obvious that although the attendance of Latinos in post-secondary education has doubled in the last 10 years, the percentages of Latinos obtaining a bachelor's and advanced degrees are very low. This is a matter of great concern, because the predictions for the year 2020 indicate that about 50 percent of the labor force in this country will be accounted for by Latinos.[6]

Other research has indicated that Latino's are "at risk" for academic failure because of their limited English proficiency and their attendance in urban public schools, which are inadequate, have low expectations, inferior instruction, and experience institutional and social racism.[7] In addition, Latino students bring cultural values, attitudes, and beliefs that affect their educational experiences in both sustaining, and also viewed as limiting, their education.[8]

Cultural factors have been viewed as presenting obstacles to and demands on students who want to focus on education on the one hand, and on the other, as providing much of the resilience needed to succeed.[9] The cultural value of familism is shared by many Latinos. Familism involves an individual's strong identification with and attachment to his or her nuclear and extended families, with strong feelings of loyalty, reciprocity, and solidarity among members of the family.[10] Familism has been viewed as positive and negative by researchers studying social support and students' adaptations in education. The positive aspect of familism is the extended family system, which has been found to contribute to psychological well being by providing social support.[11] Conversely, the negative aspect of familism espoused by Parsons and Goode, as mentioned by Valenzula and Dornbusch, derived from the explanation view that Latino culture is culturally deficient and is a source of women's oppression. Under this explanation socioeconomic success is gained by the willingness of young adults to move away from the extended family in order to pursue occupational and educational opportunities.[12] In this study, the value of familism will be viewed as a source of social support and how this value relates to adjustment to college for Latino students.

Research on Latino college students and social support has shown that "the support of family was clearly a key factor for this population of students," and many other studies have confirmed that family support and social support facilitate college adjustment.[13] Although, in a recent study investigating social support from family and friends in Latino college students the results indicated that support from the family was less important than the support of peers while attending college.[14] Ethnic and racial minorities experience an added stressor when attending a white-oriented college or university, because the culture of the institution is different from their own.[15] In many cases, ethnic and racial minorities attending predominately white universities feel isolated, alienated, and unsupported, placing them at a greater risk of academic failure and loss of retention.[16] Thus availability of social support is important for college adjustment as well as integration with campus life for these students. Finally, acculturation studies on Latino college students found consistently that those students who are acculturated to the Anglo culture experienced lower levels of stress, and were therefore better able to adjust to college.[17]

The present study will investigate how the value of familism affects college adjustment. The research methods are quantitative and correlational, examining patterns of relationships among the variables of familism, social support, acculturation, and college adjustment.

LITERATURE REVIEW

Social Support

One way social support has been researched is on how this construct is tied to a specific situation or to coping with a particular stressful event.[18] This perspective has found that social support contributes to buffering stress and benefits personal adjustment. Social support affects adjustment in two ways. In one way, the *buffering model* posits that as stress increases, social support systems are activated and buffer (or protect) the individual from the possible debilitating effects of stress.[19] Thus, individuals who are exposed to stressful circumstances and who perceive social support as available will adjust better than will those individuals who do not perceive support to be available. The second model or perspective explains that individuals who perceive social support to be available will have better adjustment levels than will individuals who do not perceive social support to be available.[20]

Research on social support and its cultural context has discussed that culture defines, directs, and gives meaning to life. Thus, culture influences people's values, beliefs, attitudes, expectations, and behaviors, therefore providing a contextual grounding for social support to be given and received.[21] The cultural context of the individual provides the basis to allow for the expression of certain needs and the provision of social support. In the case of Latino college students, familism is an important cultural value, creating a context that will influence expectations and behaviors of family support. Consequently, Latino college students will be more likely to expect family support in many areas of their life.

As discussed previously, Latino value of familism stresses support from the family.[22] Thus, when Latino college students leave the family to complete their education in a college or university, they expect that they will receive support from their families when they encounter stressors in college. Research on Latino college students and social support by Hurtado indicated that "the support of family was clearly a key factor for this population of students,"[23] although Latino college students obtain 40 percent of social support from peers and 28.3 percent from parental social support while in college. An investigation on Latino college students and social support from Solberg et al.[24] showed that social support minimized stress and that the quality of family relationships was important in facilitating college adjustment. Nevertheless, it is important to keep in mind, social support networks of Latino college students may change while attending post-secondary education due to the kind of stressors encountered, as noted by Rodrigues et al., who found that successful students shared similar support networks regardless of race/ethnicity or sex.[25]

Research on Latino College Students

Research on Latino college students began by focusing on the access to higher education, the preparation needed for students attending academic settings, and the institutional barriers confronting these students. Research from 1970 to 1990 on Latino college students and their adjustment to higher education was reviewed by Quintana et al.[26] This meta-analytic study found that Latino college students experience higher stress levels of academic and financial stressors compared with Anglo students. Comparisons between Latino and African American students on social isolation showed African American students experience higher levels of social isolation as a result of discrimination, alienation, and interracial and intercultural interactions. Studies on gender differences among Latino college students showed that Latino college females experienced higher levels of stress when compared to males. Finally, Quintana's study that looked at the relationship between acculturation and adjustment to college consistently found that Latino college students who are more acculturated to the Anglo culture experienced lower levels of stress.

A literature review from 1991 to 1998 on Latino college students identified 16 studies. The studies pertinent to this investigation were two qualitative studies, three studies that investigated gender differences in Latino college students, one on acculturation, another study on racial and gender discrimination and academic discouragement, and three on social support that were mentioned previously. Arnold's qualitative study found that pressures and stressors of Latino female college students were due to family obligations and to responsibilities because of a strong sense of familism.[27] The second study of Arellano and Padilla found that both male and female Latino college students attending one selective university were strongly supported by their families.[28]

The quantitative studies that studied social support in Latino college students were the three mentioned in the previous section on social support.[29] Of the other five studies, two reconfirm previous research on acculturation indicating that Latino college students who are acculturated to the Anglo culture adjust better to their university.[30] The other three studies investigated gender differences in Latino College students. Young found Latina college students experienced higher economic stress and higher familial obligations, which interfered with their academic aspirations.[31] Similarly, López found Mexican American females, compared to males, experience greater challenges in finances, family obligations, and domestic obligations. In addition, López found that Mexican American males, who are upper class men, experience difficulties with domestic responsibilities, such as taking care of the family and finances.[32] Finally, De Leon found in four Latino ethnic groups of males and females that Latinas have a strong sense of familism.[33]

Research on First-Generation College Students

Research on first-generation college students has been limited. The Terenzini et al. review of the literature on first-generation college students focused on three areas. One area was first-generations students' pre-college expectations, planning, and the college choice process. This research found differences between first-generation and traditional students with respect to their basic knowledge of college, personal commitment, and level of family support, with first-generation students being at a disadvantage.[34] Other studies looked at attitudes of these students both before and while in college.

The second set of studies on first-generation students examined the transition between high school to college or out to work. These studies relied on personal accounts and experiences of first-generation students and their families and found that these students face the same anxieties, dislocations, and difficulties of any college student, but with the added stressors brought about by different cultural, social, and academic transitions.

The third area of research focused on the effects of their college experience on persistence when compared with traditional students. The findings in this category of studies showed that first-generation students are less likely to persist, and therefore, less likely to attain a degree than are traditional college students because of a lower level of academic and social integration.[35]

In sum, research on Latino college students indicates that social support, support from the family, and acculturation to the Anglo culture are important for the adjustment of Latino college students. Other findings indicate Latina college students experience high stress due to finances, family obligations, and domestic obligations as well as their strong sense of familism. Similarly, Latino males also seem to experience financial and family responsibilities. Research on first-generation college students has shown that these students have difficulties finding support from the family, have problems understanding the culture of the college or university, and have lower levels of commitment and persistence to attain a degree. Most important, the research on first-generation college students indicates that these students have added stressors due to the different cultural, social, and academic transitions. Consequently, Latino students who are first-generation college students are at higher risk of not adjusting to college and dropping out of college because of lower support from the family, lack of knowledge of the culture of universities, family and financial obligations, academic disadvantages, and cultural differences.

Measurement Instruments

The rational for using the measures in this study can be found in Jean-Van Hell.[36] The following measures were used. One, the College Adjustment Scale (CAS) developed by Anton and Reed, is used to assess nine areas of difficulties such as anxiety, depression, suicidal ideation, substance abuse, self-esteem problems, interpersonal problems, family problems, and career problems.[37] This scale has been tested for its reliability and validity and is used in counseling college students. Two measures were used to quantify familism, because each measure encompasses different aspects of familism. One measure of familism is the Bardis Familism Scale, which has been used with different populations in the world and was revised by Sabogal.[38] The second measure of familism is a questionnaire developed by Valenzuela and Dornbusch, which is also supported by research to be valid and reliable.[39]

The social support scale used in this investigation was the Social Provisions Scale (SPS) created by Cutrona and Russell, which has been used widely with different populations and with populations facing specific stressful circumstances. The validity of this scale has been tested with both adult and adolescent samples.[40] Finally, the Bidimensional Acculturation Scale for Latinos was used, because it provides scores in two cultural domains (Latino and non-Latino) as well as a bicultural score. This scale has been used with Mexican Americans and with Central Americans; it represents an important contribution in particular to the recent contribution on the behavioral advantages of biculturalism.[41]

Methodology

This study is nonexperimental, quantitative, and correlational and examines patterns of relationships among the variables. The quantitative section attempts to answer the following questions: (1) Is familism in Latino college students related to adjustment to college? (2) Is acculturation in Latino college students related to college adjustment? (3) Does social support in Latino college students help adjustment to college? (4) Is familism in Latino college students related to acculturation? and (5) Are there gender differences in familism among Latino college students?

Sample

The sample of this study was composed of a total of 91 undergraduate Latino college students from which only 90 students completed all the questionnaire and scales. Sixty-eight students, male and female, were recruited from Boston College through AHANA Student Programs and through contacts in dormitories and other campus locations. Recruitment was extended also to the University of Massachusetts in Boston, from which 12 students filled in the questionnaire and scales. This sample was of undergraduate Latino college students (males and females). Finally, 12 Latino female students from Wellesley College completed the questionnaires. In total, the sample was made of 31 males and 59 females. The representation by class was 36.7 percent freshmen, 25.6 percent sophomores, 17.8 percent juniors, and 20 percent seniors. The respondents were 76.7 percent Catholic and 88.9 percent were U.S. citizens. Regarding family income, 38.9 percent had an income above $50,000 a year, and 27.7 percent had an income below $20,000. The median income of all Latinos in the United States is $28,141, as reported by the U.S. Bureau of Labor Statistics.[42] Consequently, the sample recruited for this study had a higher income than that of the total Latino population. Nevertheless there was representation of below the median income of the total Latino population in this sample of at least 24.4 percent (see Table 6.1.)

The parental educational attainment of this sample is shown in Table 6.2. Fathers with less than a high school diploma were 30.8 percent, and 27.8 percent of fathers had education beyond college and graduate degrees. The mothers' education of this sample was that 24.5 percent had not obtained a high school diploma, 25.6 percent had a high school diploma, and 13.3 percent had completed beyond college and graduate degrees.

Students participating in this study signed an informed consent prior to completion of the demographics questionnaire and the scales. Instructions indicated that participants had to complete the packet at one sitting in a quiet environment. Participants were given a code number to maintain anonymity.

Table 6.1
Family Income of the Sample

	Frequency	Percent
Under 10,000	10	11.1
15,000 to 19,990	12	13.3
20,000 to 29,990	10	11.1
30,000 to 49,990	20	22.2
50,000 to 79,990	15	16.7
80,000 to 100,000	20	22.2
Total	87*	100

Note: Three participants in the sample had an income lower than $10,000 a year (3.3%), and one participant did not fill in this question.

Table 6.2
Fathers' and Mothers' Education

	Father		Mother	
	Frequency	Percent	Frequency	Percent
Some grade school	12	13.3	14	15.6
Finished grade school	5	5.6	3	3.3
Some high school	9	10.0	5	5.6
High school graduate	14	15.6	23	25.6
Some college/two years	11	12.2	19	21.1
Four year college graduate	14	15.6	14	15.6
Some school beyond college	2	2.2	2	2.2
Professional/graduate degree	22	24.4	10	11.1
	90*	100	90	100

*One father had less than grade school

Measures

The variables of interest in the study were the following: (1) college adjustment as measured by the College Adjustment Scales (CAS); (2) familism as measured by the Bardis Familism Scale, which provides a level of familism and in addition the familism questions created by Valenzuela and Dornbusch;[43] (3) the Bidimensional Acculturation Scale for Hispanics (BAS), which gives two levels of acculturation on each domain (Latino and non-Latino) and a bicultural level; (4) social support measure by the Social Provisions Scale, which provides levels of social support, and (5) gender. Additional independent variables were socioeconomic status and parental education, which were taken from the demographics questionnaire.

Measurement Instruments

The College Adjustment Scale (CAS)

This scale assess nine areas of adjustment difficulties: anxiety, depression, suicidal ideation, substance abuse, self-esteem problems, interpersonal problems, family problems, academic problems, and career problems.[44] Students responded to 108 items on a 4-point scale ranging from False, Not at All True, Somewhat True, to Very True. Responses were entered on a self-scoring answer sheet. Scores are entered in a profile sheet. Higher t-scores indicate higher difficulty of adjustment to college and lower t-scores indicate adjustment to college. T-scores on each of the nine areas of difficulty range from 30 to 80; t-scores between 30 to 59 indicate no difficulty; 60 to 69 indicate some difficulty, and 70 to 80 high level of difficulty. The t-score of the nine dimensions was added and averaged to obtain the level of college adjustment for each participant. The CAS is intended to be used with students ages 17 to 30. Internal consistency reliability coefficients for the nine scales range from 0.80 to 0.92, with a mean of 0.86. Five studies have examined the convergent and discriminant validity of the CAS and its ability to distinguish students in counseling from those not in counseling. The results of the studies support the validity of the CAS as a measure of college adjustment problems.[45]

The Bardis Familism Scale

The Bardis Familism Scale was used to assess level of familism. The original scale contains 16 items.[46] However, the revision of the Bardis Familism Scale by Sabogal et al. redefined the construct of familism as covering three dimensions that are appropriate to use with Hispanics.[47] These dimensions are familial obligations (Cronbach alpha .64), perceived support from family (Cronbach alpha .76), and family as referents (Cronbach alpha .70). This Bardis Familism Scale was factor analyzed and tested for reliability, which showed high Cronbachs' alphas and contains 14 items. The Bardis Familism scale has 14 items that provide a level of familism. The items are responded on a 5-point likert scale (ranging from very much in agreement to very much in disagreement); high score indicates more familism. A total score is obtained from the scale that ranges from 14 to 70; a score of 14 to 28 indicates low level of familism, a score of 29 to 55 indicates medium level of familism, and a high score of familism is between 56 and 70.

In addition, questions developed by Valenzuela and Dornbusch were used to assess familism behavior, familism structure, and household structure.[48] Thus, the Bardis Familism Scale and the questions developed and used by Valenzuela and Dornbusch were both used to assess different dimensions of familism that have been used with Latino populations in research and have been proven reliable. The Valenzuela and Dornbusch questionnaire includes six items that provide a level of familism. The responses for the items are on a seven-point-likert scale (ranging from strongly agree to not at all); the total range from this questionnaires is from 6 to 42 points. The scores indicate a strong level of familism (26 to 42), a moderate level of familism (18 to 25), and a low level of familism (6 to 17).

The Bidimensional Acculturation Scale for Hispanics (BAS)

The BAS measures two cultural domains (Hispanic and non-Hispanic) and provides scores in both cultural domains plus a score that indicates biculturalism on the part of the respondent. The scale has 24 items, 12 for each cultural domain. The possible total score ranges from 1 to 4 for each domain. Scores above 2.5 in both cultural domains can be interpreted as indicating biculturalism. The response categories for items 1 through 6 and items 19 through 25 are Almost Always (4); Often (3); Sometimes (2); and Almost Never (1). The response categories for items 7 through 18 are Very Well (4); Well (3); Poorly (2); and Very Poorly (1).[49]

The scores obtained with the BAS show high internal consistency and high validity coefficients. The combined score of the four subscales showed high internal consistency for the Hispanic domain (alpha = .87), and for the non-Hispanic domain (alpha = .94), and the internal consistency for the combined score of the three language-related subscales was alpha = .90 for the Hispanic domain, and alpha = .96 for the non-Hispanic domain. The scale works well with Mexican Americans and with Central Americans. This scale represents an important contribution in particular to the recent literature on the behavioral advantages of biculturalism.[50]

The Social Provisions Scale (SPS)

The SPS was created by Cutrona and Russell and based on the model of Social Provisions of Weiss.[51] The scale has 24 items and integrates 6 factors, which reflect each dimension of social support. The six dimensions of social support are guidance (advice and information), reliable alliance (tangible assistance), attachment (caring), social integration (belonging to a group of similar others), reassurance of worth (positive evaluation), and opportunity for nurturance (providing support to others). Subjects assess their entire support network to the extent to which they feel that each of the six provisions is currently available to them. All items are rated on a four-point scale from 1 = strongly disagree, to 4 = strongly agree.

A factor analysis by Cutrona and Russell yielded a six factor in the six dimensions of support, which supported this scale's reliability. Reliability was established using three samples (college students, public school teachers, and nurses from a military hospital), which range from .87 to .915. Coefficient alphas for the total scale were .915 for the three samples. Four to six month test retest reliability was assessed using an elderly sample and was found to be .57 for the total scale. Research on populations facing specific stressful circumstances was also conducted. Thus, extensive validity evidence for the SPS among both adult and adolescent populations has been presented.[52]

The SPS assesses the subject's entire support network to the extent to which participants feel that each of the six provisions is available to them. Items are rated on a 4-point scale, and scores are obtained ranging from 24 to 96; high scores indicate a high level of social support (between 72 and 96). A low level of social support ranges from 14 to 28, and a medium level of social support ranges between 29 and 55.

Results

Preliminary descriptive analyses were conducted prior to the planned statistical tests of the data. Descriptive analyses were generated to look at the data. Next correlations and independent t-test were obtained to examine the hypotheses.

The independent variables were the following: (1) Valenzuela and Dornbusch Familism Questions (VDFAM), (2) the Bardis Familism Scale (BFS), (3) parental involvement (PARINV), (4) the Social Provisions Scale (SPS), and (5) the Bidimensional Acculturation Scale (BAS, ANGLO and HISP). The dependent variable is the College Adjustment Scale (CAS). Other independent variables used in this study were income, mother's education, and father's education, which were set on three levels—low, medium, and high.

In order to test the first question (Does familism of Latino college students relate to college adjustment?) the sample of Latino college students in this study was divided into two groups on the basis of the level of college adjustment they had obtained (with a score of < 60, the students were adjusted to college; and a score of > 60 students were not adjusted to college). The t-score below or above 60 was chosen because the standardization sample of this scale had a mean score of 50 and a standard deviation of 10[10]. The adjusted Latino group consisted of 86 participants, and the not-adjusted group consisted of 4 participants. These results indicate the majority of the participants in this study were adjusted to college.

A two-tail t-test for independent groups was used to test levels (high and low) of familism (using the two familism scales) and for levels of college adjustment. The two-tailed t-test of independent variables revealed that the mean for the BFS of adjusted Latino college students 49.42 (SD = 6.45) was not significantly different from that of the not-adjusted Latino students—44.00 t (88) = -1.575, $p > .05$. The mean for the VDFAM for the adjusted Latino students was 29.87 ($SD = 4.83$) and was significantly different from that of the not-adjusted Latino college students, 24.50 t (88) = -2.169 $p = .03$. The strength of the relationship between the two familism measures (BFS and VDFAM) and the CAS, as indicated by the point biserial correlations, was—.124 with $p > .05$. This correlation indicates that 15 percent of the variability is accounted in common by these two variables, however, because it is negative it means that as students obtained higher levels of college adjustment their level of familism decreased. To further test the measures used, correlations were done among and between these measures of familism and college adjustment as measured by the CAS.

The results indicated no relationship between the two measures of familism and the measure of college adjustment. To further test the relationships among and between the variables, correlations were done between the two familism measures and the variables in the CAS. Interestingly, the correlations demonstrated that both the BFS and VDFAM were moderately correlated (r = .426, $p > .01$), indicating that these two measures of familism assessed the construct of familism.

Other analyses were done to compare the standardization sample of the CAS ($N = 1146$) with the sample of Latino college students in this study ($N = 91$). Descriptive statistics with the nine variables of the CAS were done with the Latino sample of this study to compare with descriptive statistics reported in the standardization of the scale. The findings revealed that the two samples are similar, because the mean raw scores were one to three points lower for the Latino college students sample than for the standardization sample.

To answer the second question of this study (Is acculturation in Latino college students related to college adjustment?) again the sample was divided into two groups, not bicultural and bicultural. This was done according to the instructions of the Bidimensional Acculturation Scale (BAS), which indicates scores above 2.5 in both cultural domains (Anglo and Latino) are interpreted as bicultural, while scores below 2.5 in both cultural domains are interpreted as not bicultural. Thus, the results showed students who were not bicultural ($N = 27$) and those who were bicultural ($N = 63$). The mean for the not-bicultural group was 49.1726 ($SD = -7.1794$), and the mean for the bicultural group was 48.8567 ($SD = 6.1245$), and no correlations were found. The results of the two-tailed t-test of independent groups demonstrated that there were no significant differences in the adjustment between the these two groups t (88) = .21, $p > .05$

The third question in this study (Does social support in Latino college students help adjustment to college?) was tested by using a two-tail t-test for independent groups. Two groups were created; one had a high level of college adjustment with a score < 60 ($N = 86$), and the other group had a low level of college adjustment with a score > 60 ($N = 14$). Thus, the sample was split at the score that indicates adjustment to college.[53] The two-tailed t-test of independent groups indicated no significant differences between the two groups of college adjustment and social support. The mean for the low level of college adjustment was 59.55 ($SD = 5.76$), and the mean for high level of college adjustment was 60.71 ($SD = 5.59$) $t(88) = .633$ $p > .05$. The strength of the relationship between college adjustment and social support, as indicated by the point biserial, correlation was .032, $p > .05$.

The fourth research question (Are levels of familism related to levels of acculturation?) was investigated by doing a two tailed t-test of independent groups to find out if there were differences in familism in Latino college students who were Latino acculturated and those who were not Latino acculturated. Two independent groups were created, one Latino acculturated (> 2.50) and the other not Latino acculturated (< 2.50). The two-tail t test revealed that the mean for Latino acculturated students using the VDFAM was 29.68 ($SD = 5.07$), and the BFS mean was 49.50 ($SD = 6.68$). No significant differences were found between these two familism scales and the two groups; the Latino acculturated group had $t(88) = .166$, $p > .05$ and the not-Latino acculturated had a $t(88) = .173, p > .05$.

To further investigate the fourth question, a two-tailed t-test of independent means was used to test differences in familism and Anglo acculturation. The sample of Latino college students was divided in two groups, one group Anglo acculturated (> 2.50) (N = 85) and the other group not-Anglo acculturated (< 2.50) (N = 5). The t-test revealed that the mean for the VDFAM for the Anglo group (29.64) was not significantly different from that of the not-Anglo acculturated group (M = 29.60) $t(88)$ = .015, p > .05. The t-test also demonstrated that the mean of the BFS for the Anglo acculturated group (49.28) was not significantly different from that for the not-Anglo acculturated (M = 47.40) $t(88)$ = .601, p > .05. Thus, the results of these t-tests showed no significant differences in familism with those students who were Anglo acculturated and those who were not-Anglo acculturated.

An interesting finding was that a two-tailed t-test of independent groups revealed that parental involvement with the Latino acculturated group (M = 6.22) was not significantly different from the not-Latino acculturated group (M = 7.81) $t(88)$ = $-1.734, p$ = .057.

A question was developed to test if there was a relationship between familism and socioeconomic level and education. Correlations were run to assess if lower levels of familism were related to higher income level and higher education (Table 6.3). At the same time additional correlations were run in SPSS between and among the two familism scales, income, parental involvement, and father's and mother's education. The results of Pearson correlations demonstrated that the two measures of familism were moderately correlated—r = .42, p > 001. Then, the VDFAM was mildly correlated with parental involvement (r = .22, p = .03), with income (r = .21, p = .04), and with mother's education (r = .35, p < .001). These correlation coefficients were low but showed a relationship among the variables. Parental involvement was found to be correlated with income (r = .29, p < .001) and with mother's education (r = .46, p = .00). This last correlation coefficient was moderate, whereas the previous one was low. The correlation matrix also demonstrated that income was correlated with father's education (r = .36, p < .001) and mother's education (r = .62, p < .001); this last correlation coefficient was moderate. Finally, mother's education was correlated moderately with father's education (r = .44, p < .001).

Gender differences in familism among Latino college students were investigated by doing a two tailed t-test for independent groups in SPSS by testing for differences in familism using the two measures of familism (VDFAM and BFS) among males and females. A two tailed-t-test for independent groups was run in SPSS to test for differences in familism (using the two measures) among males and females. Two groups were created. One consisted of males (N = 31) and the other of females (N = 59). The t-test revealed that the mean for the VDFAM in males was 28.29 and was not significantly different from that of females (M = 30.34), $t(88)$ = $-1.89, p$ = .061, p > .05. The BFS t-test results indicated that the mean for the males (6.03) was not significantly different from that of the female group 6.88 $t(88)$ = $-1.028, p$ > .05. Thus, this finding indicates there were no differences between females and males [54]

Discussion

The results obtained in this investigation raise many questions that need further investigation in order to understand Latino college students in

Table 6.3
Summary of Correlations

Measures	1	2	3	4	5	6	7
1. Valenzuela & Dornbusch	—						
2. Parental Involvement	.227* .032	—					
3. Bardis Fam Scale	.426** .000	−.001	—				
4. Acculturated Anglo	.010 .925	.124 .249	−.031 .774	—			
5. Acculturated Latino	.130 .225	−.139 .194	.137 .200	−.451** .000	—		
6. Social Provisions Scale	.170 .111	−.120 .342	.012 .910	.079 .460	.106 .325	—	
7. College	−.203 —	.021	−.124	−.117	−.045		.032
Adjustment Scale	.057	.845	.245	−.275	.678		.763

*Correlations is significant at the 0.05 level (2-tailed).
**Correlation is significant at the 0.001 level (2-tailed).

post-secondary education contexts. The value of familism, in this study, was not related to college adjustment even though the sample had a high number of adjusted (86 out of 90) Latino college students. This result could have been influenced by the measure of college adjustment used in this study that assessed pathology rather than a perception of college adjustment. It would be interesting to investigate measures used in other similar studies to find out what types of measures where used to evaluate college adjustment and how college adjustment needs to be assessed.

College adjustment has also been an important focus in the literature of first-generation college students. The research done by Terenzini et al. (1996), relying on personal accounts and experiences of these students and their families, have found first-generation students and their families face the same anxieties, dislocations, and difficulties of any college student but with the added stressors brought about by different cultural, social, and academic transitions.[55] In addition, research on the effects of students' college experience on persistence when compared with traditional students has indicated that first-generation students are less likely to persist and less likely to attain a degree than traditional college students because of lower levels of academic and social integration.[56] This finding further indicates how important it is for first-generation and Latino college students to adjust to the academic environment in order to persist and complete a degree.

Another finding was a small negative correlation between familism and college adjustment, which indicates that as familism increases, college adjustment decreases. Why would college adjustment increase if familism decreases? What aspects of familism interfere with college adjustment? This finding indicates that familism needs to be better understood as it pertains to Latinos. Are there differences of familism across different Latinos groups, and are there differences of familism related to socioeconomic level and education levels? These questions need to be furthered studied.

It is not clear why familism did not imply social support as it was thought to be by some researchers in the area of mental health services and in the study of Latino college students.[57] Perhaps the social support in familism involves changes in the nature of family relationships as children and youth interact more with the society that surrounds them. Therefore, other social supports or networks develop, and social support becomes less dependent on the family. In addition, parental relationships evolve over time, with a shift of emphasis from parents serving as primary support providers to their children to parents relying on their adult children.[58] Could it be that family support is less important during the college years and that finding other sources of support is what helps college adjustment, as Hurtado et al. had mentioned in her study?[59]

Another important finding was that the two measures used to quantify the value of familism in this study, the BFS and VDFAM, had a moderate correlation, which implies that these two measures were measuring the familism construct. These measures could be used as a starting point for developing a more comprehensive measure of Latino familism.

Although the results in this study did not find a relationship between acculturation and college adjustment, and the two-tail t-test of independent groups indicated no significant differences between the two groups of college adjustment and social support, the results on acculturation indicated that 85 (out of 90) Latino college students were acculturated to the Anglo culture. This result supports previous research that has indicated that Latino students who are acculturated to the Anglo culture are better adjusted to the academic institutions.[60] Moreover, this result was reinforced by the finding that 86 out of the 90 Latino students in this study were adjusted to college by the results obtained by the CAS.[61] Other results on acculturation showed no significant differences between levels of familism and levels of acculturation for those Latino college students who were Latino acculturated and those who were not-Latino acculturated. This finding raises the question of whether familism changes are due to acculturation to the Anglo culture or to biculturalism.

In this study, levels of social support and levels of college adjustment were not found to be significantly different—a finding that was not anticipated. However, a small correlation was found between college adjustment and social support (.032, p > .05). Could this finding be influenced by the measures used in this investigation and by the size of the sample? Finally, no gender differences were found between females and males in this study. Perhaps this result was obtained because the sample in this study had a larger number of females than males.

There is a need to further investigate the value of familism in Latinos of several backgrounds and what this value implies to each Latino group, as well as how this value relates to relationships between different generations, different socioeconomic levels, different educational levels, and how it is influenced by acculturation or not, across time.

Studies relying on personal accounts of first-generation college students have shown that multigenerational family relationships influence how students adapt to college, because students have to reconcile between "conflicting requirements of family memberships and educational mobility" (London, 1992, p. 144). Laura Rendón's (1992) account of her personal experiences as a first-generation Mexican American college and graduate student from a low income background describes that as a first-generation college student she had to confront new academic demands and try to reconcile her new world with her old culture. She also mentions that academics subscribe to Euro-centered rationalism and objectivity and that in order to succeed she had to let go of her past values and culture and assimilate to this culture, which forced her to live in two cultures. Richard Rodríguez (1982) described a similar experience in his book *Hunger for Memory*.

In sum, the value of familism needs further research, which can be then used to better understand the cultural challenges Latino college students face when entering post-secondary education.

NOTES

1. "College Enrollment by Racial and Ethnic Group, Selected Years, *The Chronicle Almanac* 2004–2005 (October 2005). http//chronicle.com/weekly/almanac/2004/nation/0101603.html.

2. Hispanics: A People in Motion (Washington, D.C.: The Pew Hispanic Center, January 2005). Retrieved March 17, 2005 from http://pewhispanic.org.

3. Ibid. See also Peter Schmidt, "Academe's Hispanic Future," *The Chronicle of Higher Education* (November 28, 2003). http://chronicle.com/weekly/v50/i14/14a00801.htm.

4. Schmidt, "Hispanic Future."

5. Roberto Suro, "Educating the Largest Minority Group," *The Chronicle of Higher Education* (November, 28, 2003). Retrieved March 17, 2005 from http://chronicle.com/weekly/v50/i14/14600601.htm.

6. Hispanics: A People in Motion (Washington, D.C.: The Pew Hispanic Center, January 2005).

7. Noguera, P. *City Schools and the American Dream: Reclaiming the Promise of Public Education;* M.B. Spencer, S.M. Dornbusch, and R. Mont-Reynaud, "Challenges in Studying Minority Youth," in *At the Threshold: The Developing Adolescent*, S.S. Feldman and G.R. Elliot, Eds. (Cambridge: Harvard University Press, 1990); J. Chapa and R.R. Valencia "Latino Population Growth Demographic Characteristics and

Educational Stagnation: An Examination of Recent Trends," *Hispanic Journal of Behavioral Sciences*, 15 (1993).

8. Sonia Nieto, *Affirming Diversity: The Sociopolitical Context of Multicultural Education*, 3rd ed. (New York: Longman Publishers, 2000); Sonia Nieto, *Sociopolitical Context of Multicultural Education*, 2nd ed. (New York: Longman Publishers, 1995).

9. Enrique (Henry) Torres Trueba, 2004. *The New Americans. Immigrants and Transnationals at Work*. New York: Rowman and Littlefield Publishers, Inc.

10. G. Marín and B. Van Oss Marín, *Research with Hispanic Populations*, Applied Social Methods Series, 23 (Thousand Oaks, CA: Sage Publications, 1985); H.C. Triandis, G. Marín, H. Betancourt, J. Lisansky, and B. Chang, *Dimensions of Familism*.

11. *Among Hispanics and Mainstream Navy Recruits*, Technical Report no. 14 (Champaign: University of Illinois, 1982); Marín and Van Oss Marín, *Research*; F. Sabogal, G. Marín, R. Otero-Sabogal, B. Marín, and Pérez-Stable, "Hispanic Familism and Acculturation: What Changes and What Doesn't?" *Hispanic Journal of Behavioral Sciences* 9 (1987): 397–412; W.A. Vega, "The Study of Latino Families: A Point of Departure," in *Understanding Latino Families: Scholarship, Policy, and Practice*, R.E. Zambrana, ed. (Thousand Oaks, CA: Sage Publications, 1995).

12. In A. Valenzuela and S.M. Dornbusch, "Familism and Social Capital in the Academic Achievement of Mexican Origin and Anglo Adolescents," *Social Science Quarterly*, 75 (1994): 18–36.

13. S. Hurtado, D. Carter Faye, A. Spuler, B. Dale, and A. Pipkin, *Latino Transition to College: Assessing Difficulties and Factors in Successful College Adjustment*. Paper presented at the Association of Institutional Research Forum, 1994 (New Orleans).

14. N.P.C. Rodriguez, C.B. Mira, H. Myers, D. Cardoza, "Family or Friends: Who Play Greater Supportive Role for Latino College Students?" *Cultural Diversity and Ethnic Minority Psychology*, Vol. 9 (3), August 2003.

15. V. Perez and M.E. Kenny, "Attachment and Psychological Well Being among Racially and Ethnically Diverse 1st Year College Students," *Journal of College Student Development* 37 (1996): 527–35; M.E. Kenny and S. Stryker, "Social Network Characteristics and College Adjustment among Racially and Ethnically Diverse 1st Year Students," *Journal of College Student Development* 37 (November/December 1996): 649–58; G.R. Pierce, B.R. Sarason, I.G. Sarason, H.J. Joseph, and C.A. Henderson, "Conceptualizing and Assessing Social Support in the Context of the Family," in *Handbook of Social Support and the Family*, ed., G.R. Pierce, B.R. Sarason, and I.G. Sarason, 3–25 (New York: Plenum Press, 1996); B.C. Rollins and D.L. Thomas, "Parental Support, Power and Control Techniques in the Socialization of College Students," *Contemporary Theories about the Family* (New York: Free Press, 1979), 317–64.

16. Ibid.; Peréz and Kenny, "Attachment and Psychological Well Being," 17.

17. Suarez-Orozco, C., and Suarez-Orozco, M. *Transformations: Migration, Family Life and Achievement Motivation Among Latino Adolescents*, 1995; Hurtado et al., *Latino Transition to College*; S.M. Quintana, M.C. Vogel, and V.C. Ybarra, "Meta-analysis of Latino Students' Adjustment in Higher Education, " *Hispanic Journal of Behavioral Sciences*, 13 (1991): 155–68.

18. S. Cohen and T.A. Wills, " Stress, Social Support, and the Buffering Hypothesis," *Psychological Bulletin* 98 (1985): 310–57; Sidney Cobb, "Social Support as Moderator of Life Stress," *Psychosomatic Medicine* 38 (1976): 300–14.

19. Cohen and Wills, "Stress"; V.S. Solberg, J. Valde, P. Villareal, "Social Support, Stress, and Hispanic College Adjustment: Test of a Diathesis-Stress Model, "*Hispanic Journal of Behavioral Sciences* 16 (1994): 230–39.

20. Cohen and Wills, "Stress"; Kenny and Stryker, "Social Network"; Peréz and Kenny, "Attachment and Psychological Well Being"; Pierce et al., "Conceptualizing and Assessing Social Support."

21. P. Dilworth-Anderson and S. Marshall, "Social Support in Its Cultural Context," in *Handbook of Social Support and the Family*, ed. G. R. Pierce, B. R. Sarason, and I. G. Sarason, 66–83 (New York: Plenum Press, 1996).

22. Marín and Van Oss Marín, *Research*; D. W. Sue and D. Sue, *Counseling the Culturally Different: Theory and Practice*, 2nd edition (New York: John Wiley & Sons, 1990).

23. Hurtado et al., *Latino Transition to College*, 14.

24. Solberg et al., "Social Support."

25. N.C.P. Rodriguez, C. B. Mira, H. Myers, D. Cardoza, "Family or Friends: Who Play Greater Supportive Role for Latino College Students?" *Cultural Diversity and Ethnic Minority Psychology*, Vol. 9, No. 3, August 2003.

26. S. M. Quintana, M. C. Vogel, and V. C. Ybarra, "Meta-analysis of Latino Students' Adjustment in Higher Education," *Hispanic Journal of Behavioral Sciences, 13* (1991): 155–68.

27. K. Arnold, "The Fulfillment of Promise: Minority Valedictorians and Salutatorians," *The Review of Higher Education* 16, 1 (1993): 257–83.

28. A. R. Arellano and A. P. Padilla, "Academic Invulnerability of a Select Group of Latino University Students," *Hispanic Journal of Behavioral Sciences*, 18, 4 (1996) 485–07.

29. Hurtado et al., *Latino Transition to College*, 15; Solberg et al., "Social Support," 22.

30. Suárez-Orozco, Carola and Marcelo Suárez-Orozco. *Transformations: Migration, Family Life, and Achievement Motivation Among Latino Adolescents*. Stanford, CA: Stanford University Press, 1995; Hurtado et al., *Latino Transition to College*, 15; Solberg et al., "Social Support," 22.

31. G. Young, "Role Making among Married Mexican," *Applied Behavioral Sciences*, 14, 3 (1992) 341:52.

32. E. M. Lopéz, "Challenges and Resources of Mexican American Students with Family, Peer Group, and university: and Gender Patterns," *Hispanic Journal of Behavioral Sciences*, 17, 4 (1995): 499–08.

33. B. De León, "Sex Role Identity among College Students: A Cross-Cultural Analysis," *Hispanic Journal of Behavioral Sciences*, 15, 4 (1993): 476–89.

34. P. T. Terenzini, L. Yaeger, E. T. Pascarella, and A. Nora, "First-Generation College Students: Characteristics, Experiences and Cognitive Development," *Research in Higher Education*, 37, 1 (1996): 1–73.

35. Ibid.

36. R. Jean-Van Hell, *Hispanic College Students' Adjustment: The Influence of Familism, Acculturation and Social Support*, UMI Number 9995926 (Anne Harbor: Bell & Howell, 2000).

37. W. D. Anton and J. R. Reed, "College Adjustment Scale" (Lutz, Florida: Psychological Assessment Resources, 1991).

38. P. D. Bardis, "A Familism Scale," *Marriage and Family Livng*, 21 (1959a): 340–341.

39. A. Valenzuela and S. M. Dornbusch, "Familism and Social Capital in the Academic Achievement of Mexican Origin and Anglo Adolescents," *Social Science Quarterly*, 75 (1994): 18–36.

40. C. E. Cutrona and D. W. Russell, "The Provisions of Social Relationships and Adaptation to Stress," *Advances in Personal Relationships*, 1 (1987): 37–67. See also

D. W. Russell and C. E. Cutrona, *The Provisions of Social Relationships and Adaptation to Stress*, Paper Presented at the Annual Meeting of the American Psychological Association, Toronto (1984).

41. G. Marín and R. Gamba, "A New Measurement of Acculturation for Hispanics: The Bidimensional Acculturation Scale for Hispanics (BAS)," *Hispanic Journal of Behavioral Sciences*, 18 (1996): 297–16; Marín and Van Oss Marín, *Research with Hispanic Populations.*

42. U.S. Census Bureau 1999.

43. A. Valenzuela and S. M. Dornbusch, "Familism and Social Capital in the Academic Achievement of Mexican Origin and Anglo Adolescents," *Social Science Quarterly*, 75 (1994): 18–36.

44. Anton and Reed, *College Adjustment Scale*, 46.

45. Ibid.

46. Bardis, "Bardis Familism Scale," 47.

47. Sabogal et al., "Hispanic Familism and Acculturation."

48. A. Valenzuela and Dornbusch, "Familism and Social Capital," 48.

49. Marín and Gamba, "A New Measurement of Acculturation," 51.

50. Ibid.

51. Cutrona and Russell, "The Provisions of Social Relationships," 49.

52. Ibid.

53. Anton and Reed, "College Adjustment Scale," 46.

54. Ibid.

55. Terenzini et al., "First-Generation College Students," 41.

56. Ibid; Vega, "The Study of Latino Families," 11.

57. Marín and Van Oss Marín, *Research with Hispanic Populations*, 11.

58. Pierce et al., "Conceptualizing and Assessing," 17.

59. Hurtado et al., *Latino Transition to College*, 15.

60. Quintana et al., "Meta-Analysis of Latino Students," 20.

61. Anton and Reed, "College Adjustment Scale," 16.

REFERENCES

Achor, S., and Morales, A. (1990). "Chicanas Holding Doctoral Degrees: Social Reproduction and Cultural Ecological Approaches." *Anthropology and Educational Quarterly, 21*, pp. 269–287.

Adler Lomnitz, L., and Perez-Lizaur M. (1987). *A Mexican Elite Family, 1820–1980: Kinship, Class and Culture.* Princeton, NJ: Princeton University.

Alva, S. A. (1991). "Academic Invulnerability among Mexican-Appraisals." *Hispanic Journal of Behavioral Sciences, 13*, pp. 18–34.

Alvirez, D., and Bean, F. D. (1976). "The Mexican-American family." In C. H. Mindel and R. N. Haberstein (Eds.), *Ethnic Families in America* (pp. 271–291). New York: Elsevier.

American Association of University Women. (1991). *Shortchanging Girl Shortchanging America.* Special report prepared by Greenberg-Lake. Washington, D.C.: Author.

Anton, W. D., and Reed, J. R. (1991). *College Adjustment Scales.* Psychological Assessment Resources, Inc.

Arbona, C., and Novy D. M. (1991). "Hispanic College Students: Are There Within-Group Differences?" *Journal of College Student Development, 32*, pp. 335–341.

Arellano, A. R., and Padilla A. P. (1996). "Academic Invulnerability of a Select Group of Latino University Students." *Hispanic Journal of Behavioral Sciences, 18*, 4, pp. 485–507.

Arnold, K. (1993). "The Fulfillment of Promise: Minority Valedictorians and Salutatorians." *The Review of Higher Education, 16*, 3, pp. 257–283.

Baker, R. W., and Siryk, B. (1984). "Measuring College Adjustment." *Journal of Counseling Psychology, 31*, pp. 179–189.

Bardis, P. D. (1959a). "A Familism Scale." *Marriage and Family Living, 21*, pp. 340–341.

Bardis, P. D. (1959b). "Attitudes toward the Family among College Students." *Sociology and Social Research, 43*, pp. 352–358.

Bem, S. L. (1981). "Gender Schema Theory: A Cognitive Account of Sex Typing." *Psychological Review, 88*, pp. 354–364.

Bem, S. L. (1993). *The Lenses of Gender: Transforming the Debate on Sexual Inequality.* New Haven, CT: Yale University.

Bernal, G., and Shapiro E. (1996). "Cuban Families." In M. McGoldrick, J. Giordano, and J. K. Pierce (Eds.), *Ethnicity and Family Therapy*, second edition (pp. 155–169). New York: Guilford Press.

Berry, J. W. (1990). "Psychology of Acculturation." In John J. Berman (Ed.), *Cross-Cultural Perspectives. Nebraska Symposium on Motivation 1989, 37* (pp. 205–231). Lincoln: University of Nebraska Press.

Baca Zinn, M. (1989). "Family, Race and Poverty in the Eighties." *Signs: Journal of Women in Culture and Society, 14*, pp. 856–74.

Betancourt, H., and Regerser Lopez, S. (1993). "The Study of Culture, Ethnicity and Race in American Psychology." *American Psychologist, 48*, 6, pp. 629–637.

Burbridge, Lynn C. (1991). "The Interaction of Race, Gender and Socioeconomic Status in Education Outcomes." *Center for Research on Women ,Working Paper Series*, No. 246.

Buriel, R., and Saenz, E. (1980). "Psychocultural Characteristics of College-Bound and Non-College-Bound Chicanas." *Journal of Social Psychology, 110*, pp. 245–252.

Chacon, M., Cohen, E., Camarena, M., Gonzalez, J., and Strover, S. (1985). *Chicanas in California Post-Secondary Education: A Comparative Study of Barriers to Program Progress.* Stanford, CA: Center for Chicano Research.

Chacon, M., Cohen, E., Strover, S. (1986). "Chicana and Chicanos: Barriers to Progress in Higher Education." In M. M. Olivas (Ed), *Latino College Students.* New York: Teachers College, Columbia University Press (pp. 296–324).

Calabrese, R. L., and Poe, J. (1990). "Alienation: An Explanation of High Dropout Rates among African American and Latino Students." *Educational Research Quarterly, 14*, 4, pp. 22–26.

Chapa, J. (1990). *Minorities and the College Graduating Class of 2010: An Analysis of the Demographic and Socioeconomic Characteristics of Preschool Children in 1988.* Paper written for the Association of Governing Boards of Universities and Colleges, Washington, D.C.

Chapa, J., and Valencia, R. R. (1993). "Latino Population Growth Demographic Characteristics and Educational Stagnation: An Examination of Recent Trends." *Hispanic Journal of Behavioral Sciences, 15*, 2, pp. 165–187.

Chavez, J., and Roney, C. E. (1990). "Psychological Factors Affecting the Mental Health Status of Mexican American Adolescents." In R. Stiffman and L. E. Davis (Eds). *Ethnic Issues in Adolescent Mental Health.* California: Sage Publications.

Chickering, A. and Reisser, L. (1993). *Education and Identity.* Second edition, San Francisco: Jossey-Bass Publishers.

The Chronicle Almanac 2004–5. (2005, October). *College Enrollment by Racial and Ethnic Group, Selected Years.* Retrieved October 14, 2005, from http://chronicle.com/weekly/almanac/2004/nation/0101603.html.

Cobb, Sidney. (1976). "Social Support as Moderator of Life Stress." *Psychosomatic Medicine, 38,* 5, pp. 300–314.

Cohen, S., and Wills, T. A. (1985). "Stress, Social Support, and the Buffering Hypothesis." *Psychological Bulletin, 98,* pp. 310–357.

Cohen, R. (1979). *Culture, Disease and Stress among Latino Immigrants.* Washington, D.C.: Smithsonian Institution.

Comas-Diaz, L. (1991). "Feminism and Diversity: The Case of Women of Color," *Psychology of Women Quarterly, 15,* pp. 597–609.

Comas-Diaz, L., Lykes, M. B., and Alarcón, R. D. (1998). "Ethnic Conflict and the Psychology of Liberation in Guatemala, Perú and Puerto Rico." *American Psychologist, 83,* 7, pp. 778–792.

Cutrona, C. E. (1989). "Ratings of Social Support by Adolescents and Adult Informants: Degree of Correspondence and Prediction of Depressive Symptoms." *Journal of Personality and Social Psychology, 57,* 4, pp. 723–750.

Cutrona, C. E., and Russell, D. W. (1987). "The Provisions of Social Relationships and Adaptation to Stress." *Advances in Personal Relationships, 1,* pp. 37–67.

Dana, R. H. (1996). "Assessment of Acculturation in Hispanic Populations." *Hispanic Journal of Behavioral Sciences, 18,* 3, pp. 317–328.

De Leon, Brumilda. (1993). "Sex Role Identity among College Students: A Cross-Cultural Analysis." *Hispanic Journal of Behavioral Sciences, 15,* 4, pp. 476–489.

Dilworth-Anderson, P. and Marshall S. (1996). "Social Support in its Cultural Context." In G. R. Pierce, B. R. Sarason, and I. G. Sarason (Eds), *Handbook of Social Support and the Family* (pp. 67–83). New York: Plenum Press.

Eagle, E., and Carroll, C. D. (1988). "High School and Beyond National Longitudinal Study: Post-Secondary Enrollment, Persistence, and Attainment for 1972, 1980, and 1982 High School Graduates (Publication No Cs 89–101). Washington, D.C.: U.S. Government Printing Office, U.S. Department of Education, Office of Educational Research Improvement.

Eagly, A. H. (1987). *Sex Differences in Social Behavior: A Social Role Interpretation.* Hillsdale, NJ: Erlbraun.

Erikson, E. H. (1968). *Identity, Youth and Crisis.* New York: Norton.

Ethier, K., and Deaux K. (1990). "Hispanics in Ivy: Assessing Identity and Perceived Threat." *Sex Roles, 22,* 7/8, pp. 427–440.

Falicov, C. J. (1996). "Mexican Families." In M. McGoldrick, J. Giordano and J. K. Pierce (Eds.), *Ethnicity and Family Therapy,* second edition (pp. 169–183). New York: Guilford Press.

Gandara, P. (1982). "Passing through the Needle: High Achieving Chicanas." *Hispanic Journal of Behavioral Sciences, 4,* pp. 167–179.

Garcia-Coll C. T. (1990). "Developmental Outcome of Minority Infants: A Process Oriented Look into our Beginnings." *Child Development, 61,* pp. 270–289.

Garcia-Preto, N., (1996a). Latino Families: An Overview. In M. McGoldrick, J. Giordano and J. K. Pierce (Eds.) *Ethnicity and Family Therapy,* second edition (pp. 141–155). New York: Guilford Press.

Garcia-Preto, N. (1996b). "Puerto Rican Families: An Overview." In M. McGoldrick, J. Giordano and J. K. Pierce (Eds.), *Ethnicity and Family Therapy*, second edition (pp. 183–200). New York: Guilford Press.

Garmezy, N. (1996). "Reflections and Commentary on Risk, Resilience, and Development." In E.J. Haggerty, L.R. Sherrod, N. Garmezy, and M. Rutter (Eds.), *Stress, Risk and Resilience in Children and Adolescents: Processes, Mechanisms and Interventions.* Cambridge: University Press.

Ginorio, A. B., Gutierrez, L., Cauce, A.M., and Acosta (1995). "Psychological Issues for Latinas." In H. Landrine (Ed.), *Bringing Cultural Diversity to Feminist Psychology* (pp. 241–262). Washington, D.C.: American Psychological Association.

Gonzalez, J. T. (1988). "Dilemmas of High Achieving Chicana: The Double Bind Factor Male/Female Relationships." *Sex Roles, 18*, pp. 367–380.

Hayes-Bautista, D., Schunk, D., and Chapa, J. (1988). *The Burden of Support: Young Latinos in a Changing Society.* Stanford, CA: Stanford University Press.

Heller, Peter. (1976). "Familism Scale: Revalidation and Revision." *Journal of Marriage and the Family, 38* (August), pp. 423–429.

Hernandez, M. (1996). "Central American Families." In M. McGoldrick, J. Giordano and J.K. Pierce (Eds), *Ethnicity and Family Therapy*, second edition (pp. 214–227). New York: Guilford Press.

Hurtado, S., Faye Carter, D., Spuler, A., Dale, B., and Pipkin, A. (1994). *Latino Transition to College: Assessing Difficulties and Factors in Successful College Adjustment.* University of Michigan. Paper presented at the Association of Institutional Research Forum in New Orleans, LA.

Jones, D. J., and Watson, B. C. (1990). *High-Risk Students and Higher Education: Future Trends.* ASHE-ERIC Higher Education Report 3.

Jones, Tony Griego and Velez, William. (1997). "Effects of Latino Parent Involvement on Academic Achievement." *Paper presented at the Annual Meeting of the American Educational Research Association* (Chicago, IL, March 24–28).

Keefe, S. E., and Padilla A.M. (1987). *Chicano Identity.* Albuquerque: University of New Mexico Press.

Keefe, S. E., Padilla, A.M. and Carlos, M. L. (1979). "The Mexican American Extended Family as an Emotional Support System." *Human Organization, 38*, 2, pp. 144–152.

Kenny, M. E. (1990). "College Senior's Perceptions of Parental Attachments: The Value and Stability of Family Ties." *Journal of College Student Development, 31* January, pp. 39–46.

Kenny, M. E., and Stryker, S. (1996). "Social Network Characteristics and College Adjustment among Racially and Ethnically Diverse 1st Year Students." *Journal of College Student Development, 37*, 6, pp. 649–658.

Kohlberg, L. (1966). A Cognitive-Developmental Analysis of Children's Sex Role Concepts and Attitudes." In E. Maccoby (Ed), *The Development of Sex Differences* (pp. 82–173). Stanford, CA: Stanford University Press.

Kozol, J. (1991). *Savage Inequalities: Children in America's Schools.* New York: Harper Perennial.

Kraemer, B.A. (1997). "The Academic and Social Integration of Hispanic Students into College." *The Review of Higher Education, 20*, 2, pp. 163–179.

Laosa, L.M. (1981). "Maternal Behavior: Socio-Cultural Diversity in Mode of Family Interaction." In R. W. Henderson (Ed.), *Parent Child Interaction: Theory, Research, and Prospects.* New York: Academic Press (pp. 125–167).

Lerner, J., V., and Lerner, R. M. (1983). *Temperament and Adaptation across Life: Theoretical and Empirical Issues.* In B. P. Baltes. New York: Academic Press.

Lerner, J. V., Baker, N. and Lerner, R. M. (1985). "A Person Centered Goodness of Fit Model of Adjustment. In P. C. Kendall (Ed.), *Advances in Cognitive-Behavioral Research and Therapy, 4* (pp. 11–136). New York: Academic Press.

Loevinger, J. (1983). "Personality: Stages, Traits and the Self." *Annual Review of Psychology, 34,* pp. 195–222.

London, Howard B. (1992). "Transformations: Cultural Challenges Faced by First-Generation Students." In Zwerling, L. S., and London, H. B., (Eds.), *New Directions for Community Colleges, 80,* Winter, pp. 5–12, Jossey-Bass: San Francisco.

López, E. M. (1995). "Challenges and Resources of Mexican American Students within the Family, Peer Group, and University: Age and Gender Patterns." *Hispanic Journal of Behavioral Sciences, 17,* 4, pp. 499–508.

Marín, G., and Gamba, R. J. (1996). "A New Measurement of Acculturation for Hispanics: The Bidimensional Acculturation Scale for Hispanics (BAS)." *Hispanic Journal of Behavioral Sciences, 18,* 3, pp. 297–316.

Marín, G., and Van Oss Marin, B. (1991). *Research with Hispanic Populations.* Applied Social Research Methods Series, 23, CA: Sage Publications.

Martin, B., and Burks, N. (1985). "Family and Non-Family Components of Social Support as Buffers of Stress for College Women." *Journal of Applied Social Psychology, 15,* pp. 448–465.

Moore, L. V. (1990). *Evolving Theoretical Perspectives on Students.* New Directions for Student Services, 51. San Francisco: Jossey-Bass Publishers.

Moore, J. W. (1970). *Mexican-Americans.* Englewood Cliffs, NJ: Prentice-Hall.

Moos R. H., and Moos, B. S. (1994). *Family Environment Scale Manual,* third edition. Palo Alto: Consulting Psychologists Press.

McNairt, F. G. (1996). "The Challenge for Higher Education: Retaining Students of Color." In I. H. Johnson and A. J. Ottens (Eds.), *Leveling the Playing Field: Promoting Academic Success for Students of Color, 74* (pp. 3–15). San Francisco: Jossey-Bass Publishers.

Moyerman, D. R., and Forman, B. D. (1992). "Acculturation and Adjustment: A Meta-Analytic Study." *Hispanic Journal of Behavioral Sciences, 14,* 2, pp. 163–200.

Muuss, R. E. (1988). *Theories of Adolescence,* Fifth Edition, New York: McGraw-Hill.

Negy, C., and Woods, D. J. (1992). "The Importance of Acculturation in Understanding Research with Hispanic Americans." *Hispanic Journal of Behavioral Sciences. 14,* 2, pp. 224–247.

Nieto, Sonia. (1995). *Sociopolitical Context of Multicultural Education,* Second Edition. New York: Longman Publishers.

Nieto, Sonia. (2000). *Affirming Diversity: The Sociopolitical Context of Multicultural Education,* Third Edition. New York: Longman Publishers.

Noguera, Pedro. (2003). *City Schools and the American Dream: Reclaiming the Promise of Public Education.* New York: Teachers College Press.

Nora, A. (1987). "Determinants of Retention among Chicano College Students: A Structural Model." *Research in Higher Education, 13,* 1, pp. 31–58.

Ortiz, V. (1986). "Generational Status, Family Background, and Hispanic White Youth." In M. A. Olivas (Ed.), *Latino College Students* (pp. 29–46). New York: Teachers College Press.

Padilla, A.M. (1980). "The Roles of Cultural Awareness and Ethnic Loyalty in Acculturation." In A.M. Padilla (Ed), *Acculturation: Theory, Models and Some New Findings* (pp. 47–84). Boulder, CO: Westview.

Parker, G. and Gladstone, G. L. (1996). "Parental Characteristics as Influences on Adjustment in Adulthood." In G. R. Pierce, B.R. Sarason and I.G. Sarason (Eds.), *Handbook of Social Support and the Family* (pp. 195–219). New York: Plenum Press.

The Pew Hispanic Center (January, 2005). *Hispanics: A People in Motion.* Washington, D.C. Retrieved October 14, 2005, from http://pewhispanic.org.

Pérez, V., and Kenny, M. E. (1996). "Attachment and Psychological Well Being among Racially and Ethnically Diverse 1st Year College Students. *Journal of College Student Development, 37*, pp. 527–535.

Pierce, G. R., Sarason B. R., Sarason, I. G,. Joseph, H. J. and Henderson, C. A. (1996). "Conceptualizing and Assessing Social Support in the Context of the Family." In G. R. Pierce, B. R. Sarason and I. G. Sarason (Eds), *Handbook of Social Support and the Family* (pp. 3–25). New York: Plenum Press.

Pipher, M. (1996). *The Shelter of Each Other: Rebuilding Our Families.* New York: Ballantine Books.

Prakasa Rao, V. V., and Nandini Rao, V. (1979). "An Evaluation of the Bardis Familism Scale in India." *Journal of Marriage and the Family*, May, pp. 417–421.

Quintana, S. M., Vogel, M. C., and Ybarra, V.C. (1991). "Meta-Analysis of Latino Students' Adjustment in Higher Education." *Hispanic Journal of Behavioral Sciences, 13*, 2, pp. 155–168.

Rendon, Laura, I, (1992). "From the barrio to the academy: Revelations of a Mexican American 'Scholarship Girl.'" In Zwerling, L.S., and London, H.B., (Eds), *New Directions for Community Colleges, 80*, Winter, pp. 55–64, Jossey-Bass: San Francisco.

Rodriguez, R. (1982). *Hunger of Memory*, Boston: Godine.

Rodríguez, N. P. C., Mira, C. B., Cardoza, D. (2003). "Family or Friends: Who Play Greater Supportive Roles for Latino College Students?" *Cultural Diversity and Ethnic Minority Psychology. 9*, 3, pp. 236–250.

Rollins, B., C. and Thomas, D. L. (1979). "Parental Support, Power and Control Techniques in the Socialization of College Students." *Contemporary Theories about the Family, 1* (pp. 317–364). New York: Free Press.

Ryan R., M., and Solky J. A. (1996). "What is Supportive about Social Support? On the Psychological Needs for Autonomy and Relatedness." In G. R. Pierce, B .R. Sarason and I. G. Sarason (Eds.), *Handbook of Social Support and the Family* (pp. 249–269). New York: Plenum Press.

Sabogal, F., Marín, G., Otero-Sabogal, R., Marín, B., and Pérez-Stable. (1987). "Hispanic Familism and Acculturation: What Changes and What Doesn't?" *Hispanic Journal of Behavioral Sciences, 9*, pp. 397–412.

Sampson E. E. (1988). "The Debate on Individualism: Indigenous Psychologies of the Individual and Their Role in Personal and Societal Functioning." *American Psychologist, 43*, pp. 15–22.

Schmidt, P. (2003, November 28). "Academe's Hispanic Future." *The Chronicle of Higher Education.* Retrieved October 14, 2005, http://chronicle.com/weekly/v50/i14/14a00801.htm.

Smart, J.F., and Smart, D.W. (1995). "Acculturative Stress: The Experience of the Hispanic Immigrant." *The Counseling Psychologist, 23*, 1, pp. 25–42.

Solberg, V. S., Valdez, J., Villarreal, P. (1994). "Social Support, Stress, and Hispanic College Adjustment: Test of a Diathesis-Stress Model." *Hispanic Journal of Behavioral Sciences, 16,* 3, pp. 230–239.

Solberg, V. S., O'Brien, K., Villarreal, P., Kennel, R., and Davis, B. (1993). "Self-Efficacy and Hispanic College Students: Validation of the College Self-Efficacy Instrument." *Hispanic Journal of Behavioral Sciences, 15,* 1, pp. 80–95.

Solberg, V. S., Hale, J. Bradford, Villarreal, P., and Kavanagh, J. (1993). "Development of the College Stress Inventory for Use with Hispanic Populations: A Confirmatory Analytic Approach." *Hispanic Journal of Behavioral Sciences, 15,* 4, pp. 490–497.

Spencer, M. B., Dornbusch, S. M., and Mont-Reynaud, R. (1990). "Challenges in Studying Minority Youth." In S. S. Feldman and G. R, Elliot (Eds), *At the Threshold: The Developing Adolescent* (pp. 123–146). Cambridge, MA: Harvard University Press.

Steinberg, L., Dornbusch, S. M., and Brown, B. B. (1992). "Ethnic Differences in Adolescent Achievement." *American Psychologist, 47,* pp. 723–729.

Suárez-Orozco, Carola, and Marcelo Suárez-Orozco. *Transformations: Migration, Family Life, and Achievement Motivation Among Latino Adolescents.* Stanford, CA: Stanford University Press, 1995.

Suro, Roberto. (2003, November 28). "Educating the Largest Minority Group." *The Chronicle of Higher Education,* Retrieved October 14, 2005, http://chornicle.com/weekly/v50/i14/14b00601.htm.

Szapocznick, J., and Kurtines, W. (1993). "Family Psychology and Cultural Diversity: Opportunities for Theories and Research Application." *American Psychologist, 48,* 4, pp. 400–407.

Szapocznick, J., and Kurtines, W. (1980). "Acculturation, Biculturalism, and Adjustment among Cuban Americans." In A. M. Padilla (Ed.), *Acculturation: Theory, Models, and Some New Findings* (pp. 139–159). Boulder, CO: Westview.

Terenzini, Patrick T., Springer, L., Yaeger, Patricia M., Pascarella, E., T., and Nora, A. (1996). "First-Generation College Students: Characteristics, Experiences and Cognitive Development." *Research in Higher Education, 37,* 1, 1–73.

Timko C., and Moos R. H. (1996). "The Mutual Influence of Family Support and Youth Adaptation." In G. R. Pierce, B. R. Sarason, and I. G. Sarason (Eds.). *Handbook of Social Support and the Family* (pp. 289–313). New York: Plenum Press.

Tracey, T. J., and Sedlacek, W. E. (1985). "The Relationships of Noncognitive Variables to Academic Success: A Longitudinal Comparison by Race." *Journal of College Student Personnel, 26,* pp. 405–410.

Triandis, H. C., Marín, G., Betancourt, H., Lisansky, J., and Chang, B. (1982). *Dimensions of Familism among Hispanics and Mainstream Navy Recruits,* Technical Report No 14, Department of Psychology, University of Illinois, Champaign.

Trueba, Enrique (Henry) T. (2004). *The New Americans. Immigrants and Transnationals at Work.* New York: Rowman and Littlefield Publishers, Inc.

U.S. Census Bureau. (2000). P159H. Poverty Status in 1999, July 8, 2005. Retrieved from http://factfinder.census.gov/servlet/DTTable.

U.S. Census Bureau. (2004). Current Population Report P20–550. Retrieved October 12, 2005, http://web.lexis-nexis.com/statuniv/document?_m=9313b87a302af8 5aa6e7e92cc6e3530a.

U.S. Census Bureau. (2004). U.S. Interim Projections by Age Sex, Race and Hispanic Origin. Retrieved March 16, 2004. http://www.census.gov/ipc/wwwusinterimproj.

U.S. Department of Commerce, Economics and Statistics Administration. Bureau of the Census (1999). *Statistical Abstract of the United States: The National Data Book*, 119th Edition (p. 54). Washington, D.C.: U.S. Government Printing Office.

U.S. Department of Commerce, Bureau of the Census. (1997). Statistical Abstract of the United States. *The National Data Book*. Washington, D.C.: U.S. Government Printing Office.

U.S. Department of Commerce, Bureau of the Census. (1993). Statistical Abstract of the United States. *The National Data Book*. Washington, D.C.: U.S. Government Printing Office.

U.S. Department of Commerce, Bureau of the Census. (1991). *The Hispanic Population of the United States: March 1990.* (Current Population Reports, Series P-25 No. 995). Washington, D.C.: U.S. Government Printing Office.

Valenzuela, A. and Dornbusch, S. M. (1994). "Familism and Social Capital in the Academic Achievement of Mexican Origin and Anglo Adolescents." *Social Science Quarterly, 75*, 1, pp. 18–36.

Vasquez, M. J. (1982). "Confronting Barriers to Participation of Mexican American Women in Higher Education." *Hispanic Journal of Behavioral Sciences, 4*, pp. 147–165.

Vasquez-Nuttall, E., Romero-Garcia, I., and De Leon, B. (1987). "Sex Roles and Perceptions of Femininity and Masculinity of Hispanic Women: A Review of the Literature." *Psychology of Women Quarterly, 11*, pp. 409–426.

Vega, W. A. (1995). "The Study of Latino Families: A Point of Departure." In Zambrana, R. E. (Ed), *Understanding Latino Families: Scholarship, Policy and Practice*. Thousand Oaks, CA: Sage Publications.

Werner, E. E., and Smith, R. S. (1992). *Overcoming the Odds*. Ithaca, NY: Cornell University Press.

Williams, N. (1988). Role-Making among Married Mexicans." *Applied Behavioral Sciences, 24*, pp. 203–217.

Young, G. (1992). "Chicana College Students on the Texas Mexico Border: Tradition and Transformation." *Hispanic Journal of Behavioral Sciences, 14*, 3, pp. 341–352.

Zapata, J. I., and Jaramillo, P. T. (1981). "The Mexican American Family: An Adlerian Perspective." *Hispanic Journal of Behavioral Sciences, 3*, 275–290.

CHAPTER 7

Mexicana/Latina Mothers and Schools: Changing the Way We View Parent Involvement

Esperanza De La Vega

> Parents are being promiscuously invited into the now deficit-ridden sphere of public education; invited in "as if" this were a power-neutral partnership. Parents enter the contested public sphere of public education typically with neither resources nor power.[1]
>
> *"¿Quién tiene la última palabra?"* "Who has the last word?"
>
> (Bilingual Advisory Committee meeting December 30, 1996)

It was the frustrated edge in the parent's voice that caught my attention during the Bilingual Advisory Committee meeting. At this particular meeting I, as a Chicana/Latina novice researcher, began to see the moments of exclusion and missed communication between the school administration and Spanish-speaking parents. I found myself wondering if my native Spanish-speaking mother had experienced something similar in her attempts to be involved in her daughters' school experiences. My inquisitive mind coupled with my mother's *consejos* would take me on a four-year journey through academic and social justice landscapes to arrive at an understanding that the traditional, mainstream approach to parent involvement does not work for Mexican/Latino parents. Throughout the study, I searched for alternative and culturally responsive approaches to parent involvement that would facilitate collaboration and partnerships between schools and the Mexicana/Latina mothers who participated in this study. The parent/family involvement framework proposed in this chapter is based on the results of my study and offers an alternative to the Euro-American-centered mainstream model of parent involvement, which is unconnected to the lives of Mexican/Latino parents.

THE ETHNOGRAPHIC STUDY

The purpose of the ethnographic study was to try and understand the perspectives of Spanish-speaking, Mexicana/Latina mothers at Freedom Elementary School, which is located in the San Francisco Bay Area.[2] Freedom Elementary School received federal funds to restructure their bilingual education program at the same time that I, as a graduate student at a university nearby, took a part-time research assistant position at the school. My role was to support the school in their restructuring effort through the implementation of a strong assessment program. My interest in and relationship with the Spanish-speaking mothers at the school emerged from observing their interaction in meetings and their presence on the school grounds. The participation of bilingual or monolingual Spanish-speaking parents in school meetings and other school activities was particularly vital, because they represented a historically silent one-third of the school's population. For this reason, understanding how native Spanish-speaking mothers negotiated meaning from the social context of their encounters with school personnel became a driving question behind this study. This four-year study explored how the participants viewed the notion of parent involvement and participation at their child's school and how this perception was enacted in their daily lives and through encounters with school personnel.

It was through the Mexicana/Latina mothers' stories of their encounters with school personnel where several significant findings of this study were revealed. First of all, the data revealed that there were common binding aspects of Mexican/Latino culture among all of the participants. These aspects of culture appeared to be part of the participants' Mexican/Latino cultural way of seeing the world and seemed to be a natural or unconscious way of being. Secondly, the cultural lens through which the participants viewed the encounters influenced how they interpreted the interactions as moments of conflict or collaboration. Although encounters of collaboration were not shared as much as encounters of conflict, there were some stories of collaboration among the participants, and it was in these stories where I found hope.

In this chapter, I set out to bring forth some of the findings of the ethnographic study, which presents a view of Latino parent involvement that departs from mainstream conventions. I highlight participants' stories to illustrate the rich cultural lens in which they see the world, and I argue that schools will need to consider these aspects of culture in reaching out to their Mexican/Latino school community. In order to effectively reach out and increase their partnership with this language minority community, I believe that schools will need to shift the lens in which they see the Mexican/Latino community from a deficit view, where the parents are seen as "lacking," and move toward a resource view, where parents are seen has having valuable knowledge and resources.[3] The parent/family involvement framework proposed in this chapter will require that schools incorporate some of the important aspects of culture that are part of the Mexican/Latino culture into their perspective, approaches, and policies.

INTRODUCTION

With the birth of a child, the responsibility for that child's emotional, spiritual, physical, and intellectual growth rests within the family. More often than not, in the United States, the responsibility for the child lies with the parents. It is hard to dispute the idea that all parents want the best for their children. Being a good parent is something all would aspire to be, and so when asked about her views on being a good parent, Marta, a participant from the study, shared the following:

Una buena madre tiene que inculcar a sus niños las raíces de uno. De que sus niños no se olviden de su raíces Mexicanas—Porque están en este país y pues yo pienso que una buena madre esta con ellos, al lado de ellos, para darles la mano y el apoyo y que ellos estudien lo mejor.

A good mother has to acculturate her children to one's own roots. That their children not forget their Mexican roots—because they are here in this country and I think that a good mother is with them, by their sides, to give them a hand and support and that they study the best they can. (Interview, February 24, 2000)

Standing by a child's side is a beautiful image for how parents can support their children. However, once their child enters the educational system of public schools, the parent's role becomes one of shared responsibility. How that responsibility is shared is a topic that has been studied from the perspective of parents "participating" or becoming "involved" *within* schools. For parents who do not speak the language of the school (English), this new, shared parent-school relationship is a mystery that needs to be unraveled. Non-English speaking or limited-English speaking parents are faced with navigating this complex place called "public school" in a language and culture that is unfamiliar to them so they can stand by and support their children.

Often with good intentions, schools will invite language minority parents to become partners, to involve themselves in the education of their child, and unknowingly to participate in a bewildering world of school discourse in English. Based on her years of research on parent involvement programs in Chicago, New York, and Philadelphia, educational researcher Michelle Fine concludes that often poor, urban area parents enter the public sphere of public education without resources or power.[4] Throughout the restructuring effort at Freedom Elementary School, personnel spoke about collaborating with and including all voices in this new forum of shared-decision making. As the Spanish-speaking parent quoted at the beginning of this chapter demonstrated, the answer of who had the "last word" in the decision-making process was obscured and confusing to her. As I watched this encounter between the Spanish-speaking mother and school personnel, I felt something inside of me sit up and take notice. There was something mysterious happening here, something I didn't quite understand. It felt as if they were speaking to each other, and yet, they did not comprehend each other. It was this interaction that compelled me to search out answers of my own.

With the goal of trying to understand parents' perceptions of "parent involvement" and specifically from Mexicana/Latina mothers, I began with seminal literature in the field, such as Joyce Epstein's work on school and family partnerships.[5] I found, however, that the parent involvement typology proposed by Epstein was limiting (see Table 7.1).

I puzzled over how and where the Spanish-speaking mothers at my school would fit into the categories listed and discovered that sadly, many of them would not fit any of the types listed in Epstein's work. The types of outcomes described in the typology are activities and actions that are characteristic of white, middle-class parents. This particular view of parent participation does not address the complexities of linguistically and culturally diverse families' access and relationship with schools.[6]

In the end, I didn't use Epstein's parent involvement typology because it was not particularly helpful and because it did not include sociocultural issues of language, power, or race, which are a very real part of immigrant and language minority parents' daily lives.

Table 7.1
Joyce Epstein Proposed School/Family/Community Partnership Types

Type	Description
1. Parenting	Help all families establish home environments to support children as students.
2. Communicating	Design effective forms of school-to-home and home-to-school communications about school programs and children's progress.
3. Volunteering	Recruit and organize parent help and support.
4. Learning at Home	Provide information and ideas to families about how to help students at home with homework and other curriculum-related activities, decisions, and planning.
5. Decision-Making	Include parents in school decisions, developing parent leaders and representatives.
6. Collaborating with Community	Identify and integrate resources and services from the community to strengthen school programs, family practices, and student learning and development.

I found that Annette Lareau's research on parent involvement was useful for understanding how the socioeconomic status of parents impacted their involvement in schools.[7] Lareau provides a structure to more deeply analyze the resources or lack of resources parents bring to a particular situation and how those resources are or are not used. One of the key findings in Lareau's work points to how networks or links to others are part of one's resources. How parents utilize their resource or "social capital" will enable them to enact moments of inclusion into power structures and decision-making processes.[8]

Networks then became an integral part of this research study, in order to understand the ways Mexicana/Latina participants were linked into the life of the school. Using a sociocultural lens, I focused on the day-to-day lives and stories of 12 Mexicana/Latina mothers, in order to understand how they made decisions to become involved and participate, or not, at their children's school. Various researchers such as Concha Delgado-Gaitán, Guadalupe Valdés, and R. Shepard and H. Rose posit that culturally and linguistically diverse families are often viewed as "different" and that those differences are sources of misunderstanding when schools make cultural assumptions about the roles and participation of the parents.[9] There is a need to shift our thinking into more of a "resource" perspective when working with language minority parents and to develop relationships that are positive and respectful.[10] While researching and developing principles for restructuring schools that work with linguistically and culturally diverse families, Miramontes, Nadeau, and Commins found that underlying assumptions about different cultures and languages were critical to any restructuring effort. If a school community held a core assumption that respected and valued such differences, they were more likely to promote and effect positive change in their schools.[11] If schools held a deficit view of cultural and linguistic diversity, the impact could be quite negative, as noted by educational researcher Lourdes Díaz-Soto in Florida. Díaz-Soto worked with and conducted research on a Latino parent community that fought to save their bilingual education program. She documented the ways that district personnel and those with power silenced and oppressed the Latino parents. In the end, the school board demonstrated their lack of value for linguistic differences and dismantled a long-standing bilingual education program in the school district.[12] Holding a resource perspective and respecting and valuing diversity all became a part of the framework used for this study and later, became the basis for an alternative approach to parent/family involvement.

The work of Hoover-Dempsey and Sandler was critical to this research, as it focused not on the "types" of parent involvement, but instead on the process parents go through to become involved in their children's education.[13] Coming from a psychological research base and partly based on Brofenbrenner's ecological model, Hoover-Dempsey and Sandler provided a theoretical frame in which to view the process of parents' decisions to become involved in their children's education.[14] One of the first steps in the decision-making process involves a parents' construction of the parental role. Hoover-Dempsey and Sandler point out that the process of parental construction is influenced by parents' membership within a group. In their article "Why do parents become involved in their children's education?," Hoover-Dempsey and Sandler cite the process of parental construction to be the most important in the decision-making process.[15] The second and third influences appear to have less impact on the decision for parents to become involved. These are the parent's sense of efficacy for helping their children succeed in school and the parent's perceptions of opportunities or demands for involvement from their children and the school.

Although Hoover-Dempsey and Sandler's work does not address issues of linguistically and culturally diverse parents, there is an implicit connection to cultural influences in the construction of the parental role. The notion of being a member of a group relies on the assumption that we are culturally and socially part of a group, and that being part of a group means that we have been socialized in particular ways through membership. Thus, using a sociocultural lens with Hoover-Dempsey and Sandler's work, along with an adoption of a resource perspective that respects and values the culture and language of the Spanish-speaking mothers, I modified and utilized a framework in order to study Mexicana/Latina parent's choice to be or not be involved at this school site (see Figure 7.1).

This particular framework was useful in understanding Mexicana/Latina involvement with their children's schooling, because it represented the reality of a complex and multifaceted life. Trying to understand the

Figure 7.1
Theoretical Framework

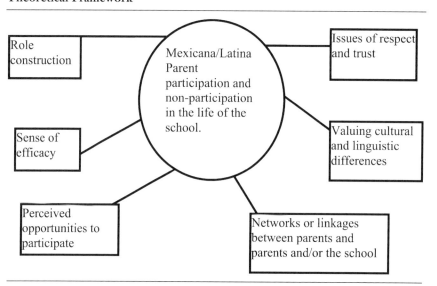

process of Mexicana/Latina mothers choices to become involved or not involved in their children's education provided more insight to me as a researcher than simply trying to fit their behavior into mainstream notions of parent involvement or a fixed typology, such as Epstein provides in her framework.

METHODOLOGY

This research began as a qualitative study of a group of Mexicana/Latina mothers whose children were enrolled at Freedom Elementary School during the restructuring of their bilingual education program. It became transformed, however, into an ethnographic study when the research continued over a four-year period and when the study began to focus on cultural issues.[16] These two main characteristics identify ethnographic studies. The fieldwork for this study was conducted during the period of September 1996 through September 1999, with follow-up interviews that extended into May 2000. Through qualitative research techniques, I was able to gather field notes, conduct interviews, and record observations that contributed to my understanding of the context at the study site and the perspectives of 12 Mexicana/Latina women whose children attended the school. Using a sociocultural framework to ground the study and qualitative research techniques to analyze the data, themes and findings emerged to highlight the ways this group of Mexicana/Latina mothers made sense of and constructed meaning from their experiences and encounters at Freedom Elementary School.

All of the participants had elementary school-age children who attended Freedom Elementary School. The participants of this study were added in a layered manner during a three-year period while I was a researcher and participant observer at the school. The first year of the study included 3 participants, the second year added 3 more, and the third year attempted to encompass all 12 of the Mexicana/Latina mothers who agreed to participate in this study. Each of the participants shared a new perspective of what it meant to be a mother of children attending this particular school. Their varied and rich backgrounds added a depth and complexity to the study that would not have been possible had I chosen to focus on a few of the women. Table 7.2 shows how the participants were added through the years of the study and the type of educational program in which their child was enrolled.

The participants in this research were unique in their own way and brought a rich depth to the research through their stories. Table 7.3 outlines the participants native language, educational experiences, current occupation, and how many children they had. The table also identifies whether their experience at Freedom School was their first encounter with an elementary school in the United States (eldest child entering kindergarten). The participants are listed in the order in which they were added to the study.

Table 7.2
Layered Addition of Participants

Parent	First Set (1996–97)	Second Set (1997–98)	Third Set (1998–99)
1. Anayeli	✓(B)		
2. Rosa Maria	✓(B)		
3. Margarita	✓(TWI)		
4. Carolina		✓(B)	
5. Mimi		✓(M)	
6. Susana		✓(B)	
7. Dolores			✓(TWI)
8. Marta			✓(TWI)
9. Chaya			✓(TWI)
10. Nazarene			✓(TWI)
11. Angelica			✓(TWI)
12. Rebeca			✓(TWI)

B = Bilingual classroom (transitional), TWI = Two Way Immersion bilingual classroom, M = Mainstream classroom (no bilingual services).

FINDINGS

"[L]anguage is inextricably linked to culture. It is a primary means by which people express their cultural values and the lens which they view the world."[17]

Valuing and building upon ones' native language is critical in a bilingual educational setting. Researchers in the field of education and linguistics agree that for children in a bilingual school setting, native language proficiency is the foundation of cognitive and social development as well as the basis for the development of academic proficiency levels (including literacy) in a second language.[18] For the parents of such children, language proficiency in their native language allows for cultural traditions to be passed on, as well as for communication to remain open and flowing between parent and child.

Sonia Nieto and other multicultural educators and researchers highlight the power of language for expression and interaction and its solid connection to ones' culture and lens for viewing the world.[19] Throughout the analysis of the data, language was not the only aspect of culture that emerged. Aspects of culture were not only consistent patterns in the data, but they also were reflected in each of the women's stories. These binding aspects of culture that appeared in their lives were *respeto, ser bien educado, dichos/consejos,* and *confianza.* These binding aspects of cultures appeared in different events and

Table 7.3
Participants' Backgrounds

Parent	Native Lang.	Occupation	Education Level	Child(ren)	First Experience with Schools?
1. Anayeli	Spanish	maid	Mexican Technical School for EMT	3	No—Eldest in High School
2. Rosa Maria	Spanish	fast food worker & office helper & parent advocate	Mexican Technical School for Secretary	2	No—Eldest in Middle School
3. Margarita	Spanish	homemaker	6th grade	3	Yes—Eldest in TWI classroom
4. Carolina	Spanish	research & pharmacy assistant & parent advocate	Mexican College degree in Nursing	3	No—Eldest in 4th grade Bilingual
5. Mimi	Bilingual (Native English)	homemaker & parent advocate	USA College degree (Education)	2	Yes—Eldest in General Education Classroom
6. Susana	Spanish	maid	6th grade	3	No—Eldest in Middle School
7. Dolores	Spanish	homemaker	Mexican College degree in Psychology	3	Yes—Eldest in TWI class
8. Marta	Spanish	homemaker	2nd grade	5	No—Eldest in High School
9. Chaya	Spanish	homemaker	Mexican College degree in Engineering	2	Yes—Eldest in TWI classroom
10. Nazarene	Spanish	homemaker	3rd grade	3	Yes—Eldest in TWI classroom
11. Angelica	Spanish	restaurant cook	6th grade	3	No—Eldest in Middle School
12. Rebeca	Bilingual (Native Spanish)	artist & midwife & homemaker	USA College degree	1	Yes—Eldest in TWI classroom

incidents throughout the study and became the thread that wove in and out of each of the women's stories. In particular, oral traditions such as *dichos* and *consejos* in many of the women's stories emerged as a way to socialize their children into framing and dealing with racism and discrimination. In this next section, I explore each of the aspects of culture that were common among the women.

Respeto and *ser bien educado*

Respeto and being *bien educado* were some of the first aspects of culture to emerge when I was a participant observer in Bilingual Advisory Committee meetings the first year of the study. During our first interview, Anayeli and I discussed the Mexican cultural value of *respeto*, which Anayeli believed was an important aspect of the culture. But first, she added, the "welcome" is very important. The way that a person is greeted is part of how you were raised, or your upbringing (manners), or in Spanish, *ser bien educado*. According to Anayeli, a person shows what a good upbringing they have by the way they greet another person. She felt that a person should never show the *acidez*[20] on their face or in the way that they speak, or in the haughtiness of having power. These comments came from her experiences and frustrations with Betty Lou, the principal of Freedom School, who treated Anayeli and other minority parents as a second-class citizen.

Betty Lou was not familiar with the Mexican/Latino culture and often missed opportunities to tap into the cultural resources of the Mexicana/Latina women's desire to be involved and connected with personnel from their children's school. In her discussion of the principal, Anayeli, felt that the responsibility of the school officials was to be a good example for others, which includes demonstrating respect to all people. The following excerpt from my interview with Anayeli explains her perspective on these issues:

As the head of a school, they should show respect to all of the others; to all races, "*no nomás enseñarle a uno . . . un lado de una cara y no la otra cara.*" "not just to show one . . . side of a face to one (person) and the other side to another (person)." Anayeli went on to tell me that other parents viewed the principal as a "monster." She added that she felt this way also. In her opinion, a person such as Betty Lou who is in an important position as the school's principal, needed to be caring and humble. Anayeli explained to me why she felt this way and what she experienced the first day of school.

According to Anayeli, the very first face that she saw on the first day of school was the vice principal. He was standing outside the entrance of the school building near the doors. There were three sets of heavy glass doors, all next to each other, that lead to stairs and upward into the hallways of the school. She thought that maybe he was nervous or something, but the first thing that he said to her was "Don't use this door. You should use the side doors, not the main, middle door." She thought to herself that a school should have all doors open and that a parent should be able to enter through whichever door they wanted. But mostly, she was caught off guard by his greeting, expecting a "good morning" instead of being told what not to do.

After dropping off her children to their classrooms, she saw some Spanish-speaking women in the hall near the office. She stopped to listen to the women and found that the parents were discussing the issue of transportation. They were worried because the bus did not come that morning, so they had brought their children to school. The parents were worried and unsure if the afternoon bus would bring their children home. Some of these parents had to go to work, which added to their uncertainty. According to Anayeli, the principal, Betty Lou, came out and "chased them" out of the hallway. "*Entonces, ella nos dijo 'pueden retirarse—aquí es el pasillo, no deben ver a uno en el pasillo. En la cafetería tenemos café si quieren sentarse allá a conocerse.*" (Then, she said, you should leave—This is the hallway and we shouldn't see anyone in the hallway. The cafeteria has coffee if you want to go and sit in there to get to know each other.) Anayeli clarified to me that it wasn't so much the words that were said to the group that distressed them, but the "manner" in which they were spoken. The women felt disrespected by the principal's words and actions. (Fieldnotes and Interview, April 8, 1997)

In this excerpt, we see the interrelatedness between *respeto* and being *bien educado* through Anayeli's interpretation of the first day welcome and encounter with the principal in the hallway. The cultural aspect of showing respect by ones' greetings and leave-takings emerged as a strong commonality among the participants. When talking about racism one encounters in a store or other places of business, Susana shared the *consejo* she gave to her daughters.

Yo siempre les digo que tienen que tener respeto para la gente mayor y un respeto para la gente menor. Pero que todos somos iguales. Todos somos personas. Y no porque ella habla más inglés que ella—porque si tú hablas español y ella no lo habla, yo no quiero que haya un problema.

Siempre tratar de llegar a un lugar dónde va a ir a comprar uno algo, y si le preguntan "¿te puedo ayudar en algo?" decirles—"sí, necesito esto, ¿por favor lo tiene?" Y cuando ya uno se va a retirar, un abrazo y thank you.

I always tell them that they have to have respect for the elders and respect for the younger. But that we are all equal. We are all persons. And just because she speaks more English than her—because if you speak Spanish and she doesn't, I don't want there to be any problems.

Always when you arrive at a store—and if they ask you "Can I help you with something?," say to them, "yes, I need this please do you have it?" And when you are ready to leave, a hug and thank you. (Interview, February 25, 2000)

Embedded in Susana's *consejo* were words about how to display appropriate behavior such as being polite in stores and greetings/leave-takings, which included a hug and an appreciation. This example reflected binding aspects of culture of *respeto* and being *bien educado*. It was also reflective of the second layer of socialization, where Susana was advising her daughter on how to avoid conflict and equipping her for future racist encounters.

According to the mothers in this study, appropriate greeting/leave-taking behavior showed that one is *bien educado*. Anayeli expected this in the principal's behavior, while Susana expected this in children's behavior as a means of demonstrating respect. Susana and Anayeli were not the only ones who discussed ideas about being well behaved or *bien educado*. For Rosa Maria,

"Una buena educación se refleja en nuestros hijos" (A good upbringing is reflected in our children) (Interview, February 24, 2000).

It was not only children's behavior that was watched, but the behavior of adults was observed and interpreted by the participants. Like Anayeli, Marta also shared her experiences with greeting adults at Freedom School. As a mother with older children, she felt comfortable about coming onto the school grounds. Whenever she was at Freedom School and she saw adults she knew, she would greet them. Marta saw the new principal, Julie Winston, as *"buena gente"* (good people), because she would take time to greet her, even though she knew Marta did not speak English. Marta appreciated this and believed that she had an open communication with most of the staff at the school. There were incidents, however, that made her feel bad. Marta shared the following:

Pues, como conoces unos varios maestros y a veces uno se siente mal porque pasa un maestro y tú lo quieres saludar y en vez se voltean por otro lado o no hablan contigo. Y allí se siente uno como, "¿por qué no la saludó?" porque si tuvo sus niños con él ¿verdad?

Well, like you know various teachers and sometimes you feel badly because you pass a teacher and you want to greet them, and instead, they turn to the other side or they don't speak to you. And there you are feeling like. "why don't they greet me?" because they had your children—right? (Interview, February 24, 2000)

The lack of reciprocity in a greeting hurt Marta's feelings and pointed to the value she placed in the cultural aspect of greetings. The participants' stories in this section reflected the cultural aspect of *respeto* and being *bien educado* as demonstrated through greetings and leave-takings.

Dichos and Consejos

In her ethnographic work about Spanish-speaking families in a Texas border community, Guadalupe Valdés points out that *dichos* (sayings) and *consejos* (counsel) are a Mexican tradition among woman.[21] There appeared to be a connection between the ways the participants' were socialized as young children and the echo of their mothers' *dichos* and *consejos* in their own parenting as adult women. Rosa Maria found comfort in the *consejos* of her mother during a particularly difficult time in her life. *"Por los consejos de mi madre, quiero darles lo mejor a mis hijos"* (because of the counsel of my mother, I want to give the best to my children) (Interview, June 4, 1999). Susana spoke lovingly about her parents and how *"nos dan buenos consejos"* (they give us good counsel). Her growing up experiences with having *"buenos consejos"* influenced her own views of what defined a "good mother." Susana had this to say: *"Ser una buena madre es también darles buenos consejos a los hijos"* (to be a good mother is to also give your children good counsel/advice) (Interview, May 28, 2000).

Dichos and *consejos* are messages offered to loved ones and children about critical issues. Often, the messages can emphasize what it means to be a person who is *bien educado*, about what's important in life, how to defend oneself against discrimination, and to never believe that someone is more important than you, but instead to treat others with respect. These messages (categorized as the second layer of socialization) were seen throughout the data in the stories of the different participants. The data pointed to the possibility that the participants' mother or caretakers voices through *dichos* and *consejos* were a link that kept them tethered to their cultural and linguistic roots. They were verbal traditions that in a few words captured a deeply serious message that was then passed from the participant's mothers to them, and then passed on to the participants' children. Generation to generation, *dichos* and *consejos* are passed from parent to child.

A particularly clear example of this second layer of socialization appeared in a story Rosa Maria shared about an incident that happened to her and her seven-year-old daughter, Alejandra, at a local grocery store. She was in the line to make her purchase when an Anglo woman entered in front of her into her line. Rosa Maria said to her "excuse me, *yo voy primero* (I'm first in line)" and the woman responded with a "No, I'm in a hurry." Rosa Maria explained to me that she argued with the woman and told her that she too, was in a hurry, but the woman rudely pushed her way in front of Rosa Maria telling her "you can wait, I'm a regular at this store." Alejandra asked her mother to not say anything else to the woman, but Rosa Maria responded to her daughter that:

Uno tiene que defenderse, no pelear, pero sí defenderse, porque si no, lo van a estar echando para atrás y no lo van a respetar a uno.

One has to defend oneself, not fight, but to defend oneself, because if you don't, they will keep pushing you back and they won't respect you. (Interview, February 24, 2000)

As the woman pushed her way to the front of the line, Rosa Maria appealed to the cashier who then called the manager. In the end, the woman was asked to step to the back of the line and wait her turn.

It grieved Rosa Maria, however, to see Alejandra exhibit nervous behavior every time they entered that particular grocery store. She explained to me that somehow her daughter had picked up the message that *"los blancos valen más"* (that whites [Anglos] have more value, or are more important) and that she had to emphasize to Alejandra that this was not true. In a previous occasion, she talked about how she appreciated her children attending a diverse school where they could learn the value of being equal to others. She shared the following:

Lo que me gustó es que hay diferentes nacionalidades—americanos, latinos, morenos,[22] y pueden aprender que todos son iguales—somos una comunidad. No porque él es latino es menos o porque él es moreno es menos. Que nos hagan menos es otra cosa—pero tienen que ver y pensar que no son menos.

What I like is that they have different nationalities. Americans, Latinos, African-American and they can learn that all are equal—we are a community. Just because he is Latino doesn't mean he is less than or because he is African American he is less than.

That they make us less than is another thing, but they (her children) have to see and think that they are not less than. (Interview, June 4, 1999)

Similar words were used by Susana when she told her daughter to treat others well, because all of us are equal. The notion that all people are the same is something that other participants said as well.

Angelica shared the *consejos* she gives to her children. She said:

Les digo que todos somos iguales, todos tenemos que tratarnos bien.
   I tell them that we are all the same and that we all have to treat each other well. (Interview, February 25, 2000)

Rebeca spoke about how she would question Daniel about why he didn't like a particular child. She would try and explain to her young son about life and that everybody is different but they are also the same. She explained:

Hay personas de todas las diferencias, de color, de raza, de clase, de lo que sea. Somos humanos.
   There are people of many differences, of color, of race, of class, of whatever. We're all humans. (Interview, February 25, 2000)

There was an undercurrent of equity and equality in the *consejo* of being the same, which the participants shared.

As mothers, one of their primary responsibilities is to socialize children in how to behave within the context of their sociocultural environment. Examples of this socialization process could include when to say "please" and "thank you," how to act around elders or youngsters, and when it's appropriate to interrupt or not. These common acts could be considered the first layer of socialization. This study revealed that within the stories of the participants, the *consejo* of "we are all the same" came up around incidents of discrimination. The message of "sameness" could be seen as a second layer of socialization and a way for the Latina/Mexican mothers to instill in their children a sense of equality.

Confianza

The University of Chicago Spanish/English Dictionary defines *confianza* as "confidence, trust; familiarity; informality."[23] The word is not easily translated into English because the notion of having *confianza* in another person emerges from a deep belief and carries more ideological weight than the English translation can hold. *Confianza* emerges from perceptions and mutual feelings of being welcomed, cared for, valued, and trusted. Confidence in another person can be another manifestation of the *confianza*, although one can have confidence in another, but not trust them. Trust in oneself, on the other hand, can be considered or translated into self-confidence or self-esteem. The other translations of *confianza* into the English words of familiarity and informality do not seem to reach the depth of trust the Spanish word exudes. The sociocultural context of the word *confianza* is deeply rooted in the Latina/Mexicana culture. It is an ideologically charged word that carries emotional connections to and respect for another person.

Rebeca shared her thoughts on this as she spoke to me about her beliefs on raising children and about their development of *confianza*. During an interview she shared that a good education should teach children how to respect and care for all types of people and

Bueno—este—no dañar su espíritu, de que tiene que ver mucho con la confianza en sí mismo y también nada de confianza. Hay una balanza. Y eso es muy importante para los niños, porque vemos muchos adultos que tienen problemas con la confianza en si mismo porque se les hizo pedazos.

Well—umm—not to hurt the spirit, that has a lot to do with the self-confidence one has and also no confidence. There is a balance. And this is very important for the children, because we see that there are many adults that have problems with self-confidence because it [the spirit] has been broken into pieces. (Interview, February 25, 2000)

Thus Rebeca's beliefs about *confianza* were associated with self-confidence and ones' spirit. She believed if adults have had their spirits broken as young children, they would eventually not demonstrate strong self-esteem as adults. It is an interesting idea to consider, in light of the notion that *confianza* can be seen manifested in several ways: self-confidence and confidence or trust in others.

The participants spoke at length about incidents at the school where they felt confident in or trusted others. Dolores and other mothers spoke highly of Julie Winston, the new principal at Freedom School. Through her warm smile and engaging style of leadership, she won the hearts of many Spanish-speaking parents at the school. Susana referred to Julie as *"buena gente"* (a good person) and felt confident enough to approach Julie and other teachers with her questions or concerns. She shared the following:

Siempre me gusta saludar a los maestros—me da mucho confianza—entonces yo siempre estoy preguntando muchas cosas.

I always like to greet the teachers and it [the communication] gives me much more confidence—and then I'm always asking questions about lots of things. (Interview, May 28, 2000)

In speaking about her level of *confianza* at the school, Carolina shared her early experiences with the former principal Betty Lou. She was able to provide a contrast about how she felt then and how she felt later when she was at the new school site with Julie Winston as the new principal. She shared:

Yo me sentía que no había mucha comunicación. O sea—como me sentía como una extraña en la escuela. Ella [Betty Lou] era muy—no es una persona que te inspira confianza . . . además

de que no le gustaba ser sociable con la gente—especialmente—bueno escuché muchos—que se molestan con latinos especialmente.

Aquí me siento mejor—porque estaba participando—entonces me siento con más confianza de venir, de platicar con el personal, de ir a los salones de mis hijos…como que ya—ya se siente más suave.

I felt that there was not a lot of communication. Well—I felt like a stranger in the school. She [Betty Lou] was very—she was not a person who inspires confidence in one … In addition she did not like to be social with people—especially—well I've heard a lot—that she was especially disturbed by Latinos.

Here I feel better because I was participating—and then I felt more confidence to come, to talk with the personnel, to go to my children's classrooms . . . like now—now things feel better. (Interview, June 8, 1999)

Having confidence in or trusting the situation allowed the participants to come onto the school grounds and talk with school personnel. This was a common theme among the participants. Marta, Rosa Maria, and Angelica shared the sentiments expressed by Susana, Dolores, and Carolina. The more that participants interacted with and built relationships with teachers, the more their confidence increased. When the participants were asked whom they approached whenever they had a school issue to resolve, most cited being able to approach and talk with their child's teacher. Angelica shared the following:

Vengo y les pregunto como están o platicamos de cualquier cosa.
I ask them how they are, or we talk about any thing. (Interview, February 25, 2000)

Marta spoke about the relationship she had with her son's teacher.

Yo tengo más confianza con la maestra de mi hijo. Como hemos platicado tengo mucha confianza.
I have a lot of confidence with the teacher of my son. Because we have spoken, I have lots of confidence. (Interview, February 24, 2000)

Rosa Maria talked about the confidence she had in the principal, the teachers, and others at the school. For her, the ability to trust school personnel was an important factor in being able to participate in her children's education. She said:

Yo tengo confianza—se puede decir que con todos. A la directora—ella conoce mis problemas, a Ann-Marie, a Deborah, al maestro Gutierrez—a los maestros de mis hijos. Porque yo creo que tenemos que sentirnos en confianza para así poder pedir ayuda. Porque si no—si yo no me siento con confianza, yo no voy a ir a platicar mi problema que yo tengo con mis hijos—¿verdad?
I have confidence—you could say with everyone. The principal—she knows my problems, with Ann-Marie, with Deborah, with teacher Mr. Gutierrez, with the teachers of my children. Because I believe that we have to feel confident in order to ask for help. Because if not, if I don't feel confident, I'm not going to go and talk about the problem I have with my children—right? (Interview, February 24, 2000)

Rosa Maria felt strongly about being able to share her problems with the school personnel, and especially sought out teachers with whom she could partner and problem solve for the sake of her children.

In summary, the aspects of culture that appeared in the participants' lives were *respeto, ser bien educado, dichos* and *consejos,* and *confianza.* These aspects of the participants' Mexican/Latino culture were part of their way of seeing the world and appeared to be a natural or unconscious way of being. In addition to the binding aspects of culture and the second layer of socialization, the data revealed language was very interwoven into the women's stories, and it was through language that their worldviews were revealed.

Many of the encounters that participants faced during this study revolved around issues of language use, both in school and in the home. Most of the participants believed that talking with their children is a way for them to be involved and to understand what was going on in school. They desired to understand what their children were experiencing and thinking. Thus, communication with one's children became a key component of parent involvement. Maintaining ones' native language also emerged in the data under this the overarching theme of multilingual considerations. Many of the parents worried about their children's bilingualism and biliteracy development and took steps to promote it in the home environment. Not only did the participants speak Spanish at home, they also encouraged writing in Spanish as well.

The data showed Mexicana/Latina mothers understood that English was the language of power and that society viewed their lack of proficiency negatively or somehow less than ideal. This tension was seen in many of their stories as they spoke about being unable to help their children with homework or their discomfort in speaking with school personnel in English. They also shared stories of how they had to legitimize their knowledge and their language skills to their children. Thus their support of bilingual education programs was a strong statement of validation and belief in developing bilingualism in their children.

The data also showed that the second layer of socialization was a way to move toward social justice and equity. It was a more personal and often unseen effort to combat racism and discrimination and these events of socialization were usually initiated through encounters of conflict. Through the second layer of socialization process the Mexicana/Latina mothers in this study socialized their children in ways that helped them deal with racism and discrimination. The participants in this study spoke about such encounters within and outside of the school environment, and the data revealed that their responses varied. At times, they simply gave *consejos* about "trying your best" or about not letting others treat you badly. At other times, they gave their children reminders about demonstrating *respeto* and being *bien educado.* Thus the desire for social justice and equity emerged in this study to support the way their words and culture were used to raise their children.

IMPLICATIONS

The implications of this study point to an alternative view of parent involvement than the traditional model. In our growing pluralistic society, multilingual and cultural considerations need to become a part of every aspect of our public school policies. Understanding that language is inextricably linked to culture is a mindset and perspective that should be understood among educational leadership and embedded in school districts' services for their English-language learners. Schools should explore their assumptions and scrutinize the climate in their schools community, in particular, how parents' native language is treated and accepted. In addition, schools should examine how the invitations are delivered to and received by their diverse parent community. Are they translated? Are they embedded within a newsletter? Are invitations being recognized as such by the parent/family community? Ultimately, school districts should look beyond sending home a newsletter with a paragraph devoted to inviting parents to join school committees. These invitations, although cost effective, are not powerful enough to reach diverse families, and especially if not translated into their native languages.

The implications of this study clearly point to creating climates that promote respect for and inclusion of diverse languages and cultures into the school environment. So how does a school go about demonstrating these attributes? In an interview, Susana shared the conditions she believed would contribute to an increase in Latino parent involvement. She felt that in order to gain the confidence and affection of the Latino community, one needed to recognize Latinos as a people who responded well when others treated them with respect and care. She said:

Si vemos que son esas personas amables, que quieren a nuestros hijos, nos quieren a nosotros, nos apoyan y siempre nos buscan para hacer algo en la escuela. Los latinos siempre van a estar presentes . . . Siempre vamos a apoyar. Siempre vamos a tratar de ir siempre adelante.

If we see that they are kind people who care about our children, who care about us, who support us, and always seek us to do something at the school, the Latinos will always be present. We will always be there. We will always be supportive. We will try to always move forward. (Interview, May 28, 2000)

Susana's perspective is a powerful one to consider as conditions for collaboration. She used the word "*quieren*," which is difficult to translate into English. We often don't think about loving a stranger or someone we barely know, but the word *quieren* is most often translated as *love*. In this situation, "care" or "affection" conveys the intent of Susana's words more accurately. From her perspective, it would appear that showing one's care for children and families was an integral part of demonstrating a willingness to collaborate. The act of inviting Latino parents to help in some way seemed to be another important consideration. According to Susana, Latino parents were always willing to help out if asked. Providing translation and interpretation services through bilingual instructional assistants, home/school liaisons, or bilingual office staff is another suggestion that will help facilitate the communication and the development of positive relationships between non-English speaking families and schools. Using a personal touch (through person-to-person contact and phone calls) when reaching out to families and inviting them onto the school grounds would help as well. In addition, when setting up meeting times and locations, schools should think "outside the box" and consider holding meetings at different times, days, and in locations other than the school. Often churches, community centers, and apartment complexes' general purpose rooms will bring more families to the gathering.

Although difficult, school personnel should not avoid dealing with injustice and inequity issues when they arise. School leadership should investigate their efforts to combat racism and discrimination at the institutional and personal level. When conflicts occur and district personnel find angry or frustrated parents at their door, they should view these encounters as an opportunity to understand the cultural perspective of those parents. For every parent who chooses to fight and speak out, there are many more who remained silent. Thus encounters of conflict can provide a deeper look at how parents are interpreting the district's policies and practices. This type of investigation could lead district personnel and administration into recognizing which policies are creating negative repercussions for schools with diverse families.

In conclusion, the Mexicana/Latina mothers had much to say about language and culture. Their stories and day-to-day lives gave insight into several important processes connected to language and culture. They had much to say about their desire to be treated with respect, care, and equality. They also were very willing to help out when invitations to help were perceived as authentic and included their input and ideas. In addition, when the need arose, the Mexicana/Latina mothers in this study would give their children *consejos* to help them combat racist or discriminatory situations. This second layer of socialization responsibility was something the mothers did in order to help their children deflect negative messages related to race, ethnicity, social class, and language. These events revealed social justice and equity efforts in more intimate private moments as the Mexicana/Latina mothers prepared their children for a world that doesn't always treat people with justice and equity.

The major implications of this study point back to the framework used for understanding parent/family involvement during the research process. The alternative to a mainstream typology of parent involvement moves us toward viewing Mexican/Latino parents/family members with new eyes. First and foremost, we need to understand that language and culture are integrated in people's lives in complicated and deeply rooted ways. Aspects of culture such as *respeto*, being *bien educado*, sharing *dichos/consejos*, and building relationships that elicit *confianza* are not simply quaint folk traditions or notions, but they are aspects of culture that are manifested in the day-to-day lives of children and families. This is an important consideration for educators to incorporate into their encounters and interactions with Mexican/Latino parents and family members. When approached with cultural sensitivity, the Mexican/ Latina mothers of this study all conveyed a willingness to communicate, collaborate, and to help the teacher and school. Secondly, our school policies should promote and value cultural and linguistic differences. Sadly, policies such as Proposition 227, which passed in California in 1998, are reflective of a trend of "English-Only" initiatives that disrespect the linguistic and cultural differences students' bring to schools. State and district parent involvement policies that explicitly affirm and value linguistic and cultural differences would support day-to-day efforts at the school level. Finally, the power of relationships should not be underestimated. Positive relationships that created feelings of care, respect, and *confianza* were important to the Mexicana/Latina mothers in this study. These were a necessary pre-requisite for creating positive environments of collaboration. The data showed that parents looked for signs or cues that principals, teachers, or other school representatives cared about them and their children. They also wanted their school personnel to be kind, respectful, supportive, and to listen to their concerns and suggestions. It is difficult to quantify qualities such as care, respect, and valuing of another person. However, small signs did not go unnoticed by the participants. It was often a warm welcome, a smile and acknowledging nod, a friendly wave from across the school yard, or making time to hold a newborn in one's arms that made a big difference in conveying feelings of inclusion and care among the Mexicana/Latina mothers in this study.

Thinking back to the Bilingual Advisory Committee meeting on a late December evening and hearing the Spanish-speaking parent question—*¿Quién tiene la última palabra?* (Who has the last word?), it reminds us of the ultimate question of who is making the decisions that impact linguistically and culturally diverse students and families? If we view parent involvement with mainstream eyes, the people in power, such as school administrators, vocal parents, and influential others, will continue to make decisions that inadvertently keep linguistically and culturally diverse families silent and oppressed. I believe that collaboration is possible and that a shared decision-making process can happen when we view the involvement of Mexican/Latino parents and families with new eyes. Adopting a culturally responsive Mexican/Latino parent involvement approach will open doors and build relationships where shared decision-making processes can occur. We can then answer the questioning parent, that we all share in the decision-making process that will directly impact the education of our children.

NOTES

1. Fine, Michelle, "[Ap]parent Involvement: Reflections on Parents, Power and Urban Public Schools," *Teachers College Record 94* no. 4 (1993): 692.

2. Pseudonyms are used for research school site and participants of this study.

3. Moll, Luis, "Bilingual Classroom Studies and Community Analysis: Some Recent Trends," *Educational Researcher* 21 no. 2 (1992): pp. 20–24. His description of the "funds of knowledge" supports a resource perspective.

4. Fine, Michelle, "[Ap]parent Involvement: Reflections on Parents, Power and Urban Public Schools," *Teachers College Record 94* no. 4 (1993): 682–709.

5. Epstein, Joyce, "School and Family Partnerships," in *Encyclopedia of Educational Research* (New York: Macmillan Publishing Company, 1992); Epstein, Joyce, "School/Family/Community Partnerships: Caring for the Children We Share," *Phi Delta Kappan* May issue (1995): 701–712.

6. Valdés, Guadalupe, *Con Respeto: Bridging the Distances Between Culturally Diverse Families and School* (New York: Teachers College Press, 1996); Moll (1992).

7. Lareau, Annette, *Home Advantage: Social Class and Parental Intervention in Elementary Education* (New York: Falmer, 1989); Lareau, Annette, and E. M. Hargot, "Moments of Social Inclusion and Exclusion: Race, Class and Cultural Capital in Family-School Relationships," *Sociology of Education* 72, no. 1 (1999): 37–53; Lareau, Annette, and W. Shumar, "The Problem of Individualism in Family School Policies," *Sociology of Education* extra issue (1996): 24–39.

8. Lareau and Hargot (1999).

9. Delgado-Gaitán, Concha, "Involving Parents in the Schools: A Process of Empowerment," *American Journal of Education* 100, no. 1 (1991): 20–46; Valdés (1996); Shepard, R., & H. Rose, "The Power of Parents: An Empowerment Model for Increasing Parental Involvement," *Education* 115, no. 3 (1995): 373–377. They also refer to Brofenbrenner's "ecological" model view individuals as belonging to interconnected, concentric environments.

10. Miramontes, O. B., Nadeu, A., and N. Commins, *Restructuring Schools for Linguistic Diversity: Linking Decision Making to Effective Programs* (New York: Teachers College Press, 1997).

11. Edwards, A.P., Fear, K.L., and M. Gallego, "Role of Parents in Responding to Issues of Linguistic and Cultural Diversity," in *Meeting the Challenge of Linguistic and Cultural Diversity in Early Childhood Education* (New York: Teachers College Press, 1995); Rosado, L.A., "Promoting Partnerships with Minority Parents: A Revolution in Today's Restructuring Efforts," *The Journal of Educational Issues of Language Minority Students*, 14, winter issue (1994): 241–254.

12. Díaz-Soto, Lourdes, *Language, Culture and Power* (Albany: SUNY Press, 1997).

13. Hoover-Dempsey, K. V., and H. M. Sandler, "Parental Involvement in Children's Education: Why Does it Make a Difference?" *Teachers College Record* 97, no. 2 (1995): 310–331; Hoover-Dempsey, K. V., and H. M. Sandler, "Why do Parents Become Involved in Their Children's Education?" *Review of Educational Research* 67, no. 1 (1997): 3–42.

14. Brofenbrenner, U., "Ecology of the Family as a Context for Human Development: Research Perspectives," *Developmental Psychology* 22 (1986): 723–742. His seminal work helps us understand the complex nature and ecology of families.

15. Hoover-Dempsy and Sandler (1997).

16. Van Maanen, J., *Tales from the Field: On Writing Ethnography* (Chicago: University of Chicago Press, 1988). See his description of and characteristics for research that is ethnographic.

17. Nieto, Sonia, *Affirming Diversity: The Sociopolitical Context of Multicultural Education* (White Plains: Longman Publishing Group, 1992), 153.

18. Collier, Virginia P., *Promoting Academic Success for ESL Students: Understanding Second Language Acquisition for School* (Jersey City: New Jersey Teachers of English to Speakers of Other Languages—Bilingual Educators, 1995); Lightbown, Patty, *How Languages are Learned* (London: Oxford University Press, 1999); Lindors, Judith Wells, *Children's Language and Learning* (Englewood Cliffs: Prentice-Hall Inc., 1987).

19. Nieto (1992); Collier (1995); García, Eugene E., *Student Cultural Diversity: Understanding and Meeting the Challenge* (New York: Houghton Mifflin, 2002).

20. *Acidez* cannot be conveyed through a direct translation. It's a cultural term that implies a bitterness or belittling attitude from someone with authority to someone with less power.

21. Valdés (1996).

22. *Moreno* is translated as "dark" or "brown" but is used to refer to people of African American or Caribbean descent, or to people with dark skin.

23. *University of Chicago Spanish Dictionary 4th Edition* (Chicago: University of Chicago Press, 1987), 87.

CHAPTER 8

Policing the Latino Community: Key Issues and Directions for Future Research

Cynthia Pérez McCluskey and Francisco A. Villarruel

INTRODUCTION

Traditionally, the relationship between Latinos and police has been characterized by mistrust and tension. A history of conflict between Latinos and police in the United States has been well documented (Acuña, 1988; Mirandé, 1985; Samora, Bernal, and Peña, 1979). Early confrontations related to immigration during Depression-era deportation movements have been cited (Mirandé, 1985), and tensions between Latinos and police continued into the 1940s with the Zoot Suit Riots. Strained interactions between Latinos and police were highlighted in the 1970s and 1980s as part of a national recognition of the breakdown in relations between police and minority communities. Mistrust and tension between police and minorities continues today and represents a source of scholarly and public attention. History of the relationship between Latinos and law enforcement is an important context for understanding the current state of affairs between Latinos and police (Escobar, 1999).

In recent years, highly visible police abuse cases have drawn attention to police and minority relations (Alozie and Ramirez, 1999; Lasley, 1994; Skolnick and Fyfe, 1993; Tuch and Weitzer, 1997). Increasingly, federal funds have been made available to examine interactions between police and minority communities in the United States. Of particular concern are the legitimacy of police within minority communities and the perceived legitimacy of the criminal justice system generally (Jesilow, Meyer, Namazzi, 1995; Miller, 1991; Walker, 1999). As Miller (1991) describes, police legitimacy emerges from the community through interactions with citizens. When those interactions are characterized by conflict, police legitimacy and trust are compromised. In the progression toward community policing and increased police presence in neighborhoods, the importance of establishing legitimacy has increased substantially (Kelling and Moore, 1999). A number of studies have found that minorities are more likely than whites to view the police negatively because of the experience of unfair treatment, racial discrimination, verbal abuse, and excessive use of physical force by police officers (Carter, 1985; Huo and Tyler, 2000; Morales, 1972; Samora, Bernal, and Peña, 1979).

To date, most knowledge of police and minority relations is based on the experience of African Americans (Herbst and Walker, 2001; Holmes, 1998). As a result, little is known about interactions between police and the Latino community. Predominantly, studies related to police and minority communities include a dichotomous race variable and do not always recognize Latinos as a distinct group (Flowers, 1990). Few studies of policing in minority communities include Latinos and examine challenges that Latino communities face with law enforcement (see Schuck, Lersch, and Verrill, 2004 for a description of Latino underrepresentation in criminal justice research generally).

Latinos have emerged as the largest minority population in the United States, surpassing the size of the African American population in the last several years (Guzmán, 2001). In spite of that, however, there remains a paucity of research on police and Latino relations. Underlying the relationship between Latinos and police is a history of conflict, mistrust, and misunderstanding (Escobar, 1999). Given the rapid growth of the Latino population in recent decades, Latino presence in metropolitan areas, and growing Latino population in areas without an historical Latino presence, the opportunity for Latino contacts with police has increased substantially.

Characteristics of the U.S. Latino Population

In recent years, it has become increasingly important that the social sciences direct attention to Latinos, considering their rapid growth in the United States generally, as well as in the criminal justice system. In population estimates released since the 2000 census, the Current Population Survey reveals that as of July 2004, Latinos number 41.3 million and comprise approximately 14 percent of the total U.S. population (Bernstein, 2005). This represents a Latino growth rate of 3.6 percent between 2003 and 2004, which is more than three times the growth rate of the national population.

In an analysis of Latino growth rates in the 100 largest metropolitan areas of the United States between 1980 and 2000, Suro and Singer find that the "growth of the Latino population is no longer limited to just a few regions" (2002, 2). While the number of Latinos increased in established Latino cities such as Los Angeles, New York, and Miami, "new Latino destinations" were identified and include Atlanta, Las Vegas, and Charlotte, North Carolina (Suro and Singer, 2002, 5). Shifts in the geographic distribution of Latinos are likely to provide unique challenges, particularly to those "new Latino destinations," in providing services to the community.

Nationally, the Latino population is characterized by rapid growth, residence in metropolitan areas, poverty, and youthfulness; all of which are associated with a higher likelihood of contact with police. Between 1990 and 2000, the Latino population increased by nearly 60 percent (22 million to 35 million), compared to a 13 percent overall growth of the U.S. population (Guzmán, 2001). Latinos are also concentrated geographically, primarily in the West and South, and the largest Latino communities are found in cities such as Los Angeles, New York, Chicago, Houston, Philadelphia, and San Antonio. Overall, Latinos are more than twice as likely as non-Latino whites to live in a central city in a major metropolitan area (Therrien and Ramirez, 2001).

By the same token, the diversity amongst and between Latino communities has increased substantially over the past couple of decades (Ramirez and de la Cruz, 2003). While Latino communities share the common language of Spanish and most are of Catholic faith, there are unique political, religious, and economic histories that have been experienced and influence both public trust and civic engagement. These personal experiences have contributed to a common misperception that Latino communities experience political, economic, cultural, and social difficulties, thus delaying their integration and acculturation into U.S. societal structures. Stereotypes of being "dirty" or "lazy" exacerbate perceived differences between Latino and non-Latino communities.

Within the Latino community the rate of unemployment is two times that of non-Latino whites. Latinos are also more likely to live in poverty (23% compared to 8% poverty for non-Latino whites). Compared with the national age distribution, Latinos are also younger than non-Latino whites. Thirty four percent of the Latino population is under 18 years of age, compared with 24 percent white and 30 percent African American youth.

Given these demographic characteristics, the likelihood of Latino encounters with the criminal justice system is substantial. Contact with the criminal justice system is exemplified by Latino overrepresentation in corrections statistics, where the ethnic group comprises 29 percent and 15 percent of persons under Federal and State correctional authorities, respectively (Maguire and Pastore, 2001). Given the limited research on policing in Latino communities, criminal justice researchers and administrators would benefit greatly from examining these ethnic groups more closely, especially with regard to police, who serve as gatekeepers to the criminal justice system.

Goal of Current Research

The purpose of this chapter is to examine the literature on police and the Latino community and to identify directions for future research. Examination of historical, organizational, and community factors may help to identify sources of misunderstanding and conflict between police agencies and Latino citizens. Although studies have begun to include Latino samples in police research, additional research is needed to enhance the understanding of police and Latino community relations. Empirical assessment of such factors may ultimately focus efforts to enhance cooperation among police and Latinos and create safer Latino communities.

LATINOS AND POLICE: KEY RESEARCH AREAS

Historical Relationship between Latinos and Police

Although the Zoot Suit Riots of 1943 served as a significant point in the relationship between police and Mexican Americans in Los Angeles, Escobar (1999) chronicles the strained history between Chicanos and police in Los Angeles, which extends back into the early twentieth century.

Most scholars cite the urban uprisings of the 1960s and the resultant findings by the National Advisory Commission on Civil Disorders (the Kerner Commission) as a predominant turning point in relations between police and minority communities. Although this was a significant event in identifying mistrust and hostility between police and minority communities, Escobar finds that for the Mexican American (Chicano) community, the relationship was impacted by events that occurred much earlier in the twentieth century. Studies that focus on events of the 1960s and 1970s are therefore seen as incomplete in providing an in-depth historical analysis of the relationship between Latinos and law enforcement; particularly between Mexican Americans and the Los Angeles Police Department (LAPD).

Escobar identifies three primary historical movements that shaped the relationship between law enforcement and the Mexican American community in Los Angeles, including societal views on the link between race and crime, police professionalism, and community activism. Societal views toward Mexican Americans shifted in the first half of the twentieth century to include inherent criminality. Mexican youth, in particular, were viewed with suspicion and were typically linked with gangs and criminal activity in the 1930s and 1940s. As Escobar describes:

At the beginning of the century, while Mexicans were certainly seen by whites as an inferior race, they were not generally regarded by government and law enforcement officials as inherently criminal. Even the LAPD articulated no such view. During the subsequent half century, however, the deterioration of the relationship between Mexican Americans and the LAPD, and especially the hysteria during World War II over juvenile delinquency, thrust Mexican American youth into the national consciousness as a criminal element in society. (1999, 10)

During this time, Chicano youth, particularly those who fit the image of a "zoot suiter" or "pachuco" were targets of racism and repression. The common image of the youthful, rebellious Chicano was magnified by the media (Trujillo, 1974) and ultimately resulted in fear and anti-Mexican hysteria (Escobar, 1999). Mirandé (1985) cites this as an example of the mobilization of bias, whereby the media was involved in spreading the image of the zoot suiter as criminal, as were other social institutions such as politicians and police.

One significant event in the history of police and Latino community is the aforementioned Zoot Suit Riots, which was a series of violent confrontations between predominantly white servicemen and Chicano youth in Los Angeles in 1943 (Mazón, 1984). As media perceptions led to the growing fear and suspicion of Chicano youth, they ultimately resulted in violent victimization of those who fit the image of the violent pachuco. Media reports of Chicano youth crime and the accusation of 17 Chicano youth in the Sleepy Lagoon Case (see Escobar, 1999 or Mazón, 1984 for an in-depth account) created an anti-Chicano movement in Los Angeles. The Zoot Suit Riots occurred between June 3 and June 10, 1943, and began with off-duty policemen conducting a vigilante hunt for zoot suiters who allegedly attacked several servicemen. During the riots, several hundred servicemen drove through the barrio and beat Chicano youth. Police condoned the violence and are reported to have escorted the servicemen to safety and arrested their Chicano victims.

Coinciding with the criminalization of Mexican youth in the media was the "professional" era in policing. According to Escobar (1999), changes in policing impacted the relationship between police and the Latino community. The professionalism movement spurred a war on crime that targeted youthful offenders, most typically minorities. As police agencies moved toward professionalism, the organizations developed efficient and effective mechanisms for fighting crime. Given societal perceptions of the link between race and criminal behavior, minority youth were the most likely targets of crime fighting efforts.

Wolcott (2001) describes the "Crime Fighting Era" in the 1920s and 1930s in Los Angeles as characterized by aggressive enforcement, even among youthful offenders. In an analysis of arrest rates, Wolcott cites an overall increase in felony arrests of males between the ages of 10 and 17 in Los Angeles during the 1930s and 1940s (2001, 357). Arrests of Hispanic males, in particular, rose during the "Crime Fighting Era." Supporting Escobar's depiction of the criminalization of Chicano youth, Wolcott suggests that arrest was used "predominantly as a mechanism to regulate boys who were darker-skinned and—allegedly—more often criminal" (2001, 357). In 1940, Hispanics comprised 32 percent of all youthful males arrested by the LAPD, and at the time, comprised 8 percent of the city population. In compiling juvenile court records of the 1940s, Wolcott (2001) also found that Hispanic youth were more likely to be petitioned to court for robbery and other violent crimes than were whites and African Americans combined (17% versus 6%, respectively). Over half of all youthful males accused of violent crime during the 1930s and 1940s were Hispanic (Wolcott, 2001).

In addition to the widespread views of Chicanos as criminal and police professionalism, Escobar also describes political activism among Chicanos in Los Angeles as a contributing factor to the strained relationship between the Mexican American community and police (1999). In an effort to endure the alienation and discrimination consistent with minority group status, Chicanos developed formal and informal coping mechanisms, including labor unions and civil rights groups. From these initial efforts grew community-based activism and the development of a Mexican American political identity (Escobar, 1999). The convergence of the three factors shaped police and Latino relations well before national attention was drawn to the fractured relationship between police and minority communities following the civil rights movement.

Organizational Responses to Latinos

The literature on Latinos and police suggests that administrative attitudes may influence police practices in terms of the utilization of resources, tolerance for the use of force, and responsiveness to Latino concerns. Within the law enforcement agency, attitudes toward Latinos may influence the distribution of manpower and police deployment tactics in Latino neighborhoods, subjecting Latinos to increased scrutiny and social control (Jackson, 1989; Mirandé, 1987; Morales, 1972).

Similarly, administrative attitudes may influence the tolerance for the use of force against Latino suspects (Acuña, 1988; Mandel, 1981; Trujillo, 1974). As described previously, common perceptions of Latinos included inherent criminality. This image has been argued to implicitly condone the use of force in controlling the violent offender. Empirical research on the use of force against minorities has produced mixed findings, however. Studies of police force have examined a variety of causal factors, including citizen characteristics such as sex, race, and social class, along with characteristics of the police-citizen encounter. In a comprehensive study of police use of force, Garner, Maxwell, and Heraux (2002) reviewed research findings on police force and found that studies are nearly evenly split on the significance of race. Three studies described higher rates of force against nonwhite citizens (Smith, 1986; Terrill and Mastrofski, 2002; Worden, 1996). Due to the limited numbers of Latinos in these samples, studies combined minorities into a single (nonwhite) category. While several studies demonstrate a significant relationship between suspect race and force, other studies failed to produce such a finding (Engel, Sobol, and Worden, 2000; Garner et al., 2002). In their analysis of 7,512 adult custody arrests, Garner et al. (2002) examine three separate racial/ethnic groups in six jurisdictions. In comparing the prevalence of physical force used against suspects, Garner et al. (2002) found African Americans and Latinos were more likely than whites to experience force (19.9% and 17.6% compared to 14.1%, respectively). In identifying the antecedents of force, Garner et al. (2002) examined a variety of factors, including situational, individual, and organizational factors that are likely to impact the interaction between police and suspect. Although there were some differences observed in the prevalence of force, suspect race/ethnicity was not a significant predictor of force once all other variables were examined. Instead, suspect behavior, such as demeanor and resistance, significantly predicted force Garner et al. (2002, 738).

Suspect resistance and demeanor toward police officers has been cited in other research as a key predictor of a variety of outcomes such as arrest (Worden and Shepard, 1996), force used by officers (Worden, 1996), and officer disrespect toward citizens (Mastrofski, Reisig, and McCluskey, 2002). In an attempt to uncover sources of suspect resistance in encounters with police, Belvedere, Worrall, and Tibbetts (2005) examined officer and suspect race as predictors of resistance along with officer and suspect race dyads to capture interactions between officer and citizen race. Interestingly, Belvedere et al. found that African American suspects were significantly more likely to resist arrest generally. Additionally, the only significant race dyad was that between Hispanic officer and Hispanic suspect, suggesting that Hispanic suspects are likely to resist arrest by Hispanic officers (2005, 40).

Given conflicting findings on the use of force and the overall lack of Latino representation in policing research, it is unclear whether the prevalence and extent of force used specifically against Latinos is consistent with other minority and nonminority populations. Even less is known about interactions between Latino immigrants and law enforcement. To address this gap in the literature, Phillips, Rodriguez, and Hagan (2002) conducted a study of deported Salvadorans and their families (n = 211) to determine whether force was used by immigration officers (INS) or police in their apprehension and detention in the United States. This study represents an important contribution to the sparse literature on Latino immigrants and the force that may be used against them in the enforcement of immigration law.

Phillips et al. (2002) described a significant increase in the arrest, detention, and deportation of immigrants between 1995 and 2000, following the passage of the Illegal Immigration Reform and Immigrant Responsibility Act (IIRIRA) in 1996. Following the terrorist attacks on September 11, 2001, this issue has become an even greater concern. In interviews with Salvadoran deportees and their family members, Phillips and colleagues (2002) asked whether physical coercion, beyond handcuffing, was used in their apprehension and deportation experience. Force was reported in 14 percent of cases. Unfortunately, extent of force was not measured in the study; however, researchers have acknowledged the difficulty in assessing excessive force (Garner et al., 2002). Phillips et al. (2002) compared the prevalence of force in their study to other samples, including the Police-Public Contact Survey (PPCS) and police officer self-report data on the use of force. Depending upon the definition of force, prevalence of force against U.S. citizens in the two studies ranges from 2 to 5 percent in police self reports and between 9 to 14 percent in the PPCS data (Phillips et al., 2002, 299). The researchers conclude that immigrants appear to experience force more often than U.S. citizens; however, the factors that predict force are similar across both populations (age, sex, location of encounter, seriousness of offense). The study of Salvadoran deportees by Phillips and colleagues (2002) raises a number of questions about the treatment of Latino immigrants in the United States. It is an initial examination of Latino immigrants and use of force and is likely to open the door to future research in this largely unexamined area.

Latino Attitudes toward Police

In assessing attitudes toward law enforcement, a number of studies have found that minorities are more likely than whites to view the police negatively because of the experience of unfair treatment, racial discrimination, verbal abuse, and excessive use of physical force by police officers (Carter, 1985; Huo and Tyler, 2000; Morales, 1972; Samora, Bernal, and Peña, 1979). In other studies, however, neighborhood characteristics have been found to mediate the relationship between race or ethnicity and perceptions of police (Reisig and Parks, 2000; Sampson and Bartusch, 1998).

Research in Chicago by Schuck and Rosenbaum (2005) has suggested that both global and neighborhood specific ratings of police are important considerations for whites, African Americans, and Latinos. In community surveys of 344 Chicago residents, African Americans and Latinos were found to be more likely to encounter police outside of their neighborhood than whites. In addition, a stronger relationship was found between global and specific attitudes of police along with greater variation in neighborhood attitudes among minorities (Schuck and Rosenbaum, 2005).

Literature on minority attitudes toward police suggests ethnic variation in experiences with police is important for understanding ratings of law enforcement (Herbst and Walker, 2001; Holmes, 1998). For example, the frequency and nature of police contacts with Latinos may shape attitudes toward law enforcement officials and the law generally (Langan, Greenfield, Smith, Durose, and Levin, 2001). In examinations of police ratings, Latinos report less favorable attitudes toward police than their white counterparts but more favorable attitudes than African Americans (Schuck and Rosenbaum, 2005; Skogan, Steiner, DuBois, Gudell, and Fagan, 2002; Webb and Marshall, 1995). In addition to the number of contacts, the diversity in the type of contact may be important to examine, particularly within one's own neighborhood (Schuck and Rosenbaum, 2005). Perceptions of poor police response to calls for service have also been reported in the literature, with Latinos citing the need for more rapid police response (Carter, 1985; Mirandé, 1981).

Weitzer and Tuch (2004) examined perceptions of police misconduct as a potential source of racial differences in general evaluations of police that were identified in earlier studies. Specifically, Weitzer and Tuch (2004) systematically examined Latino, white, and African American perceptions of four types of misconduct, including unwarranted stops, verbal abuse, excessive force, and police corruption. Their study is based on group-position thesis, which describes dominant and minority group orientations toward social institutions based on their competing interests. Specifically, Weitzer and Tuch (2004) test the hypothesis that the dominant group is more likely than minority groups to identify with police and other institutions and see them as protecting their interests. On the other hand, minority groups may view police as an institution of domination and might therefore be more likely to view police practices as inappropriate.

Weitzer and Tuch (2004) found general support for the group-position thesis, in that whites were less likely to report police misconduct. Minority groups in the study were more likely to view all types of police misconduct as occurring very often or fairly often. In addition, African Americans and Hispanics were more likely to report personal experiences of police misconduct. Media reports of misconduct appeared to reinforce minority views of police, particularly among African Americans.

While the group-position thesis was generally supported, differences within minority groups were found by Weitzer and Tuch (2004), which is consistent with other studies. Specifically, minority groups differed in their experiences and perceptions of police; African Americans were more likely to cite police misconduct than Latinos. To explore this finding in more depth, they examined nativity of Latinos in the study and found Puerto Ricans were the most likely of any Latino group to report police misconduct (2004, 317). Generally, the study by Weitzer and Tuch (2004) highlights the importance of examining experiences across racial and ethnic groups and moving away from more general conclusions about white versus nonwhite or minority groups. Differences between African Americans and Latinos were found and should be examined more closely. In addition, a preliminary examination of intragroup differences among Latinos suggests that nativity is an important consideration when drawing conclusions about race and ethnic perceptions of police.

Perceptions of Police Legitimacy

Establishing legitimacy among the public is critical in determining citizens' reaction to police. As Sunshine and Tyler describe it, "legitimacy is a property of an authority or institution that leads people to feel that that authority or institution is entitled to be deferred to and obeyed" (2003, 514). Legitimacy is thought to directly relate to public support and trust in police. Legitimacy is also expected to enhance citizen cooperation with police and ultimately lead to safer communities through cooperative crime prevention. The development of community policing is based on such cooperation. Public support and cooperation are recognized as key components of community policing (Kelling and Moore, 1999). To the extent that the relationship with Latino communities can be strengthened, efforts to control crime might prove to be more successful.

The literature on community interventions highlights the importance of cultural awareness in developing and implementing community-wide change strategies (Carter, 1983, 1985; Cryderman and Fleras, 1992; Dunham and Alpert, 1988; Marín, 1993; Trojanowicz and Bucqueroux, 1991). Recognition of the values and norms within the Latino community may lead to more successful implementation of community interventions, including community policing strategies. The nature of community policing and its reliance on community participation provides the opportunity for improving relations between Latinos and police. For example, recent evaluation of the Chicago Alternative Policing Strategy (CAPS) focused on the growing Latino population in Chicago and estimated the extent of Latino involvement in community policing efforts (Skogan, et al., 2002). Although Latinos represent one of the city's most disadvantaged groups, Latino involvement in CAPS was limited and Latinos held less favorable attitudes toward police than whites (Skogan et al., 2002). While community policing has been cited as a method of improving the racial climate, its influence within the Latino community remains unclear.

As a means of enhancing legitimacy, Huo and Tyler (2000) have drawn attention to procedural justice. Specifically, procedural justice is centered on citizen perceptions of fair treatment in encounters with authorities such as police. Sunshine and Tyler (2003) propose that perceptions of procedural justice influence general assessments of police as well as specific interactions with police officers. In their examination of legitimacy, they found that procedural justice was an important predictor of legitimacy. In turn, legitimacy shapes public cooperation with police across all racial and ethnic groups (2003, 532).

To examine perceptions of treatment in processing (procedural justice) and outcomes (distributive justice), Engel (2005) utilized data from the Police-Public Contact Survey (PPCS) collected in 1999. Specifically, citizens' were asked about experiences with police during traffic stops and reported their perceptions of fairness in treatment and outcome by race/ethnicity. In describing their encounters with police, citizens rated the legitimacy of the traffic stop to assess distributive justice and appropriateness of police behavior during the stop to assess procedural justice. Engel found that perceptions of fairness in interactions with police are important for all racial and ethnic groups (2005, 469). Although Latinos do not vary significantly from other racial and ethnic groups in their ratings of distributive and procedural justice, the interaction between ethnicity and social class revealed that Latinos from lower socioeconomic strata were 3.5 times more likely than Latinos of the middle or upper class to view police behavior during the stop as improper (2005, 464). Engel attributes this finding to increased levels of assimilation of middle and upper class Latinos into mainstream society; as a result, higher-income Latinos may experience differential treatment by law enforcement or differing perceptions of police behavior (2005, 471). Future research should assess this hypothesis empirically.

Latino Representation in Police Agencies

The literature on diversity in law enforcement suggests that underrepresentation of Latinos in police agencies has contributed to the division between police and the Latino community (Carter, 1986; U.S. Commission on Civil

Rights, 1993; Flowers, 1988; Walker, Spohn, and DeLone, 2000). Underlying efforts toward diversifying law enforcement agencies is the notion that a representative police force is likely to be more responsive to community needs (Alozie and Ramirez, 1999). Although the number of Latino officers has increased in recent years, Latinos remain underrepresented through-out the law enforcement hierarchy. Within the organization, Latino officers have cited unfair hiring and promotion practices that advance white officers (Carter, 1986). Among factors that influence Latino employment in police agencies, Alozie and Ramirez (1999) find that diversification is predicted by the proportion of Latinos within a given community. Within larger Latino communities, the need for Latino officers may be more apparent, the labor pool is likely to be comprised of Latino candidates, and political influence among Latinos in such areas is likely to be stronger than in communities with a smaller Latino presence (Alozie and Ramirez, 1999).

In an examination of Latino population growth and diversity in the 50 larg-est metropolitan police agencies, McCluskey and McCluskey (2004) found that cities with a substantial Latino population-base experienced increased Latino representation in law enforcement between 1990 and 2000. However, those cities that lacked a large Latino population, but experienced a rapidly increasing number of Latinos during the decade, were significantly less likely to experience an increase in Latino representation within local law enforce-ment. This finding is consistent with the conception of police bureaucracies as being slow to adapt to their environment. This suggests that cities with an established Latino population may be better equipped to integrate Latinos into their justice system. This finding is consistent with research by Alozie and Ramirez (1999), which suggests that cities with a higher proportion of Latinos have a larger pool for recruiting Latino officers, and may also have greater Latino political influence to address diversity issues. The impact of increased diversity in law enforcement on crime rates is an area to be studied in the future.

Sociocultural Influences

Studies on Latino cultural value systems and communication patterns iden-tifies sociocultural characteristics of the ethnic group that are likely to set them apart from non-Latino groups and ultimately influence utilization of police services (Carter, 1983; Herbst and Walker, 2001; Jesilow et al., 1995) and attitudes toward police. Cultural differences may act as a source of mis-understanding among police and Latino citizens, particularly if police lack awareness of such differences. For example, police officers may not be fully aware of various elements of the Latino value system and therefore might not take full advantage of those strengths when attempting to improve relations with the Latino community.

Cross-cultural differences can potentially impact the relationship between police and Latino community members (Carter, 1983). Unfortunately, few studies to date have examined everyday encounters between police and Latinos. One area that has been examined recently is the influence of language barriers on service provision (Herbst and Walker, 2001). Findings from the study suggested that language barriers did *not* pose significant problems in police and Latino interactions. Similarly, Cheurprakobit and Bartsch (1999) found that Spanish-speaking Latinos demonstrated a greater understanding of, and cooperation with, police work. Although not widely addressed in the literature, the relationship between police and Latino citizens in their country of origin may influence attitudes toward U.S. police agents and expectations of police in the Latino community. The potential influence of acculturation on attitudes toward police might also be examined, where differences might be observed between Latinos of different generations.

SUGGESTIONS FOR FUTURE RESEARCH

In criminal justice research, sizeable Latino populations are rarely included to examine issues specific to growing Latino communities (Schuck et al., 2004). Contributing to the paucity of data is the lack of consistent methods of race and ethnic classification and the absence of ethnicity data in national arrest statistics (Herbst and Walker, 2001; Villarruel and Walker, 2002). Increasingly, studies on attitudes toward police and fear of crime have included diverse samples. Future research should continue to build upon current studies and seek to gauge community experiences with police and attitudes toward the law generally (e.g., Langan et al., 2001). Additionally, systematic social observation research (e.g., Mastrofski, Reisig, and McCluskey, 2002; Mastrofski, Worden, and Snipes, 1995; Reiss, 1971; Smith, 1986; Sykes and Brent, 1983)—which historically has excluded samples of Latino communities (c.f. Bayley, 1986)—should strive to systematically examine daily encounters between law enforcement officers and members of the Latino community. Efforts to ensure Latino representation in data collection are particularly important as the Latino population in the United States continues to grow.

In regard to sociocultural factors, existing literature suggests that family, honor, religion, and communication patterns are important for understanding Latinos generally. As such, future inquiry should attempt to understand the role of the extended family as an informal social control network, which might explain, in part, the underutilization of police services in the Latino community. Additionally, the importance of respect in the Latino community might be better understood, as well as the implications of officers showing disrespect to Latino citizens (Carter, 1983). Law enforcement agencies might better understand the role of religious organizations within the Latino community and recognize them as a source of promoting cooperation among police and citizens. Finally, verbal and nonverbal communication patterns might also be examined to determine whether Latino cues (such as averting eye contact as a sign of respect) are misunderstood by police and labeled as suspicious or disrespectful.

Latino populations in the United States, compared to peoples from other parts of the world, have distinct and unique cultures (Umaña-Taylor and Fine, 2001). Until recently, most literature on Latino families has failed to recognize the important effects that variables such as generational status and country of origin may have on shaping lived experiences and engagement with social institutions (Massey, Zambrana, and Bell, 1995).

Researchers suggest that future studies should focus on contextual influences that impact police and minority relations (Herbst and Walker, 2001). For example, immigration trends and population shifts in Latino communities might be examined along with characteristics of law enforcement agencies and styles of policing. Fyfe (1996) has suggested that law enforcement agencies monitor and respond to population changes through ongoing officer training. Neighborhood characteristics have also been cited as a potential influence on attitudes toward the law (Jesilow et al., 1995; Leiber, Nalla, and Farnworth, 1998; Reisig and Parks, 2000; Sampsôn and Bartusch, 1998; Weitzer, 1999); therefore, future research should examine structural contexts within which police and Latino interactions unfold. Aforementioned efforts to increase research on policing in the Latino community should ultimately attempt to disentangle organizational, structural, and sociocultural influences on police and Latino relations to increase our understanding of how police service is delivered in that community.

Similarly, immigration patterns may provide a unique focus for understanding community-law enforcement relations. Mexican immigrants, for example, tend to join well-established Mexican American communities. However, large-scale immigration from Central America is relatively recent, with the two largest populations, Salvadorans and Guatemalans, immigrating to escape escalating violence and civil conflict. These immigrants tend to arrive under refugee-like conditions comprised of higher percentages of mother-only families. Clearly, responses to law-enforcement in these two contexts may vary dramatically, and as such, merit further research to understand practices that can enhance public safety in a culturally responsive manner.

REFERENCES

Acuña, R. (1988). *Occupied America: A History of Chicanos.* New York: Harper and Row Publishers.

Alozie, N. O., and Ramirez, E. J. (1999). " 'A Piece of the Pie' and More: Competition and Hispanic Employment on Urban Police Forces." *Urban Affairs Review, 34,* 456–475.

Bayley, D. H. (1986). "The Tactical Choices of Police Patrol Officers." *Journal of Criminal Justice, 14,* 329–48.

Belvedere, K., Worrall, J. L., and Tibbetts, S. G. (2005). "Explaining Suspect Resistance in Police-Citizen Encounters." *Criminal Justice Review, 30,* 30–44.

Bernstein, R. (2005). "Hispanic Population Passes 40 Million, Census Bureau Reports." *U.S. Census Bureau News,* June 9, 2005.

Carter, D. L. (1983). "Hispanic Interaction with the Criminal Justice System in Texas: Experiences, Attitudes, and Perceptions." *Journal of Criminal Justice, 11,* 213–227.

Carter, D. L. (1985). "Hispanic Perception of Police Performance: An Empirical Assessment." *Journal of Criminal Justice, 13,* 487–500.

Carter, D. L. (1986). "Hispanic Police Officers' Perception of Discrimination." *Journal of Police Studies, 79,* 204–210.

Cheurprakobkit, S., and Bartsch, R. A. (1999). "Police Work and the Police Profession: Assessing Attitudes of City Officials, Spanish-Speaking Hispanics, and Their English-Speaking Counterparts." *Journal of Criminal Justice, 27,* 87–100.

Cryderman, B. K., and Fleras, A. (1992). *Police, Race, and Ethnicity: A Guide for Police Services.* Toronto: Butterworths.

Dunham, R. G., and Alpert, G. P. (1988). "Neighborhood Differences in Attitudes toward Policing: Evidence for a Mixed-Strategy Model of Policing in a Multi-Ethnic Setting." *Criminology, 79,* 504–523.

Engel, R. S. (2005). "Citizens' Perceptions of Distributive and Procedural Injustice during Traffic Stops With Police." *Journal of Research in Crime and Delinquency, 42,* 445–481.

Engel, R. S., Sobol, J. J. and Worden, R. W. (2000) "Further Exploration of the Demeanor Hypothesis: The Interaction Effects of Suspects' Characteristics and Demeanor on Police Behavior." *Justice Quarterly, 17,* 235–258.

Escobar, E. J. (1999). *Race, Police, and the Making of a Political Identity.* Berkeley: University of California Press.

Flowers, R. B. (1990). *Minorities and Criminality.* New York: Praeger.

Fyfe, J. J. (1996). "Training to Reduce Police-Civilian Violence." In W. A. Geller and H. Toch (eds.), *Police Violence: Understanding and Controlling Police Abuse of Force.* New Haven: Yale University Press, pp. 165–179.

Garner, J. H., Maxwell, C. D., and Heraux, C. G. (2002). "Characteristics Associated With the Prevalence and Severity of Force Used By the Police." *Justice Quarterly, 19,* 705–746.

Guzmán, B. (2001). *The Hispanic Population.* Washington, D.C.: U.S. Census Bureau.

Herbst, L. and Walker, S. (2001). "Language Barriers in the Delivery of Police Services: A Study of Police and Hispanic Interactions in a Midwestern City." *Journal of Criminal Justice, 29,* 329–340.

Holmes, M. D. (1998). "Perceptions of Abusive Police Practices in a U.S.-Mexico Border Community." *The Social Science Journal, 35,* 107–118.

Huo, Y. J., and Tyler, T. R. (2000). *How Different Ethnic Groups React to Legal Authority.* San Francisco: Public Policy Institute of California.

Jackson, P. I. (1989). *Minority Group Threat, Crime, and Policing: Social Context and Social Control.* New York: Praeger Publishers.

Jesilow, P., Meyer, J., and Namazzi, N. (1995). "Public Attitudes toward the Police." *American Journal of Police, 14,* 67–88.

Kelling, G. L., and Moore, M. H. (1999). "The Evolving Strategy of Policing." In V. Kappeler (ed.), *The Police & Society* (pp. 2–26). Prospect Heights: Waveland Press, pp. 165–179.

Langan, P. A., Greenfield, L. A., Smith, S. K., Durose, M. R., and Levin, D. J. (2001). *Contacts Between the Police and the Public: Findings from the 1999 National Survey.* Washington, D.C.: U.S. Department of Justice, Office of Justice Programs, Bureau of Justice Statistics.

Lasley, J.R. (1994). "The Impact of the Rodney King Incident on Citizen Attitudes toward Police." *Policing and Society*, 3, 245–255.

Leiber, M. J., Nalla, M. K., and Farnworth, M. (1998). "Explaining Juveniles' Attitudes toward the Police." *Justice Quarterly*, 15, 151–174.

Maguire, K. and Pastore, A. L., eds. (2001). *Sourcebook of Criminal Justice Statistics* [Online]. Available: http://www.albany.edu/sourcebook/.

Mandel, J. (1981). *Police Use of Deadly Force: Los Angeles.* Washington, D.C.: National Council of La Raza.

Marín, G. (1993). "Defining Culturally Appropriate Community Interventions: Hispanics as a Case Study." *Journal of Community Psychology*, 21, 149–161.

Massey, D.S., Zambrana, R.E., and Bell, S.A. (1995). "Contemporary Issues in Latino Families: Future Directions for Research, Policy, and Practice." In R. E. Zambrana (ed.), *Understanding Latino Families.* Thousand Oaks, CA. Sage Publications.

Mastrofski, S. D., Reisig, M. D., and McCluskey, J.D. (2002). "Police Disrespect toward the Public: An Encounter-Based Analysis." *Criminology*, 40, 519–552.

Mastrofski, S.D., Worden, R.E., and Snipes, J.B. (1995). "Law Enforcement in a Time of Community Policing." *Criminology*, 33, 539–563.

Mazón, M. (1984). *The Zoot-Suit Riots: The Psychology of Symbolic Annihilation.* Austin: University of Texas Press.

McCluskey, C. P., and McCluskey, J. D. (2004). "Diversity in Policing: Latino Representation in Law Enforcement." *Journal of Ethnicity in Criminal Justice, Special Issue: Hispanics and the U.S. Criminal Justice System*, 2, 67–81

Miller, W. (1991). "Cops and Bobbies." In C. Klockars and S. Mastrofski (eds.), *Thinking About Police* (Vol. 73–87). New York: McGraw-Hill.

Mirandé, A. (1981). "The Chicano and the Law: An Analysis of Community-Police Conflict in an Urban Barrio." *Pacific Sociological Review*, 24, 65–86.

Mirandé, A. (1985). *The Chicano Experience: An Alternative Perspective.* Notre Dame: University of Notre Dame Press.

Mirandé, A. (1987). *Gringo Justice.* Indiana: University of Notre Dame Press.

Morales, A. (1972). *Ando Sangrando (I Am Bleeding): A Study of Mexican-American Police Conflict.* La Puente: Perspectiva Publications.

Phillips, S., Rodriguez, N., and Hagan, J. (2002). "Brutality at the Border? Use of Force in the Arrest of Immigrants in the United States." *International Journal of the Sociology of Law*, 30, 285–306.

Ramirez, R. R., and de la Cruz, P. G. (2003). *The Hispanic Population in the United States: March 2002.* (Current Population Reports P20-545). Washington, D.C.: U.S. Census Bureau.

Reisig, M. D., and Parks, R. B. (2000). "Experience, Quality of Life, and Neighborhood Context: A Hierarchical Analysis of Satisfaction with Police." *Justice Quarterly*, 17, 607–630.

Reiss, A.J., Jr. (1971). *The Police and the Public.* New Haven: Yale University Press.

Samora, J., Bernal, J., and Peña, A. (1979). *Gunpowder Justice: A Reassessment of the Texas Rangers.* Notre Dame: University of Notre Dame Press.

Sampson, R. J., and Bartusch, D. J. (1998). "Legal Cynicism and (Subcultural?) Tolerance of Deviance: The Neighborhood Context of Racial Differences." *Law & Society Review*, 32, 777–804.

Schuck, A.M., Lersch, K. M., and Verrill, S. W. (2004). "The 'Invisible' Hispanic? The Representation of Hispanics in Criminal Justice Research: What Do We Know and Where Should We Go?" *Journal of Ethnicity in Criminal Justice*, 2, 5–22.

Schuck, A. M., and Rosenbaum, D. P. (2005). "Global and Neighborhood Attitudes toward the Police: Differentiation by Race, Ethnicity, and Type of Contact." *Journal of Quantitative Criminology, 21,* 391–418.

Skogan, W. G., Steiner, L., DuBois, J., Gudell, J. E., and Fagan, A. (2002). *Community Policing and "The New Immigrants": Latinos in Chicago.* Research Report, National Institute of Justice.

Skolnick, J. H., and Fyfe, J. J. (1993). *Above the Law: Police and the Excessive Use of Force.* New York: The Free Press.

Smith, D. A. (1986). "The Neighborhood Context of Police Behavior." In Albert J. Reiss, Jr., and Michael Tonry (eds.), *Communities and Crime.* Chicago: University of Chicago Press, pp. 313–341.

Sunshine, J., and Tyler, T. R. (2003). "The Role of Procedural Justice and Legitimacy in Shaping Public Support for Policing." *Law & Society Review, 37,* 513–547.

Suro, R. and Singer, A. (2002). *Latino Growth in Metropolitan America: Changing Patterns, New Locations.* Washington, D.C.: The Brookings Institution Center on Urban and Metropolitan Policy and the Pew Hispanic Center.

Sykes, R. E. and Brent, E. E. (1983). *Policing: A Social Behaviorist Perspective.* New Brunswick, NJ: Rutgers University Press.

Terrill, W., and Mastrofski, S. D. (2002). "Situational and Officer-Based Determinants of Police Coercion." *Justice Quarterly, 19,* 215–248.

Therrien, M. and Ramirez, R. R. (2001). *The Hispanic Population in the United States: Population Characteristics.* Washington, D.C.: U.S. Census Bureau.

Trojanowicz, R., and Bucqueroux, B. (1991). *Community Policing and the Challenge of Diversity.* Community Policing Series No. 21. East Lansing: National Center for Community Policing, Michigan State University.

Trujillo, L. (1974). "La evolucion del 'Bandido' al 'Pachuco': A Critical Examination and Evaluation of Criminological Literature on Chicanos." *Issues in Criminology, 9,* 43–67.

Tuch, S. A., and Weitzer, R. (1997). "Racial Differences in Attitudes toward the Police." *Public Opinion Quarterly, 61,* 642–663.

Umaña-Taylor, A. and Fine, Mm. (2001). "Methodological Implications of Grouping Latino Adolescents into One Collective Ethnic Group." *Hispanic Journal of Behavioral Sciences, 23,* 347–362.

United States Commission on Civil Rights. (1993). *Racial and Ethnic Tensions in American Communities: Poverty, Inequality, and Discrimination.* Volume 1: The Mount Pleasant Report.

Villarruel, F. A. and Walker, N. E. with Minifee, P., Rivera-Vázquez, O, Peterso S., and Perry, K. (2002). *¿Dónde Está La Justicia?: A Call to Action on Behalf of Latino and Latina Youth in the U.S. Justice System.* Washington, D.C.: Building Blocks for Youth. (Report also available online at: www.buildingblocksforyouth.org.)

Walker, S. (1999). "Windows and Fractured History: The Use and Misuse of History in Recent Police Patrol Analysis." In V. Kappeler (ed.), *The Police & Society.* Prospect Heights: Waveland Press, pp. 2–26.

Walker, S., Spohn, C., and DeLone, M. (2000). *The Color of Justice: Race, Ethnicity, and Crime in America.* Belmont: Wadsworth Thompson Learning.

Webb, V. J., and Marshall, C. E. (1995). "The Relative Importance of Race and Ethnicity on Citizen Attitudes toward the Police." *American Journal of Police, 14,* 45–66.

Weitzer, R. (1999). "Citizens' Perceptions of Police Misconduct: Race and Neighborhood Context." *Justice Quarterly, 16*, 819–846.

Weitzer, R., and Tuch, S. A. (2004). "Race and Perceptions of Police Misconduct." *Social Problems, 51*, 305–325.

Wolcott, D. (2001). " 'The cop will get you': The Police and Discretionary Juvenile Justice, 1890–1940." *Journal of Social History, 35*, 349–371.

Worden, R. E. (1996). "The Causes of Police Brutality: Theory and Evidence on Police Use of Force." In W. A. Geller and H. Toch (eds.), *Police Violence: Understanding and Controlling Police Abuse of Force*. New Haven: Yale University Press, pp. 23–51.

Worden, R. E., and Shepard, R. (1996). "Demeanor, Crime, and Police Behavior: A Reexamination of the Police Services Study Data." *Criminology, 34*, 83–105.

CHAPTER 9

Cracking the Safety Net: Latina/o Access to Health and Social Programs in the Post-Welfare Era

Héctor R. Cordero-Guzmán and Victoria Quiroz-Becerra

INTRODUCTION

Over the last decade, while the number of Hispanics in poverty has increased from 6 million in 1990 to 8.6 million in 1996 to 9.3 million in 2005, Latino/a access to the shrinking social safety net in the United States and participation in Cash Assistance, Supplemental Income, and Food Stamps has declined significantly. One of the main causes of declining access to government benefit programs has been legislative and policy changes enacted since the welfare reform legislation of 1996 that have taken focus of the programs away from direct cash assistance to families and children.

Changes in welfare and immigration policy have impacted the health and well-being of poor and immigrant families by reducing their access to federally funded social programs and decreasing the level of support provided by these programs. Latino families are particularly affected by changes in regulations and policies that in most cases eliminate the rights of immigrants to seek and access cash assistance programs (AFDC\TANF and SSI), food stamps, and Medicaid. The relatively high proportion of Latino/as among immigrants, families with children, and in low income families makes the population more vulnerable and magnifies the adverse effects of changes in federal and state policies.

For example, consider the following data taken from recent government reports: in 1996 9 out of every 10 uninsured children who were eligible for Medicaid were U.S.-born, but more than 1 in 3 lived in immigrant families. Close to 11 percent of eligible uninsured children were immigrants and an additional 25 percent had at least one parent born abroad (GAO, 1998c). The same report indicates that more than 70 percent of children in uninsured immigrant families were Latino. Many of these families qualify but do not have insurance because state offices fail to provide Spanish-language staff, materials, or applications, and do not make adequate efforts to target and enroll the eligible Latino population. Loss of eligibility and lack of access to health insurance and other related social services present serious challenges to the development and well-being of the community.

The Latino population in the United States is large, growing, relatively young, and materially poor. In 1990 there were 22.4 million Latinos in the United States, or 9 percent of the population. By 2004 the Latino population had grown to 40.4 million persons or 14.0 percent of the U.S. population. Latinos are also an increasing share of the growing immigrant population. Between 1951 and 1960, 67.7 percent of immigrants were from Europe and Canada, and only 20.9 percent were from Mexico and the rest of Latin America and the Caribbean. In contrast, during the 1981 to 1990 period the proportions reversed, with only 12.5 percent of immigrants from Europe and Canada, and 37.3 percent from Asia, 22.6 percent from Mexico, 18 percent from other Latin American and Caribbean countries, and 9.5 percent from other countries (Ramirez, 2000). Continued immigration and relatively high birth rates are reflected in data that indicate that the Latino population grew at a rate of 61 percent during the 1970s and 53 percent during the 1980s compared to 9 percent and 7 percent growth rates for the non-Hispanic population. If these trends continue, Latinos are estimated to become 21.1 percent of the U.S. population by the year 2050. Hispanics are geographically concentrated and, even though there has been some dispersion in recent years, in 2000 close to 82.5 percent of the population lived in just 10 states: California (31.1%), Texas (18.9%), New York (8.9%), Florida (7.6%), Illinois (4.3%), New Jersey (3.7%), Arizona (3.7%), New Mexico (2.2%), Colorado (2.1%), and Washington (1.3%) (Ramirez and de la Cruz, 2003).

Latino children and youth are among the fastest growing segments of the U.S. population. Almost one out of every three Latinos in the country is less than 15 years of age. The number of Hispanics under 24 years of age is close to 15 million persons (or 15%) out of a total youth population of 98 million. Close to 34.4 percent of Hispanics are under 18 years of age compared to 22.8 percent for non-Hispanic Whites. Unfortunately, the Latino population is also quite poor. In 2005, there were at least 9.3 million Latinos living below poverty, and the poverty rate of the Hispanic population was 21.8 percent. For whites, the poverty rate was 8.3 percent, while for African Americans the percent below poverty was 24.9 percent (U.S. Census 2006). The prevalence of high poverty rates in the Latino community constitutes one of the main challenges to the healthy development of families, children, and youth.

This chapter will examine the role of changes in social welfare policy since 1996 on Latino access to health services and cash assistance programs with a focus on families and children. We use materials from recent government reports documenting the impacts of changes in immigration and welfare policy and interviews with a range of immigrant serving social service organizations and other key informants in government agencies and policy making positions to discuss the particular impacts on the Latino population. After a brief introduction, the second section reviews specific changes in immigration and welfare laws and discusses some of the main factors that led to these changes. The third section focuses on changes in the number of families, children, and immigrants participating in three types of programs: cash assistance (AFDC\TANF and SSI), food stamps, and Medicaid. The fourth section highlights some recent federal and state initiatives designed to provide some coverage to sub-groups excluded from participation under the 1996 laws. We also discuss other efforts to expand health insurance among low income populations. The paper concludes with a review of the main challenges to the health status of Latino populations in the post-welfare era. Our review of the evidence suggests that changes in welfare and immigration policy have had an adverse impact on Latino access to health insurance, social welfare programs, and related social services.

RECENT CHANGES IN WELFARE AND IMMIGRATION POLICY

Forces that Motivated Changes in Social Policy

There were several social forces and trends that brought about changes in welfare and immigration policy over the last two decades. First, since the mid-1980s there was a growing perception, fomented by many conservative think tanks, that individuals and families receiving some kind of welfare assistance needed to work in exchange for participating in the programs (Mead, 1986; Murray, 1984). Many commentators on the political right argued that the welfare system was too permissive, that eligibility criteria was too broad, that it encouraged dependency and out of wedlock births, and that it discouraged marriage and work (Mead, 1986; Murray, 1984).

Second, there was a growing political trend, captured in the so-called Contract with America of 1994, toward a reduction in the size of government, tax cuts, and the devolution of regulatory, administrative, and fiscal authority from the federal level to the states. States sought to increase their authority to set rules and regulations for public benefits, and many legislators at the federal level agreed and enacted legislation to accelerate this process (Morse et al., 1998). Third, there was a growing trend since the 1980s both to reduce the number of state provided social services and to increasingly privatize and the remaining services. This was a way of reducing purported government inefficiency and waste in the administration of welfare programs and became a way to continue to privatize and contract out government services. States, for example, were permitted under the new TANF laws to privatize eligibility assessments and other functions traditionally performed by state governments (GAO, 1998b).

Another set of forces that motivated the 1996 changes in immigration and welfare laws were increasing concerns over the escalating costs of health care and the growing trend toward "managed care" (GAO, 1998d; GAO, 2000). The escalating costs of health care were partly attributed to providing services to immigrant and indigent populations (Borjas, 1990; Fix and Passel, 1994). Changes in the national origin of the population and increasing immigration were additional factors that motivated changes in the laws. Immigration was at its highest point since the turn of the century with an annual average of close to 1 million persons of an increasingly diverse economic, social, political, and cultural background entering the United States during the mid-1990s (Fix and Passel, 1994).

Many conservative commentators have suggested that increases in the size and the changing composition of immigration had negative consequences for the United States. Immigrants' diversity, conservatives argued, made acculturation and adaptation more difficult, fragmented national culture, increased competition in the labor market, increased conflict over the distribution of public goods and services, and altered the political balance of power (Borjas, 1990; Brimelow, 1995). In some cases there were radical proposals to eliminate access to education and health care for the children of undocumented immigrants and projects that received voter or legislative support like Proposition 187 in California or the Sensenbrenner Bill [HR 4437] or proposals to eliminate automatic citizenship for persons born in the United States (Perea, 1997).

Electoral politics dominated policy in the late 1990s as the Republican congress and Democratic president colluded to "end welfare as we know it." For the political right it was a matter of eliminating the "welfare problem" by eliminating welfare programs. Advocates of the poor and others also argued that the system needed change but for different reasons. For welfare rights advocates the main problem was that the system treated recipients badly, that the application and enrollment process was very difficult, that the programs offered were not comprehensive and developmental in their approach, and that the programs did not make connections between recipients and other community-building processes. Advocates saw welfare as a right of persons in need who qualified for services, and they made an effort to enroll as many individuals as possible under existing rules. In the end, there were disagreements of principle and policy, but no one from conservatives to progressives defended "welfare as we knew it," and the system (what was provided, for how long, who qualified for services) was significantly changed.

In 1996, President Clinton signed into law the *Personal Responsibility and Work Opportunity Reconciliation Act of 1996 (P.L. 104–193)* [PRWORA] and the *Illegal Immigration Reform and Immigration Responsibility Act of 1996 (P.L. 104–208)* [IIRIRA]. One of the main features of the new laws was that they gave a significant amount of authority and discretion to the states to design, administer, and fund their own social welfare programs and determine eligibility. But, even though there are essentially 50 new welfare systems, there is a perception among state level policymakers that there are disincentives for states to offer more generous benefits than neighboring or other states for fear of attracting a disproportionate share of the low income population into the state (GAO, 1998a; GAO, 1998b; Singer, 1999).

Main Changes in Welfare Policy

The Welfare Reform Act (P.L. 104–193, August 22, 1996) changed several central features of the welfare system during the last decade. The new law changed eligibility and access to cash assistance programs, health insurance programs, and food stamps. Under the previous law, eligible individuals were guaranteed assistance, including child care, at levels determined by each state. The program was funded by a combination of state and federal matching dollars based on the number of individuals enrolled. Benefits were guaranteed to individuals, families, and children even during economic recessions. Under the new rules, eligibility and access have become significantly more challenging and complicated.

Temporary Assistance for Needy Families (TANF)

The 1996 law replaced Aid to Families with Dependent Children (AFDC) with a program funded with block grants and administered by the states, called Temporary Assistance for Needy Families (TANF). The new law limited eligibility to a lifetime maximum of five years for TANF benefits and ended the family lifetime entitlement to cash assistance. A clear emphasis of the new approach was to force states to ensure that a percentage of their welfare households worked, and states had to require a proportion of families to work after two years on assistance. Under TANF, states designed their own cash assistance programs including using strategies to divert potential applicants from participating (Chavkin, Romero, and Wise, 2000). A report prepared by the GAO in 1998 on TANF implementation (1998b) found that many states had begun implementing strategies to discourage potential applicants from participating in the program. Some of the methods that had been used include requiring applicants to certify that they looked for employment before processing TANF applications; requiring recipients to attend job readiness, training programs, and to engage in other job search activities; offering a onetime payment (diversion payment) to potential applicants to discourage them from enrolling in the program; eliminating access to Food Stamps; and reducing the household's total food grant as a penalty for not complying with TANF regulations.

Supplemental Security Income (SSI)

The 1996 law included a new definition of disability for children. In addition, there were changes in the use of "maladaptive behavior" in medical determinations of mental disabilities in children. All cases of children receiving SSI were to be reevaluated to determine whether they met the new definitions of disability. Unfortunately, the implications of these specific changes for Latino children have not been investigated.

Medicaid

The new laws enacted since 1996 changed the relationship between participation in cash assistance programs and Medicaid eligibility by separating the rules of the two programs. The welfare reform law also provided states with new choices regarding how to administer Medicaid and determine suitability for coverage. Previously, states were required to use one state agency to administer AFDC and Medicaid and a single application to assess eligibility. Under the new law states can use separate state agencies, forms, eligibility criteria, and application procedures for the two programs. Regardless of a state's TANF requirements, for purposes of Medicaid, the new law requires states to provide medical assistance to individuals based on the AFDC income and resource criteria that were in place in July of 1996. States can eliminate Medicaid eligibility for adults who are removed from TANF for failure to work. States also have the option of using more liberal income and resource criteria for Medicaid eligibility. As was the case under previous law, families that would lose Medicaid benefits due to increased earnings from spousal support, child support, or work remain eligible to receive Medicaid benefits for an additional period.

Food Stamps

The new legislation also tightened food stamp eligibility criteria. For example, it excluded able-bodied adults without dependents who received food stamp benefits for at least 3 months but worked less than 20 hours per week during the previous 3 years. In addition, the act gave the states more flexibility to operate their own type of food stamp programs.

Other Changes

The new law also included a number of changes related to child protection, child care, child nutrition programs (giving states the option to determine whether to provide WIC and other child nutrition benefits to undocumented persons and other noncitizens), and changes to the social services block grant (SSBG). Under the new law, states are allowed to conduct drug tests on recipients and to penalize persons who test positive for controlled substances. The law also gives universal access, independent of citizenship status, for: public health for immunizations and communicable diseases, emergency medical services, prenatal care, job training programs, short-term (noncash) disaster relief, and drug treatment programs.

Main Changes in Immigration Policy

Many Latinos have been in the United States for generations. However, the immigration status of some members of the community and linguistic and cultural barriers lead to a less informed and more vulnerable population, resulting in less access to programs that promote the development of children and youth (Padilla, 1998). Several provisions of the PRWORA limited the eligibility of legal immigrants for means-tested public assistance. These changes have had a significant impact on Latino families who are more likely to be immigrant and more likely to have an immigrant in the family or household (Fix and Zimmerman, 1999). The main focus of the legislative approaches has been to close the borders, increase the penalties, reduce the number of avenues to legalization, and selectively enforce immigration laws with the hope of augmenting the costs and reducing the number of immigrants. While the costs of migration have increased, it is not clear that this has led to a reduction in the number of immigrants that need to, want to, or will venture north.

Restrictions on Public Benefits to Immigrants

The new law prohibited legal immigrants (with certain exceptions) from obtaining food stamps and SSI while establishing screening procedures for these programs. It also excluded legal immigrants entering the United States after August of 1996 from access to most federal means-tested programs for five years and allowed states to exclude them from major federal and state programs. The new laws also increased the responsibility of sponsors (or the individuals in the United States that agree to take financial responsibility for the immigrant) by making the affidavit of support legally enforceable, imposing new requirements on sponsors, expanding sponsor-deeming requirements (where the sponsors' income counts as applicant's income when determining eligibility for programs), and lengthening the amount of time income would be deemed for program eligibility purposes. Lastly, the law explicitly excluded undocumented persons and nonimmigrants (or persons in the country with student or visitor visas) from access and required the INS to verify the status of immigrants who applied for federal programs.

Other Changes in Immigration Policy

In addition to increased restrictions on access to many government-funded programs, the new immigration law (IIRIRA) tightened the immigration system by establishing measures to increase the policing of U.S. borders, increased worksite raids, and expedited removal of individuals with criminal or other deportable offenses. The law also excluded persons seeking to re-enter the United States after having been unlawfully present (by overstaying their visas or entering the country without proper documentation) for 3 or 10 years and, among other provisions, placed additional restrictions on foreign physicians and others seeking to work in the United States.

While there was significant discussion in the fall of 2005 and throughout 2006 about a comprehensive immigration package, there was no agreement on the specific details of the project between the various branches of the Republican-controlled congress and the administration, and a significant comprehensive immigration law has not been passed since 1996. The Congress did approve the continued buildup along the U.S.-Mexico border and authorized construction of an additional 700 miles of fencing and security along the border.

THE IMPACTS OF CHANGES IN SOCIAL WELFARE AND IMMIGRATION POLICY

The legislative and policy result of the actions taken and positions expressed during the debates over immigration and welfare reform have had significant implications for the socioeconomic status and the rights of Latinos and have brought into question the country's willingness to invest in this segment of the population (Cordero-Guzman and Navarro, 2000; Perea, 1997). The evidence on changes in program participation and changes in the characteristics of participants is fragmented and incomplete, but several government studies, reports, and state level studies are beginning to shed some light on the impacts of changes in government cash assistance, food stamp, and health insurance programs.

Declining Participation in Cash Assistance Programs

Participation in both welfare and food stamps peaked in 1994 and has dropped significantly since then. Government statistics indicate that the number of welfare recipients dropped by about 43 percent, from about 14.2 million in 1994 to about 8.1 million in August 1998. About two-thirds of the decline occurred after the Welfare Reform Act was signed in August 1996 when there were close to 12.2 million welfare recipients (GAO 1999d).

Table 9.1 includes data on changes in participation in the AFDC\TANF cash assistance program among families, children, and adults and includes information on states with a significant Latino population. The data indicates that participation in the program decreased by 57.7 percent among families from 1995 to 2002. The proportion of Latinos participating in TANF increased from 20.7 percent in 1995 to 24.9 percent in 2002. However, the actual number of Latinos in the program declined by 495,772 families (49.1%) and 1,016,853 children (49%). Of the states reviewed, Illinois, Florida, and New York had the largest declines at 79.6 percent, 74.4 percent, and 62.7 percent, respectively. Texas, California, and Arizona had declines in the 40–50 percent range in the number of families participating in AFDC\TANF between 1995 and 2002. There were 5.9 million fewer children participating in the program in 2002 than in 1994, of which 1,016,853 were Latino (a 49% decrease).

Data on adults (not shown on the table) indicates that between 1997 and 2002 there were 1,365,000 fewer adults participating in the program, and of

Table 9.1
Changes in Participation in the AFDC\TANF Cash Assistance Program among Latino Families

	(1) 1995 (Oct 94–Sept 95)	(2) 2002 (FY 2002)	Net Change 95 to 02	Percent Change 95 to 02
United States	4,873,398	2,060,328	−2,813,070	−57.7%
Number of				
Latinos	1,008,793	513,022	−495,772	−49.1%
Percent Latino	20.7%	24.9%	4.2%	
Arizona	69,609	40,097	−29,512	−42.4%
Percent Latino	40.8%	51.9%	11.1%	27.2%
Total Latino	28,400	20,810	−7,590	
California	919,471	462,320	−457,151	−49.7%
Percent Latino	40.0%	48.9%	8.9%	22.3%
Total Latino	367,788	226,074	−141,714	
Florida	230,807	59,013	−171,794	−74.4%
Percent Latino	17.6%	19.5%	1.9%	−10.8%
Total Latino	40,622	11,508	−29,114	
Illinois	236,205	48,091	−188,114	−79.6%
Percent Latino	11.9%	7.6%	−4.3%	−36.1%
Total Latino	28,108	3,655	−24,453	
New York	456,929	170,258	−286,671	-62.7%
Percent Latino	36.3%	35.8%	−0.5%	−1.4%
Total Latino	165,865	60,952	−104,913	
Texas	274,505	129,937	−144,568	-52.7%
Percent Latino	44.5%	47.6%	3.1%	7.0%
Total Latino	122,155	61,850	−60,305	

Sources: (1) Administration for Children and Families (HHS), 1996. *Characteristics and Financial Circumstances of AFDC Recipients FY 1995* (June 28, 1996), Table 10; (2) Administration for Children and Families, 2004. *Sixth Annual Report to Congress* (November 2004), Tables 10:2, 10:8.

these, 284,046 were Latinos or a decline of 50 percent in one year (U.S. Dept. HHS, 1998; U.S. Dept. HHS, 2004). The main effects of changes in the rules of eligibility to cash assistance programs have been to force more individuals out of welfare and into various kinds of work. This can have many positive effects, but it has also resulted in an increase in the number of persons and families who work but do not earn above the federal poverty line, and in some cases, increases in the levels of stress and injury associated with working in the low-wage labor market combined with reduced access to social support and service programs.

TANF and Immigrants

Data on participation among immigrants and Latino immigrants is not reported in the major government studies, but interviews with immigrant service providers indicate that these groups have been among the most affected by changes in the programs (Cordero-Guzman and Navarro, 2000; Paral, 1998a, 1999; Singer, 1999). A recent government study (GAO, 1999b) indicates that almost all states decided to continue providing some TANF and Medicaid benefits for immigrants that were legally in the country before August of 1996 and to provide these benefits to new immigrants after five years of U.S. residency. However, the study also found that very few states offer assistance comparable to TANF and Medicaid to new immigrants during their first five years in the United States. Also, many of the state programs do not apply to the same number of immigrants that could have received services before, limit participation to particular categories of immigrants, or impose certain residency requirements (GAO, 1999b).

Participation in SSI among Latinos and Immigrants

Before welfare reform, SSI provided a monthly cash benefit to needy individuals who were aged, blind, or disabled whether they were immigrants or citizens. Although welfare reform ultimately kept SSI eligibility for most immigrants that were in the United States before the law was enacted, it excluded new immigrants from SSI until citizenship (with limited exceptions). A GAO study (GAO, 1999b) found that very few states replaced SSI benefits with state-funded programs. After the law was enacted the Social Security Administration (SSA) was mandated to eliminate benefits for close to 580,000 immigrants, but subsequently the laws were changed to allow SSI benefits for immigrants already in the program and to provide benefits to those in the country before August of 1996 who became blind or disabled. Immigrants who were not already receiving SSI, however, would not qualify for the program based only on their age. The GAO estimates that 20,000 prereform noncitizens in 1998 were not eligible under the new criteria and would have lost SSI assistance unless they adjusted their immigration status (GAO, 1999b).

Table 9.2 includes data on participation in the SSI program with an emphasis on changes among the noncitizen Latino population. The figures indicate that there was an increase of 388,230 participants (or 6%) between 1995 and 2003. The figures for noncitizens indicate that there was a decline of 88,638 participants in the program (or 11%) between 1995 and 2003. Noncitizen applications to SSI decreased significantly by 88,720 between 1995 and 2003 (or 40%). SSI annual reports do not include the number of Latinos that participate in the program, but other publications (see Table 9.2 for specific references) list the percent Latino at 14.2 percent or 931,042 persons in 1999.

Table 9.2
Participation in the Supplemental Security Income (SSI) Program

	1995	2003	Net Change 1995 to 2003	Percent Change 1995 to 2003
Total Recipients (1)	6,514,134	6,902,364	388,230	6.0%
Noncitizen Recipients (2)	785,410	696,772	−88,638	−11.3%
Percent Noncitizens	12.1%	10.1%	−2.0%	
Total Citizen Applications (3)	1,928,350	2,095,720	167,370	8.7%
Total Noncitizen Applications	223,540	134,820	−88,720	−39.7%
Percent Citizen Application	11.6%	6.4%		
Citizen Adults (18 to 65 years old)	1,297,050	1,542,720	245,670	18.9%
Noncitizen Adults (18 to 65 years old)	83,040	73,720	−9,320	−11.2%
Percent Citizen Adults Application	6.4%	4.8%		

	1999	2001	Net 2001 Change 1999 to 2001	Percent Change 1999 to 2001
Latino Percent (4)	14.2%	14.2%		
Latino Recipients (5)	931,042	949,765	18,723	2.0%
Percent of Latinos	31.4%	32.4%		
Noncitizens (6)				

	1999	2001 (7)
Total Noncitizen Latinos	292,220	307,610
Central America	*159,220*	*168,910*
Mexico	134,890	142,470
El Salvador	10,440	11,390
Guatemala	6,190	4,610
Other	7,700	10,440

Table 9.2 (Continued)

	1999	2001 (7)		
South America	*24,900*	*22,130*		
Colombia	6,320	6,720		
Ecuador	5,420	5,650		
Peru	4,610	4,930		
Other	8,550	4,830		
Caribbean	*108,100*	*116,570*		
Cuba	48,750	48,630		
Dominican Republic	34,630	38,640		
Haiti	10,760	12,380		
Other	13,960	16,920		
Percent of Recipients that Are Noncitizen Latinos	4.5%	4.6%		
Total Recipients (8)	6,514,134	6,902,364	388,230	6.0%
Noncitizen Recipients (9)	785,410	696,772	−88,638	−11.3%

Sources: (1) Social Security Administration, 2004. *SSI Annual Statistical Report 2003* (September 2004): Table 3; (2) Social Security Administration, 2004. *SSI Annual Statistical Report 2003* (September 2004): Table 19; (3) Social Security Administration, 2004. *SSI Annual Statistical Report, 2003* (September 2004): Tables 3, 42, 43 and 44; (4) Social Security Administration, 2000. *Social Security Bulletin* 62(4) (April 2000): 13. The Social Security Bulletin Annual Statistical Supplement (1999) lists the percentage of Latinos as 14.3%; (5) Computed from percentage given in 1999 assuming no change in proportion Latino; (6) Social Security Administration, 2000. *SSI Annual Statistical Report 1999* (June 2000): Table 26. Data for the Caribbean includes Haiti and Other; (7) Social Security Administration, 2002. *SSI Annual Statistical Report 2001* (June 2002): Table 19; (8) Social Security Administration, 2004. *SSI Annual Statistical Report 2003* (September 2004): Table 3; (9) Social Security Administration, 2004. *SSI Annual Statistical Report 2003* (September 2004) Table 19.

Also, in this year, the number of noncitizen Latinos is close to 292,220 or 31.4 percent of Latinos in the program and 4.5 percent of participants in SSI. There was a slight increase of 2 percent (or 307,610 persons) in the noncitizen Latino population from 1999 to 2001.

Declining Access to Food Stamps

Government statistics indicate that in fiscal year 1998, the Food Stamp Program spent close to $16.9 billion at an average of $170 per household each month. The monthly food stamp grant is based on household income, assets, and the number of qualified members. The Department of Health and Human Services' (HHS) poverty guidelines are used to determine who is eligible for the program. To be eligible household gross income cannot be more than 130 percent of the poverty level (about $2,167 per month for a family of four in 2006), and net income cannot be more than the poverty level. In addition, a household is limited to $2,000 in assets and a vehicle worth no more than $4,650. Food stamp households have to certify their eligibility every 3 to 12 months (GAO, 1999a).

The number of households using food stamps increases and decreases with the overall economy, but since 1996 it has declined much faster than poverty. The number of people living in poverty was at its highest level in 1993 at around 39.3 million. Since then it has declined more gradually, and it leveled off after 1995. However, close to 4 million more people were living in poverty in 1997 than in 1989. The number of people who received food stamp benefits has declined each year since fiscal year 1994, when there were close to 27 million participants in the program, with most of the decline occurring after fiscal year 1996. Between fiscal year 1996 and fiscal year 1998, use of food stamps decreased by 5.8 million persons to close to 20 million. This is 75 percent of the total decrease since 1994 (GAO, 1999a, 5).

Table 9.3 presents data on changes in participation in the food stamp program with an emphasis on Latinos and states with significant Latino populations. In 2002, close to 18.2 percent of participants in the program were Latino. The figures indicate that between 1996 and 2002 there was a decline of 22 percent or 5.2 million participants in the program. During the same period the number of Latinos declined by about 0.9 million from 4.4 to 3.4 million persons or 23 percent. From 1997 to 2002, data at the state level suggests that the largest declines took place in California, New York, and Texas. The number of Latino households in the program declined by about 61 percent in California (by 398,000) and 45 percent in New York (by 115,000) between 1997 and 2002.

There are several factors that have contributed to the significant declines in food stamp participation. First, a relatively robust economy and low unemployment rates in many areas of the country has increased work income and reduced the number of persons eligible for the program. However, the number of participants has declined twice as fast as the number of persons eligible (see Table 9.3). Second, provisions of the law made eligibility for the program more difficult and eliminated immigrant access to the program, and third, state and local initiatives were introduced that were designed to reduce the number of persons on welfare, which also impacted access to food stamps. According to a GAO report, during fiscal year 1997, participation in the program by able-bodied adults without dependents and by permanent resident aliens fell by about 714,000 people, accounting for about 25 percent of the decline in food stamp participation (GAO, 1999a, 7). As a result of changes in the law

Table 9.3
Changes in the Use of Food Stamps among Latinos

	1996	2002	Net Change 96 to 02	Percent Change 96 to 02
	(1)	(7)		
Total Participants (1)	24,272,688	19,041,000	−5,231,688	−22%
Number of Latinos (2)	4,477,000	3,467,000	−1,010,000	−23%
Percent Participants Latino	18.40%	18.20%	0%	
Total Number of Eligibles (3), (6)	35,662,325	34,693,233	−969,092	−3%
Percent of Total Eligible Enrolled	68.06%	54.88%	−13%	
Number of Latino Eligibles (4)	8,485,461	7,556,647	−928,814	−10.95%
Percent of Latino Eligible Enrolled	52.76%	45.88%	−7%	

	1997	2002	Net Change 97 to 02	Percent Change 97 to 02
	(5)			
Total Households (6)	8,446,000	8,201,000	−245,000	−3%
Latino Households	1,566,000	1,003,000	−563,000	−36%
Percent Latino Households	16.60%	12.23%	−4.37%	
Arizona				
Total Households	133,000	144,000	11000	8%
Total Latino	46,000	39,000	−7,000	−15%
Percent Latino	34.40%	27.08%	−7.32%	
California				
Total Households	1,045,000	647,000	−398,000	−38%
Total Latino	394,000	152,000	−242,000	−61%
Percent Latino	37.70%	23.49%	−14%	
Florida				
Total Households	514,000	474,000	−40,000	−8%
Total Latino	146,000	146,000	0	0%
Percent Latino	28.40%	30.80%	2%	

(Continued)

Table 9.3 (Continued)

	1997	2002	Net Change 97 to 02	Percent Change 97 to 02
Illinois				
Total Households	434,000	393,000	−41,000	−9%
Total Latino	36,000	25,000	−11,000	−31%
Percent Latino	8.40%	6.36%	−2%	
New York				
Total Households	899,000	691,000	−208,000	−23%
Total Latino	257,000	142,000	−115,000	−45%
Percent Latino	28.60%	20.55%	−8%	
Texas				
Total Households	751,000	570,000	−181,000	−24%
Total Latino	362,000	230,000	−132,000	−36%
Percent Latino	48.20%	40.35%	−8%	

Sources: (1) *Trends in Food Stamp Program Participation: Focus on September 1997.* Prepared by Laura Castner and Scott Cody of Mathematical Policy Research, Inc. for the U.S. Department of Agriculture Food and Nutrition Service (November 1999); (2) Castner and Cody (1999), *Trends in Food Stamp Program Participation*, 103–109; (3) Castner and Cody (1999), *Trends in Food Stamp Program Participation*, 103–109; (4) Castner and Cody (1999), *Trends in Food Stamp Program Participation*, 103–109; (5) Cody and Castner (1999), *Characteristics of Food Stamp Households 1997*, 125; (6) Rosso and Fowler (2000), *Characteristics of Food Stamp Households: Fiscal Year 1999.* Report No. FSP-00-CHAR. Tables A-24, A-28, B-1, B-9; (7) The Office of Analysis, Nutrition and Evaluation. *Characteristics of Food Stamp Households: Fiscal Year 2002.* Report No. FSP-03-CHAR02. Tables A-21, A-23, B-1, B-9.

and drastic reductions in access to and use of food stamps, there has been decreased food security and nutrition among poor Latino families and more reports of food-related stresses (Cordero-Guzman and Navarro, 2000).

Children and Food Stamps

There is a growing gap between the number of children living in poverty and the number of children receiving food stamps. In reference to the aforementioned GAO report, during fiscal year 1997, the number of children living in poverty declined by 350,000 (or 3%) while the number of children participating in the program decreased by 1.3 million (or 10%). As a result, the percentage of children living in poverty who received food stamps declined from 91.4 percent to 84.1 percent. In 1995, 94.6 percent of children below poverty, or 13.8 million children out of 14.6 million poor children, received food stamps. In 1997, 11.8 million children received food stamps, and between 1994 and 1997 the number of children receiving food stamps declined by an estimated 2.5 million. That same year 14.1 million children were living below poverty. Most of the decline in use of food stamps occurred during 1997, the year after changes in the law, when an estimated 1.3 million children were dropped from the program (GAO, 1999a, 10).

While participation in the food stamp program has decreased, the demand for food assistance by low-income families and requests to community-based organizations have increased in recent years (Cordero-Guzman and Navarro, 2000, GAO, 1999a). According to the study prepared by the GAO, the need for food assistance has not diminished but, instead, needy families are relying on other sources of assistance. For example, the number of children served free lunches in USDA's National School Lunch Program increased by 6 percent between 1994 and 1997 at the same time that the number of school age children receiving food stamps declined by 18 percent. Around 5 million more children obtained free lunches than food stamps during 1997 (GAO, 1999a).

Immigrants and Food Stamps

Following welfare reform, an estimated 940,000 of the 1.4 million immigrants receiving food stamps lost their eligibility for benefits. Those no longer eligible would have received close to $665 million in food stamps during 1997. Almost one-fifth of those no longer eligible were immigrant children. The U.S. Department of Agriculture (USDA) determined that most of those who remained eligible did so because they became citizens or met the exception of having 40 or more work quarters. The most recent legislation (P.L. 105–185) restored food stamp eligibility after November of 1998 to 250,000 (mostly children, the disabled, and the elderly) of the estimated 820,000 immigrants no longer eligible for food stamps in 1999 at a cost of close to $187 million.

Changes in Access to Medicaid Health Insurance and Health Care

Between 1995 and 1997, Medicaid enrollment declined at a slower rate when compared to AFDC\TANF and food stamp participation. Medicaid enrollment among the nonelderly and nondisabled adults and children declined by about 1.7 million, or 7 percent, compared with a 3.1 million, or 23 percent, decline in welfare participation (GAO, 1998d). The main reasons for the decline in Medicaid use have been strong state economies, low unemployment rates, and recent state-level reform initiatives (Chavkin, Romero, and Wise, 2000). The smaller declines in Medicaid enrollment relative to food stamps and cash assistance may also be due to expansions of Medicaid coverage for low-income children that were approved before welfare reform.

Table 9.4 includes data on changes in the use of Medicaid with an emphasis on trends among Latinos and states with a significant Latino population. The figures suggest that from 1996 to 1999, while there was an increase in participants of 12 percent (or 4.2 million persons), the number of Latinos in

Table 9.4
Changes in the Use of Medicaid by the Latino Population

	(1) 1996	(2) 1999	(3) 2002	Net Change 96 to 99	Percent Change 96 to 99	Net Change 99 to 02	Percent Change 99 to 02
Total Participants	36,117,956	40,300,394	49,754,619	4,182,438	11.58%	9,454,225	23.46%
Number of Latinos	6,314,486	6,331,084	9,233,599	16,598	0.26%	2,902,515	45.85%
Percent Participants Latino	17.48%	15.71%	18.56%				
Total Population Eligible	41,196,978	41,063,803	51,552,491	−133,175	−0.32%	10,488,688	25.54%
Percent of Eligible Enrolled	87.67%	98.14%	96.51%				
Number of Latino Eligibles	6,914,934	7,261,067	10,694,241	346,133	5.01%	3,433,174	47.28%
Percent of Eligible Enrolled	91.32%	87.19%	86.34%				

	1996	1999	2002	Net Change 96 to 99	Percent Change 96 to 99	Net Change 99 to 02	Percent Change 99 to 02
California							
Total recipients	5,106,746	6,801,371	9,301,001	1,694,625	33.18%	2,499,630	36.75%
Percent Latino	36.73%	31.74%	44.14%				
Total Latino	1,875,620	2,158,520	4,106,377	282,900	15.08%	1,947,857	90.24%

216

Florida							
Total recipients	1,638,049	2,255,182	617,133	37.67%	2,676,235	421,053	18.67%
Percent Latino	15.90%	14.06%			19.68%		
Total Latino	260,411	317,077	56,666	21.76%	487,343	170,266	53.70%
Illinois							
Total recipients	1,454,152	1,454,721	569	0.04%	1,731,398	276,677	19.02%
Percent Latino	15.10%	15.06%			18.83%		
Total Latino	219,620	219,055	−565	−0.26%	325,994	106,939	48.82%
New York							
Total recipients	3,281,016	3,234,466	−46,550	−1.42%	3,920,718	686,252	21.22%
Percent Latino	15.32%	20.86%			15.19%		
Total Latino	502,544	674,706	172,162	34.26%	595,432	−79,274	−11.75%
Texas							
Total recipients	2,571,547	2,518,016	−53,531	−2.08%	2,952,569	434,553	17.26%
Percent Latino	47.27%	46.39%			49.64%		
Total Latino	1,215,650	1,168,044	−47,606	−3.92%	1,465,561	297,517	25.47%

Sources: (1) Health Care Financing Administration (HCFA), Medicaid Statistical Information System (MSIS), *HCFA-2082 Report* (October 1997), Tables 27 (Recipients) and 33 (Eligibles); (2) Medicaid Statistical Information System (MSIS). *MSIS Tables Fiscal Year 1999.* Tables 01, 07, 14. Available at http://www.cms.hhs.gov/medicaid/msis/mstats.asp; (3) Medicaid Statistical Information System (MSIS). *MSIS Tables Fiscal Year 2002.* Tables 01, 07, 14. Available at http://www.cms.hhs.gov/medicaid/msis/mstats.asp.

the program increased only by 16,598 persons (or 0.3%). In contrast, from 1999 to 2002 there was an increase in participants of 23 percent (or 9.5 million persons) while the percent increase for Latinos was 46 percent (or 2.9 million persons). This seems to indicate that although the immediate aftermath of welfare reforms had a negative impact on the Latino population, this trend has not continued through time as a result of increased interventions by community-based organizations. The data suggest that there was a significant increase in California and more moderate increases in Florida while there were declines in Texas, Illinois, and New York (though there appears to be an increase for Latinos). Other research using data for 1995 and 1997 (Chavkin, Romero, and Wise, 2000) shows a 12.9 percent decline in Medicaid enrollment including a 15.5 percent decline in California and a 7 percent decline in New York.

In terms of the impacts of policy changes on Latino children's access to health care, studies have shown that insured children are more likely than uninsured children to get preventive and primary health care (Bindman, et al. 1995; Casanova and Starfield, 1995; Pappas, et al. 1997). Insured children are also more likely to have a relationship with a primary care physician and to receive required preventive services, such as well-child checkups (Bindman, et al. 1995; Casanova and Starfield, 1995; Pappas, et al., 1997). In contrast, lack of insurance can inhibit parents from trying to get health care for their children and can lead providers to offer less intensive services when families seek care. Several studies (GAO, 1997) have found that low-income and uninsured children are more likely to be hospitalized for conditions that could have been managed with appropriate outpatient care. Most insured U.S. children under age 18, 62 percent in 1996, have health coverage through their parents' employment (GAO, 1998c). Most other children with insurance have publicly funded coverage usually through the Medicaid program. Historically, children and their parents were automatically covered if they received benefits under the Aid to Families With Dependent Children (AFDC) program, but changes in AFDC\TANF eligibility have reduced access (Chavkin, Romero, and Wise, 2000). Children and adults may also be eligible for Medicaid if they are disabled and have low incomes or, at state discretion, if their medical expenses are extremely high relative to family income (GAO, 1998c, 3).

Government data indicate that in 1996, 3.4 million Medicaid-eligible children, or 23 percent of those eligible, were uninsured, and 35 percent of these children were Latinos. The majority were children of working poor or near poor, and their parents were often employed in the informal sector or by small firms and are also uninsured. Children who are eligible for Medicaid but do not have insurance are more likely to be in working families, Latino, and either U.S.-born to foreign-born parents or foreign-born. The report (GAO, 1998c) estimates that there were 2.4 million Latino children insured (58.8%), 1.2 million eligible but uninsured (29.2%), and another 362,000 eligible insured by other programs. The data by region suggest that of the uninsured children in the Northeast 31 percent were Latinos (140,000), 14 percent in the Northwest (or 65,000) and 27 percent in the south (407,000). Close to 56.7 percent (or

590,000) of the uninsured in the West and 64.4 percent of the uninsured in California (or 360,000 children) were Latinos. The data suggest that state outreach efforts have to make special attempts to target the eligible Hispanic population. States in the West have higher numbers and percentages of Hispanics and immigrants among their Medicaid-eligible uninsured children suggesting that these groups have been particularly excluded. Close to three-quarters of uninsured Medicaid-eligible children live in the West and the South, which suggests that states in these regions need to increase their efforts to enroll eligible Latino children (GAO, 1998c, 2).

There are a number of reasons why many eligible children in Latino families are not enrolled in Medicaid. First, some low-income working families may not realize that their children qualify for Medicaid, or they may think their children do not need coverage if they are not currently sick. Also, the creation of separate cash assistance and Medicaid programs under welfare reform has caused confusion among families, organizations, and state bureaucrats (Cordero-Guzman and Navarro, 2000; Paral, 1999). In addition, it is possible that some families believe that Medicaid carries the same negative image of dependency and inability to provide for their family that they attach to welfare. Immigrant status is also a factor, and many Latino immigrant families face additional barriers including language and culture, fear of dealing with the government, loss of eligibility among some members of the family, confusion over changing eligibility rules, and fear of future financial or other retribution for participating in the program. Finally, the enrollment process for Medicaid involves completing long forms and significant documentation that can make enrollment and participation difficult (GAO, 1998c, 2). It is important to continue to monitor access to Medicaid under the new legislation, because the potential dangers of reductions in access to health programs can be detrimental for the individuals and families affected and can be quite costly in the medium and long term (Chavkin, Romero, and Wise, 2000).

OPPORTUNITIES IN THE POST-WELFARE POLICY ENVIRONMENT

Some of the adverse effects of changes in welfare policy have been ameliorated by economic growth during the late 1990s and the recovery from the post-September 11 economic recession. For instance, a relatively high demand for labor has increased the number of work opportunities for Latinos in the labor market and has reduced the number of people eligible to participate in means tested social programs, because more people are employed and earning slightly more. The strong economy has also reduced the length of time on food stamps and other programs among some persons, because they can find new jobs faster. However, the Latino population is the first to feel economic downturns and is more vulnerable to the fluctuations of the economy. Continued economic growth and increasing opportunities in families, schools, and communities are essential to the development of Latino children and youth. In addition to policies that encourage economic growth, there have been other federal and state initiatives designed to ameliorate some of the impacts of the 1996 laws.

Some Federal Initiatives to Restore Benefits

At the federal level, recent legislation, including the Balanced Budget Act of 1997 (P.L. 105–33) and the Non-citizen Benefit Clarification and Other Technical Amendments Act of 1998, restored disability and health benefits to 380,000 legal immigrants who were in the country before welfare reform and proposed to restore eligibility for SSI and Medicaid to legal immigrants who entered after if they had been in the United States for five years and became disabled after entering the United States. This proposal was estimated to assist close to 53,000 legal immigrants by 2005, about half of whom would be elderly. In terms of nutritional assistance, the Agricultural Research Act of 1998 was expected to restore food stamps to 225,000 legal immigrant children, senior citizens, and people with disabilities who entered the United States after August of 1996. The new budget for Fiscal Year 2001 would also restore eligibility to about 165,000 legal immigrants in the United States before August of 1996 who subsequently reach age 65 or who live in households with food stamp eligible children. It bears noting that these restorations have been approved during a period of economic growth, and it is not clear whether they will remain in place during periods of economic decline. In 2002, benefits to legal noncitizens who met all other requirements were restored through the Farm Security and Rural Investment Act. Also, noncitizens receiving disability benefits and those living in the United States for five years are eligible for food stamps as of 2002 and 2003, respectively.

In terms of health care, federal initiatives included in the Balanced Budget Act of 1997 give states the option of allowing continuous Medicaid eligibility to children for a year without a reevaluation of the case. This avoids the problem of children frequently moving into and out of Medicaid as their parents' circumstances change. The new law also allows for Medicaid coverage to children on the basis of "presumptive eligibility" until a formal determination is made. This means that certain qualified providers can make an initial determination of eligibility based on income information and are assured reimbursement for services rendered. Third, the act created the Children's Health Insurance Program (CHIP), a grant program for uninsured children funded with an allocation of $20.3 billion over five years to expand coverage under state Medicaid programs to reach additional low-income children. Lastly, the new law gives states the option to extend coverage under Medicaid or State Children's Health Insurance Program (SCHIP) to low-income legal immigrant children and Medicaid to pregnant women regardless of their date of entry (GAO, 2000). By 2000, all states had implemented a SCHIP program. For 2001, 4.6 million children were enrolled either in a Medicaid expansion program (M-SCHIP) or a separate child health program (S-SCHIP). California, Florida, New York, and Texas accounted for 51 percent of SCHIP enrollment. Also, in 2001, states were given the option of enrolling adults to their SCHIP programs. As of 2001, only four states had expanded their programs to enroll adults (Ellwood, et al., 2003).

State-Level Initiatives

At the state level, there have also been recent initiatives to expand coverage to certain low income children, but the efforts have still not had the effect of providing universal coverage to all children and families. The eligibility changes under welfare reform for immigrants expanded states' administrative responsibilities and added financial responsibilities for states opting to provide benefits. As a result of the law many states, including those with significant Latino populations and where Latinos play an important role in local politics such as Florida, New York and California, are also expanding access and rethinking the methods they use to reach and enroll eligible populations in state health programs (GAO 1999a, 18). Some states have undertaken education and outreach initiatives and have tried to change the image of the Medicaid program and simplify enrollment to collect only essential information, but Welfare Reform poses additional challenges for states to reach out, educate, and enroll eligible populations, particularly Latinos, into the various programs.

CHALLENGES TO LATINO FAMILY HEALTH IN THE POST-WELFARE ERA

Recent changes in immigration and welfare laws present a number of challenges to the Latino community and its efforts to reduce risk factors and increase access to preventive health and social services among the population. These challenges include: ensuring the restoration of entitlement to benefits, increasing access to program information, increasing investments in social services, incorporating the role of culture in social services, challenges related to socioeconomic status, challenges related to migration status, increasing Latino access to policymaking, and incorporating Latino Community Based Organizations (CBOs) in service delivery and in the policy process.

The first challenge that Latinos face in the post-welfare era is ensuring the restoration of the entitlement to benefits for citizens, as time limits begin to take effect, and for immigrants who were excluded after the 1996 laws and subsequent amendments (such as able-bodied adults without dependents). So long as there are different rules and criteria for eligibility based on migration status, the Latino community is likely to participate less in such programs.

A second challenge is to increase access to information about programs and eligibility rules and to target efforts to the Latino community. There is substantial confusion by eligibility workers and applicants about the eligibility rules for both TANF and food stamps, and this is a deterrent to potential applicants (Cordero-Guzman and Navarro, 2000). Many people do not apply for food stamps, because they assume that if they are ineligible for TANF they are also ineligible for food stamps. Also, the new five-year lifetime limit on the receipt of cash assistance, for example, deters people who are eligible for Medicaid benefits from applying, fearing that Medicaid benefits will count against their time limit. Welfare reform poses additional challenges for states to educate and enroll individuals who are eligible for Medicaid. States need to make efforts to ensure that Medicaid determinations are made separate from public assistance cases and that individuals who qualify are enrolled in the programs. As the number of families on public assistance declines, there are grounds to be concerned that individuals who continue to qualify for Medicaid may not participate in the program. It is clear that in the coming years states need to make efforts to identify and enroll potential Latino Medicaid beneficiaries in order to prevent loss of benefits.

The third main challenge to the Latino community is to ensure increased investments in social services. The loss of government benefits means that other charitable and nonprofit organizations face increasing demands and pressures to provide needed social services to the community. General social services involve a wide array of economic, social, and health services and programs designed to improve the socioeconomic status of the population. Changes in immigration and welfare laws have had some impact on the work of community-based organizations and their ability to respond to the evolving needs of clients, advocate for them, and, in many instances, fulfill their mission of serving everyone in the community in need of services regardless of immigration legal status (Cordero-Guzman and Navarro, 2000). During the initial phases of the implementation of immigration and welfare reform many organizations felt that they had not been provided with the information that they needed to inform themselves and help their clients and themselves adapt to the emerging policy environment and the new eligibility rules. They also felt their ability to plan for and develop new programs was compromised by the energies that had to be spent adapting to the more restrictive policy climate (Cordero-Guzman and Navarro, 2000).

The fourth challenge is to incorporate the role of culture in social services. This is a long-standing issue (Jenkins, 1981, 1988; Cordero-Guzman, 2005), but still there are very few outreach efforts targeted to Latinos and immigrants even in states with large immigrant or Latino populations. Immigrant households, especially those in which the parents are not naturalized U.S. citizens, are likely to be a difficult group to enroll. This is due both to complex new rules and because of apprehension by some immigrants to interact with government agencies for fear of potential negative repercussions. Some immigrant families include U.S.-born children who are citizens and fully eligible for Medicaid. Moreover, some of these children live in families where one or more adults are in the country without documentation, and there might be more hesitation to participate in Medicaid. An additional complicating factor is that families in some states are asked about the immigration status of other members of the household when applying for Medicaid for their children, and this deters applications (Fix and Zimmerman, 1999; Zimmerman and Fix, 1999).

Lastly, language is often also a barrier. Individuals who do not speak English fluently, cannot read the application and other informational materials, and cannot talk to the case workers by phone or in person are very disadvantaged. This suggests that efforts need to be made to target and outreach the Latino community and to incorporate culture, translated materials, and proficient multilingual workers into the development of outreach and service strategies.

Another set of challenges faced by Latinos in the post-welfare era relate to the socioeconomic status of the population. Welfare-to-work strategies and strong state economies are leading more people into work, but poverty is still very high in the Latino community (21.9% in 2004), and large segments of the population live with minimal resources (Ramirez, 2000). While the federal minimum wage increased from $4.25 in 1995 to $4.75 in 1996 to $5.15 in 1997, many full-time workers still earn below poverty wages. There are also many difficulties after families leave welfare associated with low income and poverty. Leaving welfare might not necessarily mean that the family and the children are more secure and can meet their shelter, food, and health care needs. A government-sponsored study in Wisconsin surveyed families leaving welfare in 1998 and found that 30 percent of persons on welfare said that they had been behind in their rent or house payments compared to 37 percent of those who left welfare. The percent that said that there were times when they could not buy food was 22 percent for those on welfare and 32 percent for those who left welfare. Close to 22 percent of respondents on welfare could not afford child care in order to work compared to 33 percent of those who left welfare. Similar proportions on and off welfare said that they had been behind on a utility bill (47% on welfare compared to 49% off welfare), that somebody in their home ever got sick or hurt for lack of medical care (8% on welfare and 11% off welfare), and a similar number said that they had to go to a homeless shelter (5% on welfare versus 3% off welfare). These figures clearly indicate that though former welfare recipients are working and their incomes might have increased slightly, they still encounter a significant number of obstacles (GAO, 1999e).

Given the punitive and restrictive nature of many aspects of the new immigration legislation, it is clear that immigration status poses another significant challenge to the health status of Latinos in the post-welfare era. Immigration status and language barriers mean that the population is often less informed, more vulnerable, engages in more dangerous work, and that it has less access to programs that promote the healthy development of children and youth. Since the 1996 changes many Latino immigrants are more vulnerable to poverty and less likely to receive needed social services (Cordero-Guzman and Navarro, 2000).

An additional challenge involves ensuring increased Latino access to policymaking. There are millions of Latino families, children, and youth, but they are missing from planning, design, research, reporting, and policy on social welfare programs. Incorporating Latino expertise into policymaking is essential to identifying and replicating best practices, building and maintaining organizational networks, and to both reaching and servicing the

Latino community. A final and related challenge is to incorporate Latino Community-Based Organizations (CBOs) into the social service delivery system. This helps ensure there is cultural competence and sensitivity in the system and potentially increases access to health care among Latinos. In recent years the number and visibility of professionals, groups, organizations, and service providers in the Latino community has increased appreciably. There are many community-based organizations with significant experience in the design, development, management, and evaluation of programs that help build, maintain, and rejuvenate Latino communities and that provide much needed social services to the population. Each one of them is an asset, and it is important to draw on these resources to build leadership around Latino family health and well-being.

CONCLUSION: INCREASING ACCESS AND INVESTING IN THE HEALTH OF LATINOS

Our review of changes in welfare and immigration policy and its impact on Latinos calls for a plan of action. We believe that the Latino community needs to focus on three key issues as it looks into the future. The first is ensuring access to social programs and health services. Public health professionals in the Latino community need more specific documentation and monitoring of the broad social service needs among Latinos, the chilling effects of changes in policy, the role of employers who do not provide insurance, and a better understanding and outreach efforts to target the uninsured (32.7% of Latinos and 33.7% of the foreign born were uninsured in 2004).

The second key issue in the post-welfare reform era is monitoring changes in the health status of the Latino population and the specific causes of these changes. This involves analyzing the increased stresses and difficulties related to the work first policies and welfare diversion strategies adopted by states to discourage eligible Latino individuals and families from receiving benefits. There is also a need to monitor how reduced access to services and programs impacts particular health and related outcomes among children in immigrant and Latino families (Wise, Chavkin, and Romero, 1999).

The third key issue is to continue to argue for the need to develop preventive approaches to the reduction of health risk factors and to provide broader access to the health care system. Some of the changes in the law have the potential of reducing the amount of information that is available to Latinos about health issues, decreasing the effectiveness of prevention and other strategies aimed at reducing health risks, and can reduce the number of doctor and clinic visits, all of which might lead to potentially lethal diseases going undiagnosed or unattended for long periods of time. The policy changes also have the potential of reducing treatment among many poor, and particularly undocumented, Latino individuals and families, inducing higher levels of family stress due to lack of health care, severe financial stress among families and individuals that are affected by some diseases, and increases in the number of preventable emergency room visits and hospitalizations, leading to potentially lower quality of life and, ultimately, higher levels of mortality.

In spite of some efforts to increase health coverage among low-income populations, other elements of welfare and immigration "reform" undermine these policies and have a negative overall impact for Latinos. The United States ended "welfare as we know it," but this did not bring about universal health coverage or the elimination of poverty among millions of Latino families and children. In the final analysis, pervasive demographic changes and the complex nature of the social, economic, political, and cultural linkages that exist between the United States, Latinos, and Latin America make it imperative for U.S. social policy to adopt preventive and comprehensive approaches. Ultimately, it is in everyone's interest to make proactive investments in the kinds of social welfare programs that stimulate the socioeconomic development of Latinos in the United States. Otherwise, we may have to bear the larger risk of being besieged by the many costs of providing emergency or remedial health care and by the other negative effects and impacts of increased social inequality on the country and its population.

ACKNOWLEDGMENTS

The authors would like to acknowledge the help and encouragement received from Ana Calero, Tracy Chimelis, Jessica Conzo, Wendy Garcia, Maciel Gutierrez, Maritza Hernandez, Migi Lee, Antonio Ribeiro, Marina Rivera, and Anyiseli Rodriguez and the support from the Rockefeller Foundation, Ford Foundation, and the Aspen Institute Non-Profit Sector Research Fund. All disclaimers apply.

REFERENCES

Borjas, George. 1990. *Friends or Strangers: The Impact of Immigrants on the U.S. Economy.* New York: Basic Books.

Bindman, Andrew, et al. 1995. "Preventable Hospitalizations and Access to Health Care," *Journal of the American Medical Association.* 274 (4): 305–11.

Brimelow, Peter. 1995. *Alien Nation.* New York: Harper Perennial.

Cardenas, Gilberto, and Antonio Ugalde (eds.). 1998. *Health and Social Services among International Labor Migrants.* Austin: University of Texas Press.

Casanova, Carmen, and Barbara Starfield. 1995. "Hospitalizations of Children and Access to Primary Care: A Cross-National Comparison," *International Journal of Health Services* 25 (2): 283–94.

Chavkin, Wendy, Diana Romero, and Paul H. Wise. 2000. "State Welfare Reform Policies and Declines in Health Insurance." *American Journal of Public Health* 90 (6): 900–908.

Cordero-Guzman, Hector. 2005. "Community Based Organizations and Migration in New York City" *Journal of Ethnic and Migration Studies (JEMS)* 31 (5): 889–909.

Cordero-Guzman, Hector, and Jose G. Navarro. 2000. "What Do Immigrant Groups, Organizations, and Service Providers Say about the Impacts of Recent Changes in Immigration and Welfare Laws?" *Migration World* 28 (4): 20–26.

Ellwood, Marilyn, Angela Merrill, and Wendy Conroy. 2003. *SCHIP's Steady Enrollment Growth Continues. Final Report.* Center for Medicare & Medicaid Services, U.S. Department of Health and Human Services (CMS# 500–96–0016 (03).

Fix, Michael, and Jeffrey S. Passel. 1994. *Immigration and Immigrants: Setting the Record Straight.* Washington, D.C.: The Urban Institute Press.

Fix, Michael, and Jeffrey S. Passel. 1999. *Trends in Noncitizens' Use of Public Benefits Following Welfare Reform: 1994–1997.* Washington, D.C.: The Urban Institute Press.

Fix, Michael, and Wendy Zimmerman. 1999. *All under One Roof: Mixed Status Families in an Era of Reform.* Washington, D.C.: The Urban Institute Press.

Jenkins, Shirley. 1981. *The Ethnic Dilemma in Social Services.* New York: The Free Press.

Jenkins, Shirley (ed.). 1988. *Ethnic Associations and the Welfare State: Services to Immigrants in Five Countries.* New York: Columbia University Press.

Mead, Lawrence. 1986. *Beyond Entitlement: The Social Obligations of Citizenship.* New York: Free Press.

Morse, Ann, Jeremy Meadows, Kristen Rasmusen, and Sheri Steisel. 1998. *America's Newcomers: Mending the Safety Net for Immigrants.* Washington, D.C.: National Conference of State Legislatures.

Murray, Charles. 1984. *Losing Ground: American Social Policy, 1950–1980.* New York: Basic Books.

O'Neill, June E., and Sanders Korenman. 2004 *Child Poverty and Welfare Reform: Stay the Course.* Civic Report, No.44. New York: Manhattan Institute for Policy Research.

Padilla, Yolanda. 1998. "Social Services to Mexican American Populations in the United States." In Gilberto Cardenas and Antonio Ugalde (eds.), *Health and Social Services among International Labor Migrants.* Austin: University of Texas Press.

Pappas, G., et al. 1997. "Potentially Avoidable Hospitalizations: Inequities in Rates Between U.S. Socioeconomic Groups," *American Journal of Public Health* 87 (5): 811–22.

Paral, Robert. 1998a. *Citizenship Service Need: A Report to the Illinois Department of Human Services.* Chicago: The Latino Institute.

Paral, Robert. 1998b. *New Immigrants and Refugees in Illinois: A Profile of 1990–1995 Arrivals.* Chicago: The Latino Institute.

Paral, Robert. 1999. *The Chicago Noncitizen Service Provider Survey.* Chicago: Latino Institute.

Passel, Jeffrey S., and Rebecca L. Clark. 1998. *Immigrants in New York: Their Legal Status, Incomes and Taxes.* Washington, D.C.: The Urban Institute.

Perea, Juan F. (ed.). 1997. *Immigrants Out!* New York: New York University Press.

Ramirez, Roberto. 2000. "The Hispanic Population in the United States." Census Bureau, Current Population Reports P20–527. Washington, D.C.: U.S. Department of Commerce.

Ramirez, Roberto R., and G. Patricia de la Cruz. 2003. "The Hispanic Population in the United States: March 2002." Census Bureau, Current Population Reports P20–545. Washington, D.C.: U.S. Department of Commerce.

Singer, Audrey. 1999. "Social Welfare and Immigrants in the United States: Policy and Research Challenges." Paper Presented at the Metropolis Conference in Vancouver in 1999. Washington, D.C.: Carnegie Endowment for International Peace.

U.S. Bureau of the Census. 2006. *Current Population Survey, Annual Social and Economic Supplements.* Washington, D.C: Poverty and Health Statistics Branch/HHES Division.

U.S. Department of Agriculture. 2004. *Characteristics of Food Stamp Households: Fiscal Year 2003.* Nutrition Assistance Program Report Series (Report No. FSP-04-CHAR).

U.S. Department of Health and Human Services. 1998. *Characteristics and Financial Circumstances of AFDC Recipients FY 1997* (December 14, 1998), Table 11.

U.S. Department of Health and Human Services. 2004. *Sixth Annual Report to Congress* (November 2004), Tables 10:19, 10:22.

U.S. General Accounting Office. 2000. *Medicaid and SCHIP Comparisons of Outreach, Enrollment Practices, and Benefits* (GAO/HEHS-00–86 April 2000).

U.S. General Accounting Office. 1999a. *Amid Declines, State Efforts to Ensure Coverage After Welfare Reform Vary* (GAO/HEHS 99-163, September 1999).

U.S. General Accounting Office. 1999b. *Food Stamp Program: Various Factors Have Led to Declining Participation* (GAO/RCED-99–185, July 2, 1999).

U.S. General Accounting Office. 1999c. *Welfare Reform: Public Assistance Benefits Provided to Recently Naturalized Citizens* (GAO/HEHS-99–102, June 23, 1999).

U.S. General Accounting Office. 1999d. *Welfare Reform: States' Implementation, Progress, and Information of Former Recipients* (GAO/T-HEHS-99–116, May 27, 1999).

U.S. General Accounting Office. 1999e. *Children's Health Insurance Program: State Implementation Approaches Are Evolving* (GAO/HEHS-99–65, May 14, 1999).

U.S. General Accounting Office. 1999f. *Welfare Reform: Information on Former Recipients' Status* (GAO/HEHS-99–48, Apr. 8, 1999).

U.S. General Accounting Office. 1998a. *Welfare Reform: Many States Continue Some Federal or State Benefits for Immigrants* (GAO/HEHS-98–132, July 31, 1998).

U.S. General Accounting Office. 1998b. *Welfare Reform: States Are Restructuring Programs to Reduce Welfare Dependence* (GAO/HEHS-98–109, June 17, 1998).

U.S. General Accounting Office. 1998c. *Outreach to Medicaid Eligible Children* (GAO/HEHS-98–93).

U.S. General Accounting Office. 1998d. *Medicaid: Early Implications of Welfare Reform for Beneficiaries and States* (GAO/HEHS-98–62, February 24, 1998).

U.S. General Accounting Office. 1997. *Health Insurance: Coverage Leads to Increased Health Care Access for Children* (GAO/HEHS-98–14, November 24, 1997).

Van Hook, Jennifer, Jennifer E. Glick, and Frank D. Bean. 1999. "Public Assistance Receipt among Immigrants and Natives: How the Unit of Analysis Affects Research Findings." *Demography* 36 (1): 111–20.

Wise, Paul, Wendy Chavkin, and Diana Romero. 1999. "Assessing the Effects of Welfare Reform Policies on Reproductive and Infant Health." *American Journal of Public Health* 89: 1514–1521.

Zimmerman, Wendy, and Michael Fix. 1999. *Declining Immigrant Applications for Medi-Cal and Welfare Benefits in Los Angeles County.* Washington, D.C.: The Urban Institute Press.

The Latinization of Lawrence: Migration, Settlement, and Incorporation of Latinos in a Small Town of Massachusetts

Ramón F. Borges-Méndez

INTRODUCTION

Over the last 50 years, African American migration from the South and the immigration of Latinos and Asians has changed the racial and ethnic landscape of southern New England states. Massachusetts, Connecticut, and Rhode Island are experiencing a new racial and ethnic diversity that is challenging social, political, and economic institutions. Latinos are the largest the minority group in the region.[1] The focus of this research is the settlement and path of social and political incorporation of Latinos in Lawrence, a small mill town of Massachusetts.[2] Specifically, this chapter discusses the experience of Latinos who, in contrast to the historic settlement pattern of dense concentrations in large urban areas, are forming big *barrios* in small cities and towns.[3] Lawrence is an old mill town of some 73,000 people near the border with New Hampshire. Latinos—Dominicans, Puerto Ricans, and small groups of other Latinos—began to arrive in Lawrence in large numbers in the early 1970s and currently represent 60 percent of the population. In New England, this pattern of growth and dispersal of the Latino population, away from the traditional big urban cores, appears firmly established. For example, as of 2000, Latinos made up 7 percent (428,729) of Massachusetts' population; only about 20 percent of them live in Boston. The rest are distributed in small cities and towns across the state, where, in some cases, they account for large percentages of the population, as in Lawrence (60%), Chelsea (45%), and Holyoke (42%).[4]

A shift of settlements into small towns is slowly becoming the pattern in other areas of the country as well.[5] Traditional theories of social and political integration postulate that immigrants tend to settle and form enclaves in large urban cores where spatial concentration and their "thick fabric" of social, political, and cultural organizations paves the way to political enfranchisement and empowerment.[6] Dispersal into the suburbs takes place as immigrants acquire socioeconomic mobility and political power. These maxims bear a great deal of empirical support, as shown by a large number of studies on the political and social incorporation of immigrant and ethnic/racial groups in American cities.[7]

The literature on the incorporation of Latinos has run somewhat counter to traditional wisdom—particularly literature that analyzes the patterns of incorporation of Latinos in the Northeast in the latter part of the twentieth century. Urban restructuring and social welfare reform have altered the traditional pattern of immigrant settlements. On the one hand, the restructured urban economies of large Northeastern cities that greeted Latinos during the 1980s and 1990s fixed them in niches that did not easily promote upward mobility. On the other hand, the opportunities for organizational development that accompanied social policy and community development programs between the 1960s and early 1980s—maximum feasible participation—have almost disappeared with federal policy devolution.[8] Overall, the direction of Latino integration in the large Northeastern cities was not necessarily toward assimilation, and further suburbanization in subsequent generations, but rather toward, at best, an uneven incorporation and significant residential segregation and social exclusion. Latinos seem also to be experiencing narrowing opportunities to sustain community-organization or to grow new ones.

An examination of the path of settlement and incorporation of Latinos in smaller cities reveals that these new communities do not fit easily the traditional model of immigrants moving from the large city to smaller ones as function of socioeconomic upward mobility, or of blending into suburban political America. The new Latino settlements do not appear to represent a "spillover," or a process of suburbanization from larger urban areas. Migration to these small cities often bypasses the "big city," but it also can be the result of internal migration from larger cities. Also, immigrants into these small towns do not seem to reflect the flight of upwardly mobile sectors from the city. For Latinos in New England, the path to settle in these small cities and towns has meant high rates of poverty, even relative to the "big-city Latinos."[9]

The research's findings are informed by case studies of communities experiencing processes of change like Lawrence's,[10] supplemented by 2000 Census data and interviews with community leaders.[11] The analysis is organized around six general findings, which are organized into two large sections:

1. Settlements in small cities, like Lawrence, developed out of various migratory streams that include both direct migration from Latinos' countries of origin and internal migration from other U.S. cities.

2. Latinos have experienced an uneasy fit into the economy of the city. Latinos have been incorporated into the dying manufacturing and the low-end service sectors. As a result, wages are low and poverty rates are among the highest in the region.

3. Latinos are highly concentrated in specific neighborhoods, where they have lived since they initially settled, and have moved to concentrate in newer ones. They have faced urban renewal and isolation, but contrary to the situation of Latinos in large urban areas, they have managed to remain.

4. The social incorporation of Latinos in these small cities has been strongly contested by established residents and institutions. This dynamic has been affected by federal devolution in two fundamental ways: (a) It has affected the local government's capacity (and willingness) to serve a rapidly changing and demographically different population; and (b) It has affected the ability of Latinos to form the types of service-oriented organizations that have characterized the organizational environment (and might) of Latinos in large cities.

5. The social organization of Latinos in these small cities is independent, community-sustained, not grounded on Community-Based Organizations (CBOs) established during the Civil Rights Era, or during the years of federal activism.

6. Latinos have increased their political representation using multiple strategies: (a) recurrent challenges against the local political machine, (b) the channeling of activism of the small community organizations into a pan-Latino framework for collective action, and (c) the management of intra-Latino differences or tensions.

ORIGIN, ECONOMIC RESTRUCTURING, AND SETTLEMENT

The Roads to Lawrence: Immigration and Internal Migration

Increased immigration from Latin America to the United States during the 1980s and 1990s, and the specific characteristics of the regional economy, propelled the formation and expansion of the Latino settlement in Lawrence, as well as in other small cities. According to the common story of immigrant geographic mobility, these settlements would be considered "spillovers" from larger cities such as Boston and New York City. In fact, the findings underscore the importance of this as a factor. But the evidence also reflects that Latino migrants and immigrants made their way to these cities through a variety of pathways that often bypassed the large cities, sometimes recruited directly in the countries of origin by specific manufacturing and agricultural employers and governmental institutions, or by way of a complex web of mature social and family networks connecting small, mid-size, and large cities throughout the entire northeast.

Between 1960 and 2000, the Latino population in Massachusetts grew from about 5,000 to almost half a million people (see Table 10.1).

For the 1980–1990 decade, Massachusetts was one of the five states with the highest rate of growth of Latinos.[12] In 1960, while Latinos represented about 0.3 percent of the total population of the state, by 2000 they were almost 7 percent. The makeup of the Latino population has also changed. For 40 years, Puerto Ricans have been the largest group in the New England

Table 10.1
Massachusetts Population by Race and Latino Origin, 1960–2000

	1960 Total	%	1970 Total	%	1980 Total	%	1990 Total	%	2000 Total	%***
Total	5,148,578	100.00	5,689,063	100.00	5,737,037	100.00	6,016,425	100.00	6,349,097	100
White	5,023,144	97.60	5,484,685	95.90	5,294,151	92.30	5,280,292	87.80	5,367,286	84.50
Black	111,842	2.20	173,376	3.00	213,615	3.70	274,464	4.60	343,454	5.40
*Latino	N.A.		64,680	1.10	141,043	2.50	287,549	4.80	428,729	6.80

* Latinos may be of any race. In 2000, 393,062 Latinos identified with one racial category and 35,667 with two or more races. The discrepancy between the categories and the total population is due to this double count.
** In 1960, Puerto Ricans were the only Latino group identified by the Census.
*** Percentages are approximated.
Source: U.S. Dept. of Commerce. Bureau of the Census. Massachusetts: General Characteristics of the Population. Census Tracts: 1960. Government Printing Office. Washington, D.C. 1962; U.S. Dept. of Commerce. Bureau of the Census. 1970 Census of the Population. Detailed Population Characteristics: Massachusetts. PC80-1-D23. Government Printing Office. Washington, D.C. 1983d; U.S. Dept. of Commerce. Bureau of the Census. 1980 Census of the Population; Detailed Population Characteristics: Massachusetts. PC80-1-D23. Government Printing Office. Washington, D.C. 1983d; U.S. Dept. of Commerce. Bureau of the Census. 1990 Census of the Population and Housing. Summary Social, Economic and Housing Characteristics: Massachusetts. 1990 CPH-5-23 Government Printing Office. Washington, D.C. 1992a; DP1 Profile of Several Demographic Characteristics: 2000 Census 2000. Summary File 1 (SFI) 100. Percent Data.

region, although they are changing fast in Lawrence. As of 2000, they represented about 37 percent of Latinos of the city. Dominicans represented almost 38 percent of Lawrence's Latinos (see Table 10.2 and Table 10.3).

Several phenomena converge to fuel the growth of the Latino population and its diversity. The first has to do with the evolution of U.S. policy toward Puerto Rico and the use of Puerto Rican migrants in the economic transformation of the Eastern seaboard. The U.S. capital investment in the island, through a program known as *Operation Bootstrap*, resulted in the accelerated industrialization of the island's economy, the mechanization of agriculture, and massive migration of Puerto Ricans to the United States,[13] just as northern cities in the United States were demanding low-wage labor for their dying urban manufacturing industries and expanding service sectors. Between 1945 and 1965, over half a million Puerto Ricans—about half of the active workforce of the island—migrated to the United States.[14]

The settlement of Puerto Ricans in small Massachusetts' cities such as Lawrence, Holyoke, and Lowell began in the early 1950s. Mainly seasonal agricultural workers in the apple orchards bordering New Hampshire (Lawrence) and tobacco farms of the Connecticut River Valley (Holyoke) dropped out of the migrant stream and settled there. In the 1960s and 1970s, however, Puerto Ricans were attracted by manufacturing employment.[15] The interconnection between the island and the mainland has become tighter and faster during the last 15 years, allowing Puerto Ricans to move at ease through a broader migratory circuit much beyond the traditional destinies in and around New York City.

The second factor that affects the growth and diversity of the population is the increasing number of immigrants from Latin America, propelled by both a more lenient U.S. immigration policy (before the USA Patriot Act) and a series of economic and political crises in their countries of origin. In the case of Dominicans, the other most important group in Lawrence, close to one fifth of the population of the island has migrated to the United States in the last 40 years.[16] At first, repression under the dictatorship of Rafael Leonidas Trujillo, which ended with his assassination in 1961, expelled large numbers of Dominicans to New York City and the other northeastern cities. The subsequent political turmoil during the 1960s and recurrent economic crises until this day have continued to fuel migration.[17] In New England, labor migrants from the Dominican Republic came from New York City during the 1960s to work in the remaining manufacturing industries in Massachusetts and Rhode Island (shoes, textile, leather, jewelry, etc.).[18] Although most Dominicans arrive legally from the Dominican Republic or via New York City, limitations on the quotas of U.S. visas allotted to the country force many Dominicans to be undocumented. Accounts from the period reveal that Puerto Rico and New York City are often intermediate stops between Santo Domingo and Providence, Boston, and Lawrence.[19]

The Immigration Reform and Control Act (IRCA) of 1986 and the Immigration Act of 1990 provided avenues for the legalization of undocumented

Table 10.2
Population of Lawrence by Race and Latino Origin, 1970–2000*

	1970 Total	% of Total	1980 Total	% of Total	% Change 1970–1980	1990 Total	% of Total	% Change 1980–1990	2000 Total	% of Total	% Change 1990–2000
Lawrence											
Total	66,915		63,175		−5.60	70,207		11.10	72,043		2.60
White	65,930	98.50	51,371	81.30	−22.10	38,401	54.70	−25.30	35,044	48.60	−8.80
Black	682	1.00	865	1.40	26.80	1,195	1.70	38.20	3,516	4.90	194.20
Latino	2,327	3.50	10,296	16.30	342.50	29,237	41.60	184.00	43,019	59.70	47.10
Asian/ Nat. Am./ Other	N.A.		643	1.00		1,374	2.00	113.70	1,910	2.70	39.00

*In 1970, racial/ethnic categories were not mutually exclusive. For that reason, the sum of the racial/ethnic categories does not equal the Total Population. In 1980 racial/ethnic categories were mutually exclusive.
Source: U.S. Dept. of Commerce. Bureau of the Census. 1970 Census of the Population. Detailed Population Characteristics: Massachusetts. Government Printing Office. Washington, D.C. 1972(d); U.S. Dept. of Commerce. Bureau of the Census. 1980 Census of Population. Detailed Population Characteristics: Massachusetts. PC80-1-D23 Government Printing Office. Washington, D.C. 1983(d).

Table 10.3
Distribution of the Latino Population by Ethnic Group: Lawrence 1970–2000

	1970 Total	% of Latinos	1980 Total	% of Latinos	1990 Total	% of Latinos	2000 Total	% of Latinos
Latino	2,123		10,296		29,237		43,019	
Puerto Rican	385	53.30	5,726	55.60	14,661	50.10	15,816	37
Mexican	0	0.00	92	0.90	165	0.60	316	1
Cuban	685	32.30	417	4.10	463	1.60	408	1
Other	419	19.70	4,061	39.40	13,948	47.70	26,479	62
Dominican	N/A	N/A	N/A	N/A	10,870	37.20	16,186	38
Central Am.	N/A	N/A	N/A	N/A	433	1.50	1,001	2
South Am.	N/A	N/A	N/A	N/A	839	2.90	725	2

* In the 1970 Census, there is a discrepancy between the summation of the Latino subgroup numbers and the total number of Latinos. The aggregate number of Latinos for each city is larger than the summation of the Latino subgroup categories. In here, the total number of Latinos being used is the smaller number, product of the summation of the Latino subgroup categories. Such discrepancy may be the result of the Census ethnic/racial classification procedures. The problem does not exist in 1980, 1990, and 2000.

Source: U.S. Dept. of Commerce. U.S. Bureau of the Census, 1972(a), 1972(b), 1972(c) 1983(a), 1983(b), 1983(c).

workers, although not enough to improve the legal status of a significant segment of this community. The causes and conditions of migration of newcomers from Central and South America are also diverse. The presence of these groups exploded in the 1980s and 1990s. Most Salvadorians, Guatemalans, and Hondurans came escaping war, repression, and economic hardship. Among Colombians are small groups of long-term legal immigrants who came to work in hospitals, in higher education, or as skilled workers in textiles and jewelry manufacturing, as well as a more recent group of undocumented immigrants who came escaping the violence in their country.

Latinos came to Lawrence both directly from their country of origin and from other cities in the United States. Some have more settlement experience in other areas, such as New York, Hartford, or Boston. The presence of industrial work and the networks of family reunification are strong pulls for other family members who now come directly to the smaller city. Living in smaller cities is also attractive because of the perception that they are safer and more tranquil than large cities.

A Poor Local/Regional Economic Fit: Latinos and Economic Restructuring in New England

The formation of Latino settlements in small cities responds to the specific dynamic of immigrant flows from the different Latin American nations. But the particular characteristics of the local and regional economy and ways Latinos fit into those economies also explain part of the attraction to the region. Puerto Ricans and other Latinos have been the labor power of fading New England industries for almost half a century, helping to breathe some life into this dying sector. These jobs are characterized by instability, low wages, and poor working conditions and have meant high rates of poverty for Latinos in the region. The restructured economy's high tech and biotechnology industries have largely bypassed Latinos, who in the new economy are concentrated in the low end of the service sector.

By the time Latinos arrived in the region, New England had already undergone several waves of deindustrialization. By the end of the 1970s, the new industrial structure of New England (and especially Massachusetts) consisted of five sectors: (1) declining labor-intensive, mill-based industries employing tractable labor and old technologies; (2) surviving mill-based industries producing mainly consumption goods through a combination of product specialization, substantial mechanization, computerization, and the use of relatively cheap sources of labor; (3) subcontracting manufacturing firms making capital goods for domestic and foreign producers; (4) high-tech firms making computers and peripherals and a wide variety of military, scientific, and medical equipment; and (5) expanding service sectors. Except for the 1982 recession, economic expansion continued until the late 1980s, mostly in Massachusetts—associating the state with the image of "Economic Miracle."[20]

Through the 1950s and 1960s, Latinos were making their way into the rapidly declining manufacturing industries, or into the still viable mostly labor-intensive manufacturing that remained in areas such as Lawrence and other mill towns: shoes, garments, paper and cardboard, and a few into electrical appliances and equipment. Notwithstanding, their insertion was precarious, because the sector truly did not promise any long-term prospects of mobility, although it solved the problems of immediate employment.

During the 1970s and 1980s, Latinos were hardly able to enter the growing segments of the booming New England economy, especially in Massachusetts. The miracle, to a large extent, was primarily a phenomenon reduced to some cities along Route 128 (analogous to Silicon Valley), which left untouched other parts of the state and the region. Also, the over-concentration of Latinos in the declining manufacturing industry fueled Latino poverty in Massachusetts and the region. In the 1980s, Latinos in Massachusetts showed the highest poverty rate of Latinos in any other state (Table 10.4).

Latinos also doubled in number during the 1980–90 decade (Table 10.1). In 1970, 29 percent of the whites and 26 percent of the blacks in Massachusetts were employed in manufacturing, and 38 percent of the employed Latinos were in that sector. By 1980, the percentage of whites and blacks in manufacturing as a share of each group's total employment had decreased to 26 percent and 23 percent respectively; for Latinos, the share had increased to 42 percent. Boston aside, the concentration of Latinos in manufacturing in selected standard metropolitan statistical areas (SMSAs) was even higher. For instance, in 1980 in the Lawrence-Haverhill SMSA, 37 percent of the whites and

Table 10.4
Percentage of Latino Individuals in Massachusetts and Lawrence below the Federal Poverty Line, 1969–1999

	1969	1979	1989	1999
Massachusetts				
Latinos	22.40%	37.60%	36.70%	29.80%
Whites	8.00%	8.40%	7.00%	7.40%
Blacks	25.60%	25.30%	23.00%	21.20%
Lawrence				
Latinos	20.40%	45.40%	45.50%	31.20%
Whites	11.40%	15.60%	18.50%	17.70%
Blacks	19.70%	21.50%	33.00%	29.00%

Sources: U.S. Bureau of the Census. 1970 Census of the Population. Detailed Population Characteristics: Massachusetts; U.S. Bureau of the Census. 1980 Census of the Population. Detailed Population Characteristics: Massachusetts. PC80-1-D23. U.S. 1990 Census of the Population and Housing. Summary Social, Economic and Housing Characteristics: Massachusetts; U.S. Bureau of the Census. 2000. STF3/STF.

58 percent of the blacks employed had manufacturing jobs; of the total number of Latinos employed, 72 percent were employed in manufacturing.[21] The decline of manufacturing dominated the employment picture of New England (and of Lawrence) at least from 1967 until 1988. This seclusion into declining manufacturing in occupational terms has translated into concentration in low-skill occupations with little prospect for upward mobility, moreover in a sector that continues to decline. Occupational data for the 1990s shows that there are new avenues opening for Latinos, although for the most part these are in low-skill, low-wage occupations: clerical, sales, and personal services. In Lawrence, the most recent data indicates that occupational diversification among Latinos has taken place, yet still 35.1 percent were laborers; a significantly higher share than for the total population (see Table 10.5).[22]

Did this story of regional/local labor market insertion continue into the 1990s? During the 1990s, the Massachusetts economy underwent an expansion[23] fueled by the growth of the knowledge-based economy in high-tech, bio-tech, and financial services, which this time around seems to have been even more closely integrated into the economy of the immediate Boston area and Cambridge, with some employment and growth spillover into the northern suburbs, but not as far as Lawrence.[24] In Massachusetts, the knowledge-based economy and the internal sophistication of the sector created a profile of jobs that are not likely to be filled by Latinos, especially given the high educational requirements those jobs demand.

Caught in this roller-coaster ride, Latinos barely hold on. In the 1990s, Latinos apparently derived some benefits from the overall economic bonanza. The poverty rate in Lawrence, according to the 2000 Census, dropped significantly, as can be seen in Table 10.4, but nevertheless it remains high, still almost four times the white rate. Although Latinos in the 1990s experienced both occupational and sectorial diversification, the persistence of high rates of poverty makes it difficult to argue that they have been able to improve their integration into the local and regional economies.

Dense Concentration in Neighborhoods: The Struggle for Spatial Integrity and Continuity

In many small and mid-size cities, like Lawrence, Latinos have been highly concentrated in certain neighborhoods, where they have lived since they initially settled. They have faced urban renewal, isolation, displacement, and urban "benign neglect." But contrary to the situation of Latinos in large urban areas (for the most part), they have managed to remain. "Staying in place," preserving the spatial integrity of the initial *colonias* and of to-be *barrios*, has been critical to spinning several territorially-based, as well as cultural, organizations. It has also provided an anchor to the growing Latino population base of the cities. The process, however, is far more complex and rich than the dry dynamics of "neighborhood replacement," strongly marked by "white flight."

Table 10.5
Occupational Distribution of the Employed and Latino Populations
16 Years Old and over Lawrence, 1970–2000

Prof.; Tech.; Managers

Administrators	1970	%	1980	%	1990	%	2000	%
Total Population	4667	0.162	3678	0.143	6134	0.209	5322	20.7
Latino	40	0.045	208	0.07	935	0.094	2014	14.6
Clerical and Sales								
Total Population	6378	0.221	6863	0.266	6836	0.233	6225	0.242
Latino	25	0.028	340	0.114	1662	0.168	2911	0.212
Craftsmen; Foremen								
Total Population	3498	0.121	3475	0.135	4020	0.137	N.A.	N.A.
Latino	53	0.059	473	0.159	1353	0.136	N.A.	N.A.
Operatives; Laborers (except farm)								
Total Population	10726	0.372	8525	0.331	7432	0.253	7178	0.279
Latino	738	0.826	1767	0.595	3841	0.387	4828	0.351
Construction								
Total Population	N.A.	N.A.	N.A.	N.A.	N.A.	N.A.	1932	0.075
Latino	N.A.	N.A.	N.A.	N.A.	N.A.	N.A.	905	0.066
Farm Workers								
Total Population	13	0	108	0.004	201	0.007	115	0.004
Latino	0	0	12	0.004	30	0.003	108	0.008
Service and Private Household Workers								
Total Population	3537	0.123	3133	0.122	4714	0.161	5000	0.194
Latino	38	0.043	170	0.057	2093	0.211	2995	0.218
Total Employed Pop 16+	28819	1	25782	1	29337	1	25722	0.503
Latino Employed 16+	894	1	2970	1	9914	1	28104	0.49

Source: U.S. Bureau of the Census, 1970–2000.

The process has been fraught with conflict and to a large extent illustrates the tensions of social and political incorporation in the cities.[25]

Latinos in Lawrence did not settle in a section of the city slated for urban renewal or transformation; in other words, they did not occupy valued real estate, and thus the concentration took place without significant interference. In Lawrence, the paucity of urban renewal initiatives and municipal neglect allowed Latinos to plant roots in several neighborhoods and housing projects in the northern part of the city, albeit under heavy ostracism, which made living conditions deteriorate as years went by. Latinos settled in the mainly Irish Lower Tower Hill and the Italian Newbury Street neighborhoods.[26] In Lawrence, Model Cities monies and Community Development Block Grant (CDBG) funding went into constructing high-rise buildings for the retiring old white ethnic population.[27] The extent of the concentration can be further appreciated at the Census Tract level. Lawrence is divided into 18 Census Tracts (see Table 10.6).

In 1970, in all 18 tracts whites represented between 80–100 percent of the population, and in all of them Latinos represented between 0–19.9 percent of the population. Through the 1970s and 1980s, Latinos slowly "climbed the ladder of concentration." By 1990, only two of such tracts had white shares

Table 10.6
Distribution of Census Tracts by Share of White and Latino Populations, 1970–2000 Lawrence

	1970	1980	1990	2000
% White				
80–100%	18	11	2	0
60–79.9%		6	3	1
40–59.9%		1	5	2
20–39.9%			7	10
0–19.9%			1	5
Total Tracts	18	18	18	18
% Latino				
80–100%			1	6
60–79.9%			5	6
40–59.9%		3	5	5
20–39.9%		7	5	0
0–19.9%	18	8	2	1
Total Tracts	18	18	18	18

Source: U.S. Bureau of the Census, 1970, 1980, 1990, and 2000.

between 80–100 percent. Latinos in 1 tract had reached the 80–100 percent plateau, and in 10 more tracts they represented over 40 percent of the population. In 5 tracts, Latinos represented between 20 percent and 39.9 percent of the population. By 2000, Latinos had moved into southern Lawrence, previously rather off-limits to them. Also, the number of census tracts with over 80 percent Latinos increased rapidly from one tract in 1990 to six in 2000 (see Table 10.6). Although for different reasons—resilience, resistance, or institutional obliviousness—Latinos have managed to "stay in place." Such long-term anchoring separates the experience of Latinos in Lawrence from that of Latinos in Hartford, New York, and, especially, Boston, where the forces of urban renewal, gentrification, and displacement unleashed by restructuring have kept the base of the Latino community "moving" from neighborhood to neighborhood and without the possibility of consolidating social capital and political power.[28]

DEVOLUTION, SOCIAL ORGANIZATION, AND POLITICAL EMPOWERMENT

Contested Social Incorporation: White Resistance in the Midst of Devolution

Although Latinos have managed to "stay in place" and consolidate their presence in the city, the history of tensions between Latinos and local institutions cuts through Lawrence's neighborhoods. The social incorporation of Latinos has been uneven, slow, and fraught with contention and perhaps more violent than in comparable cities.[29] This struggle came to the consciousness of the state on a hot night in August 1984, when a "big brawl" between Latino and white youth escalated into two days of racial/ethnic rioting. The riots, although many government officials insisted in that it was just a "big brawl," marked the opportunity to assail the city for its failure to move forward on social and economic integration. In the aftermath of the riots, the city responded to the plight of Latinos with a number of policy measures that marked the beginning of a more open—although uneasy—sociopolitical relationship between Latinos and Anglos. Municipal and state authorities moved to: (1) create Lawrence's Human Rights Commission, (2) subcontract with *Inquilinos Boricuas en Acción* in Boston to create a social multiservice agency (*Centro Panamericano*), (3) build a recreational area, (4) rehabilitate the housing projects in the area, (5) open a Neighborhood Housing Services Office in the Lower Tower neighborhood, and (6) step-up efforts to employ Latinos in municipal jobs. Some of the proposed changes were not carried out to any significant extent, as the incorporation of Latinos in more city hall jobs. The mild adjustments however, paved the road to more serious political encounters between City Hall and the emerging Latino local power base.

In Lawrence, Latinos have experienced social exclusion from the white dominated mayoral offices, as well as state and federal agencies. But what are the specific conditions that reinforce such exclusion? It is critical to emphasize the effect that federal devolution has had both on the delivery of public services in small cities and on the capacity of minority groups to develop their own solutions. Devolution has had a critical impact, on the one hand, on the local bureaucracies' ability to maintain quality public services and their willingness to adapt these services to the new populations that are now its citizens. This has meant that public services do not serve Latinos well in the city. On the other, devolution has deeply reduced the funding for specialized services directed to specific racial/ethnic communities. This has left Latinos without the possibility of developing, for and by themselves, at least a basic layer of supportive services.

The geography of the new immigration has come in tandem with policies that have underscored the role of localities in the funding and delivery of public services. Just as Latinos began to arrive in small cities and towns in large numbers, federal devolution began to create new challenges for local public administration and public policy. Bureaucracies were called upon to modernize and to become more accountable to citizens while at the same time, local "no-taxes" initiatives reduced the fiscal leeway of local governments. The "New Federalism" of the 1980s challenged the basic premises of the "War on Poverty" programs of the 1960s and 1970s, not only on the role of the federal government in guiding and delivering social policy programs, but also on the role of social services as vehicles for the empowerment of the poor. What began as an attack on "welfare" policies, spilled over into other areas, including neighborhood revitalization and services to newcomers.[30] Federal devolution has meant greater discretion in local policy and the use of market-driven instruments as the engines of local policymaking. Market-driven principles have replaced public-institution building, distributive equity, and the earlier mandated "maximum feasible participation."

The political changes point to a very uneven process of engagement between the old political machines and the Latino community in its search for political space and empowerment. Federal, formula-driven allocations for programs are clearly not enough for the local bundle of problems. In addition, fiscal measures that limit expanding the local revenue base, like the Massachusetts' 2 1/2 percent cap on property taxes, and the general resentment shown by "old timers"—who feel threatened or invaded by the new populations—hinders political change, or delays power-sharing, coalition-building, or outright power transfers. Part of the resistance shown by the local machines is related to the fact that government jobs in small cities and towns are a very important source of employment and part of the system of rewards and incentives used by the political machines to hold onto power. But the resistance to change seems way more complex than a battle for jobs: in the vortex of power-sharing, or power-transfer, economic interests combine with institutionalized racism, administrative insufficiencies, mutual distrust, and shifting demographics.

Ineffective Services: Education, Health, and Urban Economic Development

Education has been an area of high contention between Latinos and local government in Lawrence (and in other cities). By 1990, about 70 percent of students in Lawrence were Latinos, yet Lawrence was one of the cities with the worst school outcomes for Latino children in Massachusetts. Following the Educational Reform Act of 1993, the state attempted to equalize funding across school systems and introduce measures of accountability.[31] As a result, during the 1990s Massachusetts' schools, including Lawrence, received substantial additional funding. But Lawrence (as well as other cities such as Holyoke), quickly became a "poster city" of educational reform gone wrong. This was due to incompetence and mismanagement, as well as resistance to change on the part of past superintendents, as well as school committee members. Lawrence received more than $250 million between 1993 and 1997 to improve its schools.[32] The city was well known for under-funding its school system, refusing to increase its property tax base to fund the schools. Under the Educational Reform, the budget of the school system more than tripled. This funding was to be directed to increasing the teacher core, reducing class size, purchasing books and equipment, professional development for teachers, and building maintenance.[33]

The fact is that educational reform, like devolution, assumed capable leadership at the local level. And this proved to be hard to come by in Lawrence. In a 1997 report on the use of Educational Reform funding in the Lawrence district, the State Auditor called the management practices of the district "horrific," pointing to such "chaos in management" that there were millions of dollars in funding for which there was no accounting. The School Board, under strong pressure from the State Department of Education, fired James Scully, who had been Superintendent of the Lawrence Public Schools since 1987 and had lived in Lawrence all of his life.[34] But the saga was not over. In collaboration with the State Board of Education and the State Department of Education, the Lawrence Public Schools embarked on a search for a Superintendent, which yielded Mae Gaskins, a former Superintendent of the public schools in St. Paul, Minnesota. Her tenure would last less than two years. In January 2000, the Mayor of Lawrence called for her resignation for misspending $600,000.[35] Gaskins left Lawrence just as the economy faltered in 2000 and was replaced by Wilfredo Laboy, a top administrator in the public schools of New York City and a Puerto Rican. By 2002, Educational Reform funding was greatly reduced due to the State's budget crisis. Wilfredo Laboy was the first Latino superintendent in Lawrence, a system that has been predominantly Latino for over 20 years. His tenure has been equally fraught with all kinds of managerial problems.

Undoubtedly, education is a critical battleground between Latinos and the local established bureaucracy and service systems. But it is not the only one. Health services and urban/economic development are also areas of contention.

One of the effects of devolution and funding reductions has been the privatization of public services and the rise in the numbers of actors that deliver publicly funded services to communities. States and cities contract with private nonprofits for the delivery of services. In places like Lawrence, these contracts take place with established agencies and do not demand delivery that is fully accessible to the Latino population. The outsourcing has created barriers, such as: (1) the lack of bilingual information about public services and eligibility; (2) the lack of trained interpreters or bilingual personnel in public services, courts, and hospitals; and (3) the lack of Latino personnel in mid- and upper-level decision-making jobs in service delivery agencies (and the commissions that regulate the services for City Hall). Community health advocates and community economic development planners in the nonprofit sector of the city also assert that local government can no longer be, as it has been, so acquiescent with the reduction in funding resulting from devolution and the fiscal crisis. According to advocates and planners, local government offices require reframing their limited participatory approach toward the Latino community, as well as their poor handling of community development policies, project development, and approval. In the face of devolution and fiscal constraints, local developmental synergies among stakeholders require openness and collaboration.[36]

The Social Organization of Latino Communities in Small Cities

Latinos in small cities are caught between mainstream public and private nonprofit systems resistant to serve them and policies that strongly restrict Latinos' possibilities for building a social service institutional capacity of their own. The results are communities with few formal social supports and few avenues—because of language and cultural barriers—to access public, community, and social services.

Closely related to the capacity of Latinos to prevail in their neighborhoods is the possibility for the development of independent, community-sustained organizations that serve their needs. The formation of these organizations, although at one point they were interpreted as a "lag from the past" and a barrier to social incorporation by strict assimilation scholars, has proven to be the formal expression of the dense and strong networks characteristic of immigrant communities and the vehicles for social support and political activism among these groups.[37] Accounts of the process of formation of Latino communities in the region underscore the role of community-based organizations and further highlight (1) the role of social networks, both local and transnational, in the formation and development of communities; (2) the plethora of small, formal and informal organizations present in communities ranging from storefront churches and "*bodegas*" (small Latino markets) to sports and cultural organizations to political organizations; (3) how the networks evolved from such groups grow into the formal organizational of the community, usually more visible to outsiders; and (4) the role of community-based organizations in the process of leadership development.[38]

In Lawrence, as in many other cities in Massachusetts, organizations reflect a process of maturation. At the early moments of community formation, the organizations that grow are longing for the land left behind and for the need to reaffirm national culture. "*Los Juanadinos Ausentes*," for example, was an organization formed by persons from a particular town, in this case Juana Diaz in Puerto Rico, to provide a nest for basic social exchange and support. "*Los Trinitarios*," a Dominican social, sports club also illustrates the point. Cultural maintenance and dissemination, sports, entertainment, the celebration of patriotic dates, and the organization of yearly festivals are the focus of activity of many of these organizations, such as the *Semana Hispana*. Organizations of this type also carry out significant transnational activity related to the country of origin, including political and economic activity. "*Bodegas*" are perhaps the most visible marker of Latino communities. These small businesses provide Latino groceries, newspapers, and music. In Lawrence, the impact of the Latino business community, especially Dominican, is considerable. A commercial strip of Latino businesses practically dominates Main Street.[39] The city also has a robust Latino small business community that has helped create the Minority Business Council and the Minority Relations Committee of the Greater Lawrence Chamber of Commerce and maintains a small business development fund with the City's Office of Economic Development and banks.[40] There is also evidence that Latinos in Lawrence are utilizing the networks already mobilized around the national, cultural, and sports associations to take action around issues affecting the broader community. The emergence of advocacy for political activity directed to the problems immigrants face in their communities represents the fruition of a subtle process of maturation of community leadership and organizational capacity.[41] During the 1980s in Lawrence, organizations that at first strictly organized along national lines started developing a pan-Latino framework of action, which in the 1990s opened the path to local political empowerment.[42]

New Strategies Bring Substantial Electoral Success

Analysts and observers of Latino politics in Massachusetts and New England believe that a new era in Latino electoral politics has arrived.[43] Lawrence's local political system has a nine-member City Council, with six members elected by the district and three members elected at-large. With the Mayor as the Chair of the School Committee, the city's six-member School Committee is also elected, with all seats elected by the district. In Lawrence, the history of Latinos running candidates dates from the 1980s. Since 1981 into the early 1990s, a dozen or so candidates ran, but their candidacies failed badly.[44] It was not until 1991 that a Latino, Ralph Carrero, was elected to the School Committee. This marked the start of a string of electoral victories by Latino candidates—a clear process of coming of political age during the 1990s. In the

1999 local election, Latinos fielded 11 candidates.[45] Dominicans and Puerto Ricans have shared the electoral victories, with significant participation from women, and the victories have been "scaling up" from the very local to the state level. Currently, the level of Latino representation stands at: two members on the School Committee; three city councilors, including an at-large member who is also the Council's President; and one of the three state representative seats (16th Essex District) in the Massachusetts' House of Representatives. However, it would be a mistake to think that this rapid ascent and breakthrough in the late 1990s was relatively easy.

In Lawrence, there is evidence that, although electoral results still trail Latinos' percentage in the electorate, the 1990s brought political maturity and unprecedented penetration of the political arena. Latinos evidence some political power and expertise by winning state senate and house races in Massachusetts, Rhode Island, Connecticut, and even New Hampshire; gaining numerous school committee and city council posts; and running some very visible mayoral challenges and triumphs, as in Hartford. Apparently, we are beginning to combine our "numbers" with the effective use of the American political institutions, resource mobilization, pan-Latino campaigning and coalition building, leadership development, and other forms of political learning and strategies.

Managing the internal relationships within the community is one of the most critical variables, and these relationships are currently battered in this region by contradictory forces that reflect the evolving dynamics of intragroup leadership. One critical piece is the evolving role of Puerto Rican leadership. Puerto Ricans are the oldest and still the largest Latino group in many parts of the region. Having historically spearheaded and mediated political mobilization in communities throughout the Northeast, Puerto Ricans are experiencing their own set of political dilemmas as the new local political reality exacts a different type of political maturity. Puerto Ricans are citizens by birth and, historically, among Latinos in the East Coast, Puerto Ricans were most able to use the avenues offered by public policy and public programs to gain a measure of political empowerment. In many ways, Puerto Ricans were the brokers of that relationship for Latino communities, and in this region, to their credit, the benefit was often well shared with other Latino groups. But during the 1980s and 1990s, as was mentioned earlier, social policy reforms driven by devolution, privatization, and cutbacks greatly curtailed these avenues. For Puerto Ricans, this is a time of redefinition.

Simultaneously, some "new" Latino immigrants, especially from the Dominican Republic, are coming to the fore with great political strength. Better known for their involvement in transnational politics than in local ones, Dominicans seem to begin to be able to use one to push the other. Many elected officials in New England are Dominican. The most critical variable in this development has been time—time for Dominicans to achieve citizenship and for the second generation of Dominicans, born and raised in U.S. cities, to exercise their power.

Latinos seem to be coming of political age in this city. However, political ascendancy is connected to a long and heated political history of inter-Latino conflict, and to a contentious and explosive relationship with the local white political machines of Irish, Italian, and French-Canadian background. The intercommunity conflict was predominantly between Puerto Ricans and Dominicans, which has been subsiding in more recent years. The city's Latino community has evolved to show a well-defined set of leadership arenas in education, politics, business, religious, communications, and social clubs. In all of them there are Latino leaders pitching in one way or another into the pool of social and political capital of the community at large. The conflicts between Latino leaders from different national groups, or between the different leadership arenas, of the 1970s and 1980s have not necessarily disappeared; at times they still flare with viciousness, yet they are being well enough managed not to erode the accumulated political capital.[46] This shows, according to former Dominican City Council member Julia Silverio, political maturity. In addition, the passing of time has allowed the Dominican community to amass and activate a larger number of people with citizenship status who can directly influence local political outcomes.

Regarding the relationship of Latinos with City Hall, it remains contentious yet is becoming more amenable to negotiations, framed by the terms of the old ethnic political machines yearning for "restoring a glorious past."[47] Most important, this relational framework forestalls Latino appointments to meaningful posts in, and power sharing and managerial collaboration within, the numerous administrative commissions and departments that run municipal affairs.[48] Some Latinos have been appointed to various posts, such as the Human Rights Officer and Affirmative Action Director, yet the appointees come from smaller Latino groups (Chilean, Mexican American) that have nonthreatening power bases.[49] Most recently, appointments of Latinos to the School Superintendent and Police Chief posts perhaps indicate a shift for the better.

The process of political empowerment in Lawrence seems to have "taken-off" once Latinos began to effectively manage internal strife. This has enabled diverse leadership and a more focused electoral strategy while external pressures have forced some change upon the local political machine. Political electoral gains seem to be opening access into the administrative arena of municipal affairs. Latino strategies of political incorporation have been combining electoral and confrontational strategies with more weight on the electoral side. To illustrate the matter, in 1998, responding to urgent complaints by citizens, the U.S. Justice Department filled a suit against the City of Lawrence for violating the Voting Rights Act.[50] Three issues were at the core of the suit: (1) districts and at-large seats may have been created or used to weaken voting power of Latinos; (2) not all election materials were provided in Spanish;[51] and (3) the city had not provided sufficient Latino poll workers or a propitious environment to Latino political participation. After some political and legal haggling, the City negotiated a deal with the U.S. Department of Justice. It included more resources and provisions to enhance and safeguard Latino participation in the electoral process.[52] Although it did not include provisions to overhaul the structure of the districts, the fresh resources, according to local Latino political leaders and other observers, have greatly improved the prospects of political empowerment.[53] Along the same lines, the combined strategy comes out clearly in the process of redistricting that carved the Massachusetts' State House Representative seat for the 16th Essex District, and in the election of a Latino to that seat (already alternately occupied by two Latinos of Puerto Rican and Dominican descent). The first victory was possible due to strong and well-organized grassroots and media activity among Latinos, including managing the tensions of a vote recount, transportation to get voters to the polls, and information about the voting process.[54]

CONCLUSION

The Latino community in Lawrence developed out of various migratory streams that include both direct migration from Latinos' countries of origin and internal migration from other U.S. cities. These new Latino settlements do not represent "spillover settlements," nor are they the result of the process of suburbanization of larger urban areas. Migration to these small cities can be direct, thus bypassing the "big city," as well as it can be internal, mainly through network vines grounded in cities through the Northeastern seaboard (and abroad). Our examination of this path of settlement and incorporation of Latinos into what amounts to "big *barrios* in small cities" reveals that these new communities do not fit easily, or only partially, into the classical paradigm of immigrant spatial assimilation, which predicts a path from the "big-city to the suburbs," largely as a result of socioeconomic upward mobility. Moreover, as a result of these multiple streams, Lawrence's Latino community has diversified to include not only Puerto Ricans, but also equally large numbers of Dominicans.

Latinos have experienced an uneasy fit into the economy of the city of Lawrence. They have been incorporated into the dying manufacturing and low-end service jobs. As a result wages are low and poverty rates are among the highest in the region. Likewise, they have not been able to enter the rising industries, at least into some of the good occupational categories. They remain concentrated in low-end, low-pay occupational categories, although there has been some improvement within the last decade. Such poor fit took place in the prosperous mid-1980s and appeared to have repeated itself in the mid-to-late prosperous 1990s. Lawrence has been "redlined," to some extent, in spite of being so close to the Route 128 high-tech corridor and to other areas of economic activity in the Greater Boston. The city saw a brief period of recuperation in the 1990s, yet not enough to call it an economic revival.

In Lawrence, Latinos are highly concentrated in specific neighborhoods, mostly in the northern part of the city, where they have lived since they initially settled. Contrary to the situation of Latinos in large urban areas, they have managed to remain. In North Lawrence, the main story is of "benign neglect," and the paucity of renewal allowed communities to prevail spatially, yet at the expense of other malaises such as disinvestment and isolation. This capacity to "stay in place" has allowed Latinos to develop some primary organizations. These organizations became an important building block toward further political incorporation. Yet they are not powerful enough to contend with other forces such as local ostracism, institutional racism, and exclusion by political machines, and devolution. Such forces detracted these organizations from the traditional path that the organizations of previous immigrants might have followed. In the path to political incorporation, so the story goes, immigrants develop a spatial power base—city trenches with marked ethnic identity, or an enclave—that catapults the group into power. In Lawrence's case, although there has been progress, this "path" has severely curtailed.

In recent years, the welfare state has been undermined and replaced by a much less responsive subsidiary state. In this transformation, cutbacks dressed as the overrated advantages of devolution, local autonomy, and flexibility have had an ambiguous effect on the prospects of Latino political and social incorporation. The social incorporation of Latinos in Lawrence, as in many small cities, has been affected by devolution in two fundamental ways. First, devolution has limited the local governments' capacity (and willingness) to serve a rapidly changing and demographically different population. Secondly, it has made it more difficult for Latinos to form the types of service-oriented organizations that have characterized the organizational environment (and might) of Latinos in large cities.

What is the value and importance of Latino social organization in the small cities and towns? The independent, community-based social organization of Latinos in Lawrence was initially characterized by the development of small, independent nationality-based organizations. These organizations are the base of active political organization in these communities. They also go through several stages prior to becoming building blocks for Latino empowerment. At first, small cultural organizations, organized along national and even hometown lines, serve as meeting point. But they pave the way for broader political activity, even incorporating transnational politics. Within time, the matrix of social organization also diversifies to show differentiated spheres of leadership in business, politics, religious life, cultural life, and even media. In some instances, organizational maturity opens the door to the formation of "coordinating organizations," leading into a pan-Latino framework that leaves behind the cultural specificity of the small national organizations of the moment of communal formation. The pan-Latino organizations are coterminous with a moment of communal expansion and consolidation. But as we mentioned, this process is by far not linear and has been interrupted by various forces such as urban renewal and social ostracism. For the most part, the consolidation of a pan-Latino organizational outlook marks sufficient maturity to penetrate the local political structure. In Lawrence, such processes seem to be taking place.

Latinos in the region have been increasing their political representation. The strategies to increased representation have included (1) recurrent challenging of the local political machine, (2) the channeling of activism of the small community organizations into a pan-Latino framework for collective action, and (3) and the management of intra-Latino differences or tensions. But the choice of strategy is no accident or random. Latinos have chosen strategies to match their counterparts, the political machine of old, white ethnic groups. Albeit dying and decrepit, these machines continue to resist. A very important factor to Latino political/electoral empowerment in Lawrence has been the remarkable contribution of the Dominican community. Such contribution is mediated by a strong set of transnational linkages that connect Dominican communities in the United States and the politics and resource mobilization tactics of political parties in the Dominican Republic. Current and past presidents of the Dominican Republic make a point of visiting Lawrence's Dominican community. The new political landscape has been also shaped by the changing role of Puerto Ricans, whose power as political brokers in local politics has been subsiding. Historically, Puerto Ricans have been the connecting group between Latino communities and political structures in most cities of the Northeast. That might be the result of the complex changes that have taken place as a result of devolution and other social dynamics that are beyond the scope of this chapter.

NOTES

1. U.S. Bureau of the Census, 2002. American Fact Finder, Census Bureau Home Page. Online at www.census.gov.

2. For a broader account of the incorporation of Latinos, including other case studies see: Borges-Méndez, Ramón & Miren Uriarte (2003). "Tales of Latinos in Three Small Cities: Latino Settlement and Incorporation in Lawrence and Holyoke, Massachusetts and in Providence, Rhode Island." Paper Presented at *The Color Lines Conference: Segregation and Integration in America's Present and Future*, Harvard University, Cambridge, Massachusetts. August 30–September 1, 2003.

3. In general terms, a *barrio* is the Spanish word used to identify concentrations of Latinos in a particular district(s), neighborhood(s), or area(s) of a city where they represent the majority of the population. *Barrios* vary in size and extension depending on the city. The origin and development of *barrios* in urban areas of the United States obeys to the diverse circumstances of urban development and change of cities, the history of migration, settlement, and labor market insertion of the different Latino subgroups, and to their sociocultural background.

4. Similarly, a large population of Latinos has settled in Providence and Central Falls (RI), where they represent 30 percent and 47 percent of the population, respectively. Hartford, Connecticut, is another example. In 2000, Latinos represented 41 percent of its total population. U.S. Bureau of the Census, 2002. American Fact Finder, Census Bureau Home Page. Online at www.census.gov.

5. Suro, Robert & Audrey Singer (2002). "Latino Growth in Metropolitan America: Changing Patterns, New Locations." Washington, D.C.: The Brookings Institution. Survey Series. Census 2000.

6. For a review of these theories see: Portes, Alejandro, and Robert Bach (1985). *Latin Journey*. Berkeley: University of California Press. An exception to the "traditional"

path took place when immigrants were attracted to small company towns in search for mining or manufacturing jobs, but concentration in large cities, for the most part, was the rule.

7. See, for example, Glazer, Nathan, and Daniel P. Moynihan (1970). *Beyond the Melting Pot.* Cambridge: MIT Press; Katznelson, Ira (1981). *City Trenches.* Chicago: University of Chicago Press; Alejandro Portes and Robert Bach (1985). Op.cit. For a recent collection on immigrant and ethnic/racial politics see Jones-Correa, Michael (ed.) (2001). *Governing American Cities.* New York: Russell Sage Foundation. For a broad review see: Schmidt, Ronald, Rodney Hero, Andrew Aoki, and Ivette Alex-Assensoh (2002). " Political Science, The New Immigration and Racial Politics in the United States: What Do We Know? What Do We Need to Know?" Presentation at the 2002 Annual Meeting of APSA. Boston, MA. August 31, 2002.

8. On the experience of political empowerment in New England, see, for example, Cruz, José E. (1998). *Identity and Power.* Philadelphia: Temple University Press; Hardy-Fanta, Carol, and Jeffrey Gerson (eds.) (2001). *Latino Political Representation: Struggles, Strategies, and Prospects.* New York: Garland Publishing; Jennings, James (1984). "Puerto Rican politics in two cities: New York and Boston." In *Puerto Rican Politics in Urban America.* James Jennings and Monte Rivera (eds). Westport: Greenwood Press. On the experience of social development and Latinos in the racial order of the region see, for example; Levitt, Peggy (2001). *The Transnational Villagers.* Berkeley: University of California Press; Uriarte, Miren (1993a). *Contra Viento y Marea (Against all Odds): Latinos Build Community in Boston.* In Miren Uriarte, Paul Osterman and Edwin Meléndez, eds. *Latinos in Boston: Confronting Poverty, Building Community.* Boston: The Boston Foundation; Uriarte, Miren (1993b). "A Challenge to the Racial Order: Boston's Latino Community." *Boston Review,* September/October.

9. Ibid., U.S. Bureau of the Census, 2002.

10. Findings of these independent case studies are reported in Borges-Méndez, Ramón (1994). *Urban and Regional Restructuring and Barrio Formation in Massachusetts: The Cases of Lowell, Lawrence and Holyoke.* Ph.D. Thesis. Dept. of Urban Studies and Planning. MIT; Borges-Méndez, Ramón (1993a). "Migration, Social Networks, Poverty and the Regionalization of Puerto Rican Settlements: Barrio Formation in Lowell, Lawrence and Holyoke, Mass." *Latino Studies Journal.* May 1993, pp. 3–21; Borges-Méndez, Ramón (1995). "Industrial Change, Immigration, and Community Development: An Overview of European and Latinos." *New England Journal of Public Policy.* Spring/Summer. Vol. 11. pp. 43–58; Borges-Méndez, Ramón (1993b). "The Use of Immigrant Labor in Mass. Manufacturing: Evidence from Lowell, Lawrence and Holyoke." In *Latinos and Economic Development in Massachusetts.* Edwin Meléndez and Miren Uriarte, eds. Boston: UMass Press; Uriarte, Miren (2001). *Rhode Island Latinos: A Scan of Issues Affecting the Latino Population of Rhode Island.* Providence: The Rhode Island Foundation (funding for this case study was provided to Miren Uriarte by The Rhode Island Foundation in 2001).

11. The original case study included analysis of census data, review of administrative records of organizations, and interviews with community leaders, community residents, and employers conducted between 1989 and 1993 (about 40 interviews). For a full account of the methods used in these case studies see Borges-Méndez, 1994 (Ch. 2). In the summer of 2003, additional interviews were conducted and 2000 U.S. Census data was analyzed.

12. Rivera, Ralph (1992). *Latinos in Massachusetts and the 1990 U.S. Census.* Mauricio Gaston Institute, p. 8. All figures are from the U.S. Census of 1960, 1970, 1980, and 1990.

13. History Task Force/Centro de Estudios Puertorriqueños (1979). *Labor Migration Under Capitalism: The Puerto Rican Experience.* New York: Monthly Review Press.

14. Vazquez Calzada, José (1979). "Demographic Patterns of Migration." In *Labor Migration Under Capitalism: The Puerto Rican Experience*, ed. the History Task Force, Centro de Estudios Puertorriqueños. New York: Monthly Review Press, 1979, p. 224.

15. Piore, Michael (1973). *The Role of Immigration in Industrial Growth: A Case Study of the Origins and the Character of Puerto Rican Migration to Boston.* Massachusetts Institute of Technology. Department of Economics Working Paper, no. 112, May 1973.

16. Torres-Saillant, Silvio, and Ramona Hernández (1998). *The Dominican Americans.* Westport: Greenwood Press, 1998, p. 61.

17. Leavitt, Peggy (2001). *The Transnational Villagers.* Berkeley: University of California Press.

18. Selby, John (1985). *En la Brega: Economía Política Popular para Trabajadores Latinos: El Caso de Massachusetts.* Boston: Red Sun Press, p. 85.

19. Selby (1985). Op.Cit. p. 85.

20. Borges-Méndez (1993a), (1993b), (1994), (1995). Op.Cit.

21. Ibid.

22. U.S. Census, Summary Tape File 4, 2000.

23. Congdon-Martin, et al. (2001). "Economic Performance of the New England States in 2000: An Overview." *New England Economic Indicators.* June 2001, FED Boston, p. vii.

24. Forrant, Robert, Philip Moss, Chris Tilly (2001). *Knowledge Sector Powerhouse. Reshaping Massachusetts Industries and Employment during the 1980's and 1990's.* Boston: Donohue Institute. UMass.

25. Lawrence was planned and built as a manufacturing city during the first two decades of the nineteenth century. Its urban form is influenced by the layout required for large-scale textile (wool) manufacturing, including railroad lines, water canals for power generation, large and long multistory buildings to house looms, and a clear class division between working-class quarters on the one hand and middle-class and industrial bourgeoisie Victorian houses on the other.

26. Borges-Méndez, 1994.

27. Model Cities and CDBG are programs from the U.S. Federal Dept. of Housing and Urban Development. Funds for these initiatives are usually intended for community improvements.

28. Uriarte (1993a). Op.Cit.; Cruz (1998). Op.Cit.

29. For a full-length discussion see: Borges-Méndez and Uriarte (2003). Op.Cit.

30. For an analysis of the impact of welfare reform in inner-city neighborhoods, including neighborhoods in Lawrence, Mass., see Jennings, James (2003). *Welfare Reform and the Revitalization of Inner City Neighborhoods.* East Lansing, MI: Michigan University Press.

31. With the 1993 educational reform, further reinforced in 2002 by the Federal "No Child Left Behind" Act, Massachusetts embarked in a testing program, the Massachusetts Comprehensive Assessment System (MCAS), which for the first time provided comparative data on educational outcomes by race across school systems. The implementation of the MCAS and the high failure rates among Latinos and other minority and disadvantaged students has been the source of much debate and controversy. Indeed, the high failure rates and other educational disparities negatively affecting Latinos are critical problems that need close attention, yet they are beyond the scope of this chapter.

32. Zernike, Kate. "Audit Finds Aid Wasted in Lawrence $8.9 Million in State School Money Misspent." *The Boston Globe*, June 13, 1997, p. A1.

33. Ibid.

34. For an account of the situation in Lawrence see: Zernike, Kate. "Audit Finds Aid Wasted in Lawrence $8.9 Million in State School Money Misspent." *The Boston Globe*, June 13, 1997, p. A1, and "Lawrence Schools Face State Takeover." *The Boston Globe*, January 29, 1997, p. A1; Hart, Jordana. "Panel's Steps Could Lead Lawrence Schools into Receivership." *The Boston Globe*, June 17, 1997, p. B3; Daley, Beth. "Audit of Lawrence Schools Scathing." *The Boston Globe*, May 14, 2000, p. B2.

35. Daley, Beth. "Lawrence Schools Chief Told to Resign\Gaskins Rebuff Mayor, Denies Misusing Funds." *The Boston Globe*, January 25, 2000, p. B1.

36. From Interviews by the author with staff from Lawrence Latino Health Reach 2010 and Lawrence Community Works. Lawrence, MA. June–November, 2003.

37. Most recently, the literature on social capital and social networks has reaffirmed the principle that organizational density is a fundamental component of collectivities accumulating civic culture and eventually political consciousness and power for all groups. See Putnam, Robert D. (2000). *Bowling Alone*. New York: Simon & Schuster; Skocpol, Theda, and Morris P. Fiorina (1999). "Making Sense of the Civic Engagement Debate." In *Civic Engagement in American Democracy*. Theda Skocpol and Morris P. Fiorina, eds. Washington, D.C.: Brookings Institution Press.

38. For examples of work on Latino communities in New England see: Jennings, James (1984). "Puerto Rican Politics in Two Cities: New York and Boston." In *Puerto Rican Politics in Urban America*. James Jennings and Monte Rivera, eds. Westport: Greenwood Press; Uriarte-Gaston, Miren (1989). *Organizing for Survival: The emergence of a Puerto Rican Community*. Department of Sociology, Boston University: Ph.D. Dissertation.; Hardy Fanta, Carol (1993). *Latina Politics, Latino Politics*. Philadelphia: Temple University Press; Uriarte (1993); Borges-Méndez (1993a); Borges-Méndez (1994); Amy Moreno, Angel (1998). "An Oral History of the Puerto Rican Socialist Party in Boston, 1972–1978." In *The Puerto Rican Movement*. Andrés Torres and Jose E. Velazquez, eds. Philadelphia: Temple University Press; Cruz (1998); Levitt (2001); Uriarte (2002); Hernández, Ramona, and Glenn Jacobs (2001). "Beyond Homeland Politics: Dominicans in Massachusetts." In *Latino Political Representation: Struggles, Strategies, and Prospects*. Carol Hardy-Fanta and Jeffrey Gerson, eds. New York: Garland Publishing.

39. Santiago, Jorge (2003). *The Latino Business Community in Lawrence, Massachusetts: Profile and Analysis (2000 and 2003)*. Institute for Community and Workforce Development Northern Essex Community College. Lawrence, MA.

40. Borges-Méndez, 1994.

41. Accounts of these organizational processes in Latino communities abound. For examples, see: Sanchez-Korrol (1983). *From Colonia to Community*. Westport: Greenwood Press; Cruz, José (1998). *Identity and Power*. Philadelphia: Temple University Press; Felix Padilla (1988). *Puerto Rican Chicago*. Notre Dame: University of Notre Dame Press; Uriarte, Miren (1989). *Organizing for Survival: The Emergence of a Puerto Rican Community*. Department of Sociology, Boston University: Ph.D. Dissertation. For Salvadorians see: Menjivar, Cecilia (2000). *Fragmented Ties: Salvadorian Immigrant Networks in America*. Berkeley: University of California Press.

42. Borges-Méndez, 1994.

43. See Hardy-Fanta, Carol, and Gerson, Jeffrey N. (2002). *Latino Politics in Massachusetts: Struggles, Strategies and Prospects*. New York and London: Routledge. In

this volume see the chapter by Lindeke, William (2002). "Latino Political Succession and Incorporation: Lawrence."

44. Borges-Méndez (1993); Andors, Jessica (1999). "City and Island: Dominicans in Lawrence." Masters Thesis. DUSP, MIT; Lindeke (2002).

45. Lindeke (2002).

46. Lindeke (2002). Interviews with Julia Silverio, City Councilor; and Gilda Duran, Administrative Director of Latino Health Reach 2010.

47. Lindeke (2002).

48. Interviews with Julia Silverio, City Councilor; and Gilda Duran, Administrative Director of Latino Health Reach 2010.

49. Lindeke (2002).

50. Lindeke (2002).

51. Under the Act, any city with more than five percent of a given language group requires translated materials. Lindeke (2002).

52. Lindeke (2002).

53. Lindeke (2002). Interview with Julia Silverio. City Council member.

54. Lindeke (2002).

CHAPTER 11

Social Networks and Latino Immigrants in the Labor Market: A Review of the Literature and Evidence

Luis M. Falcón

INTRODUCTION

An outcome of the process of globalization embracing economies across the world has been the thinning of national boundaries and the increased flows of people across these borders. Migration to the United States—historically a major receiver of immigrants—has maintained a steady pace over the last few decades increasing the plurality of groups already present (Rumbaut, 1994). The continuation of country and area specific inflows contributes to the maintenance and renewal of existing immigrant communities in major cities across the country. With the growth in ethnic communities, questions on social and economic progress—not only of immigrants, but also of those residing in urban centers with large immigrant populations—become more salient. The character of immigration to the United States has changed markedly over the last three decades. Not only are immigrants coming from areas different than in the past, but the dynamics that surround the flows and settlement of migrants have become more complex as refugees, legal and undocumented workers from very distinct regions and countries, continue to arrive.

This globalization of migration to the United States has augmented the scope of resources—in terms of information, social contacts, and opportunities—that individuals have, not only within the United States, but also in places as remote as Seoul or as close as San Juan. This can, indeed, be termed the internationalization of social networks. While the social sciences have traditionally recognized the role that social contacts play in the organization and functioning of societies, more than ever before in the history of world migration, social relationships permeate every aspect of the process by which individuals relocate themselves from countries of origin to destination. From immigration laws that give preference to relationships of blood and kinship to migration circuits that originate in remote villages and through social ties uproot, over time, a portion of its residents connecting communities across national borders. Migration has been defined by some as a network-creating process because of the range of contacts migrants and nonmigrants create and build upon in the process of relocating (Portes, 1995). That is the case today, perhaps, more than ever before.

Within the migration literature, social network research has lately received increasing attention, but recognition of the role that social networks play is not new (Boyd, 1989; Gurak and Caces, 1992; Portes, 1998, 2000; Ritchey, 1976). Social networks are seen as a form of social capital from which migrants can mobilize to gain access to resources such as employment, housing, and financial assistance. As individuals build ties to others, the range of resources available increases. In the long run, the broadening of these networks across space decreases the risks and costs associated with migration and ensure the continuity of the process (Garcia, 2005; Lindstrom and Massey, 1994; Reyes, 2004). Portes, Massey, and others have suggested that through these social networks, migration takes a life of its own and becomes a driving force that stimulates migration even at times when the original incentives to migrate disappear (Boyd, 1989; Massey et al., 1993; Portes, 1995, 1996).

The migration literature is replete with discussions of the origin and development of social networks and how they influence decisions such as whether to migrate or not, where to settle, and how to search for housing and employment. Until recently, the conceptualization of social networks remained largely at a theoretical level with the empirical examination of the role of social networks being scant. In some instances, social networks are seen as an explanatory mechanism for understanding the behavior of migrants but are seldom incorporated in verifiable analytical models. The lack of adequate data sources to examine pertinent questions contributed to limited empirical examination and opportunities to advance the theory. More recently, the rapid growth in the number of applied studies exploring the connections between social networks and migration tend to support, with varying degrees, the contributing role of social networks (Aguilera and Massey, 2003; Garcia, 2005; Krissman, 2005; Reyes, 2004; Wilson, 2004).

There is also a literature that is concerned with how social networks not only influence migration but also impact the social and economic mobility of immigrants. This is the case with migratory flows to the United States and, in particular, the study of Asian and Latino immigrant groups (Aguilera and Massey, 2003; Nee and Sanders, 1985; Nee and Wong, 1985; Poros, 2004). A fundamental explanation to the socioeconomic success of various Asian groups has been their use of social networks to organize socially and economically. Examples include Chinese immigrants arriving to California after the 1840s who used clans as an organizing feature, to the use of rotating credit associations by both Chinese and Japanese immigrants at the turn of the century to work around the lack of access to mainstream capital (Granovetter, 1995;

Light, 1972; Nee and Sanders, 1985; Nee and Wong, 1985). More recently, the use of churches and business associations by Korean immigrants has been suggested as the basis for their rapid entry and establishment in the small business sector (Kim, 1985; Min, 2000). The notion of a model minority has become entangled with the Asian American experience despite some evidence that undermines this hypothesis (Gold and Kibria, 1989).

Even within the Latino immigrant population we find a social network-based success story. The Cuban experience in the United States has been consistently described as rooted in ethnic social bonds that facilitate economic transactions (Nelson and Tienda, 1985; Portes's, 1987; Portes and Bach, 1985; Portes and Grosfoguel, 1994; Portes and Zhou, 1992; Tienda, 1989b; Wilson and Portes, 1980). From Wilson and Portes (1980) analysis of the economic incorporation of Cuban immigrants into distinct labor market sectors, to the careful analysis presented in *City on the Edge* (Portes and Stepick, 1993), the idea of a vibrant Cuban American community built on the foundation of a structure of social networks remains very vivid.

Until recently, however, there was little concern with the potential negative aspects of social networks (Portes and Landolt, 1996). Most of the research suggested that social networks facilitated processes for immigrants, and other outcomes were disregarded. This reflected a concern with, as Gurak and Caces (1992) have referred to it, short-term adaptive assistance. The possibility that, in the long run, social networks contribute to social inequality for some groups was not given much attention. A few works (Aguilera and Massey, 2003; Falcon 1995; Falcon and Melendez, 2001; Gurak and Caces, 1992; Nee, Sanders, and Sernau 1994; Poros, 2004; Portes and Zhou 1992; Sanders and Nee 1996; Sanders, Nee, and Sernau, 2002; Waldinger, 1995) have begun to explore the consequences of social networks, not only for those who have them, but also for those who are excluded from them.

While this notion of social capital has received increased attention within the sociology and economics literature, there are still large gaps in the understanding of how social capital affects the lives of immigrants and racial minorities once they settle in the United States. Most of the attention has been given to the role of social capital in the ethnic enclave economy and the contribution of social networks and social capital to their growth and continued success. This is, however, also an important issue for other immigrant and native groups whom, because of historical circumstances, have not developed an ethnic enclave.

In this chapter, I review some of the literature on the use of social networks and immigrants in the labor market and frame it in the experience of recent immigrants, particularly racial minorities. In particular, I examine the impact of social networks on three important aspects of immigrants' settlement: whether immigrants had networks in place at arrival to the area; whether they used those networks to secure housing; and, whether they used those networks in the initial job search upon arrival. To examine the evidence of what is known about Latino and other immigrants' settlement upon arrival, I use data from the Multi-City Study of Urban Inequality (MCSUI). The MCSUI is a survey that sampled the working age population in four urban centers in the United States. The four cities are Los Angeles, Boston, Atlanta, and Detroit. For this analysis, I used the data from the cities of Boston and Los Angeles, the only cities in the MCSUI with large immigrant populations.[1] For this analysis, the sample was restricted to only foreign-born individuals who were residing in their country of origin by age 16 and who had arrived to their respective area of residence at age 18 or older.[2] The MCSUI data are particularly useful to assess labor market dynamics. The survey included an extensive set of questions regarding recent labor market experience and the use of various search strategies in recent employment searches. In addition, for migrants to the area, questions were asked regarding the presence and use of social networks during settlement. Questions were also asked about individual characteristics at the time of arrival.

SOCIAL NETWORKS AND IMMIGRANTS' SETTLEMENT

Social networks have always been an organizing feature of migratory flows. When individuals relocate from one area to another, social contacts and relationships are established to facilitate the process. As stated earlier, migration is a network-building process. Over time, the networks established through personal migration, or because of the migration of others, increase the range of options of individuals to act upon opportunities to move and to settle.

Among immigrants, social networks have substantial overlap with kin (Gurak and Caces, 1992; Sanders, Nee, and Sernau, 2002). This is largely because of the strain that distance can place on weaker ties. It becomes far more difficult to maintain weak ties to friends than to maintain ties to kin. Networks change over time as new relationships are established and older ones dissolve. Social networks affect major aspects of the process of migration and in turn affect the composition of migration flows (Gurak and Caces, 1992). A principal mechanism through which networks affect migratory flows is by lowering of the cost of migration (Lindstrom and Massey, 1994). Networks channel information, financial and emotional assistance to those within its range. Migration selectivity, the area of settlement, and magnitude and direction of migratory flow are all interrelated aspects of the migration that are sensitive to network-building.

It is a well-established fact that migration is a highly selective process (Ritchey, 1976). Not everyone migrates. A large number of studies have documented how immigrant communities are, at least initially, far different from the population of the country they came from. In some cases, social networks contribute to selectivity by providing access to the mechanisms essential for making a move. Accordingly, individuals with social access to other migrants or with previous migratory experience will be more likely to respond to migratory pressures than those without it (Massey and Basem, 1992; Massey and Espinosa, 1997). The expanse of the social network is inversely related to the cost of migration. Because later migrants benefit from the experience and resources of earlier ones, Massey, et al. (Massey, 1987, 1988; Massey, et al., 1987) have suggested that migration becomes a self-perpetuating process. Over time, however, this same process contributes to a decline in the selectivity of the migration flow. As more people migrate, the potential number of social contacts increases rapidly and, in turn, reduces the cost of migration for a larger number of potential migrants. This latter process can make migratory flows less sensitive to the initial economic forces that led to the migration or to changes in the economic climate (Portes and Bach, 1985; Massey, 1988; Massey et al., 1987). Social networks and migration flows become dependent on each other for survival.

Relations of kin, friendship, and ethnicity are common features of immigrant networks. Social networks organized along those lines tend to channel migrant flows to areas where networks are already in place (Garcia, 2005; Wilson, 2004). Heller, et al. (2004), working with a sample of Mexican Americans, suggest that those with "resource-in-place support" were more likely to indicate a sense of control or mastery over their immediate environment. Recent data from the Multi-City Study of Social Inequality shows that, within a cross-section of immigrants in the cities of Los Angeles and Boston in 1994, most immigrants had social networks in place before arrival (Falcón, 1997). The available evidence indicates that, for immigrants, reliance on social networks is common. The vast majority of immigrants arriving into the Los Angeles and Boston areas reported having friends or relatives already living in the area. In reference to Table 11.1, in Los Angeles, 88 percent of Mexican migrants and 85 percent of Asians had networks in place. In Boston, more than 90 percent of Puerto Ricans and Dominicans reported the presence of networks prior to arrival. Salvadorean immigrants in Los Angeles were least likely to know someone but still, about 80 percent reported that they did.

Table 11.1
**Networks in Place at Arrival to Area: Ethnic/
Racial Groups in Los Angeles and Boston***

	Los Angeles	Boston
Non-Hispanic White	65.7%	68.8%
Black	80.0%	80.7%
Asian	84.5%	—
Hispanic	86.7%	93.1%
Mexican	87.9%	—
Puerto Rican	—	93.9%
Salvadorean	79.3%	—
Dominican	—	92.3%
Other	86.5%	75.0%

*Includes only those who arrived after age 18.

Immigrants use social networks to find housing once they arrive to an area where they would like to find employment and settle. Salvadoreans in Los Angeles and Puerto Ricans in Boston have the highest rates of network use to find housing after arrival, with 96 percent and 94 percent, respectively. Of Dominicans in Boston and Mexicans in Los Angeles, 88 percent use social networks to find housing, while Other Hispanics have a slightly lower rate of 85 percent and 81 percent in Los Angeles and Boston, respectively (see Table 11.2).

These results on immigrants' use of network upon arrival are very consistent with the literature on this topic, which suggests high use of social networks across all immigrant groups. Work by Massey and others (Massey, 1987, 1988, 1990; Massey, et al., 1987) on Mexican migrants, and by Grasmuck and Pessar (Grasmuck, 1984; Grasmuck and Pessar, 1991) on Dominicans have suggested that social networks orient migrants to areas where network contacts are already in place. Other studies of migrants within Europe also lend support to this argument (Wilpert, 1992).

Social networks also facilitate the permanent settlement of immigrants. Again, work by Portes and Bach and by Massey, et al., provide empirical evidence that individuals who decide to settle on a more permanent basis are more likely to have pre-existing networks in place. In the three wave study reported in Latin Journey, Portes and Bach (1985) show that most Mexican immigrants who were legal entrants had familial networks already in place. Among Mexican entrants, less than 1 percent of first-time legal entrants and 3 percent of return migrants did not have a social network contact in their place of settlement. Similarly, among Cuban legal entrants only 1 percent did not have any contacts in place. Over time, these networks become a critical

Table 11.2
Networks Used for Housing at Arrival to Area: Ethnic/Racial Groups in Los Angeles and Boston*

	Los Angeles	Boston
Non-Hispanic White	64.3%	46.9%
Black	79.8%	82.0%
Asian	92.1%	—
Hispanic	88.5%	90.9%
Mexican	87.9%	—
Puerto Rican	—	93.6%
Salvadorean	95.9%	—
Dominican	—	88.2%
Other	85.4%	81.1%

*Includes only those who arrived after age 18.

part of the process of settlement. In the third wave of interviews, Portes and Bach (1985) report much higher rates of assistance by social networks than were expected by the immigrants themselves. At arrival, about one-third of Cubans and over half of Mexican immigrants expected no assistance from family and friends. In subsequent interviews, only 13 percent of Cubans and about 30 percent of Mexicans reported having received no assistance at all (Portes and Bach, 1985).

SOCIAL NETWORKS AND LABOR MARKET PENETRATION

Research on immigrant communities has been central to the exploration of the concept of social capital—largely because immigrant adaptation into a new society entails integration into various social entities, most of which will have dramatic effects on their social and economic outcomes (Portes, 1998, 2000; Portes and Sensenbrenner, 1993). Access to the right social networks may facilitate penetration into the labor market. There is increasing evidence about the differences in the characteristics of social networks of immigrants versus those of natives. Wierzbicki (2002), using data from the MCSUI study, shows how immigrants do not have as many strong ties as natives do, and when they do have strong ties within their networks these tend to be neighborhood bound. The networks of immigrant Asians and Hispanics are more likely to be more similar educationally and ethnically to the respondent than are the networks of native born (Mouw, 2003; Wierzbicki, 2002).

Information flows on the availability and quality of employment serve to organize the process of matching a worker to a job both from the worker's and the employer's viewpoint. From the employer's side, social networks are used to attract and retain workers, particularly in times of scarcity (Johnson-Webb, 2002). Pessar (1987) has documented how social networks are used by employers in the garment industry to maintain a supply of labor that fits the organizational requirements of the workplace. Social networks are used to attract and release workers as needed. In many instances, exploitative conditions are glazed over by the mere presence of kinship or ethnic ties between employers and workers or across workers. As Portes and Bach (1985) suggested, what should be a class struggle between employers and workers gets softened by the presence of relations of kin, friendship, or ethnicity.

There are other important reasons for employers' reliance on social networks to recruit workers. Worker recruitment by employers through their own labor forces' social networks reduces the cost of recruitment (versus formal mechanisms) and adds a screening element to the process. The information being conveyed to those being recruited will tend to be more accurate, because it is coming from someone already in the workplace. Workers serving as conduits of information will tend to select those potential workers who fit the requirements of the job. Hiring through networks reduces risk by bringing workers who share some of the characteristics of the existing workforce (Bailey and Waldinger,

1991). Further, by bringing a relative or acquaintance into the workplace, a worker puts their own status within the workplace on the line, which may be used by an employer to maintain control and exercise pressure on noncomplying workers (Grasmuck, 1984; Grasmuck and Pessar, 1991; Lado, 1995; Montgomery, 1991; Pessar, 1987). Waldinger (1994, 1996) has suggested that network driven recruitment encourages the creation of ethnic niches within the labor market. As employers and workers steer recruitment to a particular group, the character of the sector becomes increasingly associated with the group.

Similarly, from the point of view of the worker, social networks are readily available mechanisms to search for employment. By organizing the flow of information, they facilitate the ability of the newly arrived to connect to potential employers (Waldinger, 1994). Aguilera (2003) presents findings that indicate that social capital use in job searching leads to longer tenure in the job found.

Data from the MCSUI suggest high rates of use of social networks to search for employment by those newly arrived (see Table 11.3). The numbers are not as consistently high for the use of networks to find a job as they were to find housing. However, Latino Immigrants in Los Angeles and Boston report very high rates of use of networks for a job search after arrival. Further, despite the fact that social network-based job search is quite widespread across ethnic/racial groups, immigrants have a much higher rate of entry into jobs through social networks than do other groups (Falcón, 1997). Of those who reported having looked for a job after arrival, the highest proportion reporting use of social networks were the Dominicans in Boston (96%), while the lowest proportion was for Asians (70%) in Los Angeles. Puerto Ricans in Boston

Table 11.3
Networks Used for Job Search at Arrival to Area: Ethnic/Racial Groups in Los Angeles and Boston*

	Los Angeles	Boston
Non-Hispanic White	33.1%	29.4%
Black	48.6%	63.2%
Asian	69.3%	—
Hispanic	81.2%	93.1%
Mexican	81.2%	—
Puerto Rican	—	91.1%
Salvadorean	82.5%	68.8%
Dominican	—	95.6%
Other	85.6%	—

*Includes only those who arrived after age 18.

also had a high rate of network use (91%), followed by Salvadoreans (83%) and Mexicans (81%) in Los Angeles. Social network use for job searching has implications for sector of employment also. Aguilera and Massey (2004) find that using social capital in the job search influences how the job is found and if it is going to be in the formal sector. Further, they also find that having members in your social network who have had migratory experiences has a positive impact on the efficiency of the job search and leads to higher wages. There is also evidence that over-reliance on social networks is associated with searching for jobs with low socioeconomic prestige (Sanders, Nee, and Sernau, 2002). Green, Tigges, and Diaz (1999) make a similar point when examining the high use of social networks among Hispanics and how it leads to poor quality jobs. The social networks buffer the effects of having limited cultural competency and language skills and facilitate entering the labor market (Sanders, Nee, and Sernau, 2002).

SOCIAL NETWORKS AND ETHNIC ECONOMIES

The embeddedness of social networks within economic behavior is central to the theoretical development of the Ethnic Enclave concept. The ethnic enclave hypothesis was developed as an alternative explanation to the apparent success of some immigrant groups whose economic activities were largely circumscribed to the boundaries of the ethnic community and who exhibited high rates of self-employment (Wilson and Martin, 1982; Wilson and Portes, 1980). Light (1984) proposed that the propensity toward self-employment among some immigrant groups is rooted in both the disadvantage they face competing in open markets and their collective experience as immigrants. Employment in the ethnic enclave provides opportunity for training and, more important, exposure to entrepreneurial behavior and access to capital— both social and financial (Portes and Zhou, 1992). Perhaps more important is the notion that, within the enclave, these social networks are the context for a situation of advantage. That is, immigrants use social networks at a higher rate than other groups, because it gives them an edge in a particular context. This idea is embedded on much of the literature on immigrant adaptation. Wilson and Portes's well-cited work on the existence of an ethnic enclave economy that provided greater returns to human capital investments by immigrants was one of the first to emphasize ethnic ties as a paramount factor in the emergence of an ethnic entrepreneurial group (Wilson and Portes, 1980). Subsequent work by Portes and colleagues has carefully detailed how social networks played a major part in the rise to prominence of a Cuban exile entrepreneurial class (Portes and Stepick, 1993).

Social networks can also dramatically alter the composition of occupational sectors. Waldinger's (1994) analysis of how an immigrant niche develops illuminates how social networks facilitate a shift in the ethnic composition of the holders of an occupational category. The shift over time in the ethnic composition of professional occupations within the government agencies in the city of New York is described using data gathered from field interviews. Waldinger concludes that social networks are not the determinant factor in this context, but do serve to facilitate the transition from what was an ethnically Anglo domain to one where Jews and Italians were highly represented, and then to one where Asians were the most visible and fastest growing group. It is the convergence of changes in the supply of native versus immigrant workers and in the regulations dominating government bureaucracies that allow for shifts in which social networks dominate the flow of information within the workplace. Once the door is open to other groups and the relative supply and influence of the dominant group declines, then newcomers can take advantage to enter the sector.

Another example comes from Kim's (1996) work on the Korean business owners in New York City. In this instance, while social networks had initially restricted employment within Korean-owned businesses to other Koreans, a transition is ongoing where bounded solidarity is giving way to economic necessities. Latinos are increasingly becoming a source of cheap labor in these businesses as Korean labor becomes more expensive. While social networks are still central to this transition, it does present an example of what the author calls "the limits of ethnic solidarity."

SOCIAL NETWORKS AND EXCLUSION

Another important aspect of the social organization of social networks is the ability to exclude those not within the network. The ability of one group to mobilize resources to advance their own collective position results, often at the exclusion of other groups from these same resources. Kim details how the social organization of Korean green grocers in New York City served to push out other ethnic vendors from the market or facilitate the succession (Kim, 1985). Waldinger's (1996) work on entrepreneurs in the building trade, also in New York City, details the way in which ethnic mobilization serves to create social closure for other groups by denying access to information or resources that could advance their mobility. This raises important questions on the ability of groups with lesser reservoirs of social capital to compete or even to get access.

Portes and Zhou (1992) position the community and the web of relationships that are established within squarely at the center of the debate on what accounts for the success of some groups and the disadvantage of others. In their words, "Lost in the fray is the community itself, with its networks, normative structure, and supporting or constraining effects on individual economic action" (Portes and Zhou, 1992, p. 492). Their argument is that the debates between individualistic and structural views have allowed little room for other relevant actors, in this case the community, to emerge in the literature (Portes and Zhou, 1992). From here, they go on to describe why we observe different socioeconomic outcomes for groups who differ in terms of the structure of social networks in their communities. Portes and Zhou argue that it is the dissolution of two of the key aspects of social capital-bounded solidarity and enforceable trust—which lie at the center of the lower propensity toward entrepreneurship among African Americans, Mexicans, and Puerto Ricans. Sanders and Nee (1996) offer a somewhat divergent interpretation in examining self-employment among Asian and Latino Immigrants. While they reemphasize the role of family-based networks on the higher propensity toward self-employment among some Asian and Latino groups, they argue that lower human capital also has an important effect on the self-employment of Puerto Ricans and Mexicans.

While there is not a fully defined paradigm on how social networks and social capital may contribute to creating disadvantage among some groups, the idea of social closure and of community constraints on economic action are important. In order to advance the understanding of how social networks can mediate success and disadvantage, we need to draw from concepts in the study of urban poverty and social isolation.

SOCIAL NETWORKS AND RACIAL MINORITIES

Some of the recent literature on urban poverty is concerned with the role that social networks play in the situation of the urban poor, largely by focusing on the connections that the urban poor have to other individuals and to mainstream institutions. Isolation from mainstream social institutions is seen as an important factor behind the increased poverty of Latinos and blacks in the United States (Elliot and Sims, 2001; Tienda, 1989a; Wacquant, 1989; Wilson, 1987, 1988).

This concern with social networks aside, little connection exists between the migration literature and the literature on urban poverty on the overlapping role that social networks play. A better understanding of how social networks function may contribute to explaining continued social inequality in the United States between racial and ethnic minorities (particularly immigrants) and the white majority. Work by Granovetter (1995) calls attention to the lack of understanding of how network processes contribute to the production and reproduction of social inequities.

The poverty literature emphasizes the importance of social resources to the process of social mobility. In his seminal work on blacks, Wilson (1987, 1991) proposed that isolation from mainstream social relationships was a determining factor in the social disadvantages experienced by blacks in the inner city. Residence in poor neighborhoods in the inner city restricts the amount of social capital that blacks can mobilize to obtain jobs. Wilson (1991) sees this lack of social capital as a function largely of the concentration of poverty in inner-city areas—a process concomitant with the transformation of the economy of cities from manufacturing to services and with the flight of the black middle class to suburban areas, among other factors. Accordingly, this dynamic has led to the growth of a sector among the black poor known as the underclass (Jencks and Peterson, 1991; Wilson 1987, 1991).

The underclass literature has mainly focused on the experiences of blacks in inner-city areas. The discussion of the situation of Latinos from this underclass perspective has been marred by debates about the applicability of underclass theoretical models and analytic methods to the situation of Latinos (for a review see Melendez, 1994; Massey 1993). Some of this debate has centered on the immigrant character of Latinos and how this distinguishes them from blacks. Massey has used this argument to criticize the analysis by Wilson and colleagues of the situation of Mexicans and blacks in Chicago. According to Massey, the issue is that selectivity influences the characteristics of Latino communities in such a way that any comparisons that do not take migration effects into account are essentially flawed. For example, Massey (1993, 711) suggests that through *circular migration* Mexicans may export their unemployment, which would cause researchers to underestimate poverty among them when compared with blacks. Another example comes from Falcón and Gurak's (1994) work on Puerto Rican women in New York City, which shows that migration contributes to the increase in the New York City Puerto Rican population of women with characteristics associated with poverty (i.e., in female-headship, less likely to be employed).

For African Americans, the poverty literature has shown the importance of social isolation from social networks in creating weak labor attachment and socioeconomic disadvantage (Kasinitz and Rosenberg, 1996; Van Haitsma, 1989; Wacquant and Wilson, 1989). This social isolation is grounded, partly, in the lack of access to informal sources of information on jobs. If African Americans suffer from social isolation due to the conditions they experience in the inner city, then what can we say about immigrants in general who are the quintessential example of reliance on social networks?

The literature suggests that the advantage of groups such as Cubans and Koreans is rooted in the social structure that surrounds their economic behavior. A first step in understanding the differences in socioeconomic position between groups in areas with large immigrant and minority communities is to account, then, for how their social networks contribute to their labor-market position. There is substantial evidence that Latino poverty can be largely explained based on labor-market disadvantage (Melendez, 1994; Sassen, 1995). Immigrants have a different sensitivity to local labor markets, which reflects differential search areas and a more narrow focus on particular labor market sectors (Sassen, 1995).

Social isolation from the right kind of networks can be detrimental to the life chances of minorities in urban areas. African Americans appear to be the most disadvantaged, in part because they have been the most exposed to the social closure that results from the mobilization of white ethnic's social capital (Waldinger, 1994). There is some evidence that Puerto Ricans have experienced some of the treatment afforded to African Americans (Torres, 1992). Following the social capital model, we need to better understand the position of African Americans and Puerto Ricans from a perspective that emphasizes not a romanticized notion of immigrants (migrants) using social

networks, but the long-term consequences of closure and racially circumscribed social networks.

CONCLUDING REMARKS

While there is some debate on the basis of the advantage (and disadvantage)
of some immigrant groups, there are some important consistencies in the
literature briefly reviewed. Social capital matters, but it matters differently
depending on where a particular group stands. Groups who share similar geographic areas may find themselves competing for similar resources or conspir-
ing to maintain social closure.

Entrepreneurship is important, but there is still some disagreement as to
the basis for its presence or absence among some groups. While Portes's work
is important in advancing the conceptualization of how community structure
translates into collective economic behavior, there is the potential for cultural
interpretations of social disadvantage to creep in. There is some evidence
that, while social capital is important, other contextual factors may facilitate
or impede the deployment of group resources. Both Waldinger's (1996) and
Kim's work (1996) serve as examples. Sanders and Nee (1996) also underscore
that human capital endowments are still important.

Within ethnic economies, the process of entering a job involves a substantial number of personal transactions. Little is known, however, about the different steps of the process. The number of actors involved includes not only
the worker that is searching, but also their network plus the employer and
the methods they use to seek workers. More research is needed on the different sides of this process and how social networks operate within. How much
organization is there to the flow of information within networks? Are employers the only actors with some semblance of organization in the way they use
social networks? Do immigrant groups whose livelihood is based within ethnic
economies (i.e., Koreans, Chinese) differ in the quantitative character of their
networks from those groups that are nonethnic economy-based (i.e., Puerto
Ricans, Mexicans), or is it just a matter of network quality?

Another issue revolves around the use of social networks in employment
searches. Changes in the overall economy have bifurcated the occupational
distribution to the point that the divide between low-skill and high-skill jobs
is quite large. What are the differential effects of social ties or networks on
these different types of workers (i.e., low-skill versus high-skill workers)?
Does, the function of social ties for most low-skill workers not extend further
than the provision of a job?

The review of the literature and assessment of available evidence suggest that
social networks in place and the use of social networks seem to facilitate settlement and economic activity for both Latino and Asian immigrants. However,
little is know about how continued embeddedness into these networks hurts
immigrants in the long run. A corollary of this proposition is that immigrants
who move away from embedded networks could do better in labor market

outcomes than those that remain within the confines of segmented labor market boundaries. Because immigrant networks tend to be largely composed of members of the same ethnic group, a movement away from using social networks may also imply a move out of the ethnic market. These are questions that require further exploration. We need to provide more detail on the types of job settings that immigrant networks provide access to and how they differ from those immigrants that maneuver the market through mechanisms other than social networks.

A problem with most comparisons of the various Latino (Cubans, Mexicans, and Puerto Ricans) and Asian (Korean, Chinese, Filipino, etc.) communities is the disregard for the level of evolution of the communities and how this impacts the reproduction of social networks. While some immigrant communities remain fairly stable over time, others continue to reconstitute themselves as new immigrants arrive. How does this impact the stability of social networks? What happens to social network use over time as ethnic communities age and native-born ethnic generations emerge? Little is known about these issues.

Gender differences in the use of social networks and related outcomes are critical. The limited evidence on the characteristics of social networks by gender suggests important differences between the networks of men and women (Moore, 1990; Sanders, 1995). Women's networks are more kin based than men's. Differences in the propensity and characteristics of employment, in family composition, and in life cycle account for some of the gender differences (Moore, 1990). When we consider, for example, the cases of Puerto Ricans and Dominicans for whom female-headed households account for a sizable proportion of those in poverty, then the importance of over reliance on networks becomes apparent.

The study of social networks and economic behavior is a fascinating and very fruitful area that could provide important answers to questions on the continued disparities in the position of immigrant groups, and Hispanics in particular, in U.S. society. Some of the notions proposed by those writing in the field need to be tested empirically and better refined in order to advance the understanding of how social networks can produce both social mobility and inequality.

NOTES

1. The Boston sampling area is the Massachusetts portion of the Boston Consolidated Metropolitan Statistical Area. This geographic area reaches from Lawrence, 25 miles north of Boston, to Brockton, which is about 20 miles south. The Boston interviews were conducted between May 1993 and November 1994 with a total of 1,820 individuals (589 whites, 701 Latinos, 465 blacks, and 65 others). In Los Angeles, the sampling area included the total Los Angeles County area. Data collection in Los Angeles began in September of 1993 and concluded in August of 1994 with a total sample of 4,025 individuals (among these are 835 whites, 1,020 Latinos, 1,103 blacks, and 1,055 Asians).

2. In addition, all immigrants from non-Spanish speaking countries in the Caribbean are excluded. This restriction brings the combined two-city sample down to about 1,900 cases including only Latinos and Asians.

REFERENCES

Aguilera, Michael B. 2003. "The Impact of the Worker: How Social Capital and Human Capital Influence the Job Tenure of Formerly Undocumented Mexican Immigrants." *Sociological Inquiry* 73 (1) (February): 52–79.

Aguilera, Michael B., and Douglas S. Massey. 2003. "Social Capital and the Wages of Mexican Migrants: New Hypotheses and Tests." *Social Forces* 82 (2) (December): 671–701.

Bailey, Thomas, and Roger Waldinger. 1991. "Primary, Secondary, and Enclave Labor Markets: A Training Systems Approach." *American Sociological Review* 56 (4): 432–445.

Boyd, Monica. 1989. "Family and Personal Networks in International Migration: Recent Developments and New Agendas." *International Migration Review* 23 (3): 638–670.

Elliott, James R., and Mario Sims. 2001. "Ghettos and Barrios: The Impact of Neighborhood Poverty and Race on Job Matching among Blacks and Latinos." *Social Problems* 48 (3) (August): 341–361.

Falcón, Luis M. 1995. "Social Networks and Employment for Latinos, Blacks, and Whites." *New England Journal of Public Policy* 11 (1): 17–28.

Falcón, Luis M. 1997. "Social Networks and the Settlement Process." Paper read at American Sociological Association, August, at Toronto, Canada.

Falcón, Luis M., and Douglas T. Gurak. 1994. "Poverty, Migration, and the Underclass." *Journal of Latino Studies* 5 (2):77–95.

Falcón, Luis M., and Edwin Melendez. 2001. "Racial and Ethnic Differences in Job Searching in Urban Centers." In *Urban Inequality: Evidence from Four Cities.*, ed. Alice O'Connor, Chris Tilly and Lawrence D. Bobo. New York: Russell Sage, 341–371.

Garcia, Carlos. 2005. "Buscando Trabajo: Social Networking among Immigrants from Mexico to the United States." *Hispanic Journal of Behavioral Sciences* 27 (1) (Feb): 3–22.

Gold, Steven J., and Nazli Kibria. 1989. "Vietnamese Refugees in the U.S.: Model Minority or New Underclass?" Paper read at American Sociological Association (ASA), San Francisco, California, August.

Granovetter, Mark. 1995. "The Economic Sociology of Firms and Entrepreneurs." In *The Economic Sociology of Immigration: Essays on Networks, Ethnicity, and Entrepreneurship*, ed. A. Portes. New York: Russell Sage Foundation.

Granovetter, Mark. 1995. *Getting a Job: A Study of Contacts and Careers.* Chicago: The University of Chicago Press.

Grasmuck, Sherri. 1984. "Immigration, Ethnic Stratification, and Native Working Class Discipline: Comparisons of Documented and Undocumented Dominicans." *International Migration Review* 19 (3): 692–713.

Grasmuck, Sherri, and Patricia Pessar. 1991. *Between Two Islands: Dominican International Migration.* Berkeley: University of California.

Green, Gary Paul, Leann M. Tigges, and Daniel Diaz. 1999. "Racial and Ethnic Differences in Job-Search Strategies in Atlanta, Boston, and Los Angeles." *Social Science Quarterly* 80 (2) (June): 263–278.

Gurak, Douglas T., and Fe Caces. 1992. "Migration Networks and the Shaping of Migration Systems." In *International Migration Systems: A Global Approach*, ed. M. M. Kritz, L. Lean Lim, and H. Zlotnik. Oxford: Clarendon Press.

Heller, Peter L., David F. Briones, Salvador F. Aguirre-Hauchbaum, and Alden E. Roberts. 2004. "Source of Support and Mastery: The Interaction of Socioeconomic Status and Mexican-American Ethnicity." *Sociological Spectrum* 24 (2) (March–April): 239–264.

Jencks, Christopher, and Paul E. Peterson. 1991. *The Urban Underclass*. Washington, D.C.: The Brookings Institute.

Johnson-Webb, Karen D. 2002. "Employer Recruitment and Hispanic Labor Migration: North Carolina Urban Areas at the End of the Millennium." *Professional Geographer* 54 (3) (August): 406–421.

Kasinitz, Philip, and Jan Rosenberg. 1996. "Missing the Connection: Social Isolation and Employment on the Brooklyn Waterfront." Paper read at American Sociological Association (ASA), New York, August.

Kim, Dae Young. 1996. "The Limits of Ethnic Solidarity: Mexican and Ecuadorian Employment in Korean-Owned Businesses in New York City." Paper read at American Sociological Association (ASA), at New York, August.

Kim, Illsoo. 1985. "The Koreans: Small Business in an Urban Frontier." In *New Immigrants in New York*, ed. N. Foner. New York: Columbia.

Krissman, Fred. 2005. "Sin coyote ni patron: Why the 'Migrant Network' Fails to Explain International Migration." *International Migration Review* 39 (1, 149) (spring): 4–44.

Lado, Karen. 1995. "Immigrant Workers in the Cleaning Industry: The Experience of Boston's Central Americans." *New England Journal of Public Policy* 2 (1): 29 42.

Light, Ivan. 1972. *Ethnic Enterprise in America: Business and Welfare Among Chinese, Japanese, and Blacks*. Berkeley: University of California.

Light, Ivan. 1984. "Immigrant and Ethnic Enterprise in North America." *Ethnic and Racial Studies* 7: 195–216.

Lindstrom, David P., and Douglas S. Massey. 1994. "Selective Emigration, Cohort Quality, and Models of Immigrant Assimilation." *Social Science Research* 23 (4): 315–349.

Massey, Douglas, Rafael Alarcon, Jorge Durand, and Humbert Gonzalez. 1987. *Return to Atzlan: The Social Process of International Migration from Western Mexico*. Berkeley: University of California.

Massey, Douglas S. 1987. "Understanding Mexican Migration to the United States." *American Journal of Sociology* 92 (6): 1372–1403.

Massey, Douglas S. 1988. "Economic Development and International Migration in Comparative Perspective." *Population and Development Review* 14 (3): 383–413.

Massey, Douglas S. 1990. "The Social and Economic Origins of Immigration." *Annals of the American Academy of Political and Social Science* 510: 60–72.

Massey, Douglas S. 1993. "Latinos, Poverty, and the Underclass: A New Agenda for Research." *Hispanic Journal of Behavioral Sciences* 15 (4): 449–475.

Massey, Douglas S., Joaquin Arango, Graeme Hugo, Ali Kouaouci, Adela Pellegrino, and J. Edward Taylor. 1993. "Theories of International Migration: A Review and Appraisal." *Population and Development Review* 19 (3): 431–466.

Massey, Douglas S., and Lawrence C. Basem. 1992. "Determinants of Savings, Remittances, and Spending Patterns among U.S. Migrants in Four Mexican Communities." *Sociological Inquiry* 62 (2): 185–207.

Massey, Douglas S., and Kristin E. Espinosa. 1997. "What's Driving Mexico-U.S. Migration? A Theoretical, Empirical, and Policy Analysis." *American Journal of Sociology* 102 (4): 939–999.

Melendez, Edwin. 1994. *Latino Poverty and Public Policy: Competing Explanations of Latino Poverty.* Boston: The Boston Foundation.

Min, Pyong Gap. 2000. "Immigrants' Religion and Ethnicity: A Comparison of Korean Christian and Indian Hindu Immigrants." *Bulletin of the Royal Institute for Inter-Faith Studies* 2 (1) (spring): 121–140.

Montgomery, James D. 1991. "Social Networks and Labor Market Outcomes: Toward an Economic Analysis." *The American Economic Review* 81 (5).

Moore, Gwen. 1990. "Structural Determinant's of Men's and Women's Personal Networks." *American Sociological Review* 55 (October): 726–735.

Mouw, Ted. 2003. "Social Capital and Finding a Job: Do Contacts Matter?" *American Sociological Review* 68 (6) (Dec): 868–898.

Nee, Victor, and Jimy M. Sanders. 1985. "The Road to Parity: Determinants of the Socioeconomic Achievements of Asian Americans." *Ethnic and Racial Studies* 8 (1): 75–93.

Nee, Victor, Jimy M. Sanders, and Scott Sernau. 1994. "Job Transitions in an immigrant Metropolis: Ethnic Boundaries and the Mixed Economy." *American Sociological Review* 59 (6): 849–872.

Nee, Victor, and Herbert Y. Wong. 1985. "Asian American Socioeconomic Achievement: The Strength of the Family Bond." *Sociological Perspectives* 28 (3): 281–306.

Nelson, Candace, and Marta Tienda. 1985. "The Structuring of Hispanic Ethnicity: Historical and Contemporary Perspectives." *Ethnic and Racial Studies* 8 (1): 49–74.

Pessar, Patricia. 1987. "The Dominican's: Women in the Household and the Garment Industry." In *New Immigrants in New York*, ed. N. Foner. New York City: Columbia University Press.

Poros, Maritsa V. 2004. "Networks of Inclusion and Exclusion in the Economic Concentrations of Asian Indian Immigrants in New York and London." *Research in the Sociology of Work* 14: 35–61.

Portes, Alejandro. 1987. "The Social Origins of the Cuban Enclave Economy of Miami." *Sociological Perspectives* 30 (4): 340–372.

Portes, Alejandro. 1995. "Economic Sociology and the Sociology of Immigration: A Conceptual Overview." In *The Economic Sociology of Immigration*, ed. A. Portes. New York: Russell Sage Foundation.

Portes, Alejandro. 1996. "Global Villagers: The Rise of Transnational Communities." *American Prospect* 25: 74–77.

Portes, Alejandro. 1998. "Social Capital: Its Origins and Applications in Modern Sociology." *Annual Review of Sociology* 24: 1–24.

Portes, Alejandro. 2000. "The Two Meanings of Social Capital." *Sociological Forum* 15 (1) (March): 1–12.

Portes, Alejandro, and Robert L. Bach. 1985. *Latin Journey: Cuban and Mexican Immigrants In the United States*. Berkeley: University of California.

Portes, Alejandro, and Ramon Grosfoguel. 1994. "Caribbean Diasporas: Migration and Ethnic Communities." *Annals of the American Academy of Political and Social Science* 533: 48–69.

Portes, Alejandro, and Patricia Landolt. 1996. "The Downside of Social Capital." *American Prospect* 26: 18–21.

Portes, Alejandro, and Julia Sensenbrenner. 1993. "Embeddedness and Immigration: Notes on the Social Determinants of Economic Action." *American Journal of Sociology* 98 (6): 1320–1350.

Portes, Alejandro, and Alex Stepick. 1993. *City on the Edge: The Transformation of Miami.* Berkeley: University of California.

Portes, Alejandro, and Min Zhou. 1992. "Gaining the Upper Hand: Economic Mobility among Immigrant and Domestic Minorities." *Ethnic and Racial Studies* 15 (4): 491–522.

Reyes, Belinda I. 2004. "U.S. Immigration Policy and the Duration of Undocumented Trips." In *Crossing the Border: Research from the Mexican Migration Project.*, ed. Jorge Durand and Douglas S. Massey. New York: Russell Sage Foundation, 299–320.

Ritchey, Neal P., ed. 1976. *Explanations of Migration.* Ed. A. Inkeles, Coleman, James, and Neil Smelser. Vol. ii, *Annual Review of Sociology.* Palo Alto: California.

Rumbaut, Ruben. 1994. "Origins and Destinies: Immigration to the United States Since World War II." *Sociological Forum* 9 (4): 583–621.

Sanders, Jimy M., and Victor Nee. 1996. "Immigrant Self-Employment: The Family as Social Capital and the Value of Human Capital." *American Sociological Review* 61 (April): 231–249.

Sanders, Jimy, Victor Nee, and Scott Sernau. 2002. "Asian Immigrants' Reliance on Social Ties in a Multiethnic Labor Market." *Social Forces* 81 (1) (September): 281–314.

Sanders, Karin. 1995. "The 'Gift' and 'Request' Network. Differences between Women and Men in the Receipt and the Effect of Information Concerning the Labour Market." *European Journal of Women's Studies* 2 (2): 205–218.

Sassen, Saskia. 1995. "Immigration and Local Labor Markets." In *The Economic Sociology of Immigration: Essays on Networks, Ethnicity, and Entrepreneurship*, ed. A. Portes. New York: Russell Sage, 87–127

Tienda, Marta. 1989a. "Puerto Ricans and the Underclass Debate." *Annals of the American Academy of Political and Social Science* 501: 105–119.

Tienda, Marta. 1989b. "Race, Ethnicity and the Portrait of Inequality: Approaching the 1990s." *Sociological Spectrum* 9 (1): 23–52.

Torres, Andres. 1992. "Nativity, Gender, and Earnings Discrimination." *Hispanic Journal of Behavioral Sciences* 14 (1): 134–143.

Van Haitsma, Martha. 1989. "A Contextual Definition of the Underclass." *Focus* 12: 27–31.

Wacquant, Loic J.D. 1989. "The Ghetto, the State, and the New Capitalist Economy." *Dissent* 4 (157): 508–520.

Wacquant, Loic J.D., and William Julius Wilson. 1989. "The Cost of Racial and Class Exclusion in the Inner City." *Annals of the American Academy of Political and Social Science* 501: 8–25.

Waldinger, Roger. 1994. "The Making of an Immigrant Niche." *International Migration Review* 28 (1): 3–30.

Waldinger, Roger. 1995. "The 'Other Side' of Embeddedness: A Case-Study of the Interplay of Economy and Ethnicity." *Ethnic and Racial Studies* 18 (3): 555–580.

Waldinger, Roger. 1996. *Still the Promised City?* Cambridge: Harvard University Press.

Wierzbicki, Susan Kuhs. 2002. "Isolation and the Enclave: The Presence and Variety of Strong Ties among Immigrants." Ph.D. diss., University of Washington.

Wilpert, Czarina. 1992. "The Use of Social Networks in Turkish Migration to Europe." In *International Migration Systems: A Global Approach*, ed. M. M. Kritz, L. Lean Lim, and H. Zlotnik. Oxford: Clarendon Press.

Wilson, Kenneth, and Allen Martin. 1982. "Ethnic Enclaves: A Comparison of the Cuban and Black Economies." *American Journal of Sociology* 78 (May): 135–160.

Wilson, Kenneth L., and Alejandro Portes. 1980. "Immigrant Enclaves: An Analysis of the Labor Market Experiences of Cubans in Miami." *American Journal of Sociology* 86 (2): 295–319.

Wilson, Tamar Diana. 2004. "Wage-Labor Migration and Class in Jalisco and the United States." *Latin American Perspectives* 31 (5, 138) (September): 100–117.

Wilson, William Julius. 1987. *The Truly Disadvantaged: The Inner City, the Underclass, and Public Policy*. Chicago: University of Chicago.

Wilson, William Julius. 1988. "American Social Policy and the Ghetto Underclass." *Dissent* 1 (150): 57–64.

Wilson, William Julius. 1991. "Studying Inner-City Social Dislocations: The Challenge of Public Agenda Research: 1990 Presidential Address." *American Sociological Review* 56 (1): 1–14.

Index

About the Contributors

RAMÓN F. BORGES-MÉNDEZ, is an Assistant Professor in the Department of Public Policy and Public Affairs, at the University of Massachusetts-Boston with research interests and specialties in: Labor Economics, Economic Development, Political Economy, Latino Studies, Governance and Institutional Development, Evaluation and Methodology. He has held academic positions at American University's School of International Service, The Johns Hopkins' School of Advanced International Studies, and the University of Chile's Public Policy Program. Professor Borges-Méndez has also served as a Research Associate at the Mauricio Gaston Institute for Latino Community Development and Public Policy at UMass Boston. He has also worked as a consultant for the Ford Foundation, the World Bank, the Economics Commission on Latin American and the Caribbean of the United Nations (ECLAS), the Inter-American Development Bank, the Brookings Institute, the Japanese International Cooperation Agency and the government of Chile. His publications are on various public policy issues ranging from Latino poverty and community development in the United States (especially in Massachusetts) to decentralization and civil society matters in Latin America. Most recently, he has been evaluating participatory practices in sustainable forestry and environmental services in Costa Rica; assessing programmatic options to support innovative practices in local government, participation and plural networks in Chile and Peru; assessing the value-added contributions of community-based organizations to workforce development in various U.S. cities; and the implementation of regional workforce development strategies in the United States.

SUNG CHANG CHUN is Assistant Professor of Sociology at Bethel College and former Director of the Census Information Center at the Institute for Latino Studies at Notre Dame. He specializes in immigrant religions, immigrant demographics, and higher education policy issues in the United States. He is in charge of the Census Information Center for the Inter-University Program for Latino Research (IUPLR) and conducts demographic analyses and writes about a variety of Latino issues. He was involved in creating the Chicago Fact Finder and conducting the Chicago Area Survey. He has written about Latino-origin group population underestimates, Latinos in distressed communities, wave effect on Cuban political ideology, and black Latinos. He is now conducting research on Latinos' remittance behavior, Latinos' religious participation and ministry needs, and Latinos' geographical mobility.

HÉCTOR R. CORDERO-GUZMÁN is an Associate Professor and Chair of the Black and Hispanic Studies Department at Baruch College of the City University of New York and a member of the faculty in the Ph.D. programs in Sociology and Urban Education at the CUNY Graduate Center. Dr. Cordero-Guzman is working on a study of immigrant community-based organizations, a project examining transnational community economic development practices, a paper on the economics of micro-lending, and a study of self-employment patterns and trends in the Latino community. Dr. Cordero-Guzmán received his M.A. and Ph.D. degrees from The University of Chicago and is on the Board of Directors of ACCION-New York, the Community Service Society of New York (CSS), and the Upper Manhattan Empowerment Zone (UMEZ).

ESPERANZA DE LA VEGA is a Visiting Professor at Willamette College. She received her Ph.D. in Language Literacy, and Culture in Education, from the University of California, Berkeley in 2005. She has been a teacher and advocate for linguistically and culturally diverse children and families in Oregon and California for over 16 years, and has presented papers nationally and internationally on various topics, but more recently on her dissertation work titled: "Mexicana/Latina Mothers Establishing Voice in School Contexts: The Culture, Conflict, and Collaboration of Parental Involvement."

LUIS M. FALCÓN is Vice-Provost for Graduate Education at Northeastern University in Boston, MA. He holds a tenured faculty appointment in the Department of Sociology and has served as chair of the department of Sociology and as Associate Dean for Faculty Affairs in the College of Arts and Sciences. He received a Ph.D. in Sociology from Cornell University. His research interests are in the areas of labor markets, migration, urban poverty, and social gerontology. His prior research has been on the mechanisms that mediate the matching of workers to jobs in urban centers, the relationship of social capital to social and economic inequality, and the impact of the welfare to work and workforce investment legislation. His current research, funded by NIA, focuses on studying the social and psychological correlates of health disparities among the Puerto Rican population in the greater Boston area.

HUGH GLADWIN is Associate Professor of Sociology/Anthropology and Director of the Institute for Public Opinion Research at Florida International University. His major area of research is the application of survey research and GIS tools to understand large urban settings of high cultural and demographic diversity. Within that framework, a particular interest is to better model the interactions between the human population and natural systems such as the South Florida ecosystem and extreme natural events like hurricanes. For this latter area, integrating human decision models with GIS are a major task. He is a co-editor (with Walter Gillis Peacock) and contributor to the book *Hurricane Andrew: Ethnicity, Gender, and the Sociology of Disaster.* He received his Ph.D. from Stanford in 1970.

GUILLERMO J. GRENIER is Professor of Sociology at Florida International University in Miami and a Visiting Scholar at the Institute for Latino Studies at the University of Notre Dame. Until recently, Dr. Grenier was the director of the Florida Center for Labor Research and Studies. Born in Havana, Cuba, Dr. Grenier received his undergraduate education at Emory University and Georgia State University in Atlanta. He received his Ph.D. from the University of New Mexico. He is the author of *Inhuman Relations: Quality Circles and Anti-Unionism in American Industry* (1988). His other books include *Employee Participation and Labor Law in the American Workplace; Miami Now: Immigration, Ethnicity and Social Change; Newcomers in the Workplace: Immigrants and the Restructuring of the U.S. Economy;* and *This Land Is Our Land: Newcomers and Established Residents in Miami* (forthcoming). He has written numerous articles on labor and ethnic issues in the United States and conducts yearly surveys on the attitudes of the Cuban American community toward Cuba.

RAMONA HERNÁNDEZ is the Director of the CUNY-Dominican Studies Institute & a Professor of Sociology at The City College of New York. She has written several important works including *The Mobility of Workers Under Advanced Capitalism: Dominican Migration to the United States* (2002), which received the *Choice* award for "Outstanding Academic Title" in 2003, among prominent articles, book chapters, excerpts, and journal articles relating to labor history, migration studies, and Dominicans/Latinos in the United States.

REGINA JEAN-VAN HELL is an instructor in human development at Wheelock College and a researcher at Lesley University for the Say Yes to Education Project. Her interests are college student development, college adjustment of Latinos, college student's stressors, at-risk students, program evaluation of at-risk populations and counseling. She published "A New Way of Thinking about Person-Environment Interaction: Ecological Counseling." *PsycCritiques*, American Psychological Association, November 9, Vol. 49, Supplement 7.

EDWIN MELÉNDEZ is Professor of Management and Urban Policy at Milano The Graduate School of Management and Urban Policy at the New School in New York City. Dr. Meléndez has conducted considerable research in the areas of Latino studies, economic development, labor markets, and poverty. In over 20 years of experience as principal investigator, he has managed over 35 research, outreach or demonstration projects, and supervised or collaborated with over 60 researchers in projects that resulted in several edited books, special issues of academic journals, and other publications. In addition to numerous scientific papers and other publications, he is the editor of the recently published *Communities and Workforce Development* (2004), the author of *Working on Jobs: The Center for Employment Training* (1996), and a coauthor of *In the Shadow of the Sun: Caribbean Development Alternatives and U.S. Policy* (1990) and *La Empresa Comunal: Lecciones de Casos Exitosos en Puerto Rico* (1999). He has also coedited *Hispanics in the Labor Force* (1991), *Colonial Dilemma: Critical Perspectives on Contemporary Puerto Rico* (1992), *Latino Poverty and Economic Development in Massachusetts* (1994), *Borderless Border* (1998), and *The Economic Impact of Puerto Rico's Political Alternatives* (1998). He has a Ph.D. in economics from the University of Massachusetts–Amherst.

MARTHA MONTERO-SIEBURTH is an Associate Professor in the Department of Leadership in Education at the Graduate College of Education of the University of Massachusetts-Boston where she teaches in the Leadership in Urban Schools Doctoral Program and the Educational Administration Masters Program. She has published extensively in English and Spanish and co-edited *The Struggle for a New Paradigm: Qualitative Research in Latin America*, with Gary L. Anderson and *Latino Adolescents: Making the Invisible, Visible* with Francisco A. Villarruel, both from Garland Press. Her research has been in U.S. urban schools and communities in the greater Boston metropolitan area and in rural and urban schools in Costa Rica, Honduras, Mexico, and Guatemala with diverse international agencies and national educational ministries. Dr. Montero-Sieburth received the Research in Elementary, Secondary, or Postsecondary Education Award 2005 from the Hispanic Research Issues SIG of the American Educational Research Association (AERA) and a William J. Fulbright Senior Scholar Lecturing Fellowship in 2006.

LISANDRO PÉREZ is Professor of Sociology at Florida International University and the former Director of the Cuban Research Institute. For the

1997–98 academic year, Dr. Pérez was on sabbatical with the Russell Sage Foundation in New York. He received his Ph.D. in Sociology from the University of Florida. He taught at Louisiana State University where he was promoted to Associate Professor and Coordinator of Graduate Studies, and in 1985, he accepted the position of Chair of the Sociology and Anthropology Department at FIU. During his six-year term as Chair, he led the Department in the establishment of M.A. and Ph.D. degree programs. In 1991, Dr. Pérez founded the Cuban Research Institute, dedicated to the study of Cuba and the Cuban-American community. He has published on Cuban demographics, society, and culture, as well as on the dynamics of the Cuban American community.

CYNTHIA PÉREZ MCCLUSKEY is an Associate Professor in the Department of Criminal Justice at the University of Texas at San Antonio. She earned her Ph.D. in Criminal Justice in 1999 from the University at Albany, State University of New York. Her research interests include developmental perspectives of crime and delinquency, substance use, and school achievement. Her work focuses primarily on the experience of Latino/a youth and families.

VICTORIA QUIROZ-BECERRA (M.A., M.Phil.) is a Ph.D. student in Political Science at the New School. She holds a M.A. and M.Phil. from Columbia University. Ms. Quiroz-Becerra has conducted independent research focusing on women's organizations networks and processes of institutionalization. For her research, she conducted ethnographic fieldwork and in-depth interviews among women's organizations in Chile and Mexico. Currently she is working on the New York Immigrant Organizations Project at Baruch College.

FRANCISCO A. VILLARRUEL is a University Outreach Senior Fellow and a Professor of Family and Child Ecology at Michigan State University. Dr. Villarruel's research focus is on Latino youth and families, positive youth development, and youth policy/juvenile justice. Villarruel has published 48 journal articles and book chapters, edited 6 books, and coauthored 5 state or national policy reports, including the first national report on Latino youth in the juvenile justice system. He has received numerous awards and distinctions during his career, including a W.K. Kellogg Foundation National Fellowship, an MSU-Lilly Foundation Teaching Fellowship, the HACU-ETS Policy Fellowship, and the 1996 MSU Teacher-Scholar Award for dedication and skill in teaching and scholarly promise.

PENNSYLVAN
OHIO
Philadelphia
Gettysburg July 63
NEW JERSEY
Antietam Sept 62
Washington
WEST VIRGINIA
Bull Run July 61 & Aug 62
DELAWARE
Fredericksburg Dec 62
MARYLAND
Chancellorsville May 63
62
65
Richmond burned April 65
Appomattox surrender April 65
VIRGINIA
NORTH CAROLINA
SOUTH CAROLINA
Fort Sumter bombarded April 61
64
ORGIA
FLORIDA
The American Civil War 1861-65
Union States
Confederate States
Union Campaigns
Confederate Campaigns
0 200Km
0 150miles

LONGMAN GROUP LIMITED
Longman House
Burnt Mill, Harlow, Essex, UK

Produced by Cameron & Tayleur (Books) Ltd.,
25 Lloyd Baker Street, London WC1X 9AT

First published 1981

Printed in Belgium
by Fabrieken Brepols n.v, Turnhout
Setting by Input Typesetting Ltd., London
Reproduction by Brian Gregory Associates Ltd,
St Albans, Herts

Series editors: Ian Cameron, Jill Hollis
Designed by Ian Cameron

British Library Cataloguing in Publication Data

Kolpas, Norman
    Abraham Lincoln.—(Longman great lives; 3).
    1. Lincoln, Abraham—Juvenile literature
    2. Presidents—United States—Biography—
    Juvenile literature
    973.7'092'4   E467

    ISBN 0-582-39030-3

Picture credits
BBC Hulton Picture Library: 55
The Bettmann Archive, Inc., New York: 6; 9; 14b; 17;
    22; 24; 25; 27; 28a, b; 39b; 40b; 43; 47a; 48; 49b;
    57; 60; 62; 64b; 65; 66b
Collection of the Boatman's National Bank of St
    Louis: 20
Cameron & Tayleur: 5; 14a; 15a; 32b; 47b; 53a; 53b;
    59
Chicago Historical Society: 56; 38
The Cincinnati Art Museum: 33
Mary Evans Picture Library: 11
Illinois State Historical Society: 36–37
Library of Congress: 30; 42a, b; 45; 61
The Mansell Collection: 13; 40a; 41; 49a; 50; 51; 52;
    53
Peter Newark's Western Americana: 19; 35b; 39a; 44;
    54; 58a, c; 64a; 66a
Orbis Publishing Limited: 15b; 20; 30; 32a; 35a;
    36–37; 37b; 42a, b; 45; 51a; 56; 61
Schomburg Collection: 35b
US Signals Corps (Brady Collection, National
    Archives): 51a

Maps by Creative Cartography Ltd. (Terry Allen and
    Nicholas Skelton)

Contents

Abraham Lincoln

NORMAN KOLPAS

Longman

1.

A Frontier Boyhood

Thomas Lincoln's log cabin stood on a barren strip of land in the west-central part of the state of Kentucky. The one-roomed building had only a single door, and its floor was made of earth, packed and stamped down to make it hard and even.

A bed constructed of poles was built into one corner of the cabin. In that bed, under a pile of bearskins to keep out the winter cold, Thomas's wife, Nancy Hanks Lincoln, gave birth to a son on a Sunday morning, 12th February 1809. The boy was named Abraham after Thomas's father, who had also been a Kentucky farmer. The first Abraham Lincoln had been shot dead by an Indian in 1784, when he was working in the fields with his three sons. Thomas, who was six at the time, was also nearly killed by the Indian. Only quick thinking and straight shooting by his elder brother Mordecai saved him.

Baby Abraham, the son of a struggling farmer, would grow up to become the President who led the United States of America through the greatest crisis in its history, the Civil War between the North and the South. At the time of his birth in the winter of 1809, the American nation was only 32 years old; in the short period since the Declaration of Independence on 4th July 1776, the country had grown

The birthplace of Abraham Lincoln.

quickly beyond the borders of the 13 British colonies that became the founding states of the Union.

Eager to have its expanding territory securely settled, the United States government encouraged Americans to move west, offering them the chance to buy virgin land for as little as 50 cents an acre. As the population grew, local governments were established, and eventually the new territories became fully fledged states. Lincoln's native Kentucky became a state in 1792. Many people were attracted by the chance to forge a new life in an untried land. Although some of them were the romantic pioneer figures of American legend, bear-fighting woodsmen, solitary fur-trappers and dashing rivermen, the majority were simple farmers like Abraham's father and grandfather, struggling to build a new life in often hostile surroundings.

When Abe was two, Thomas sold Rock Spring Farm and moved with his family to another log cabin ten miles away next to Knob Creek, where he had 30 acres of more fertile land which nestled among the rolling hills.

As soon as Abe could walk, he began to help on the farm, fetching water and firewood, gathering wild nuts and berries, and hoeing the soil where the family grew corn, beans, potatoes, onions and pumpkins. The farm work left little time for Abe and his elder sister Sarah to go to school. When there was no planting or harvesting to be done and school was in session, which was usually in the summer, Abe and Sarah walked to a schoolhouse two miles away. The school was a log cabin not much bigger than their home, like which it had only one door, one window and a dirt floor.

Like other boys from struggling pioneer families, all Little Abe wore was a long-tailed shirt of homespun cotton and wool; trousers of blue jean or buckskin and leather moccasins were too costly to be worn except during harsh winter weather.

In the school, boys and girls of every age sat on rough wooden benches. When the teacher was not calling on individuals to recite before the class, they all read their lessons aloud at the same time, or they repeated together lessons spoken by the teacher. The popular name for this sort of establishment was a "blab school". It may not have been educationally very effective, but at least Abe learned numbers from one to ten, the alphabet, and the beginning of reading and writing. A love of learning, and most of all, of words, was sparked in his mind: at every opportunity, with a stick on the ground or with a piece of coal by the hearth of the cabin, Abe practised his writing. He read and reread the three books his family possessed a Bible, a book of religious instruction and a spelling book.

A new home In 1816, Thomas Lincoln was forced to set out again in search of a new home as he was having difficulties with the farm on Knob Creek. Incorrect and incomplete records had been kept of land ownership in the area, and Thomas became involved in legal disputes over the title to his farm. This time, he headed to the northwest, across the Ohio River to the territory of Indiana, which was, at the end of 1816, to become the newest state in the Union.

Near Little Pigeon Creek, almost a hundred miles from the Knob Creek farm, he found a promising tract. He marked its boundaries by cutting notches in trees and by stacking piles of brushwood — clear signs, in frontier law, that a man had decided to claim some unsettled land.

In the late autumn of 1816, the Lincoln family loaded its possessions on a pair of horses, and set off for its new home. Compared to Kentucky, which was already 14 years old as a state and comparatively well settled with families, Indiana was a wilderness, a rolling land densely forested with elms, oaks, birches, maples, poplars and sycamores. Thomas Lincoln, helped by Abe, who was now almost eight years old, sometimes had to cut a trail through the thick undergrowth of the woods.

After seven days of hard travelling, the family reached the small clearing at the heart of Thomas Lincoln's claim on a rise of ground near the creek. With winter approaching, their first need was shelter. Abe helped his father build what was known as a "half-faced camp", a rough structure of logs and branches with a roof and three walls. The side facing south had a curtain of skins, but was otherwise open to catch the sunshine, and in front of it a fire was kept burning for warmth and protection from wild animals. Fortunately, Thomas Lincoln was a sure shot with a rifle. He was able to shoot enough game to keep his family well fed while the trees were felled to build their new log cabin and the fields were cleared for farming.

A crude cabin, windowless and with a low doorway, was built before Abe's eighth birthday. It was square, 18 feet each side, with a loft just below the roof to which Abe climbed on pegs in the wall; it was his bedroom. From the cabin, Abe himself tried his hand at shooting, when a flock of wild turkeys approached.

The harvest. Even for much more prosperous farmers than the Lincolns, this was a time of extremely hard work, as the crops were harvested by hand.

Abe's reaction to seeing a bird die at his own hand was surprising for a pioneer boy. As he later recounted, "I have never since pulled a trigger on any larger game." Once, as his father took aim at a young deer, Abe purposely moved to startle it away; scolded and beaten for this, Abe explained that perhaps God loved deer as much as he loved people.

A tragedy

After about a year alone in the Indiana wilderness, the Lincolns were joined by their first close neighbours. Nancy Lincoln's foster parents, Aunt Betsy and Uncle Tom Sparrow, and Abe's nineteen-year-old cousin Dennis Hanks, followed them from Kentucky and moved into the disused half-faced camp the Lincolns had built. Dennis became a sort of big brother to Abe and shared with him the joys of the frontier, exploring the woods, stalking animals, wrestling and working in the newly cleared fields. They also shared the first great tragedy of young Abe's life.

On the frontier at that time a disease was rife that medical men there called simply "the milk-sick", because it struck down cattle as well as humans and may have been passed on through milk. It started with severe stomach ache and vomiting, a dark-coated tongue, chills and exhaustion; within three to fourteen days, most sufferers died. In October 1818, Tom and Betsy Sparrow fell ill with the milk-sick. Within a few days, they were dead. Soon after, Abe's mother showed signs of the disease. Seven days later, Nancy Lincoln blessed her two tearful children, told them to "be good to one another" and died. Nancy Lincoln and Tom and Betsy

Sparrow were buried side by side in a forest clearing, in coffins made by the grieving Thomas Lincoln.

The hardships of frontier life were even harder now for Thomas Lincoln, his two motherless children and Dennis Hanks. After they had fended for themselves for a winter, Thomas set out from home once again, this time to find a new wife.

Sarah Bush had been his first sweetheart. She had married a jailkeeper named Daniel Johnston and was the mother of three children. Thomas, who had heard of Daniel's death, travelled to Kentucky to propose to Sarah.

At the beginning of 1819, Thomas Lincoln returned to Little Pigeon Creek driving a wagon with four horses. Down from the wagon after him stepped a tall, handsome, smiling woman. Then the three Johnston children scrambled off: John, who was nine years old, just a bit younger than Abe, Matilda, who was ten, and 13-year-old Sarah Elizabeth.

The Johnston family possessions were unloaded: a feather bed and pillows, bedstead, clothes chest and bureau, a table and chairs, good pots, pans, plates and dishes, with knives and forks and spoons. The Lincolns' wooden plates, which were nothing more than discs cut from a tree, were thrown away. Sarah Bush Lincoln also brought good new clothes for her step-children.

The little log cabin was now crowded with eight people and a lot of furniture. But Sarah began to set things in order. She told her husband that they must have a proper floor, and he made them one of split and planed logs called puncheons. The chinks between the logs of the cabin walls were closed up to keep out draughts; a proper door was made, and windows were cut to let in the sunshine.

Sarah Bush Lincoln loved Thomas Lincoln's children and Dennis Hanks as if they were her own. She felt a special love for solemn little Abe. "Abe was a good boy, the best boy I ever saw" she said years later when she was in her old age. "His mind and mine, what little I had, seemed to run together – move in the same channel."

With a mother's attentiveness, Sarah Bush Lincoln noticed Abe's zeal for learning. A tiny new schoolhouse, barely taller than a grown man, had been built four miles away, and Sarah saw to it that Abe went there at every opportunity. Not that the opportunities came at all often: Abe was needed to share in the farm work, and the school lessons had to be paid for in kind with hams, corn and hides that could not always be spared by the newly enlarged Lincoln household.

Later, Abe was to estimate that "all my schooling did not amount to one year." But Abe's new mother also encouraged him in his desire to continue reading on his own. One phrase young Abe often repeated to his friends was: "The things I want to know are in books. My best friend is the man who'll git me a book I ain't read."

But few people on the frontier owned books. Among the books Abe managed to borrow were *Aesop's Fables, Robinson Crusoe* and *The Pilgrim's Progress*, as well as arithmetic books and a history of the United States, which gave him for the first time a full idea of his young country's heritage. In his quest for new things to read, he also studied the *Revised Laws of Indiana*, which gave him his first understanding of the way that civilized society forms rules by which people can live together in peace.

Abe carried books to the fields with him during the day and up into his loft at night. Once, he borrowed, *The Life of George Washington* from a neighbour. Abe was thrilled by the brave life of the great general of the American Revolution and the country's first president, but one night, rain seeped through the ceiling of the loft and soaked the book. Abe had to work in the lender's cornfields for three days to pay for it, but damaged though it was, the book became his.

Abe learned in other ways, too. In place of books and formal education, the people of the frontier had a rich tradition of jokes, stories and songs, many outlandishly funny and all containing some nugget of wisdom. Abe listened to their talk and song, impressed by vivid tales and sayings that he would remember and elaborate upon throughout his life.

A village school in the first half of the 19th century. Even as modest an establishment as this one would have seemed quite grand in comparison to the school that Abe attended.

Around his twelfth year, Abe started to grow quickly. Someone described him at that time as "the ganglingest awkwardest feller . . . he appeared to be all joints." At 16, Abe was already six feet tall; by 17, he was nearly six feet four inches. Although he weighed little more than eleven stone, all his work in the fields had given him the strength to match his height. Abe's skill with an axe was admired by everyone near Little Pigeon Creek. "He could sink an axe deeper into wood than any man I ever saw," one neighbour remembered. Another remarked, "If you heard him fellin' trees in a clearin', you would say there was three men at work by the way the trees fell."

With Abe's physical confidence came new confidence in dealing with people. Another book he read and studied with care was *Lessons in Elocution* by a Scottish schoolmaster, William Scott. It presented pieces of verse and prose to recite and gave advice on public speaking. Abe was also fascinated by the preachers who roamed the countryside, delivering Bible-thumping sermons. He was determined to try his hand at public speaking, at holding an audience's attention with voice and gesture alone.

He worked out ideas for his speeches on paper. These essays on the merits of American government, on the importance of education, on the need for people to respect the law, were all written and rewritten until the flow of thought was logical and clear. Then, at his work or in the nearby village, wherever a possible audience was present, he mounted an imaginary speaker's platform, a tree stump or a fence. A neighbour remembered how Abe "explained things hard for us to understand by stories, maxims, tales and figures. He would almost always point up the lesson or idea by some story that was plain and near us that we might instantly see the force and bearing of what he said."

Abe's father, Thomas Lincoln, who had worked hard for years with little success, found it more and more difficult to understand his son, who would much rather put pen to paper, talk the ears off his neighbours or bury his nose in a book than apply himself to honest farm work. Thomas often had to drag Abe away in mid-speech, and more than a few times the tall, gentle boy was clouted on the head by his uncomprehending father.

The time was coming when, rather than continue in conflict with his father, Abe would have to strike off on his own. His intellect yearned for wider experiences, and the first opportunity came just after his nineteenth birthday.

2.

Abe on His Own

A mile and a half from the Lincoln cabin a village known as Gentryville had grown up. It tooks its name from James Gentry, a wealthy man who had moved to Little Pigeon Creek in 1818 and set up a store in his house, attracting other pioneers to settle nearby.

Gentry's business prospered. He was soon conducting trade with larger towns and cities, sending boatloads of Indiana produce, corn, flour and meat, down the Ohio River to the Mississippi and on to the great port of New Orleans.

In April 1828, Abe Lincoln was hired to man one of Gentry's New Orleans-bound shipments with the businessman's son, Allen. The flatboat on which the two young men set off with their cargo was made of poplar logs, like a giant raft more than 60 feet long. In all, their trip took three months, for which Abe was paid the grand sum of 24 dollars. The money, by law and custom, went to Abe's father. Of far greater importance to Abe was the chance to be his own master and to experience some of the vastness of his country.

The only dramatic moment in an otherwise uneventful journey came one night, when they were moored on an uninhabited stretch of the Mississippi just outside New Orleans. Out of the quiet night, seven black river-pirates came aboard the boat and were, Lincoln related, "intent to kill

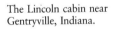

The Lincoln cabin near Gentryville, Indiana.

Poster for a slave auction in New Orleans.

and rob us." Abe and Allen Gentry fought so furiously to defend themselves and their cargo that they managed to knock some of the pirates overboard; the others fled back into the night. Only when Abe and Allen were again floating safely downstream could they tend to their wounds. A deep cut over Abe's right eye left a scar that he carried for life.

New Orleans was the first real city Abe had ever seen. Here were grand mansions with balconies of wrought iron; majestic steamboats like floating palaces were docked one alongside the other on the riverside; great sailing ships from faraway countries lay in the harbour; and people from all over the world thronged the city streets, speaking languages that Abe had never heard.

He also saw one of the most pitiful sights to ever meet his eyes: gangs of black slaves in chains on the way to market to be sold at auction. Of course, Abe had seen slaves before; some of the wealthier families in Kentucky owned slaves. But never had the human misery of slavery appeared to him so openly. What shocked Abe most, though, was the seeming indifference of the citizens of New Orleans, who regarded the blacks as they would so many horses or cattle.

Slavery was an established part of the way of life in the American South and an important factor in its agricultural economy. On the vast farming estates, or plantations, owned

Western scene: raft on a river, painted around 1830.

ANTI-SLAVERY RECORD.

VOL. I.   MAY, 1835.   NO. 5.

CRUELTIES OF SLAVERY.

Above: the cargo deck of a ship bringing slaves from Africa. Its three compartments (men in the bows, boys amidships, women in the stern) held 292 slaves. Shelves along the sides of the ship allowed a second layer to be crammed in. The slaves, whether on the shelves or under them, had at most 31 inches of height in which to exist. *Right:* an anti-slavery publication.

by single aristocratic families, slaves planted, tended and harvested the tobacco and cotton that found eager markets in Europe. With the invention in 1793 of the cotton gin, a machine for quickly and efficiently separating cotton seeds from fibre, the South increased its cotton production, and slaves became an even greater necessity. At slavery's peak, well over three million blacks, men, women and children, were owned by white people in the South.

To be sure, many slaves were well treated. They were decently clothed and fed; some were given basic educations, taught the beliefs of Christianity and entrusted with positions of responsibility in the household and on the farm. Nevertheless, all slaves were still little more than possessions. The slave masters and indeed most white people, in both the North and the South, thought black people were inferior to whites.

Slavery was less necessary to the states of the North, which relied largely on industry, trade and shipping for their economy. Over the years, slavery had gradually been abolished in the northern states. Every state had the power, if it

15

chose, to outlaw slavery at any time within its own boundaries, by action of the state legislature. Some Northerners, known as Abolitionists, were in favour of ending slavery all at once throughout the country, but this could be done only by an amendment to the Constitution of the United States. Since the northern and southern halves of the country were represented fairly equally in the federal government, any attempts to legislate on slavery were doomed to deadlock. The issue that *was* battled out in Congress was the admission of new states to the Union, and whether they would be slave or free states.

Bad fortune seemed to plague Abe's family. Abe was away in. New Orleans when his sister Sarah, who had married in 1826, died while giving birth to her first child in 1828. The winter after her death saw the return of the milk-sick to Indiana. No-one in the family caught it this time, but fear of the sickness, added to his continuing failure to prosper as a farmer, led Thomas Lincoln to move once more to a land of greater promise. He sold his Indiana farm and in March 1830 moved his family westward to find land in the state of Illinois.

Abe was now 21 and, in the eyes of the law, an adult, a fully fledged American citizen. After he had finished helping his family to settle on their new farm, he intended to set off on his own.

The Lincolns stopped this time near Decatur, Illinois, where they claimed ten acres of land, built a log cabin, cleared a field and raised a crop of corn. But whatever promise their latest home held seemed to disappear with a harsh autumn. The entire family fell ill with colds and fevers. Autumn was followed by the worst winter in memory, with two-and-a-half feet of snow and sub-zero temperatures.

With spring, Thomas Lincoln decided to move again, about a hundred miles east to Coles County, Illinois. But this time, Abe did not go with his family. Accompanied by his step-brother John Johnston, and a cousin, John Hanks, 22-year-old Abe set to work building an 80-foot flatboat. They were working for a big-talking drunkard of a frontier businessman, Denton Offutt, whose cargo of pickled pork, hogs and corn the young men would float down to New Orleans for a salary of twelve dollars each per month.

Just a few days out, the flatboat stuck on the dam of a mill near the town of New Salem, Illinois. Cool-headed Abe supervised the shifting of the heavy cargo to prevent the

Pioneers travelling down the Ohio river in flatboats.

boat from sinking. Next, he drilled a hole in the end of the boat overhanging the dam, so that the water it had taken on could drain away. Then he plugged the hole and managed to free the boat. Denton Offutt, impressed by Abe's handling of the problem, was also impressed by the looks of New Salem. He decided that he would settle in the town after the trip, open a store and hire Abe Lincoln as its clerk.

Abe returned to settle in New Salem in July 1831. The citizens of the town quickly took a liking to the long-boned stranger with his ill-fitting clothes and his shaggy black hair. They found sympathy and warmth in the young man's deep-set, dark eyes, his thoughtful face and his shy smile.

With Denton Offutt, Abe set up a small shop in New Salem. They stocked a wide variety of goods, like a frontier department store: seeds and farm equipment, guns and ammunition, liquor, cloth and clothing, horse saddles and ox yokes, fruit and vegetables, meat and cheese. While Offutt spent much of his time sampling their stock of alcoholic beverages, Abe, who disapproved of heavy drinking, soberly tended the counter. He was always ready to have a chat or a serious discussion with his customers, and had a book at hand to study when business was slow.

But life was not all calm business and reading for the shop clerk. Offutt had seen Abe put his back into hard physical labour and bragged drunkenly about the young man's strength and skill. These boasts reached the ears of a gang of young toughs from nearby Clary's Grove, and Jack Armstrong, their leader, challenged Abe to a wrestling match.

Although Abe disliked fighting, he was not one to back down from a challenge. One afternoon, a crowd gathered outside Offutt's store to watch the contest between Armstrong and Lincoln. Some men made bets on the outcome.

After a hard struggle in which Armstrong fought unfairly, Abe grabbed him by the neck, lifted him off the ground and shook him hard. With their leader embarrassingly defeated, the Clary's Grove Boys charged in to finish Abe off. He faced them all and offered to do battle with any of them. At that moment, the beaten Armstrong surprised everyone; he offered Abe his hand in friendship, calling him "the best feller that ever broke into this settlement." Now Abe had everyone's respect.

One way in which the people of New Salem showed their respect for Abe was in looking to him in legal matters. He was asked to sign as a witness on land deeds. With his skill in writing, he was called on to compose contracts and documents, a task he applied himself to with the help of Mr. Bowling Green, New Salem's Justice of the Peace.

But Abe was still dissatisfied with himself. Feeling his lack of education more and more, he approached the village schoolmaster, Mentor Graham, for help. Graham was surprised by the request of the 23-year-old shopkeeper, but when he saw that Abe was seriously set on learning, he agreed to work with him on his studies in the evenings.

Abe walked six miles to borrow a textbook on English grammar, so that he could improve his writing and speaking. By lamplight, evening after evening, he was taught and tested by Graham. The schoolmaster introduced him to great works of literature such as *Don Quixote*, to books of poetry and history, science and medicine. Graham went on to teach Abe some higher mathematics, geometry and trigonometry, subjects which often kept Abe up late at night. Abe, Graham remembered, "was so studious he somewhat impaired his health and constitution," but he was also the "most studious, diligent straightforward young man in the pursuit of knowledge and literature than any among the five thousand I have taught in schools."

In March 1832, after less than one year in Salem, Abe felt ready to run for political office. In the *Sangamon Journal*, the newspaper for the Illinois county which included New

Salem, he announced that he would be a candidate for the office of the county's assemblyman in the state legislature. Abe called for the improvement of the county's rivers, so that big steamboats could reach towns such as New Salem, bringing trade and prosperity. He also wanted more widespread education to enable every citizen "to read the histories of his own and other countries, by which he may duly appreciate the value of our free institutions." The statement ended with characteristic humility: "If the good people in their wisdom shall see fit to keep me in the background, I have been too familiar with disappointments to be very much chagrined."

On the move

But Abe's campaign did not get going straight away. By April 1832, Denton Offutt's business was failing. In spite of Abe's efforts to make the shop profitable, Offutt cared more for drink and wild gambles than he did for keeping proper accounts or a well-stocked store. Faced with unemployment, Abe, along with the other men of New Salem, heard a call for troops.

An Indian war chief, Black Hawk, had led his men across the Mississippi River into Illinois. The southern part of the state, along with parts of Indiana, had been his people's traditional homeland, but treaties that had given this land to the white settlers had forced them westward. Now the Indians were fighting back, and Black Hawk's warriors were burning log cabins and killing settlers.

Indian raid on a homestead. A late 19th century illustration by R. F. Zogbaum from *Harper's New Monthly Magazine.*

Abe borrowed a horse and enlisted in a local company of volunteers. He was elected their captain. Many of his men

were Clary's Grove Boys, who were not used to obeying orders. Abe's first command to one of them was met with the reply, "Go to hell!" Then the soldier respectfully added, "Sir!"

In a month and a half, Abe and his men encountered no Indian marauders and had nothing to do except drill and march. After Abe's enlistment reached its end, he re-enlisted twice more as a private, the rank in which he served until August 1832. Only once did he and his fellow soldiers stumble on the horrors of battle, at Kellogg's Grove, where an Indian party had ambushed a white detachment: "They lay heads towards us on the ground. And every man had a round red spot on the top of his head, about as big as a dollar where the redskins had taken his scalp."

Elections

Back in New Salem, Abe had only two and a half weeks left to campaign before the 1832 election. He travelled around the country, making speeches, helping with harvests, joining in friendly wrestling bouts and even breaking up the odd fist fight. But there was not really enough time for Abe to make himself known. On election day in New Salem, Abe won 277 of the 300 votes; in the vote across the whole county, however, he failed to win a seat in the state legislature.

Stump Speaking, a painting of a rural election campaign by George Caleb Bingham.

"The Railsplitter" – after the failure of his business in New Salem, Abe labours to pay off his debts.

Again he was at a loose end. He thought of studying law, but had little money and feared his education would not be enough. He considered becoming a blacksmith, but finally, he was offered a partnership in another New Salem store. Abe signed a note promising to pay his share, and once more he was in business. But Lincoln and his partner very soon began to sink deeply into debt.

Abe did have one piece of luck. A traveller passing through New Salem sold him for fifty cents a barrel which was said to contain nothing of special value. Only weeks

21

later did Abe bother to empty it. At the bottom, he found a complete edition of Blackstone's *Commentaries on the Laws of England.* "The more I read, the more intensely interested I became. Never in my whole life was my mind so thoroughly absorbed. I read until I devoured them."

Abe's business venture failed, leaving him 1100 dollars in debt. He was helped out by influential friends in New Salem; they had him appointed to the job of postmaster. He also took on extra work as a surveyor laying out the boundaries of farms and establishing the plans of new Illinois towns. Abe was conscientious about his huge debt: "I went to the creditors and told them that if they would let me alone I would give them all I could earn over my living, as fast as I could earn it." Although it took Abe 17 years to pay back the money, his sense of responsibility earned him the nickname of "Honest Abe". In what spare time he had from his two full-time jobs, he took on any additional work he could find. He stripped the husks from harvested corn faster than anyone else in those parts. He split fence rails from logs (a task known simply as railsplitting) by driving pegs into the wood with a sledgehammer. He repaired houses, made simple furniture, wrote letters and deeds.

In the autumn of 1834, Abe stood again in his county for the office of Illinois state assemblyman. This time, he was elected with the largest majority ever received by a candidate for that office. In his eight years in the legislature, he was re-elected three times.

Abe and the other assemblymen had to deal with the needs of a growing state. He voted in favour of increased spending on public education and schools for orphans. He

The old State House in Springfield, Illinois, where Lincoln served as an assemblyman.

dealt with bills for the development of roads, bridges, canals and navigable rivers. He supported motions to ease the burdens of poor settlers, allowing a farmer to keep a work horse or a yoke of oxen no matter how far he was in debt.

When the Assembly was not meeting, Abe continued to work and study in New Salem. A fellow assemblyman, John T. Stuart, was by profession an attorney. He encouraged the talented young man to study law and loaned Abe the necessary books.

At this point in his life, Abe fell in love for the first time. He had always been shy with women, tongue-tied and at his most awkward. But he took a special liking to Ann Rutledge. She was the most popular girl in New Salem, beautiful, intelligent, witty and sweet-natured.

Before Abe's love for her grew, however, she had become betrothed to someone else. After the engagement, the man left New Salem. He was headed for New York, he told Ann, to bring his mother, brother and sisters back to Illinois. Three years later, he had not returned, and the sympathy the grieving girl received from the adoring Abe Lincoln finally won her heart. They were to be married after her unfaithful fiancé had released her from her vow.

But soon after, in the late summer of 1835, Ann Rutledge fell ill and died of a fever. Abe fell into the deepest depression of his life; the people of New Salem feared that he might go mad. To one friend, Abe sobbed, "I can never be reconciled to have the snow, rains and storms beat upon her grave!"

A year later, he began a half-hearted courtship of another woman, Mary Owens. But his attentions spoke more of the emptiness Abe still felt in his soul than of any love he may have felt for Mary. It would be several more years before Abe loved again.

Abe the lawyer   In March 1837, the name of Abraham Lincoln was entered on the roster of attorneys allowed to practise law in the state of Illinois. He was invited by John T. Stuart to share his office in Springfield. Stuart, who was pursuing a career in national politics, needed someone to perform the day-to-day work of his thriving legal practice.

Abe left New Salem in April with only seven dollars in his pocket. His law books and his few clothes were in saddlebags, slung across the horse Abe had borrowed for the journey. His first stop in Springfield was the store of Joshua Speed, where Abe asked the cost of bedding. Seventeen dollars, was Speed's answer. "Cheap as it is," Abe replied, "I have not the money to pay. But if you will credit me until Christmas, and my experiment as a lawyer here is a success, I will pay you then. If I fail in that I will probably never pay you at all." Confronted with such a pitiful sight, Joshua Speed immediately offered to share his own lodgings above the store. The new lawyer accepted gratefully, and thus began a lasting friendship.

In his law practice, Lincoln continued to deserve the nickname of Honest Abe, never taking a case if he felt he would have to conceal or disguise the truth for his client's sake. In the middle of a trial, if Abe realized that a client was actually guilty though claiming to be innocent, he seemed to lose heart in his work. One of Abe's first clients, accused of committing murder in a drunken fight, was found guilty and hanged.

Lincoln in court, defending in a murder case.

But for honest, hard-working people, Abe was the ideal attorney. Anyone bewildered by the law, worried or troubled, found refuge in the office of Stuart and Lincoln. One summer day, for example, a simple farmer came to Abe, needing official papers to prove that he owned his farm. As court was not then in session, Abe walked with him, in the intense afternoon heat, out of town to where the local judge was working on his own farm. They finally tracked him down and, in the middle of a cornfield with the men in their shirtsleeves, the judge signed the necessary papers. Then Abe and the poor farmer pitched in and helped the judge with his farm work. When the time came for the man to pay the fee for having his papers endorsed, the judge told him that payment had been made by his honest labour.

Abe expected and received little money from such needy clients, but the work satisfied him, as did his continuing participation in the state Assembly. Meanwhile, all around him and in the newspapers were instances of the way passion and violence could make people break the law. In St. Louis, Missouri, for example, a free black man, accused of stabbing and killing a sheriff, was burned to death by an angry mob before he could stand trial.

An educated respect for the law, Abe knew, could help to repair the wrongs of society. In a speech he delivered to the Springfield Young Men's Lyceum in January 1838, Abe put forward his beliefs: "Reason – cold, calculating, unimpassioned reason – must furnish all the materials for our future support and defence. Let these materials be moulded into general intelligence, sound morality, and in particular, a reverence for the Constitution and the laws."

3. Rivalries and Principles

At the rear of Joshua Speed's store in Springfield was a large fireplace. Most evenings after work, Abe Lincoln, Speed and other men interested in politics gathered around the fire, put their feet up and talked. More likely than not, Abe would find himself in argument with Stephen A. Douglas, another legislator and the prosecuting attorney of the local court, a man whose short stature, noble head and booming voice would earn him the nickname of "the Little Giant".

At the time, the two main political parties in the United States were the Whigs and the Democrats. The Whig Party believed, above all else, that the country should have a strong central, or federal government with the right to regulate such matters as banking, trade and improvements in transport. Abe supported the Whigs. Stephen Douglas was a Democrat and believed in the right of the individual states to look after their own affairs without the interference of the federal government, a policy which the Whigs believed would weaken the United States as a nation. The Democrats, who were in the majority in Illinois, had as their slogan, "All Whigs ought to be whipped out of office like dogs out of the meat house."

A street in Springfield, Illinois, photographed in 1837, when Lincoln first lived in the town. The next to last house in the block housed the law firm of Lincoln and William Herndon from 1844 to 1860.

Abe continued campaigning in the 1840 presidential election, in which the Whig candidate, William Henry Harrison, defeated the Democratic President, Martin Van Buren. At one point, Abe's friend Edward Baker, a fellow Whig, was addressing a meeting in the courthouse on the floor below Lincoln's law office. Abe listened to the speech through a trap door in his floor, which opened directly into the courtroom ceiling. Suddenly, the Democrats in the crowd were roused by Baker's remarks, and there were angry shouts that he should be pulled down from the stand. The audience was then startled to see a long pair of legs suddenly come dangling from the ceiling. Abe lowered himself to the platform beside his friend, grabbed a stone water jug and threatened to bring it down on the head of the first man to touch Baker. Thus gaining silence, Abe said, "Hold on, gentlemen, this is the land of free speech. Mr. Baker has a right to speak and ought to be heard. I am here to protect him, and no man shall take him from this stand if I can prevent it." Baker's speech went on, uninterrupted.

Abe gets married Not only in politics were Abraham Lincoln and Stephen Douglas rivals. In late 1839 both men found themselves attracted to Mary Todd, the 21-year-old daughter of a wealthy banker from Kentucky. Mary was in Springfield staying with her sister, who was married to a politician, a friend of Abe's. She was also the cousin of his law partner, John Stuart. Mary Todd was an attractive young woman, short, pleasantly plump, well-educated and lively in conversation. Coming from a family that had always known money and power, she was also ambitious. As she once confided to her married sister, she felt "she was destined to be the wife of some future President."

Both Lincoln and Douglas showed presidential potential, and both often visited Mary Todd. Abe, however, was the more persistent suitor. In spite of his humble background, Mary's sister and brother-in-law gave support to Abe's cause. Eventually they became engaged. The wedding date was set for 1st January 1841, but Abe was suddenly bothered by the thought of marriage. There is no way of telling exactly what caused his doubts. Even after coming so far by his own efforts, Abe may still have felt unable to live up to the sophisticated social level of the Todd family: he once joked, "One 'd' is enough for God, but the Todds need two." Maybe Abe still suffered from his memories of the death of Ann Rutledge.

Whatever the reasons, Abe failed to appear for his wedding. Mary wrote, formally breaking off their engagement. Abe wrote to his partner Stuart, "I am now the most miserable man living. If what I felt were equally distributed to the whole human family, there would be not one cheerful face on the earth." He missed attending most sessions of the State Assembly. At times, his friend Joshua Speed feared that Abe might even try to kill himself: "Knives and razors, and every instrument that could be used for self-destruction, were removed from his reach."

It was Speed who most helped Lincoln out of his gloom. In the spring of 1841, Joshua moved back to his home town of Louisville, Kentucky. Late that summer, he coaxed Abe into visiting the Speed family's beautiful mansion. Abe

27

Mary Todd Lincoln, painted in 1864.

stayed for several months and enjoyed animated conversation, good food and happy outings with Joshua, his mother and sister. Abe's gloom began to be a little less deep.

Then the tables turned for Abe and Joshua. Speed became engaged. Just before his wedding, he too became moody, worrying whether he was doing the right thing, and Abe was able to help him. Speed's marriage went ahead as planned, and his joy must have served as a lesson to Abe. In the summer of 1842, Abraham Lincoln and Mary Todd became engaged again. They were married on 4th November and settled straight away in a modest boarding house ran by a widow above a tavern in Springfield, at a cost of only four dollars a week.

At the end of their first year of marriage, Abe and Mary Lincoln had a baby son. They named him Robert Todd, after Mary's father. Abe's life had changed: he had a wife and a child, and with his new responsibilities came renewed ambitions.

In early 1843, Abe tried to get the nomination of the local Whig party to run for election to the United States Congress. But when the party met, the nomination went to Abe's friend Edward Baker. Abe was nominated only as a delegate to the Whig party's district convention. He took his defeat with good humour, but was determined not to fail a second time. He continued his legal work with full dedication. His law business was growing, and he had a new partner, William Herndon. In May 1844, Abe and Mary moved into their first house, which Abe bought for 1500 dollars. Abe's work took him from courthouse to courthouse in his district of Illinois, where he met and won the respect of more and more members of the Whig party.

The Lincolns' first house.

His determination paid off. In May 1846, two months after a second Lincoln son was born and named Edward Baker Lincoln, Abe won his party's nomination to Congress. Abe's friends among the Whigs raised 200 dollars, which they presented to him to cover his personal costs in campaigning. Abe was not used to this political high finance. After the election, in which Abe defeated his Democratic opponent by 6,340 votes to 4,829, he sent a note to his Whig supporters, saying that he had travelled "on my own horse; my entertainment, being at the houses of friends, cost me nothing; and my only outlay was 75 cents for a barrel of cider, which some farmhands insisted I should treat them to." With the note, Abe enclosed the remaining $199.25.

War and slavery   In December 1847, when Abe Lincoln entered the United States Congress, the country was at war with Mexico. The war had been started almost entirely at the instigation of the current American president, a Democrat named James Polk. Like many Americans, Polk believed that the United States had a "Manifest Destiny", a God-given right, to extend the nation's territory from coast to coast. At the end of 1845, part of this ambition was achieved; Texas, a former territory of Mexico which had been settled by Americans and had won independence, became an American state. But Polk wanted territories further west, all the way to the Mexican territory of California along the Pacific coast.

The only way to get the land was by defeating Mexico in war. But first a war had to start, and Polk wanted it to seem as if Mexico itself had struck the first blow. He took advantage of an old border dispute between Texas and Mexico. Although the actual southern border of the state was the Nueces River, Texans always claimed that it was further south, at the Rio Grande. President Polk sent American troops across the Nueces to the Rio Grande. When they were attacked by Mexican soldiers, Polk informed Congress that Mexico had invaded American territory and shed American blood on American soil. War was then declared, and American troops marched on Mexico and its territories of New Mexico and California.

When Congressman Lincoln moved to Washington, D.C., the United States was close to winning the war. In Congress, Abe introduced resolutions that criticized the President's aggressive conduct, requesting that Polk should specify precisely where American blood had first been shed, so that he would have to admit publicly that the blood had fallen not

A daguerreotype photograph of Lincoln taken in Springfield in 1846.

on American soil but on Mexican land invaded by American military force. Clever and true though Abe's resolutions were, they unwisely ignored the fact that most of the people who had voted for him had friends or relatives fighting and dying in the American army as it neared its victory over Mexico. Abe's impassioned speeches went ignored in Congress and won him few friends at home in Illinois.

Beyond the question of whether the United States was right or wrong to fight with Mexico, the war raised another, more threatening question. A line between free and slave states had been drawn in the Missouri Compromise of 1820, and most of the land taken from Mexico would fall to the south of it. Texas had already entered the Union as a slave state, but many Northerners were now alarmed at the idea of the sudden shift in the North-South balance that would be caused by these vast new territories joining the South in allowing slavery. In 1846, David Wilmot, a congressman from Pennsylvania, had proposed a bill that came to be known as the Wilmot Proviso, forbidding slavery in any lands taken from Mexico.

Lincoln was morally opposed to slavery. Yet, as long as it was legal in the South, his respect for the law and his desire to see his country stay united made him reject the idea of forcing abolition on the South. He was in favour of leaving slavery alone where it already existed, in the hope that it would dwindle and disappear, but he was firmly opposed to letting slavery be extended to any new states.

Along with a majority of other congressmen, Abe supported the Wilmot Proviso. But the motion was defeated in the United States Senate. Although the balance between free states and slave states established by the Missouri Compromise was maintained, the whole question of the Wilmot Proviso once again brought to the surface the tensions between North and South. With the United States continuing to expand westward and new territories growing towards statehood, the Compromise was not likely to hold for very much longer.

In the following years, each brief solution to the differences that split the country would be more uncertain than the one before. The Compromise of 1850, for example, made concessions to both sides. For the North, California was admitted to the Union as a free state at the request of its people, and trading in slaves was abolished in the nation's capital, Washington, D.C. For the South, it was agreed that the territories of Utah and New Mexico would be free to choose which way they would go when they reached statehood, and a strict law required the return of slaves who ran away to the North.

Northern resistance to slavery increased. The thriving "underground railway" was a system of safe hideouts that could be used by runaway slaves as they escaped northwards to Canada. People who had not seen slavery in action learned about its horrors from literature. A novel called *Uncle Tom's Cabin* was written by a Northern woman, Harriet Beecher Stowe, and published in 1852. It won thousands of new supporters to the anti-slavery movement with its sentimental story of the plight of slaves.

In 1848, Abe Lincoln did not seek re-election to Congress. His outspoken opposition to the Mexican war had not helped his popularity, and he knew he would have lost the election. So Abe returned to his law practice in Springfield, and set out enthusiastically to rebuild his side of the partnership, apparently relieved to be out of the public eye. Half of his time he spent "on the Circuit", travelling on horseback, by rickety buggy or stagecoach from one courthouse to another across twenty Illinois counties.

Abe's law office was dingy and disorganized, with an unswept floor covered with letters, papers and journals. His two little sons visited him and added to the chaos by playing with the books and documents. Abe's office also extended into the tall stovepipe hat he always wore. Inside the hatband, he carried all manner of correspondence. Once, when a colleague asked why he had been slow in replying to a letter, Abe wrote, "I put it in my old hat, and buying a new one the next day, the old one set aside, and so, the letter was lost sight of for a time."

An advertisement for *Uncle Tom's Cabin*, offering four different editions, including one in German. *Right:* Topsy and Eva, from an illustrated edition of the book.

Abe's untidiness followed him home, much to the exasperation of his neat and formal wife. When he came home from work, he would sprawl on the floor and read aloud for hours from books or newspapers. But though Mary Lincoln often lost her temper with Abe, she knew that she

The Underground Railroad, the route by which runaway slaves reached Canada. A late 19th century painting dramatizing the harsh conditions that the fugitives had to endure.

had a generous and kind husband; she made sure in many ways that Abe, so often lost in thought and disorganized, kept clear sight of his responsibilities and goals.

Together, Abe and Mary shared sorrow, for in February 1850, their second son, four-year-old Edward, died. Mary, always emotional and nervous, grieved terribly. Abe comforted her and cried with her; although not a church-going man, he went with her to church to pray for their lost child. Ten months later, they had another son, William, and in April 1853 a fourth, Thomas.

A new Party

During the five years in which Abe kept out of public life, the Whig party went into decline. Its old leaders were dying, and younger men felt that the party was not doing enough about the pressing problems of the country. Instead of strongly opposing slavery, it was advocating feeble compromises with the South, and there were Southern Whigs who actually supported slavery.

In 1854, Abe suddenly felt the need to speak out again in politics. His old Springfield debating adversary, Stephen Douglas, now one of the United States Senators from Illinois, introduced in the Senate his Kansas-Nebraska Bill. This aimed to encourage settlement in the two western territories, so that a transcontinental railway, passing through the city

33

of Chicago, Illinois, could be organized. Douglas needed support for his plan from Southern senators, and it happened that both Kansas and Nebraska were north of the dividing line set by the Missouri Compromise. Douglas therefore proposed allowing Kansas and Nebraska to decide for themselves the question of whether or not to allow slavery, just as Utah and New Mexico had done in 1850. With Southern backing, the Kansas-Nebraska Act was passed; the Missouri Compromise was effectively broken and replaced by the Democratic party's principle that each individual state had the right to decide for itself on slavery.

Lincoln made speeches opposing Douglas's Act. "In his view," he said of Douglas, "the question of whether a new country shall be slave or free is a matter of as utter indifference as it is whether his neighbour shall plant his farm with tobacco or stock it with horned cattle". Abe stressed that slavery was a "monstrous injustice", not just some problem of farm management. "I admit that the emigrant to Kansas and Nebraska is competent to govern himself: but I deny his right to govern any other person without that person's consent."

Abe resolved to run for the United States Senate where, he hoped, he could oppose Douglas and his supporters. But as a Whig he was unable to gather enough support.

However, new political parties were forming, and Abe found increasing favour in the young Republican party. It had been formed by Northern politicians in 1854 and was dedicated to preventing the extension of slavery in the new territories. In the South, the party was known sneeringly as the "Black Republicans".

Abe remained loyal to the Whigs as long as he could, but the tide of events continued to worsen. The Kansas-Nebraska Act worked out as its opponents had dreaded. Nebraska was an agricultural state that was not suited to a slave economy, but Kansas, which was further south, attracted a flood of settlers from North and South, with each side determined to swing the territory its own way. Bloody battles broke out between opposing factions. Neither side played fair: one Northern abolitionist, a religious maniac named John Brown, led a midnight massacre of unarmed pro-slavery settlers. The fighting in "Bleeding Kansas", as it was known, was a prelude to a more widespread conflict.

In Bloomington, Illinois, at the end of May 1856, Abe joined in the founding of his state's branch of the Republican party, a gathering of men firmly devoted to defeating the

Dred Scott.

spread of slavery. The meeting ended with a stirring speech from Abe. Although no record was made of his words, Lincoln's partner, Herndon, later described the effect of the event: "If Mr. Lincoln was six feet four inches high usually, at Bloomington that day he was seven feet, and inspired at that." Abe immediately started campaigning for the Republican candidate in the 1856 Presidential Election, John C. Fremont, but a Democratic President, James Buchanan, was elected with widespread support in the South.

The cause of slavery won a further victory early the following year, when the decision of the United States Supreme Court in the Dred Scott case dealt the final blow to the Missouri Compromise. Scott, a slave, claimed freedom on the ground that his master had twice taken him north of the Missouri Compromise line. The Court's decision against Scott stated that as a black man, he was not a citizen and had no right to sue. It also stated that slaves were private property and that the U.S. Congress could not pass laws depriving white citizens of their property. In effect, this meant that any new territory, north or south of the Missouri Compromise line, was open to slavery.

Lincoln against Douglas

James Buchanan, President of the United States at the time of the Dred Scott case.

Abraham Lincoln's efforts for the Republican cause won him the respect of his Republican colleagues and other opponents of slavery throughout the North, but also made him widely hated in the South. Abe's hard work was rewarded in June 1858, when the Republicans of Illinois unanimously adopted him as their candidate for United States Senator against his old opponent Stephen Douglas, who was running for re-election.

Douglas and Lincoln immediately began to criticize each other in public speeches and seemed to spend as much time defending themselves against accusations as they did in clearly stating their own positions. So, on 24th July Abraham Lincoln wrote to Douglas, inviting him to join in a series of public debates, and Douglas agreed.

In seven different towns in Illinois, the "Little Giant" and "Long Abe", as one reporter described the adversaries, met and argued before thousands of spectators. Their debates added nothing new to the positions already adopted by them and their parties; the two men continued to attack each other's beliefs with great eloquence, both in the debates and elsewhere. In one speech, Lincoln referred to Douglas's persuasive and deceptive arguments with a saying that was to become famous: "You can fool all of the people some of

An open air debate between Abraham Lincoln and Stephen Douglas at Charleston, Illinois, on 18th September 1858.

the time and some of the people all of the time, but you cannot fool all of the people all of the time."

Douglas did manage to "fool" enough of the people to win re-election to the Senate by a narrow margin. But the Lincoln-Douglas debates were reported across the country, and Abe came out of the campaign with a national reputation as one of the Republican party's leading spokesmen.

Abe Lincoln's role as a spokesman for the Republicans became crucially important at the end of 1859. The mad abolitionist John Brown, who had caused his own share of the bloodshed in "Bleeding Kansas", set off on a wild new scheme. In October, he and 22 armed followers attempted to seize the United States arsenal at Harper's Ferry in Virginia, a slave state. They called on the slaves to join them by revolting against their masters, in the hope of starting a revolution in the South. No-one answered their call, and all except Brown and four others were killed. In December, Brown was found guilty of treason, murder and criminal conspiracy, and was executed. To militant abolitionists in

Opposite page: the trial of John Brown at Charlestown, Virginia.

the North he was a martyr. In the South, he was a sure sign that Northerners were willing to defeat slavery by violence, and many on both sides feared that the rising Republican party might be in favour of swift and violent abolition.

In February 1860, Abraham Lincoln was called on to speak for the Republicans at the Cooper Institute in New York City. Reporters from the country's major newspapers were there to hear him explain his own and his party's position. With wisdom, wit and passion, the tall man from Illinois, who spoke with a quaint backwoods accent, answered the questions on everyone's minds. Southerners had said that the election of a Republican president was sure to destroy the Union, and that they would thus blame this destruction on the Republicans. "That is cool," replied Lincoln. "A highwayman holds a pistol to my ear and mutters through his teeth, 'Stand and deliver, or I shall kill you, and then you will be a murderer!' "

Abe sought to reassure people that the Republicans had nothing to do with John Brown. Of Brown's plot, he said that "it was so absurd that the slaves, with all their ignorance, saw plainly enough it could not succeed." He addressed the South directly in saying that although the Republicans thought slavery was wrong, they would not risk destroying the Union by trying to stamp it out in the states where it was established. But the Republicans, Abe

stressed, would not stand for the spread of Southern slavery
into any new territories: "Thinking it wrong, as we do, can
we yield to them?"

The audience at the Cooper Institute cheered and threw
their hats in the air. The reporter from one newspaper cried
out, "He's the greatest man since St. Paul," then wrote in
his article, in words only slightly more measured, "No man
ever before made such an impression on his first appeal to
a New York audience."

In May 1860, Abraham Lincoln, now 51, was selected by
the Republican party as its candidate for United States President. The following month, the Democratic nomination
went to Stephen Douglas. The Democrats of eleven slave
states, no longer wishing to be represented by a Northerner,
withdrew from the party and nominated their own man for
president, John C. Breckinridge, who years before had called
for the Southern states to leave the Union in an act of
secession.

In the campaign, Lincoln's supporters made much of
Abe's humble background. He was cheered as "Honest
Abe", the "Railsplitter", a man of the people who was born
in a log cabin and would wind up in the White House.

Lincoln, a tinted photograph from around 1860.

An 1858 election parade in front of Lincoln's house (now extended to two storeys) in Springfield.

And they were right. The split in the ranks of the Democrats cut deeply into Stephen Douglas's vote; he won more votes than Breckinridge in total, but the secessionist had a much wider following among Southerners. Abraham Lincoln, however, won the backing of every Northern state, enough to give him the presidency. A surprisingly large number of votes had been cast for a fourth candidate named John Bell, who ran for a minority party and who, like an ostrich with its head in the sand, did not mention slavery once during the campaign.

But the citizens of the United States could no longer hide from their problems. They had a Northern President, who had little if any following in the South. At the end of 1860, a newspaper in Atlanta, Georgia, expressed the thoughts of many Southerners when it wrote: "Let the consequences be what they may ... the South will never submit to such humiliation and degradation as the inauguration of Abraham Lincoln."

4. The Civil War

President Abraham Lincoln was due to take office on 4th March 1861, some four months after his election. His final days in Springfield were spent putting his personal affairs and his legal practice in order, clearing the way for the awesome duties ahead of him.

Befitting his new position, he bought new clothes: dark, dignified suits and silk hats. He also strove for even greater dignity by growing a beard. During the campaign he had received letters from staunch Republicans suggesting that whiskers would improve his image. An eleven-year-old girl had sent Abe a note telling him he should have a beard: "You would look a great deal better for your face is so thin." The beard did indeed make him seen firmer in his determination, more serious, more like a President.

Abraham Lincoln also spent a great deal of time considering the government appointments that he had to make as President. Abe disliked these tasks because they meant having to satisfy men who felt they had given him vital help in his rise to Presidency. Men's wives even asked Mary Lincoln to persuade Abe to give their husbands important jobs.

Abe had one more welcome duty to perform before he went to Washington. He rode by freight train to Charleston, Illinois, and from there travelled another eight miles to the

Lincoln after he had grown a beard, and his step-mother, Sarah Bush Lincoln, at the age of 76.

cabin where Sarah Bush Lincoln, his widowed stepmother, lived. The old woman embraced Abe and told him of her prayers for him in the fearful years ahead. He hugged her, smoothed her hair and wiped away her tears; with a kiss, he said goodbye and returned to Springfield.

Abe left Springfield on the rainy day of 11th February 1861. A thousand people crowded into the station to see him go. From his railway carriage, he asked them to pray for him: "Without the assistance of that Divine Being, I cannot succeed. With that assistance I cannot fail... To His care commending you, as I hope in your prayers you will commend me, I bid you an affectionate farewell."

The presidential train stopped at many American towns and cities on the way to Washington: Indianapolis, Indiana; Cincinnati and Columbus in Ohio; Pittsburgh and Philadelphia in Pennsylvania; Utica, New York and New York City. Towards the end of the journey, detectives working for the Republicans heard of a plan to murder Lincoln on the night of 26th February as his train passed through Baltimore, Maryland. With armed guards, Abe left the presidential train and travelled in secret through the night to the capital.

The situation in the United States was growing more desperately tense. By the time Lincoln arrived in Washington, seven Southern states had already decided, either in their legislatures or by the votes of their citizens, to withdraw, or secede, from the United States. On 4th Feb-

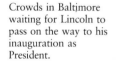

Crowds in Baltimore waiting for Lincoln to pass on the way to his inauguration as President.

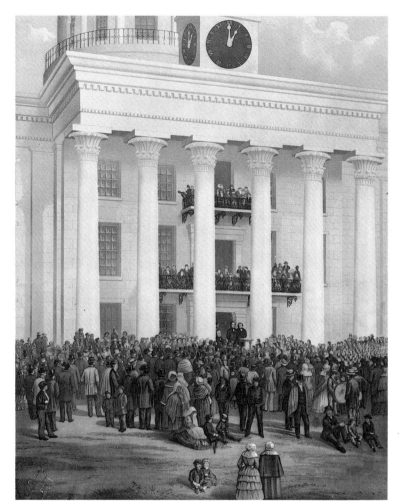

Jefferson Davis and his inauguration as President of the Confederate States of America at Montgomery, Alabama, on 18th February 1861.

ruary, the states in the South organized a new government, which they named the Confederate States of America, with former United States Senator Jefferson Davis of Mississippi as President. In preparation for the conflict, they began to raise their own troops and demanded that United States soldiers withdraw from their garrisons in the South.

With the country moving nearer to war, Abraham Lincoln was sworn into office. The presidential oath of office includes the promise to "preserve, protect and defend" the United States Constitution. In his inaugural speech, the new President reminded his countrymen in the South of his position and his duty: "In *your* hands, my dissatisfied fellow countrymen, and not *mine*, is the momentous issue of civil war. The government will not assail *you*. You can have no conflict without being yourselves the aggressors. *You* have no oath registered in Heaven to destroy the government, while I shall have the most solemn one to 'preserve, protect and defend' it." Abe made it clear that he intended to save the United States, but that he would not begin a war against his countrymen.

Fort Sumter

The South's first act of aggression came just over a month later at Charleston in South Carolina, the first Southern state to have seceded. The United States garrison at Fort Sumter, on Charleston harbour, continued to fly the United States flag, resisting Southern attempts to take it over. Major Robert Anderson, the fort's commander, reported by messenger to Lincoln that he only had food supplies for a month. But before fresh provisions could reach the fort, further Southern demands came for its surrender. Anderson refused, and on 12th April, Southern guns opened fire on Fort Sumter. After 33 hours of bombardment, with the garrison in flames, the food gone and one soldier dead, Major Anderson and his men surrendered. They were allowed to evacuate the fort by ship and head for New York City.

On the day Fort Sumter was taken, President Lincoln issued a call for 75,000 soldiers to subdue the South. His call was answered throughout the North by volunteers who

The inauguration of Abraham Lincoln as President of the United States of America on 4th March 1861 in front of the Capitol in Washington D.C.

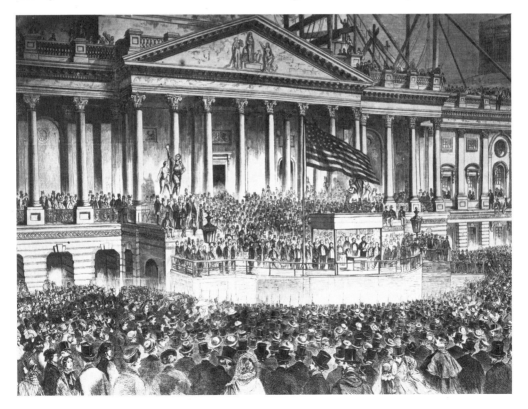

Firing the first shot in the American Civil War, Fort Sumter, 12th April 1861.

were outraged at the attack on Fort Sumter. They were enlisted for an initial service of only 90 days; few Northerners could imagine the war lasting much longer than that.

It is easy to understand why the North felt so confident. The Union side included 23 states, with more than twenty million people. After four more states had seceded from the Union, the Confederate States still numbered only eleven, with some nine million people, more than a third of whom were slaves. The industrialized North had a vast network of railways, which could be used for transporting troops; they had factories for producing guns and ammunition. They also had a well-developed navy, which was swiftly dispatched by the President to blockade all Southern ports. With its shipping cut off, the South could not sell its cotton to Europe and buy badly needed armaments and supplies.

However, the South did have a great advantage in military skill. Its troops had begun to organize and drill many months before those of the North, and some of the most skilled generals of the United States army came from the South. One of them, Robert E. Lee of Virginia, had been offered command of the Union armies by Lincoln before his state had seceded. Lee was a true gentleman and was opposed to slavery, but he realized that Virginia would soon join the Confederacy: he could not honourably fight against his native state and so he declined the President's offer and went on to lead the armies of the South. One Union general felt that the loss of Lee was as bad as losing 50,000 soldiers.

The South's other advantage was that the war was being fought largely on its home ground. If the war dragged on long enough, it was felt that the Union would tire of battle and allow the South to remain independent.

What the Southerners did not count on, however, was the willpower of President Lincoln. His foremost goal was to preserve the Union. He saw the purpose of the United States government as being "to elevate the condition of men" by having them join together to work for harmony, peace and freedom; the Southern states could not withdraw from this system without making a mockery of the American idea of government.

But what upset Abe most was that the South had seceded because of slavery. Although he was morally opposed to slavery, Abe had told the South that he was willing to let it continue there for the sake of the Union. As the President was later to say to his countrymen in a letter that was widely

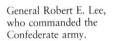

General Robert E. Lee, who commanded the Confederate army.

circulated in newspapers: "My paramount object in this struggle is to save the Union, and is not either to save or to destroy slavery." This, Abe stressed, was his "official duty", in spite of his "personal wish that all men everywhere could be free."

The first battle

Any optimism the North felt about its chances was shattered in July 1861 by the first battle of the Civil War. The United States capital, Washington, D.C., was uncomfortably close to the enemy: just across the Potomac River, in Virginia, Confederate troops were massing. With the three-month enlistment of the first Northern troops almost over without their having seen any real fighting, the American public was anxious for some action.

The division between Union and Confederate States at the start of the Civil War. Part of Virginia refused to secede and was admitted to the Union as the state of West Virginia in 1863.

President Lincoln unwisely gave in to public opinion by authorizing some 30,000 inexperienced troops under General Irvin McDowell to fight 22,000 Confederate soldiers at Manassas, an important railway junction in Virginia. On

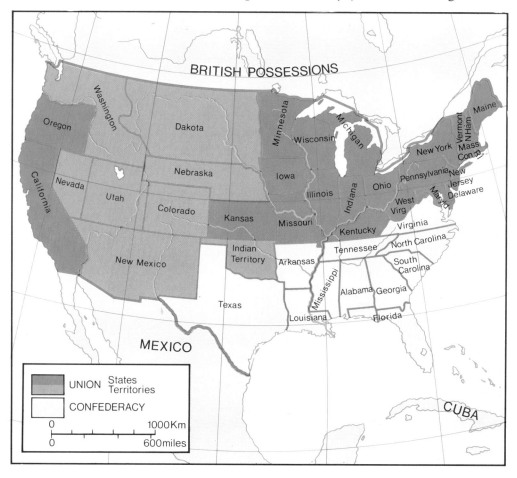

46

The first battle of Bull Run, in which the Union forces were put to flight by the Confederates.

21st July, the armies met at a small river called Bull Run. Although the Northern numbers were greater, they were no match for the Southerners, whose rural lives had given them skill as horsemen and marksmen. The Union troops panicked and fled back to Washington. Only inadequate organization of the Southern troops kept them from pursuit and the possible capture of Washington.

After Bull Run, both sides spent the rest of the year building up their forces for the more serious battles ahead. To lead the Union forces, President Lincoln appointed 34-year-old General George B. McClellan. The Army of the Potomac, as United States forces in the East were called, continued to train and drill under McClellan's careful guidance; by November 1861, it numbered 160,000 men. But they were only involved in minor skirmishes such as one that occurred in October at Ball's Bluff, Virginia, where a small detachment of Union men, led by Lincoln's old friend Edward Baker, was defeated in a raid on a party of Confederate soldiers. Baker was killed. On hearing the news, Lincoln was said to have had "tears rolling down his furrowed cheeks, his breast heaving."

Lincoln's friend, Edward Baker, who was killed in October 1861.

With the tensions of war growing all around him, President Lincoln found some welcome relief in his two young sons, eleven-year-old Willie and seven-year-old Thomas, or "Tad". (The eldest Lincoln son, Robert, was away studying at Harvard University.) Willie and Tad brightened the solemn spirit of the White House with their high spirits.

In February 1862, Willie Lincoln caught a cold from riding his pet pony in the rain. A fever developed, and within a few days, Willie Lincoln was dead. Abe, with the weight of the Civil War on his shoulders, hid his sorrow. But Mary Lincoln sobbed for days. Her grief came on top of her personal worries about the war, in which some of her family had joined the Confederate side. She never fully recovered from her depression.

Two fronts

During 1862, the war developed on two fronts. In the West, Union troops were trying to secure control of the great Mississippi River, which was the main artery of transport for the western half of the Confederacy. In the East, the fighting was mainly in Virginia, where Union troops tried to push towards the Confederate capital of Richmond.

The Union forces had greater success in the West. Under the leadership of a hard-drinking Mexican War hero named Ulysses S. Grant, they took Nashville, the capital of Tennessee, in February 1862. This gave the Union some control over the area near the northern end of the Mississippi. The following month the United States Navy, commanded by Admiral David Farragut, captured the city of New Orleans, at the mouth of the river.

A few days later, Grant's armies won the decisive battle of Shiloh, extending their control of the Mississippi basin

Mary and Abraham Lincoln with their three sons, Robert, Willie and Tad.

48

David Farragut, a Southerner by birth, who became the first Admiral in the United States navy.

further south in Tennessee. The battle was won largely through Grant's stubborn spirit; the cost in men was high, with over 13,000 Union soldiers dead. There was an angry outcry among Northern politicians; but Lincoln, saddened though he was at the waste of lives, recognized a brave commander when he saw one, and dismissed the criticism of Grant, saying, "I can't spare this man – he fights!"

The President could not say the same of his commanders in the East. In May and June, 100,000 men led by General McClellan advanced up the peninsula between the James and the York Rivers towards Richmond. But McClellan's painstakingly slow pace gave the Confederates enough time to muster their defences. After seven days' fighting outside the capital, the Union troops were turned away, and in August, the North suffered a humiliating defeat in a second battle at Bull Run. This time the South, although heavily

Lincoln and his son Tad.

An 1862 engraving of action in the battle of Shiloh, showing Union troops recapturing artillery from the Confederates.

outnumbered by more than two to one, succeeded in driving off the Union troops.

From the start of the war, Abe had actively avoided making an issue of slavery. But after a year and a half of near-fruitless battle, he resolved to take stronger actions to restore the Union. If he came out officially against slavery, he would be able to win the moral support of European countries, who up until then had either stayed neutral or, as in the case of England, had shown admiration for the pluck of the Southern underdogs. Even more important, every able-bodied male slave he freed was a potential soldier for the Union side. It would have been poor tactics, though, for the President to make such a major move while his side was losing battles. To the world, it would have looked merely like an act of desperation.

But the tide turned in September 1862. Confederate troops led by Robert E. Lee, encouraged by their recent successes against the North, invaded Maryland, one of four slave states on the border between the North and the South who were not participating in the Southern cause. General McClellan engaged with Lee's troops at Antietam. More

The Bull Run river,
scene of two defeats for
the Union army.

General Ulysses S. Grant
(third from the right)
with members of his
staff.

51

President Lincoln at the battlefield of Antietam, a photograph taken by Alexander Gardener for the great Civil War photographer Matthew Brady.

than 20,000 men on both sides were lost in two days of fighting, at the end of which Lee and his men retreated southwards. Although McClellan, with his usual wariness, failed to pursue them, Antietam could be claimed as a Northern victory.

On 22nd September, President Lincoln issued a warning to the South that, in the eyes of the United States government, all slaves in rebel states would become free as of 1st January 1863. The Emancipation Proclamation would not affect the border states who did not oppose the North; after the war, Abe reasoned, slavery could easily be phased out there. The Emancipation Proclamation did have the desired effect. Sympathy for the South in Europe, particularly in Britain, dwindled. Most significantly, more than 100,000 black soldiers eventually fought in the Union army.

President Lincoln still had to deal with the problem of his generals. After Antietam, General McClellan had sat still with his armies. Lincoln continually questioned the general, trying to prod him into action. When McClellan complained that their mounts were too footsore for fighting, Abe asked, "Will you pardon me for asking what the horses of your army have done since the battle of Antietam that fatigues anything?" Another time, Abe wrote irritably to him, "Are

Part of the Emancipation Proclamation in Lincoln's own handwriting, stating that "all persons held as slaves . . . are and henceforward shall be free."

you not overcautious when you assume that you cannot do what the enemy is doing?" But still McClellan did nothing, and Lincoln was finally forced to the conclusion that "McClellan has got the slows."

On 5th November 1862, the President relieved McClellan of his command. He was replaced by General Ambrose Burnside, who went on to lose 12,000 men in defeat at the battle of Fredericksburg the following month. Burnside, in turn, was succeeded by General Joseph Hooker, who, in

Matthew Brady photograph of Union soldiers wounded at the battle of Fredericksburg.

May 1863, suffered a demoralizing defeat from Generals Lee and Jackson at Chancellorsville.

Once again the Confederates pushed northwards, this time into the Union state of Pennsylvania. The Union army, now led by General George Meade, pursued them. On 1st July, the armies met at Gettysburg, Pennsylvania. Reinforcements poured in on both sides for what became one of the war's bloodiest battles. In three days of fighting before the Union's victory, Northern casualties, killed, wounded or missing, were 23,000 men, while those of the South were 28,000. The Confederate army retreated to Virginia.

This most stirring and tragic Union victory was commemorated the following November with the dedication of a memorial to the fallen soldiers on the Gettysburg battlefield. Lincoln had no time to prepare a speech in advance, but jotted down some notes just before his arrival. When he spoke at the end of several hours of other speeches, few of the tired spectators paid much attention to his words. But reprinted in newspapers, Lincoln's Gettysburg Address impressed people everywhere with the simple, sincere way in which it summed up all that he believed in, all that the war was being fought for. It became his most famous speech:

Abraham Lincoln photographed on 15th November 1863, four days before he delivered the Gettysburg Address, by Alexander Gardener.

"Four score and seven years ago our fathers brought forth on this continent, a new nation, conceived in Liberty, and dedicated to the proposition that all men are created equal.

"Now we are engaged in a great civil war, testing whether that nation, or any nation so conceived and so dedicated, can long endure. We are met on a great battlefield of that war. We have come to dedicate a portion of that field, as a final resting place for those who here gave their lives that the nation might live."

But, he said, the ground had already been consecrated "far above our poor power to add or detract" by "the brave men, living and dead, who struggled here. . .It is for us the living, rather, to be dedicated here. . .to the great task remaining before us. . .that these dead shall not have died in vain, that this nation, under God, shall have a new birth of freedom, and that government of the people, by the people, for the people, shall not perish from the earth."

Union victory was now almost complete in the western
campaigns. The day after the battle of Gettysburg, Grant
had successfully completed a siege of the last major Confederate stronghold on the Mississippi, Vicksburg. At the time
of Lincoln's Gettysburg Address, Grant and his fellow generals were advancing through Tennessee, heading for the
heart of the Confederacy.

By the beginning of 1864, the South was nearing defeat
but was still unwilling to surrender. In March, Abe gave
command of the Union armies to the man he knew would
finish the job, Ulysses S. Grant. He told him, "If there is
anything wanting which is within my power to give, do not
fail to let me know it. And now, with a brave army and a
just cause, may God sustain you."

During the late spring and summer, Grant doggedly went
at Lee's troops in Virginia, trying to make his way to Richmond. But, although short of food and supplies, the Confederates rallied bravely and kept Grant at bay.

Union troops in the West met with greater success. Led
by General William Tecumseh Sherman, 99,000 Northern
soldiers advanced south from eastern Tennessee along the
railway towards Atlanta, Georgia, which they captured at

the beginning of September; in the destruction of the city's warehouses, factories and military depots that followed, much of the city itself was destroyed by fire.

Sherman left half of his army in the vicinity of Atlanta, and set off with the other half on one of the war's most infamous campaigns, the "March to the Sea". In mid-November Sherman's troops began their march 250 miles east across Georgia towards the Atlantic Ocean, laying waste to everything they encountered in a path that was sometimes as much as 60 miles wide. Livestock were slaughtered, houses, crops and goods burned, family valuables confiscated, and slaves were set free. Before Christmas, the coastal city of Savannah was taken.

Election and victory

A Northern sea victory. Admiral Farragut at the battle of Mobile Bay in 1864. On the right is a southern ironclad. The Civil War marked the first important use of these armoured warships.

In the late summer and autumn of 1864, Abraham Lincoln stood for re-election as President. The Democrats opposed him with his former general, George McClellan. The Democrats' election policy was to stop the fighting straight away and restore the Union.

Their approach was simple-minded. The Confederate President, Jefferson Davis, was still insisting that he would only accept a peace proposal based on the recognition of Southern independence; as he had written in a message to

Lincoln in 1864 and part of a poster for his election campaign in that year.

President Lincoln, "It will be useless to approach me with any other." But after almost four wearying years of war, the Democrats' promises appealed to a lot of people in the North. As late as the end of August, Abe feared he might lose the election. In a personal memorandum, he wrote, "It seems exceedingly probable that this administration will not be re-elected. Then it will be my duty to co-operate with the President-elect to save the Union between the election and

General Sherman and his troops marching through Georgia.

The burning of
Richmond, Virginia.

the inauguration, as he will have secured his election on
such ground that he can not possibly save it afterward."

Lincoln was saved by his general. News of Sherman's
successes and of Grant's slow progress towards Richmond
bolstered the morale of the North. On 8th November 1864,
he was re-elected by a sound majority.

On 3rd February 1865, with Sherman's armies now advancing north towards Virginia, and Grant ever closer to
victory over Lee, President Lincoln received three delegates
from the Confederate government on board a steamer at
Hampton Roads, Virginia. The South still hoped for both
peace and independence. But Lincoln made his position clear
to them. The South must lay down its arms and then return
to the Union; nothing less would be acceptable. The two
sides parted without agreement.

The war was nevertheless coming to an end. On 2nd
April, Richmond, Virginia was evacuated by the Confederacy. The only inhabitants of the city to stay behind were
freed slaves. Their freedom was now a matter of law: on
31st January, Congress had passed the Thirteenth Amendment to the United States Constitution, prohibiting slavery.

The freed slaves in Richmond could hardly believe their
eyes when, a few days later, they saw a man they recognized
as President Lincoln walking through the streets of the fallen
city. Hundreds of black people crowded around Abe, cheer-
ing, laughing and crying with joy. One old man fell to his
knees before the President, and praised him as "the great
Messiah". Abe said to him, "Don't kneel to me. You must
kneel to God only and thank Him for your freedom."

59

General Ulysses S. Grant drafts the terms of the South's surrender at Appomattox Courthouse, Virginia, on 9th April 1865. Seated facing him is General Robert E. Lee, who signed for the South.

On 9th April, the great generals Robert E. Lee and Ulysses S. Grant met face to face at Appomattox Courthouse in Virginia. Lee, a gentleman to the last, was in his finest dress uniform. Grant, wearing the ragged clothes of the battlefield, was there to accept Lee's surrender. But the two men, brave and courteous soldiers, first chatted cordially about the Mexican War, in which they both had fought. Then Grant drew up the terms of the South's surrender, and Lee signed. Lee's soldiers would lay down their arms, but keep their horses for the hard work of rebuilding their war-ravaged lands, and Grant ordered that the starving Confederate soldiers be fed at once. He sent a telegram to the President: "General Lee surrendered the army of Northern Virginia this morning on terms proposed by myself." The war was over.

That night, jubilant crowds gathered outside the White House. President Lincoln spoke briefly to his people of their victory. He finished his speech with a gesture that showed his desire for a swift reconciliation with the former rebels. The anthem of the South during the war had been the rousing tune called "Dixie". "I propose closing up this interview by the band performing a particular tune," Abe told the crowds. "I have always thought 'Dixie' one of the best tunes I have ever heard."

5. Assassination

A great problem faced the country and its President at the end of the Civil War. The South was completely shattered. Its finest young men had died in battle. Its farms had been laid to waste, many of its cities and towns were in ruins, its businesses had collapsed, and its schools and churches were closed. A once wealthy society was now poor, and the basis of its economy, slavery, was gone. A massive programme of reconstruction would be needed.

Three million slaves were now free, but were without the work, homes, food and clothing that slavery had provided for them. Some chose to stay on and work for their old masters, but many tried, mostly with little success, to find work in towns and cities. Many did not yet know how to deal with their freedom: they had never before had the opportunity to run their own lives. Most white people still regarded them as sub-human. The country would need a lot of guidance before the freed slaves could take a proud and rightful place in American society.

Abraham Lincoln touched on the subject of reconstruction shortly before the end of the war, in the speech he delivered

The ruins of Richmond, Virginia, in 1865.

Mary Todd Lincoln in formal dress, photographed by Matthew Brady in 1864.

at his second inauguration on 4th March 1865. He first reminded his countrymen of the most common bond between the people of the North and South, a bond forgotten in war. "Both read the same Bible and pray to the same God, and each invokes his aid against the other." There were people in the North who would want to punish the South when the war was over. To them, the President made clear what his own attitude to the South would be after the war: "With malice toward none; with charity for all . . . to do all which may achieve and cherish a just and lasting peace among ourselves, and with all nations."

Abe's greatest fear was that he would not survive long enough to guide his country through the trying period of reconstruction. He knew that there were people in the South who would be glad to see him dead, although he had won respect even there. He resigned himself to the idea that, no matter how well he might be guarded from assassination. "If it is to be done, it is impossible to prevent it."

He was plagued by a nightmare in which he awoke to the muffled sound of sobbing. He got up and went downstairs, where the sobbing grew louder. The rooms of the White House were well lit, yet he could not find anyone sobbing. Then he arrived at the East Room, and found a shrouded corpse, guarded by soldiers. He asked the soldiers who had died in the White House. Their answer was, "The President. He was killed by an assassin."

On Good Friday, 14th April 1865, President Lincoln had a full day of work set out for him, and in the evening he was to visit the theatre with Mrs. Lincoln and some friends.

Abe spent much of the morning at his desk and seeing individual visitors. He signed papers granting pardons for soldiers who had deserted and had been sentenced to death when they were caught. Other papers that he signed discharged soldiers who had served dutifully.

In a meeting with his cabinet later in the morning, the President stressed his feelings about fairness to the Southern states, and in particular to the members of the Confederate government. "I hope there will be no persecution," he told them, "no bloody work. . . . None need expect me to take any part in hanging or killing them."

In the mid-afternoon, the President relaxed for a short while by taking a drive alone with his wife in a carriage. Mary had suffered during the war. Now he tried to reassure her with their hopes for the future. "We have had a hard time since we came to Washington," she remembered him saying, "but the war is over, and with God's blessings, we may hope for four years of peace and happiness, and then we will go back to Illinois and pass the rest of our lives in quiet. We have laid by some money, and during this time, we shall save up more, but shall not have enough to support us . . . I will open a law office at Springfield or Chicago and practise law, and at least do enough to help give us a livelihood."

After the late afternoon's business, dinner and a few evening appointments, President and Mrs Lincoln left for Ford's Theatre, accompanied by a 28-year-old Union major, Henry Rathbone, and his fiancée, Clara Harris. They arrived at the theatre around 8.30 and were shown to the grandest box, which was festooned for the occasion with red, white and blue bunting and a portrait of George Washington. A comfortable rocking chair was provided for Abe to sit in.

The play that evening was *Our American Cousin*, an English comedy about an American who throws away a huge inheritance to his English relatives by accidentally using a will to light his cigar. The President, in a relaxed mood, enjoyed the play, chuckling contentedly at the jokes. He even felt a little romantic: seeing the young major and his bride-to-be holding hands, Abe took Mary's hand in his.

During the play, the door leading to the President's box should have been guarded by John Parker, a 35-year-old former carpenter, soldier and policeman. That evening, though, Parker grew bored and slipped out to have a drink with the President's coachman and footman.

While Parker was away, a man appeared at the door of the President's box. He was John Wilkes Booth, an out-of-work actor who felt a deep bitterness at the South's defeat. In the afternoon, Booth had drilled a tiny spyhole in the door. He now used it to observe the occupants of the box and make sure that the play had their full attention.

Booth quietly opened the door and moved to a point five feet behind Abraham Lincoln. From his waistcoat pocket he took a small, single-shot brass derringer pistol. With a straight arm, Booth aimed the gun at the back of the President's head. A burst of laughter from the audience muffled the sound as he pulled the trigger.

Mrs. Lincoln, Major Rathbone and Miss Harris turned to see Booth. "*Sic semper tyrannis*," he said softly to them in Latin. "Thus be it ever to tyrants." Mary Lincoln screamed. Major Rathbone went for Booth, who drew a knife and wounded his right arm. As pandemonium broke loose in the

John Wilkes Booth, and a contemporary print of him about to shoot Lincoln.

theatre, Booth leapt from the box to the stage. In the jump, he broke his left foot, but he managed to run limping out to the stage door, where he had a horse saddled and ready for his escape.

The bullet entered Abe Lincoln's head three inches above the left ear, and lodged in his brain behind his right eye. The President lost consciousness immediately. He was carried from the theatre by four soldiers, to a lodging house across the street where doctors attended him. But nothing could be done. At seven o'clock the following morning, Abraham Lincoln died.

The funeral was held at the White House on Wednesday 19th April. Then the President's body lay in state in the U.S. Capitol building, where the people of Washington, D.C., filed past in their thousands.

Abe was to be buried in Springfield, Illinois. He returned home in a funeral train that travelled 1,700 miles and took two weeks to reach Illinois. Along the route, the tracks were

Procession with Lincoln's remains in Chicago.

The locomotive that pulled Lincoln's funeral train.

lined with Americans grieving for their dead President. At major cities such as New York and Chicago, the coffin was taken from the train to a government building, where the mourners could file past, leave flowers and gaze at Abe's careworn but now peaceful face.

While Abraham Lincoln was on the way to his final resting place, a search party was hunting down the assassin John Wilkes Booth and his fellow conspirators. He was finally trapped in a barn near Bowling Green, Virginia, on 26th April. The barn was set on fire. Booth was shot through the neck and dragged out of the burning building; he died a short while later.

Andrew Johnson, Lincoln's successor as President.

The new President was Andrew Johnson, who had been chosen as Lincoln's Vice-President in the 1864 campaign. Like Lincoln, Johnson was born of a poor family, in a slave state. But he did not have the moral strength or the courage of Abe Lincoln. Although he tried to put forward moderate policies aimed at a just reconstruction of the South, he was overruled by radical Republicans in Congress whose hatred of the South was increased by the feeling that the Southerners were to blame for Lincoln's death.

Little was done by the United States government to help the black population after the Civil War and racial tensions escalated. Although the Southern states rejoined the Union, no real efforts were made to reconstruct the bonds of brotherhood between North and South. A hundred years later, distrust between North and South had not vanished entirely, and black people in America were still fighting for equality. Perhaps the country's wounds would not have taken so long to heal had the just, honest, wise and good man named Abraham Lincoln lived to complete his work as President of the United States.

Chronology

This list of dates gives the main events in the life of Abraham Lincoln together with some of the many other things that were happening in the world at the time and are not mentioned elsewhere in this book. Events in bold type are mentioned in the main text of the book.

1809 **Birth of Abraham Lincoln.** Napoleon divorces Josephine. Beethoven's *Piano Concerto No. 5 (The Emperor).*
1812 United States declares war on Britain. Napoleon's Russian campaign ends in disastrous retreat from Moscow.
1814 Napoleon abdicates and is banished to Elba. British burn Washington, D.C. War between Britain and USA ended by Treaty of Ghent.
1815 Napoleon escapes from Elba and is finally defeated at Waterloo. First steam warship, the *Fulton* (built for US Navy).
1816 **Lincoln family moves to Kentucky.** Gioacchino Rossini's opera *The Barber of Seville.*
1818 **Death of Nancy Hanks Lincoln.** 49th Parallel agreed as border between USA and Canada. Mary Shelley's novel *Frankenstein.*
1819 **Thomas Lincoln marries Sarah Bush.**
1820 **Missouri Compromise.** Walter Scott's novel *Ivanhoe.*
1821 Michael Faraday discovers principle of electric motor.
1823 Simon Bolivar proclaimed Emperor of Peru. Charles Macintosh invents waterproof rubberized fabric.
1824 Beethoven's Symphony No. 9 (The Choral).
1825 Opening of Erie Canal and of Stockton and Darlington Railway, the first passenger line. Michael Faraday isolates benzene.
1827 George Ohm states Ohm's Law. Metallic aluminium first extracted. First volume of J. J. Audubon's *The Birds of America.*
1828 **Lincoln goes by river boat to New Orleans.** Synthesis of urea, first organic compound to be produced artificially.
1831 **Lincoln settles in New Salem.** Belgium becomes independent. Start of Charles Darwin's voyage as naturalist on H.M.S. *Beagle.* Michael Faraday discovers principle of electromagnetic induction.
1832 **Lincoln stands for Illinois State Assembly, enlists in volunteer militia against the Indians and is defeated in election.**
1834 **Lincoln elected to Illinois State Assembly.**
1835 **Death of Ann Rutledge.** Samuel Colt patents revolver. Hans Andersen's first *Fairy Tales.*
1836 Texas declares itself independent of Mexico.
1837 **Lincoln becomes an attorney in Springfield.** Accession of Queen Victoria.
1838 Start of regular steamship service across Atlantic.
1839 First Opium War in China. Charles Goodyear vulcanizes rubber. Louis Daguerre perfects daguerreotype photographic process.
1840 Queen Victoria marries Prince Albert. Penny post and first adhesive postage stamps in Britain.
1842 **Lincoln marries Mary Todd.** Chartist riots in England. First use of ether as anaesthetic.
1844 Samuel Morse inaugurates first telegraph line in USA (Washington to Baltimore).
1845 Texas (previously a republic) becomes a State of the USA.
1846 **Wilmot Proviso. War between USA and Mexico.** Brigham Young leads Mormon emigration to Utah.
1847 **Lincoln enters Congress as a Whig.** Liberia proclaimed independent. Gold discovered in California. Charlotte Brontë's novel *Jane Eyre.* Emily Brontë's novel *Wuthering Heights.*
1848 Wave of revolutions in Europe. Louis Napoleon elected French President. Charles Dickens publishes first parts of *David Copperfield.*
1850 **Death of Edward Lincoln.** Slave trade forbidden in District of Columbia.
1851 Isaac Singer puts sewing machine into production. Great Exhibition in London. Herman Melville's novel *Moby Dick.*
1852 **Publication of *Uncle Tom's Cabin.*** Louis Napoleon proclaimed Emperor Napoleon III.
1854 **Kansas-Nebraska Act opposed by newly formed Republican Party.** Trade treaty with USA opens Japan to world trade. Start of Crimean War. Henry David Thoreau's book *Walden.*
1856 **Lincoln joins in founding Republican Party in Illinois. James Buchanan (Democrat) elected US President.** Treaty of Paris ends Crimean War. William Perkin prepares first aniline dye (mauve).
1857 **Dred Scott case.** Irish Republican Brotherhood (Fenians) founded in USA. Start of Indian Mutiny against British.
1858 **Lincoln-Douglas debates. Douglas elected to Senate.** Bernadette Soubirous's first vision of Virgin Mary at Lourdes.
1859 **John Brown's raid on Harper's Ferry. Brown executed.** Charles Darwin publishes *The Origin of Species.* Work starts on Suez Canal (opened 1869). First American oil well drilled.
1860 **Lincoln elected President.** Garibaldi proclaims Victor Emmanuel of Sardinia King of Italy.
1861 **Inauguration of President Lincoln. Confederate States secede. Attack on Fort Sumter. First Battle of Bull Run.** Charles Dickens's novel *Great Expectations.*
1862 **Death of Willie Lincoln. Battles of Shiloh, Bull Run (Second), Antietam, Fredericksburg. Emancipation Proclamation.** Bismarck becomes Prime Minister of Prussia. Richard Gatling patents machine gun.
1863 **Battles of Chancellorsville, Gettysburg, Vicksburg. Gettysburg Address.** Edouard Manet's painting *Le Dejeuner sur l'Herbe.*
1864 **Sherman leads march across Georgia. Lincoln re-elected President.** Louis Pasteur invents pasteurization (for wine).
1865 **Thirteenth Amendment. Union Army occupies Richmond. Confederacy surrenders at Appomattox. Assassination of Lincoln. Andrew Johnson becomes President.**

Books to Read

This list includes some of the many books in which you can read more about Abraham Lincoln and his times. Some of them are short and very readable, while others are large and detailed books that you may want to look at in libraries. The names of the British and American publishers and the date of first publication are given after each title. Where only an American publisher is given, the book is also distributed in Britain by the American publisher. Many of the books have been published in paperback.

ABRAHAM LINCOLN
Abraham Lincoln Lord Longford (Weidenfeld and Nicolson/Putnams, 1974)
Abraham Lincoln (Two volumes: *The Prairie Years* and *Abraham Lincoln: The War Years*) Carl Sandburg (Harcourt Brace, 1926, 1939; new edition 1975)
Lincoln in Photographs: An Album of Every Known Pose Charles Hamilton & Lloyd Ostendorf (University of Oklahoma Press, 1968)
With Malice Towards None: The Life of Abraham Lincoln Stephen B. Oates (Allen & Unwin/ Harper & Row, 1977)
Lincoln and His America edited by David Plowden (Thames & Hudson/Viking, 1970)

THE CIVIL WAR
America's Bloodiest Day: The Battle of Antietam 1862 William A. Frassanito (Mills & Boon/ Scribner's, 1978)
The American Civil War A. H. Allt (Then & There series, Longmans, 1961)
Illustrated History of the American Civil War edited by Henry Steele Commager (Orbis/ A&W, 1979)
Battles of the American Civil War Curt Johnson & Mark McLaughlin (Sampson Low/ Crown, 1977)
The Centennial History of the Civil War (Three volumes: *The Coming Fury, Terrible Swift Sword, Never Call Retreat*) Bruce Catton (Gollancz/Doubleday, 1961, 1963, 1965)
The Army of the Potomac (Three volumes: *Mr. Lincoln's Army, Glory Road, Never Call Retreat*) Bruce Catton (White Lion/Doubleday, 1951, 1952, 1953)

THE CONFEDERACY
Biographical Dictionary of The Confederacy edited by Jon L. Wakelyn (Greenwood Press, 1977)
Confederate Women Dell Irvine Wiley (Greenwood Press, 1974)

Index

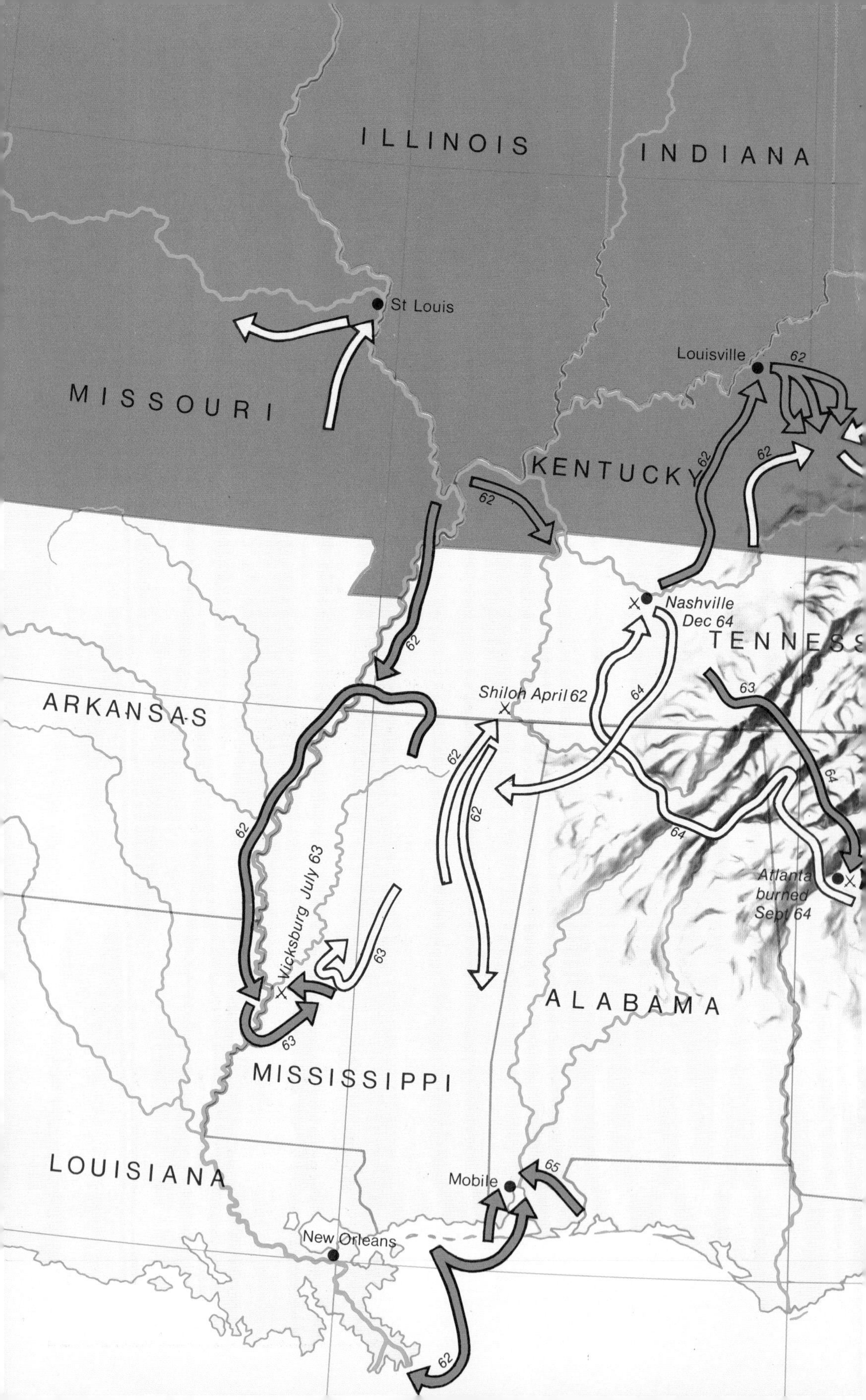

ILLINOIS

INDIANA

MISSOURI

St Louis

Louisville

62

KENTUCKY

62

62

62

ARKANSAS

62

Nashville
Dec 64

TENNESS

Shiloh April 62

62

64

63

62

62

64

64

Vicksburg July 63

63

Atlanta
burned
Sept 64

MISSISSIPPI

63

ALABAMA

LOUISIANA

Mobile

65

New Orleans

62